Trade and Income Distribution

William R. Cline

Trade and Income Distribution

Institute for International Economics
Washington, DC
November 1997

William R. Cline, *Senior Fellow*, is currently on leave as Deputy Managing Director and Chief Economist at the Institute of International Finance. He was formerly a Senior Fellow at the Brookings Institution (1973–81); Deputy Director for Development and Trade Research at the US Treasury (1971–73); Ford Foundation Visiting Professor in Brazil (1970–71) and Assistant Professor at Princeton University (1967–70). He is the author of 21 books including *Predicting External Imbalances for the United States and Japan* (1995), *International Debt Reexamined* (1995), *The Economics of Global Warming* (1992), *The Future of World Trade in Textiles and Apparel* (revised edition 1990), *United States External Adjustment and the World Economy* (1989), *International Debt: Systemic Risk and Policy Response* (1984), *Trade Policy in the 1980s* (1984), *World Inflation and the Developing Countries* (1981), and *Trade Negotiations in the Tokyo Round* (1978).

INSTITUTE FOR INTERNATIONAL ECONOMICS
11 Dupont Circle, NW
Washington, DC 20036-1207
(202) 328-9000 FAX: (202) 328-5432
http://www.iie.com

C. Fred Bergsten, *Director*
Christine F. Lowry, *Director of Publications*

Printing and Typesetting by Automated Graphic Systems
Cover painting: "The Sea" by Marian Harwood Cline

Printed in the United States of America
99 98 97   5 4 3 2 1

Library of Congress Cataloging-in-Publication Data

Cline, William R.
Trade and income distribution / William R. Cline.
    p. cm.
Includes bibliographical references and index.
    1. Income distribution.   I. Institute for International Economics (U.S.)   II. Title.
HB523.C58 1996   96-2659
339.2—dc20   CIP
ISBN 0-88132-216-4

The views expressed in this publication are those of the author. This publication is part of the overall program of the Institute, as endorsed by its Board of Directors, but does not necessarily reflect the views of individual members of the Board or the Advisory Committee.

Contents

Preface   **ix**

Acknowledgments   **xiii**

1 Trends in Income Distribution and Wages   **1**
Long-Term Patterns   1
Family Income, Poverty, and Wealth   4
Wage Distribution   14
Education and Skills   23
Experience and Unexplained Variation   28
Productivity and Wage Levels   29
International Patterns   31
Overview   32

2 A Critical Review of the Literature   **35**
Stolper-Samuelson and Factor-Price Equalization   35
Development Economists 1   46
Labor Economists 1   49
Labor Economists 2   65
Trade Economists 1   89
Trade Economists 2   110
Development Economists 2   127
Trade Economists 1 Revisited   133

Labor Economists 1 Revisited   136
Overview   139
Appendix 2A   149

3   Experiments with the Krugman Model   151
Introduction   151
The Krugman Model   152
Constant-Elasticity-of-Substitution Reformulation   158
Elasticity of Substitution between Skilled and
   Unskilled Labor   161
CES Estimates with Limited Substitutability   163
Decadal Outlook with the CES-Krugman Model   165
Appendix 3A   171

4   The Trade and Income Distribution Equilibrium (TIDE) Model   173
Model Structure   173
Factor Data   178
Trade Data   182
Model Calibration   193
Backcast and Counterfactuals   198
TIDE Model Forecasts   223
Model Sensitivity   231
Conclusion   234
Appendix 4A   240

5   Conclusion   253
Overview of the Study   253
An Illustrative Synthesis   263
Absolute versus Relative Wage   269
Policy Implications   272

Appendix A Employment and Wage Growth in Europe and the
   United States   **277**

References   285

Index   295

Tables
Table 1.1 Distribution of family money income   5
Table 1.2 Change in real hourly wage by education, 1973–93   23
Table 1.3 Education and income   25

Table 1.4 Enrollment of college-aged population, 1960–92   27
Table 1.5 Educational distribution of the US labor force   28
Table 2.1 Decomposition of estimated sources of relative wage
           changes, 1979–88   52
Table 2.2 Trends in employment and wages by broad sector and
           years of education, 1967–86   72
Table 2.3 Alternative estimates of the impact of trade on rising
           US wage inequality   140
Table 3.1 Experiments with the Krugman model   156
Table 3.2 Trade response to relative wage increase   163
Table 4.1 Country shares in global factor endowments and output,
           1973–93   183
Table 4.2 Trends in factor endowments, 1973–93   184
Table 4.3 Actual net trade in manufactures by factor intensity
           and partner   188
Table 4.4 Revealed comparative advantage by manufactured product
           group   192
Table 4.5 Factor shadow prices in the TIDE model   200
Table 4.6 Optimal trade matrix in the TIDE-CD model, 1993   204
Table 4.7 Percent deviation of factor prices from baseline: backcast
           counterfactuals, TIDE Cobb-Douglas model   208
Table 4.8 Factor shadow prices in the TIDE model: forecasts   226
Table 4.9 Percent deviation of factor prices from baseline: forecast
           scenarios, TIDE Cobb-Douglas model   228
Table 4A.1 Classification of 2-digit SITC codes by major factor input 240
Table 4A.2 Actual exports and imports by product group   241
Table 4A.3 Estimated distances between countries   244
Table 4A.4 Assumed tariff equivalents of total protection   245
Table 4A.5 Technical efficiency coefficients   246
Table 4A.6 Percent deviation of factor prices from baseline: backcast
           counterfactuals, TIDE-CES model   247
Table 5.1 Illustrative sources of increase in the ratio of skilled
           to unskilled wages in the United States   264

Figures

Figure 1.1 Median money income and poverty, 1967–93   7
Figure 1.2 Poverty by family status, 1959–93   8
Figure 1.3 Family status, 1959–93   9
Figure 1.4 Actual and hypothetical poverty, 1959–93   10
Figure 1.5 Composition of national income, 1959–94   14

Figure 1.6 90th/10th percentile wage ratios for full-time wage
and salary workers, 1969–93   17
Figure 1.7 Skilled/unskilled wage ratio, 1961–93   19
Figure 1.8 Wage inequality, males 16 years and older with positive
earnings, 1968–87   21
Figure 1.9a Wage inequality for men, 1973–93   22
Figure 1.9b Wage inequality for women, 1973–93   22
Figure 1.10 Hourly wages by education, 1973–93   29
Figure 1.11 Deindustrialization and developing-country import
penetration for OECD countries, 1970–90   33
Figure 2.1 The Lerner-Pearce diagram of the Stolper-Samuelson
theorem   39
Figure 2.2 Samuelson's diagram for factor-price equalization   42
Figure 2.3 R&D per worker versus wage differentials for college
and high school workers, 1963–88   55
Figure 2.4 Estimated wage change by percentile, 1964–88   58
Figure 2.5 Durable goods trade deficit and the return to skills,
1949–90   80
Figure 2.6 Trade and factor prices   97
Figure 2.7 Locus of minimum costs for inputs produced in the
North and South   121
Figure 2.8 Real income in countries 1 and 2 as a function of
the efficiency of country 2 in the production of good B   126
Figure 2.9 Interaction of supply and demand for skilled and
unskilled labor   146
Figure 3.1 Output and imports of manufactures of industrial
countries, 1971–93   166
Figure 3.2 OECD manufactured imports from LDCs   169
Figure A.1 Real wages for the G6 countries, 1970–93   280
Figure A.2 Wages and job creation, 1970–90   281

Preface

The impact of expanded trade on American wages is one of the hottest topics in the current debate over globalization. Advocates of liberalization argue that export jobs pay far more than the national average and that increased trade improves American income levels. Opponents charge that foreign competition, especially from developing countries, depresses American wages and worsens income distribution in this country.

This controversy has spawned an enormous amount of economic analysis as well as political debate. Virtually all studies agree that increased imports do place downward pressure on American wages; most characterize the impact as "modest" though a few have found much greater impact. A similar range of views has developed over the effect of immigration on our economy. Important policy implications derive from judgments on these issues.

This new study by William Cline has two central objectives. First, it reviews the vast literature on the topic that has already emerged in an effort to show how and why the different analysts came to different conclusions. Second, it offers its own assessment of the issue via two major innovations: a comparison of prior events with what would have happened to American wages solely as a result of changes in the *supply* of skilled versus unskilled workers, and projections over the coming twenty years to suggest what developments are likely on this front in the future. Dr. Cline also seeks to draw out the implications of his analysis for American policy—with respect to the labor market as well as trade policy itself. No single study can resolve either the intellectual or policy debate on these topics but we hope that Dr. Cline's book will promote a greater consensus on what factors lead to different viewpoints on them and how policy can best respond to these differing perceptions.

The Institute for International Economics is a private nonprofit institution for the study and discussion of international economic policy. Its purpose is to analyze important issues in that area and to develop and communicate practical new approaches for dealing with them. The Institute is completely nonpartisan.

The Institute is funded largely by philanthropic foundations. Major institutional grants are now being received from The German Marshall Fund of the United States, which created the Institute with a generous commitment of funds in 1981, and from The Ford Foundation, The Andrew W. Mellon Foundation, and The Starr Foundation. A number of other foundations and private corporations also contribute to the highly diversified financial resources of the Institute. About 12 percent of the Institute's resources in our latest fiscal year were provided by contributors outside the United States, including about 6 percent from Japan.

The Board of Directors bears overall responsibility for the Institute and gives general guidance and approval to its research program—including identification of topics that are likely to become important to international economic policymakers over the medium run (generally, one to three years), and which thus should be addressed by the Institute. The Director, working closely with the staff and outside Advisory Committee, is responsible for the development of particular projects and makes the final decision to publish an individual study.

The Institute hopes that its studies and other activities will contribute to building a stronger foundation for international economic policy around the world. We invite readers of these publications to let us know how they think we can best accomplish this objective.

C. FRED BERGSTEN
Director
September 1997

Acknowledgments

I am grateful to the following persons for comments on previous drafts of all or portions of this study: C. Fred Bergsten, Gary Burtless, Richard N. Cooper, Morris Goldstein, Gary C. Hufbauer, Daniel S. Hamermesh, Marvin H. Kosters, Paul Krugman, Marcus Miller, Marcus Noland, Fredrick L. Pryor, Dani Rodrik, and Adrian Wood, as well as participants in an Institute for International Economics study group meeting on 16 December 1996. None of these individuals should be held responsible for remaining shortcomings of the study. Dan Magder provided vital research assistance. I also thank my daughter, Marian Harwood Cline, for the use of her painting, "The Sea," on the cover.

Trends in Income Distribution and Wages

In the early 1990s it began to be clear that there had been a significant increase in inequality in the distribution of US income and wages during the 1980s. There was soon an explosion in the economics literature analyzing the causes of this trend. One of the most controversial issues in this literature has been the possible role of international trade and immigration in contributing to rising inequality in the United States and, to a lesser degree, elsewhere in the industrial world. This debate has taken place within a charged policy environment, as best illustrated by the bitter debate on whether the United States should join with Mexico and Canada in the North American Free Trade Agreement (NAFTA).

This book seeks to analyze the impact of trade and immigration on US wage inequality. The first chapter reviews the evidence that inequality has in fact been rising. The second chapter provides a comprehensive analytical survey of the economics literature on the link between these external influences and widening wage inequality. Chapters 3 and 4 then present new economic models for the purpose of shedding further light on this issue, including prospects for future international pressures on wage inequality. The final chapter synthesizes the results of the study as a whole and presents summary quantitative estimates of trade and immigration effects.

Long-Term Patterns

Historically, the US economy has provided real income growth to most Americans. From 1870 to 1965, average real per capita output grew at 1.9

percent annually in the United States, well above growth in Europe—where it was 1.7 percent in Germany, 1.6 percent in France, and 1.2 percent in the United Kingdom—and only slightly lower than in Japan—where it was 2.0 percent (calculated from Maddison 1970, 18).

Over the half century after 1929, US growth was accompanied by at least constancy in the distribution of income if not more equality. Williamson and Lindert (1980, 5) provide the following synthesis:

> inequality among *free* Americans before the Revolution was not too different from that which we experience today. Yet, inequality was hardly stable . . . the main epoch of increasing inequality was the last four decades before the Civil War. The Civil War itself reduced inequalities within regions, but it also increased inequality . . . between North and South. . . . trending inequality emerges once more between the turn of the century and World War I. World War I administered a brief, strong dose of equality, but the effects had worn off by 1929. The Kuznets-Lampman finding of considerable equalization in income and wealth between 1929 and mid-century appears to survive all the critical adjustments one might care to perform. After World War II, there was no sharp reversion to high degrees of inequality, as happened after World War I. Instead, postwar distributions appear to us to exhibit a curious stability; a slight increase in pretax and pretransfer inequality has been offset by the impact of taxes and transfers.

Similarly, Juhn and Murphy (1995, 26) use census data going back to 1939 to confirm the "dramatic fall in wage inequality during the 1940s and the relative stability of wage inequality during the 1950s and 1960s" and emphasize that "the rise in inequality witnessed during the 1970s and 1980s stands in sharp contrast" to the previous postwar experience.

The broad rise in inequality over the century preceding 1929, followed by the brisk reduction and then stabilization of inequality, led Kuznets (1955) to postulate the "inverted U-curve" to describe the path of inequality as an economy developed. The hypothesis was that greater proportionate asset accumulation by the rich, combined with urbanization, would generate rising inequality in the earlier phases of growth, while in the later phases the eventual rise of political influence of low-income groups would reduce inequality.

By the 1960s, the tenets of mainstream economic theory seemed to reinforce the notion of secular improvement or at least stability in equality. The neoclassical model of production, as mathematically related to the inputs of capital and labor, implied that, under the usual assumptions (constant returns to scale and less than unitary elasticity of substitution between capital and labor), the process of saving and investment would tend to equalize the distribution of income. The reason was that capital deepening (the rise in capital per worker) would tend to reduce the marginal product of capital and increase the marginal product of labor. With less than unitary elasticity of substitution, the rising quantity of capital would not offset the falling price of capital; thus, labor's share in the economy would tend to rise (Cline 1975).

The introduction of human capital in mainstream economic theory complicated the picture somewhat. Individuals that invested in their education (human capital) would thereafter tend to require higher earnings to compensate for lost work time (Mincer 1958). Inequality in the observed income distribution between educated and uneducated workers would result. Even so, there was room for a rising relative wage for raw labor (labor without an investment in human capital): returns to human capital would fall as human capital became abundant relative to raw labor.

The "neoclassical synthesis" of the 1960s also seemed to take care of the principal gap in the well-behaved model of production and distribution: unemployment. It was thought that properly sized and timed government intervention could make severe business-cycle downturns and their impact on unemployment relics of the past.

In the postwar period through the early 1970s, experience seemed to confirm the overall optimism about growing prosperity and equity. The proportion of US families with incomes below $5,000 in 1967 prices (about $20,000 at 1994 prices) steadily declined from 57.1 percent in 1947 to 23.9 percent in 1970 (US Department of Commerce [DOC] 1975, 290; Council of Economic Advisors [CEA] 1995, 344).

This favorable combination of rapid growth and falling or stable inequality in the quarter century after World War II gave way to a period of slow growth and rising inequality during the next quarter century. The growth of real GDP per capita slowed from 2.2 percent during 1947-73 to 1.3 percent during 1973-93 (CEA 1990, 296; 1995, 276, 311). The proportion of families with incomes below $25,000 (in 1992 prices) stagnated, moving only from 33.5 percent in 1970 to 32.3 percent by 1992 (DOC 1994, 469). The incidence of poverty, which had fallen by half, from 22.4 percent of all persons in 1959 to 11.1 percent by 1973, began to edge up again and by 1993 had climbed to 15.1 percent (DOC 1995, D13).

The slowdown in growth reflected in part the resurgence of more-severe business cycle downturns: the 1974-75 and 1982 recessions were the worst since the 1930s. However, income erosion at the lower end of the distribution also seemed to reflect a new, unfavorable trend in the distribution of income. As discussed below, there was a shift from the "curious stability" (Williamson and Lindert 1980) of the postwar period through the 1970s toward rising inequality in the 1980s.[1]

By the end of the 1980s there was increasing evidence that the new trend toward inequality was closely related to falling real wages for

---

1. Levy (1987, 196) finds that after correcting for taxes and for nonmoney benefits received, family income distribution by 1984 was more equal than in 1949 but less equal than in 1979. The share of the poorest 40 percent in this corrected income rose from 18.9 percent in 1949 to 23.2 percent in 1979 but fell to 20.7 percent by 1984. The share of the top 20 percent declined from 39.3 percent to 34.0 percent and then rose again to 36.8 percent over the same period.

workers on the lower rungs of the skill ladder and a widening differential between real wages for those with and without college degrees.

This study examines the influences of immigration and international trade, particularly with developing countries, on the relative erosion of unskilled wages. This chapter first documents trends in income distribution, wage dispersion, and skill differentials. Chapter 2 reviews literature on the causes of these trends, with special emphasis on the question of whether immigration and international trade have played important roles. Chapters 3 and 4 set forth model-based analyses of the issue and apply them to examine future trends under alternative assumptions about economic policy. Chapter 5 draws policy conclusions.

Family Income, Poverty, and Wealth

Income

Table 1.1 reports the US distribution of family money income over the past two decades.[2] Whereas there was little change in the distribution from 1970 to 1980, in the next dozen years there was a substantial increase in concentration, focused at the ends of the distribution. The income share of the poorest 20 percent of families declined by about one-sixth and that of the richest 5 percent increased by about one-sixth. The ratio of the income of the top 5 percent of families to that of the bottom 40 percent rose from about 7:1 in 1970 and 1980 to about 9.5:1 by 1992. Other measures also show rising income inequality. For example, Wolff (1994, 153) estimates that the Gini coefficient for household income rose from 0.43 in 1962 to 0.48 in 1983 and 0.52 in 1989.[3] Meanwhile, the income share of the broad middle class did not change much: the group from the 40th to the 80th percentile received 41.8 percent of family income in 1980 and 40.5 percent in 1992. However, the real income growth of the middle class was sluggish, as real median family income rose by only 2.7 percent from 1980 to 1992, about 0.2 percent per year. The lower-income groups lost

---

2. The distributions exclude households of unrelated individuals. These individuals numbered 15.4 million (7.5 percent of the total population) in 1970 and 28.3 million (11.1 percent) by 1992.

3. In a diagram with the cumulative percentage of households on the horizontal axis and the cumulative percentage of wealth (or income) on the vertical axis, absolute equality is represented by the diagonal from the lower-left origin to the upper-right corner. The actual distribution is a bowed curve (the Lorenz curve) lying below this diagonal. The Gini coefficient is the ratio of the area between this curve and the diagonal to the total area below the diagonal. With complete equality, the Gini coefficient is zero; with complete inequality (all wealth held by a single household), the coefficient is one.

Table 1.1 Distribution of family money income

	Percentage of income			Percentage change 1980-92
	1970	1980	1992	
Quantile				
Number (millions)	51.95	60.31	68.14	13.0
0–20	5.40	5.20	4.40	−15.4
20–40	12.20	11.50	10.50	−8.7
40–60	17.60	17.50	16.50	−5.7
60–80	23.80	24.30	24.00	−1.2
80–95	25.30	26.20	27.00	3.1
95–100	15.60	15.30	17.60	15.0
Income levels (thousands of 1992 dollars)				
Ceiling				
0–20	na	17.54	16.96	−3.3
20–40	na	29.64	30.00	1.2
40–60	na	41.99	44.20	5.3
60–80	na	58.87	64.30	9.2
80–95	na	92.16	106.50	15.6
Median	33.48[a]	35.84	36.81	2.7
Average[b]	na	40.96	44.62	8.9
Bottom 40[c]	na	17.10	16.62	−2.8
Average income ratios				
top 5/bottom 40	7.09	7.33	9.45	28.9
top 20/middle 40	1.98	1.99	2.20	10.9
Memorandum				
GDP per capita (1987 dollars)	na	16,582	19,495	17.6
Bottom 40 GDP per capita, hypothetical[d]	na	6,923	7,262	4.9

na = not available.

a. 1971.

b. Estimated as $[20/S3]ym$, where $S3$ is the share of the 40–60 percentile and ym is median income.

c. Estimated as $[S1\&2/40]ya$, where $S1\&2$ is the share of the 0–40 percentile and ya is estimated average income.

d. If the relative per capita income of the bottom 40 percent of families is the same as relative family income. Estimated as $[S1\&2/40]qa$, where qa is GDP per capita.

Sources: DOC (1994, 470; 1975, 289–93); CEA (1994, 304).

ground even in absolute terms. Thus, the average real family income of the poorest 40 percent fell by 2.8 percent from 1980 to 1992.

Ethnic differentials in the distribution of family income have also widened. Median family income for blacks fell from 59.2 percent of that for whites in 1967 to 56.6 percent in 1979 and 54.8 percent in 1993, and the ratio of median family income for Hispanics fell from 69.3 percent of that for whites in 1973 and 1979 to 60.2 percent in 1993 (Mishel and Bernstein 1994, 32). This chapter shows that wage differentials by skill class are widening. Because black workers generally have less education and lower levels of skills than do their white counterparts, the trend toward higher skill differentials is likely to have contributed to widening income disparities by race (Murphy and Welch 1991, 51).

Table 1.1 also reports real per capita GDP and an estimate of per capita GDP accruing to the poorest 40 percent of families. Per capita GDP grew 17.6 percent from 1980 to 1992, far exceeding the 8.9 percent growth in average real family income. Correspondingly, an estimate of real GDP per capita accruing to the poorest 40 percent of families suggests that there was a modest real increase of 4.9 percent over the period, rather than a real decrease of 2.8 percent as suggested by the income data. One factor that accounts for the divergence is that the income data deflate by the adjusted consumer price index (CPI),[4] whereas GDP deflates by the GDP deflator. As discussed below, adjusted consumer prices that rise more rapidly than do producer prices (e.g., computers) in the 1980s imply a paradox of wage and income growth more sluggish than real output growth. Nonetheless, the contrast suggests that the family income data may tend to understate improvement in the 1980s.[5]

Figure 1.1 shows the median real money income of families and households for 1967-93 (again deflating by the adjusted CPI, CPI − U − X). The figure shows that family income (in constant 1993 dollars) had fallen significantly by 1993 from its 1989 high because of the recession and slow growth of 1990-91. For the period as a whole, the growth of median family income was relatively low. Based on endpoint averages for 1967-68 and 1992-93, the growth rate was only 0.58 percent per year. A regression trend that removes the influence of the business cycle and captures the slowdown after 1979 shows that real median family income grew 0.76 percent per year from 1967 to 1979 but then slowed down to only 0.1 percent from 1980 to 1993.[6]

---

4. CPI − U − X, urban consumer prices adjusted to treat housing prices consistently. In 1983, the consumer price index shifted treatment of housing from home prices to rental equivalency. Bosworth and Perry (1994, 321) note that because this shift occurred at a high point in mortgage interest rates, "the [unadjusted] CPI greatly overstates the rise in the price level and understates real wage gains since the late 1970s."

5. Little of the discrepancy can be explained by the change in average family size, which was 3.14 persons in 1970, 3.29 in 1980, and 3.16 in 1993 (DOC 1975, 41; 1994, 63).

6. The regression is

$$\ln y = 4.491 + 0.00755t - 0.0077du + 0.0704D2 - 0.00658[D2 \times t];$$
$$\quad (0.01) \quad (0.0009) \quad (0.0018) \quad (0.019) \quad (0.0013)$$

$\bar{R}^2 = 0.863$; where $\ln y$ is the natural logarithm of median family income in 1993 dollars, t

Figure 1.1 Median money income and poverty, 1967-93

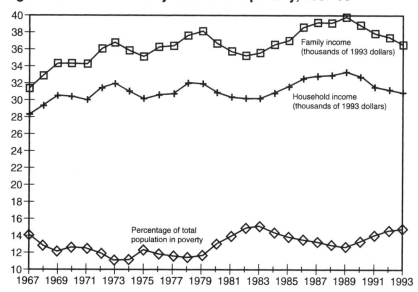

The most recent US Census Bureau estimates show a rebound of about 4 percent in real median household income from 1993 to 1996 (*New York Times*, 30 September 1997). Despite gains in relative income of women and blacks, however, overall income concentration remained virtually unchanged over this period.

Overall, based on family income, the rich got richer and the poor got poorer in the 1980s and early 1990s. Although the middle-income groups held on to a practically unchanged share—contrary to the common perception of a shrinking middle class—the overall growth of real income was so lackluster that the broad middle class failed to make the economic progress characteristic of the previous three decades.

The process of fiscal redistribution does not seem to have ameliorated trends in family income distribution. Mishel and Bernstein (1994, 86) note that federal, state, and local taxes in the United States have commanded a relatively constant share of GDP since the early 1970s—about 31 percent. They find that after-tax income has become more unequally distributed, just as before-tax income has. Indeed, changes in tax law aggravated trends in inequality in 1977-89, although this was partially reversed by the reforms of the Omnibus Budget Reconciliation Act of 1993.

---

is the year (1967 = 1), *du* is the year's unemployment rate minus the average unemployment rate for 1967-93, 6.37 percent, and *D2* is a dummy variable set at 0 until 1979 and 1 thereafter.

Figure 1.2 Poverty by family status, 1959-93

Percentage in poverty

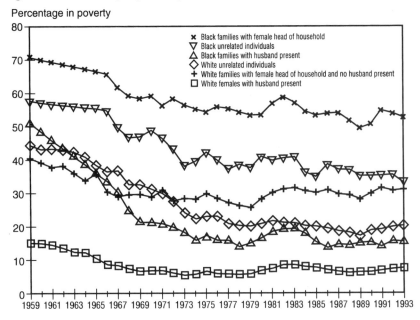

Poverty

Whereas family (and household) income merely showed a slowdown in long-term growth after 1979, the incidence of poverty has substantially increased—first with the severe recession of 1982 and then again in the early 1990s (figure 1.1).[7] Figure 1.2 shows poverty incidence by broad social categories. The striking feature of the more disaggregated data is that they show the incidence of poverty has been about constant or declining in almost every major category in recent years, except for white families with female head of household and no husband present. This means that the increase in overall poverty has come to an important degree from a shifting composition of the population toward those categories with higher poverty incidence, rather than from a generalized deterioration within each category.

The overall incidence of poverty for persons fell from 22.4 percent in 1959 to a low plateau averaging 11.6 percent in 1973-79 and then rose again to reach 15.1 percent in 1993 (DOC 1995, D13). Figure 1.2 shows dramatic reductions in poverty incidence from 1959 to 1979 for black

---

7. The US poverty line has traditionally been set at three times the amount required for a basic household budget for food. The standard data are for money income only, but, for example, inclusion of noncash benefits only reduces the 1991 rate from 14.2 percent to 12.4 percent (Mishel and Bernstein 1994, 257-8).

Figure 1.3   Family status, 1959-93

Percentage in poverty

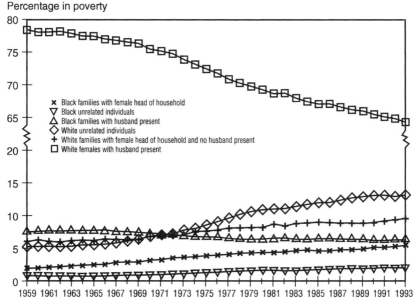

families with female head of household, black unrelated individuals, white families with female head of household, black families with husband present, and white unrelated individuals. There was a much gentler decline in poverty, from a far lower starting point, for white families with husband present.

Then from 1979 to 1993, there was little change in poverty incidence within most of these categories. Poverty incidence increased substantially for white families with female head of household, from 25.2 to 31.0 percent, and rose modestly from a low base for the numerically dominant category of white families with husband present, from 5.4 percent to 7.5 percent. Nonetheless, the rise in overall poverty incidence for persons, from 11.7 percent to 15.1 percent, came to a considerable extent from a reallocation of household types toward the higher-poverty categories. Figure 1.3 shows a persistent and accelerating decline in the share of white families with husband present in the total population and a sharp increase in the share of white unrelated individuals in the population. There are also increases in white and black families with female head of household—both have higher poverty incidence than the corresponding families with husband present.

Figure 1.4 shows what would have happened to the overall incidence of poverty among persons if the within-category poverty rates had experienced their actual paths (figure 1.2) but the composition of population across family categories had remained unchanged, at either the 1959 or

Figure 1.4 Actual and hypothetical poverty, 1959-93

Percentage in poverty

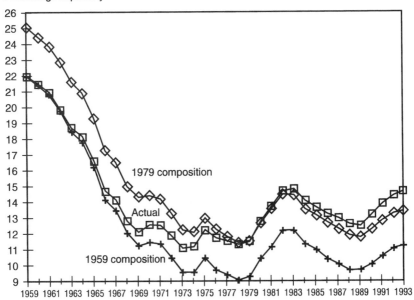

1979 profile. The poverty rate actually increased 3.2 percentage points from 1979 to 1993, about one-fourth. If family status had remained at its 1979 composition, the poverty rate would have increased by only 1.9 percentage points. From a longer perspective, if family composition had remained unchanged from 1959 to 1993, the poverty rate among persons would have been 3.5 percentage points lower in 1993 than it actually was.[8]

Figures 1.2 through 1.4 imply that changing social patterns, including not only the well-known increase in female heads of households but also the less-publicized rise in individuals living alone rather than with families, have played a major role in poverty's resurgence and account for about 40 percent of the increase in poverty since 1979. Thus, America's resurgent poverty problem is only partly due to economic factors and, more fundamentally, seems to reflect social changes.[9]

---

8. The "actual" rate in figure 1.4 is $\Sigma_i \phi_{it} p_{it}$, where N_i is the population share in category i, p_i is the percentage of persons in poverty in this category, and t is the year in question. Note that the six categories considered cover only 97.3 percent of the population, so the estimated overall actual rate is slightly different from the true overall rate (figure 1.1). The hypothetical rates in figure 1.4 are $\Sigma_i \phi_{i59} p_{it}$ and $\Sigma_i \phi_{i79} p_{it}$.

9. Nor is it clear that the social changes are caused by economic deterioration. For example, it might be expected that in hard times there would be consolidation of family households and, thus, a decline rather than increase in the number of persons in households of "unrelated individuals" rather than families.

Ethnic differences in poverty are pronounced, as suggested in figure 1.2. However, the most striking incidence of poverty is perhaps in the overlap between two categories that tend to have high poverty: nonwhites and children. In 1993, 46.1 percent of blacks and 40.9 percent of Hispanics under the age of 18 years were in poverty, compared to 17.8 percent of white children and youths (DOC 1995, D-18 to D-20). The trend was unfavorable, as poverty incidence among black children and youths had been at about 41 percent in 1975-79 (earlier data are not available).

For all races, poverty incidence for those under 18 declined from 27.3 percent in 1959 to 14.4 percent in 1973, but then rose to 22.7 percent by 1993—meaning that two-thirds of the progress in the 1960s was rolled back. The turning point coincided with the fall in the growth of US output and labor productivity that began after 1983, suggesting that weaker trends in the economy spilled over disproportionately to children, presumably through interaction with adverse trends in family structure.

In contrast, the elderly fared well. Poverty incidence among those 65 years or older fell from 35 percent in 1959 (higher than for children) to 15.2 percent by 1979 and 12.2 percent by 1993 (about half that for children). Once again, then, changes in social structure undoubtedly amplified whatever poverty trends would otherwise have emerged from the underlying economic forces.[10]

Wealth

Wolff (1994) has used data from the Federal Reserve Board's Survey of Consumer Finances to examine the distribution of wealth in 1962, 1983, and 1989. He finds little change between the first two benchmark years, but a substantial increase in concentration of wealth between the second two.

Wolff (1994, 171) considers net worth of households, including the market value of owned homes. He concludes that

> The most striking result is the sharp increase in inequality of household wealth between 1983 and 1989. While median wealth grew by 1.3 percent per year in real terms, mean household wealth increased at an annual rate of 3.4 percent. Moreover, the share of the top half of one percent (the 'super-rich') increased by 5 percentage points [from 26.2 percent to 31.4 percent] and the Gini coefficient also showed a marked increase, from 0.80 to 0.84. Whereas the average wealth (in 1989 dollars) of all households increased by 23 percent from [$162,000 in] 1983 to [$199,000 in] 1989, that of the super-rich grew by 47 percent. Of the 4.9 trillion dollar increase in family wealth between 1983 and 1989, 46 percent accrued to the top one-half of one percent of households and 53 percent to the top one percent.... [I]n sharp contrast ... [t]here was virtually no difference in wealth inequality in 1983 and 1962.

---

10. In this case, the social change was the growth in entitlement programs for the elderly, which in turn reflected the group's growing political strength.

Wolff does not quantify the causes of the increased concentration of wealth in the 1980s, but he suggests three likely sources. First, income inequality was rising (especially for after-tax income), so savings from income could have widened wealth dispersion. Second, stock prices were rising faster than housing prices, and stocks constitute a higher fraction of net worth of the rich, whereas homes represent a higher share of that of middle- and lower-wealth groups. Third, inflation in this period was lower (at 3.7 percent) than in 1962-83 (5.7 percent), providing less scope for inflationary erosion of debts—and it is the lower-wealth groups that have proportionately higher debts.

Wealth is much more concentrated than income. Thus, in 1989 the Gini coefficient for wealth was 0.84, whereas that for income was 0.52 (Wolff 1994, 155). Similarly, in 1989 the average net worth of the bottom 40 percent of families ranked by income stood at $50,600 whereas that of the top 5 percent was $1.77 million (160). Thus, the ratio of the top 5 to the bottom 40 percent was 35:1, more than three times their corresponding ratio of incomes (table 1.1).

Weicher (1996) has challenged the view that concentration of wealth in the United States increased from 1983 to 1989. Although using the same Federal Reserve survey data as Wolff, he emphasizes that the way the survey is expanded to the population critically affects the estimates.[11] Weicher argues that unadjusted sample data are preferable to the adjusted data used by Wolff, and he concludes that "it would be . . . reasonable to argue either that concentration [the top 1 percent share] *increased* from 32 to 37 percent between 1983 and 1989 or that it *decreased* from 36 to 35 percent" (10).

Weicher's broad conclusion that the distribution of income has not changed would seem to contradict his own central results, however. They indicate that, even in Weicher's (1996, 11) preferred, unadjusted data, the estimated range for the share of the richest one percent rose from 32-36 percent of total wealth in 1983 to 35-37 percent in 1989. Whereas Weicher cites alternative pairs of extremes to argue that the change could have gone either way, the more natural comparison would be between the two ranges as a whole. On this basis, there was a clear increase in concentration from 1983 to 1989, as both the range averages and endpoints increased even in the unadjusted data.

Overall, the data on wealth serve to sharpen the picture of widening inequality in the 1980s that emerges from consideration of income inequal-

---

11. If the survey is expanded using adjustments that harmonize sample estimates with aggregate values in the Federal Reserve's Flow of Funds Accounts, the measured share of the top 1 percent in net worth falls by 1½ percentage points from the unadjusted sample share, in 1983, and rises by 1 percentage point in 1989. There is much larger household debt in the Flow of Funds data than in the Survey of Consumer Finances data. Weicher notes that sample adjustment to resemble the Flow of Funds aggregates results in idiosyncra-

ity and poverty incidence. Perhaps the one potentially divergent trend in the wealth data is that median household wealth grew as rapidly as 1.3 percent annually from 1983 to 1989. In contrast, the analysis above suggests that trend growth in real family income from 1979 to 1993 was only 0.1 percent annually. The difference suggests that much of wealth accumulation in the 1980s stemmed from asset appreciation rather than from saving, because saving could not be expected to grow rapidly when real incomes were stagnant.

This interpretation would help explain the collapse in the personal saving rate, from 8.4 percent of disposable income in 1980-82 to 4.6 percent in 1989-93 (CEA 1995, 306). Weak growth in family income would have limited the supply of saving, just as asset appreciation would have induced additional consumption. Trends in median wealth could also help explain the environment of eroding consumer confidence and the public's perception of losing economic ground in the early 1990s. As Wolff notes (1994, 170), for the bottom 80 percent of households, the gross value of owned residences accounts for 60 percent of net worth. Yet in the early 1990s, the boom in house prices turned into a minibust as housing prices fell. Whereas wealth in owner-occupied real estate grew from $4.47 trillion (in 1987 dollars) in 1983 to $5.47 trillion in 1989, it fell to $5.2 trillion in 1990 and by 1992 was back up to only $5.48 trillion, practically the same as the 1989 level (CEA 1995, 405). Thus, the asset appreciation of the 1980s that gave the impression of progress despite stagnant family income growth gave way to asset depreciation in the early 1990s that reinforced the weakness of income growth.

Finally, more recent data from the Federal Reserve's Survey of Consumer Finances indicate that there was a modest reduction in wealth concentration from 1989 to 1995. The US recession at the beginning of the 1990s reduced the absolute level of household net worth by 7.5 percent on average from 1989 to 1992. Then by 1995, whereas median family net worth had recovered to virtually its same level as in 1989 ($56,400 at 1995 prices), mean family net worth was still 5 percent below its real 1989 level (at $205,900) (Kennickell, Starr-McCluer, and Sunden 1997, 6). The ratio of mean to median family wealth, a measure of concentration, had risen by 13 percent from 1983 to 1989 (based on Wolff's estimates) before falling 5 percent in 1989-95. In the first half of the 1990s, then, there was a rollback of about two-fifths of the 1983-89 increase in wealth inequality.

Importantly, the moderate reversion toward less wealth concentration in the first half of this decade came from an absolute decline in wealth at the top only, whereas the earlier increase in concentration had come from an absolute increase in wealth that was more pronounced at the top than at the bottom. However, the surge in the US stock market in 1995

sies, such as the reclassification of a particular household from the top 1 percent of wealth holders to the bottom 1 percent.

Figure 1.5 Composition of national income, 1959-94

Percentage of national income

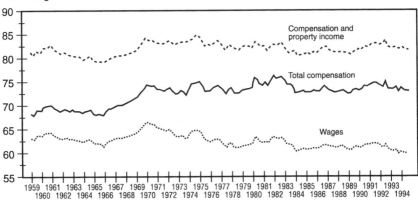

Sources: NIPA historical; SCB various.

through early 1997 suggests that more recently both absolute real wealth and its concentration have once again begun to increase (the latter in view of the greater proportion of wealth that the rich hold in stocks).

Wage Distribution

Wages and other employee compensation account for about three-fourths of national income (figure 1.5). Thus, it is likely that increasing inequality in the distribution of wages is an important source of increasing inequality in the distribution of family income. The bulk of recent literature relating international economic influences to domestic distribution focuses on the differential effects of those influences on skilled and unskilled labor, and the present study adopts this focus as well.

The emphasis on wage inequality stems in part from the stylized fact that there has been little change in the distribution of income between overall wages and capital. Figure 1.5 suggests that the share of employee compensation in national income has been relatively steady over the past quarter century. Using household survey data, Cutler and Katz (1991) confirm that labor's share in total factor compensation remained essentially unchanged over the 1980s.[12] This finding counters the attribution

---

12. The authors do find that labor's share in "market-based family income" fell from 80.3 percent in 1979 to 76.0 percent in 1989. However, the rising capital share was mainly driven by higher dividends and interest earnings. They note that the rise in dividends stemmed mainly from a corporate shift toward paying out rather than retaining earnings and so was primarily an accounting rather than economic shift. More questionably, their corresponding deemphasis of the rise in interest earnings invokes "one's view of the incidence of the taxes required to pay for government debt service." The authors judge that "the increase in

of increased income inequality to a shift in the "functional distribution of income" from labor to capital.

This constancy in factor shares is somewhat surprising given the close association of the rise in wealth concentration with rapid growth of financial and other assets owned by the rich relative to home and other assets owned by lower-income groups (as just reviewed). Nonetheless, falling real interest rates during the late 1980s and early 1990s could have limited the translation of growing concentration of wealth into any corresponding increase in concentration of income.

The difference between capital and labor income does mean that the level of inequality for income among families would be expected to exceed that for wages among workers, because capital income will tend to be more concentrated. Wolff (1994, 172) estimates the Gini coefficient for household income at 0.52 in 1989, up from 0.48 in 1983.[13] In contrast, the Gini coefficient for wage inequality among all earners in the same period was about 0.46 (Karoly as reported in Levy and Murnane 1992, 1343). This difference in levels of the two types of inequality is in fact surprisingly small, suggesting that the extremes in wages (for example, between earnings of corporate executives and the minimum wage) are not much smaller than those in capital earnings.[14] A modest difference between the concentration of labor and capital income may be less surprising given that "labor" income actually includes returns on an important, arguably the most important, type of capital: human (education and other training).

This study deals with two central questions about the trend in wages. First, how much has wage inequality increased? Second, how much of the increase can be explained by international economic factors: trade, immigration (both examined in the models developed in this study), and foreign investment (not examined in the models)? Chapter 2 finds that there is relatively broad agreement that in the 1980s there was a substantial increase in wage inequality. On the second, however, there is considerably less agreement. The majority view attributes rising wage inequality primarily toward skill-biased technological change, but there is a strongly held minority view that trade and immigration have played an important role as well.

---

overall inequality is dominated by increased inequality of labor income rather than nonlabor income" (Cutler and Katz 1991, 19).

13. Note, however, that because single-person households and those comprising other unrelated individuals are not included among families, the household and family distributions differ somewhat. The ratio of mean income to median income is one measure of concentration. In 1993, this ratio was 1.33 for the 97.1 million households in the United States but only 1.28 for the 68.5 million families (DOC 1995; 5, 11).

14. The small difference between the family and wage Gini coefficients may also reflect the fact that the coefficient is more sensitive to differences near the middle of the distribution than at the extremes (Levy and Murnane 1992, 1339), yet the contribution of capital earnings to family income would tend to widen the extremes.

In view of the seeming consensus that inequality has increased, the limited change of some overall inequality measures for wages is a bit surprising. Karoly (1988, as reported in Levy and Murnane 1992, 1343) estimates that the Gini coefficient for annual wages and salaries of all persons 16 years and older fell from an average of 0.458 in 1970-73 to 0.447 in 1979-80 but then rose to 0.459 in 1985-86. Although this pattern is a mild confirmation of the stylized fact of decreasing inequality (at least by educational differentials) in the 1970s, followed by rising inequality in the 1980s, surely wage dispersion would be a nonissue if there were only a net increase over the whole period of 0.001 on the most traditional measure of inequality (or, for that matter, an increase of 0.012 from the interim trough to the terminal peak).[15]

As it turns out, the Karoly estimate of the Gini coefficient for wages is probably biased toward constancy, because her data do not exclude part-time, and especially part-time female, workers. Data sets that focus on full-time, year-round workers do find an increase in inequality for all workers. Moreover, they find an even greater increase in inequality among male workers and among female workers separately, mitigated only modestly by a reduction in the wage gap between males and females.

Figure 1.6 shows estimates from Current Population Survey (CPS) data by Burtless (1995b) that measure wage inequality by the ratio of the wage at the 90th percentile of the distribution to the wage at the 10th percentile. Burtless uses benchmark years in which the economy was at comparable high points in the business cycle (1969, 1973, 1979, 1989, and—as the most recent year with data—1993). For full-time, year-round male workers this ratio rose from 4.0 in 1979 to 5.2 in 1993. For full-time, year-round female workers, the ratio rose from 3.4 to 4.2 over this period. For all such workers, the ratio rose from 4.3 to 4.9. Measured by the 90th/10th percentile ratio, then, from 1979 to 1993 wage inequality rose by 28.6 percent for males, 23.5 percent for females, and 13.4 percent for all workers. The overall rise in wage inequality was thus only about half that for either males or females individually.[16]

As shown in the figure, the trend line for the overall distribution was more gently sloped than that for males over the entire period or females in the 1980s. This pattern reflects the narrowing wage differential between

---

15. Other measures show similarly muted trends for the overall wage distribution. Bluestone (1989, as reported in Levy and Murnane 1992, 1343) shows the variance of the logarithm of wages oscillating from an average of 1.96 in 1963-65 to 1.80 in 1970-73, 1.79 in 1979-80, and 1.85 in 1985-87.

16. Somewhat counterintuitively, the overall inequality is not simply a weighted average of—and hence, is not necessarily intermediate between—the group inequality measures. To see this, consider two groups, each with absolute within-group equality but with widely disparate group wage averages. Overall inequality would be high, but a weighted average of group inequality would be zero.

Figure 1.6 90th/10th percentile wage ratios for full-time wage and salary workers, 1969-93

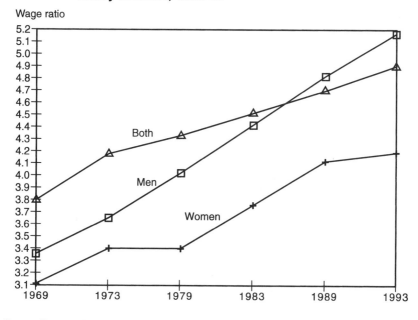

Source: Burtless (1995a).

men and women over this period. Thus, the ratio of female to male median earnings for full-time, year-round workers was stagnant at 0.58 from 1970 to 1979, but rose to 0.67 by 1987 (Levy and Murnane 1992, 1355). Female wages, accordingly, rose by almost 16 percent relative to male wages in the 1980s.

This move toward gender equality does not seem to stir much enthusiasm in the literature as an offset to the widening male disparities.[17] The inattention to what we might call the "partial gender offset" could be construed to represent a view in which wages of females are of only secondary importance because the male is the breadwinner and female work is in the end voluntary. That view seems anachronistic. As shown in figure 1.3, about 15 percent of the US population lives in households headed by females without a husband present. Another 8 percent of the population comprises females in the category of unrelated individuals,

17. For example, Juhn, Murphy, and Pierce (1993) do not even consider females in their analysis of growing wage inequality. Katz and Murphy (1992, 35) do recognize that "Although the male and female wage structures widened considerably . . . the average wage of women increased by about 8 percent relative to the average wage of men from 1979 to 1987." Yet the authors do not explicitly examine the contribution of intergender narrowing to the offsetting of intragender widening in determining the path of the overall distribution.

of whom about one-third live alone (DOC 1995, 22). So, for nearly one-fourth of the US population, the relative gains of females' incomes in the 1980s were especially important.

It is possible that the narrowing male-female wage differential reflects a link between the structure of production and comparative advantage by gender. To the extent that the US economy shifted away from occupations requiring brawn to those requiring brains, there should have been a reduction in the comparative disadvantage of female workers, who have less brawn than males. Other things being equal, it would not be surprising to see the relative wages of females rise as the economy shifts from manufacturing employment to services employment.[18]

As for the limited credit given in the literature to the narrowing gender differential, one explanation might be that the absolute decline in low-end male wages commands much more concern than the relative rise of female wages. Another may be an implicit bow to the argument that America may have struck a bad bargain in the past two decades when it sent its wives to work, in contrast with the worker deal in Europe that kept wives home and held wages high.[19] A more legitimate basis for downplaying the gender offset would be the possibility that there is a close correlation between wage levels of spouses. Such a correlation would help explain a worsening family distribution in the face of a constant distribution of overall wages.[20]

Returning to the Burtless estimates of figure 1.6, an important pattern is that they show the 1980s widening of inequality, for at least males, as an almost linear continuation of trends already present in the 1970s. This information confirms Juhn and Murphy's (1995) findings of rising wage inequality through both decades. However, both results stand in tension with much of the literature, which emphasizes that educationally based wage differentials tended to narrow during the 1970s before widening sharply in the 1980s. This literature (reviewed in chapter 2) points to the rising relative supply of college-educated workers in explanation of the trend toward narrower education differentials in the 1970s. The contrasting secular widening for male workers, based on the percentile measures, suggests that there were other more persistent factors at work.

---

18. Certainly with respect to, say, the manufacturing of steel. An important exception might be the apparel industry, where sewing requires dexterity rather than brawn and a high proportion of workers are females.

19. The trade-off between jobs and wages in the US and European context is examined in appendix A.

20. Suppose spousal earnings were completely correlated, and suppose that over time wives' earnings rose from half of the husbands' to parity. There would be a marked reduction in inequality measures for wages but no change for the more meaningful measures of family income.

Figure 1.7   Skilled/unskilled wage ratio, 1961-93

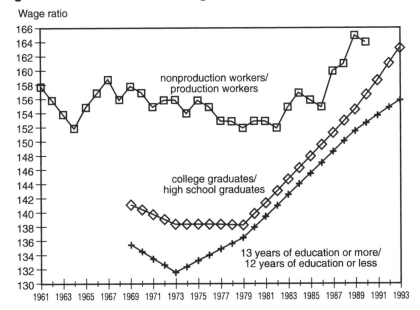

Sources: Sachs and Shatz (1995); Feenstra and Hanson (1995); Burtless (1995b).

As developed in chapter 2, most of the literature has examined skill differentials rather than pure distributional quantile ratios. Wage differentials by skill tend to show moderation in the 1970s and steep increases in the 1980s. As will be seen (e.g., table 2.5 in chapter 2), there have been two predominant definitions of skill classes. The first uses educational attainment. Those workers that are college educated or more tend to be classified as skilled; those that are high school educated or less, unskilled; and those with some college, as an intermediate group. Data using educational categories typically come from the CPS.

The second popular definition of skill classes stems from the popularity of the database in the Annual Survey of Manufactures, which groups employees as "production workers" or "nonproduction workers." Many studies consider the former to be unskilled and the latter skilled, but, as discussed in chapter 2, this dichotomy leaves much to be desired. Frequently, skilled workers are included with the production group, and conversely.

Figure 1.7 shows the trends for the ratio of skilled to unskilled wages, using these two definitions. The wage ratio for nonproduction (NPR) to production (PR) workers shows the stylized fact of a decrease in wage inequality during the 1970s and the decided increase in the 1980s. The NPR/PR wage ratio fell by about 3 percent from 1969-70 to 1979-82. A falling skill differential, despite rising overall wage inequality in the 1970s, underscores the role of unexplained increases in inequality among workers of identical education and experience, a trend discussed below. As for the 1980s, by the NPR/PR measure the increase in skill differentials during the decade was rather modest, from a ratio of 153 percent in 1979-80 to 165 percent in 1989-90, a 7.8 percent increase. Correspondingly, the net increase of the NPR/PR wage ratio over the two decades as a whole was only about 5 percent.

The trends for the educationally based skill classes indicate sharper widening of differentials in the 1980s and an earlier reversal of the 1970s trend of moderation. The frequently used wage ratio for college graduates to high school graduates fell from 1.41 in 1969 to 1.38 in 1973, remained at 1.38 until 1979, and then rose persistently to 1.63 by 1993.[21] This ratio did show the conventional moderation in the 1970s. Moreover, the subsequent increase in the wage differential was much sharper than that for NPR/PR workers. From 1979 to 1989 the increase amounted to 11.7 percent, and by 1993, the ratio stood 17.8 percent above its 1979 base. The trends were similar with skilled workers defined more comprehensively as those with 13 years of education or more (ED2) and unskilled as those with 12 years of education or less (ED1). The principal difference is that this ratio reached its trough in 1973 and rose almost linearly thereafter. From a 1979 base of 1.366, this ratio rose by 11 percent through 1989 and by a cumulative 14.2 percent through 1993.

In sum, during the 1980s the ratio of skilled to unskilled wages rose by about 10 to 15 percent, with the lower end of the range for the occupationally based distinction and the upper end for an educationally based skill classification. Because the educationally based estimates seem superior, this study uses a benchmark of 18 percent relative wage increase over the period of 1973-93 (the estimate given by both ED2/ED1 and CG/HSG in figure 1.7).

Additional evidence on wage inequality trends is shown in figure 1.8, which reports estimates by Karoly (1988, as reported in Levy and Murnane 1992, 1344) of four measures of inequality among males (annual wages and salaries, men 16 years and older with positive earnings). In addition to the more familiar Gini coefficient, these include the coefficient of variation, the variance of the natural logarithm of wages, and Theil's "entropy" index. The latter two measures have a greater sensitivity to redistributions within the lower range (Atkinson 1970 and Love and Wolfson 1976, as discussed in Levy and Murnane 1992, 1339).

The measures of inequality for wages among males show increased inequality in the 1980s. The Gini coefficient rises marginally in the 1970s

---

21. The educationally based data in figure 1.7 are from Burtless (1995b). Burtless selects the years 1969, 1973, 1979, and 1989 as benchmarks because they were all years of high employment, and he includes 1993 as the most recent observation available.

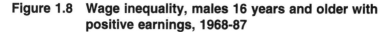

Figure 1.8   Wage inequality, males 16 years and older with positive earnings, 1968-87

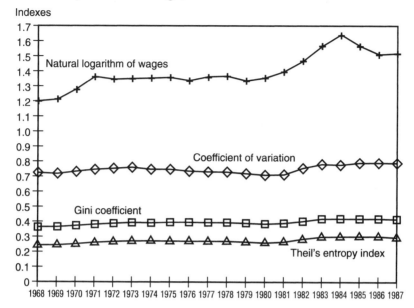

Source: Karoly (1988) as reported in Levy and Murnane (1992, 1344).

from an average of 0.388 in 1970-73 to 0.392 in 1980-81 and then increases more substantially to 0.423 in 1986-87. The most evident increase is in the variance of logarithms, although the coefficient of variation also shows a more marked rise than the Gini coefficient. This contrast suggests that the worsening of the distribution in the 1980s was concentrated in the lower quintile or so (as just discussed).

Increased wage inequality in the 1980s is also evident in wage quantile ratios. Like Burtless (1995b), Mishel and Bernstein (1994) have shown a substantially rising trend in the ratio of wages at the 90th percentile relative to the median and the median relative to the 10th percentile for both males and females separately (figure 1.9). However, the increase for females is somewhat at odds with the series of Gini coefficients estimated by Karoly (1988).[22] For males, Juhn, Murphy, and Pierce (1993) estimate that the real wage at the 90th percentile rose by 40 percent from 1963 to 1989, whereas that at the 10th percentile fell by 5 percent.

In short, there is ample evidence of widening wage inequality in the 1980s. Moreover, Levy and Murnane (1992, 1334) stress that this increase

---

22. Which falls from an average of 0.462 in 1970-73 to 0.444 in 1979-80 and then rises only modestly to 0.452 in 1986-87 (as reported in Levy and Murnane 1992, 1345).

Figure 1.9a   Wage inequality for men, 1973-93

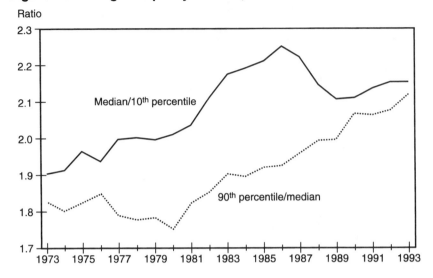

Figure 1.9b   Wage inequality for women, 1973-93

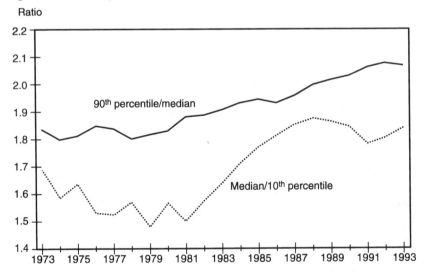

Source: Mishel and Bernstein (1994).

Table 1.2 Change in real hourly wage by education, 1973-93
(1993 dollars and percentages)

Year	High school dropout	High school graduate	Some college	College graduate	College plus 2 or more years
Real hourly wages (1993 dollars)					
1973	10.16	11.63	12.86	16.99	20.91
1979	10.06	11.23	12.24	15.52	18.80
1987	8.74	10.49	11.96	15.98	19.77
1989	8.44	10.21	11.82	15.90	20.36
1990	8.21	10.04	11.81	15.99	20.29
1993	7.87	9.92	11.37	15.71	19.93
Percentage change					
1973–79	− 1.1	− 3.5	− 4.8	− 8.6	− 10.1
1979–89	− 16.1	− 9.1	− 3.5	2.4	8.3
1989–93	− 6.7	− 2.8	− 3.8	− 1.2	− 2.1
1990–93	− 4.2	− 1.2	− 3.8	− 1.7	− 1.8
1973–93	− 22.5	− 14.7	− 11.6	− 7.5	− 4.7
Share of workforce					
1973	28.5	41.8	15.1	8.8	3.6
1979	20.1	42.2	19.1	11.0	4.9
1989	13.7	40.5	22.3	14.0	6.9

Source: Mishel and Bernstein (1994).

was driven by a hollowing out of middle-class male wage groups and a swelling of the ranks at both the low and the high ends of the distribution. In 1979 only 10 percent of men 25 to 54 years old earned less than $10,000 (in 1988 prices), and only 9.4 percent earned more than $50,000. By 1987 the two groups stood at 14.3 percent and 9.4 percent, respectively. Correspondingly, the substantial concentration of 31.3 percent of workers in the income class of $20,000 to $30,000 in 1979 moderated to 24.5 percent by 1987. The enlargement of the pool of workers with wages below $10,000 signifies an absolute deterioration, a trend that gives much more basis for concern than if the rising inequality were simply relative and absolute wages were rising along the whole distribution.

Education and Skills

Most analysts have stressed that the skill differential in wages widened during the 1980s. Figure 1.6 confirms this proposition, using two definitions of skill. Mishel and Bernstein (1994) have emphasized, moreover, that the widening resulted not from a surge in real wages of highly educated workers, but from a general decline in real wages that is proportionately greater for less-educated workers. Although their wage data ignore the growing share of compensation in fringe benefits, Mishel and Bernstein's estimates (table 1.2 and figure 1.9) are sobering. They show that real wages of high school dropouts have fallen by more than 20 percent in the last two decades. Strikingly, real wages have fallen in every educational category, although the percentage decline is smaller for the higher educational levels.[23]

For workers with a high school education or less, the wage decline persisted throughout the last two decades. In contrast, there was a more rapid decline for workers with at least some college during the 1970s, followed by an increase in the 1980s. One major explanation for this reversal is that in the 1970s the stock of college graduates rapidly expanded, in part because of the rise in college attendance in the late 1960s in the face of the alternative, the military draft. Subsequently, the deceleration of college enrollment and graduation in the early 1980s slowed the growth of the college-educated workforce.

If one postulates at the same time a persistent or accelerating trend in the demand for college graduates relative to high school graduates, the result is that the outward shifting supply dominated in the 1970s, reducing educational wage differentials, whereas outward shifting demand dominated in the 1980s, raising them again. This reversal is one of the stylized facts of the wage differential literature (e.g., Levy and Murnane 1992; Katz and Murphy 1992; Kosters 1994; and Juhn, Murphy, and Pierce 1993). As reviewed in chapter 2, whether the 1980s outward shift in demand for college graduates relative to high school graduates was primarily attributable to technological change, trade and immigration, or other influences is at the center of the debate on the relevance of international factors for trends in US wage and income distribution.

The 1980s rise in the education differential has been the largest for young male workers. For males aged 25 to 34, the ratio of wages of workers with 16 years of education to those with 12 years eased from 1.22 in 1971 to 1.13 in 1979 and then surged to 1.38 by 1987. In contrast, for workers older than 34, this educational differential was about the same or lower in 1987 than in 1971 (albeit higher than in 1979) (Levy and Murnane 1992, 1355).

Table 1.3 reports summary data on educational status and corresponding income differentials. Among white males 25 years or older, the proportion with 16 years of education rose relatively rapidly from 1960 to 1970 and even more rapidly from 1970 to 1980. In each decade this segment's

---

23. Similarly, using regression analysis, Gottschalk (1997, 30-31) finds that the "college premium" in wages for all US workers fell from 37 percent in 1971 to 31 percent in 1979 and then rose to 53 percent by 1993. The swings were even sharper for the college educated with only 1-5 years experience, reflecting the impact of the upsurge of new college graduates in the 1970s. He too attributes the rising college premium primarily to a decline in real wages for less-educated workers and not so much to a rise for the college educated. He estimates that from 1979 to 1994, real weekly earnings of college graduates rose by only 5 percent and those of high school graduates fell by 20 percent.

Table 1.3 Education and income (percentages)

	1960	1970	1980	1991
Education				
White population 25 years and older				
Males				
less than 8 years	21.1	13.3	8.2	5.8
8 years	18.7	13.9	8.3	4.5
9–11 years	18.9	15.6	12.5	9.9
12 years	22.2	30.9	33.1	36.1
13–15 years	9.1	11.3	15.8	18.4
16 years and more	10.3	15.0	22.1	25.4
median (years)	10.7	12.2	12.5	12.8
16 and more/12 and fewer	12.7	20.4	35.6	45.1
Females				
less than 8 years	17.9	11.7	7.8	5.1
8 years	17.8	13.4	8.4	4.5
9–11 years	19.6	17.3	13.7	10.5
12 years	29.2	39.0	41.6	41.8
13–15 years	9.5	10.1	14.5	18.8
16 years and more	6.0	8.6	14.0	19.3
median (years)	11.2	12.2	12.5	12.7
16 and more/12 and fewer	7.1	10.6	19.6	31.2
Income relative to high school graduate				
	All	All	White	All
Males	mean	mean	median	mean
less than 8 years	50.4	48.3	49.9	na
8 years	70.7	65.7	60.9	na
9–11 years	86.8	83.1	69.4	62.9[a]
12 years	100.0	100.0	100.0	100.0
13–15 years	123.6	118.6	107.1	108.0
16 years and more	165.1	157.1	155.7	189.5

na = not available
a. Up to 11 years.

Source: DOC (1975, 381; 1982–83, 143, 146; 1992, 144; 1994, 158).

share in the relevant population rose by about one-half. But from 1980 to 1991, this segment's share grew by only about one-seventh, albeit from a much higher base, bringing the college-educated share to one-fourth of this population group. For white females in the same age group, there was an even greater proportional increase in the college educated in the 1970s and a similar slowdown of this increase in the 1980s. The data thus confirm the notion of a rapidly expanding supply of college graduates in the 1970s, followed by much slower expansion in the 1980s.

Table 1.3 also reports incomes relative to those for high school graduates. For 1960-91, there was a persistent pattern of falling relative incomes for workers with less than a high school education. However, high school-educated workers gained relative to those with at least some college education from 1960 to 1980. This falling wage differential for the college educated reflected their growing availability. Then, from 1980 to 1991, the income ratio of college educated to high school graduates rose sharply, to a level higher than it was three decades earlier. Considering that from 1960 to 1991 the ratio of college educated or more to high school educated or less rose from about 13 percent to 45 percent for white males and from 7 percent to 31 percent for white females, factors other than just shifting relative supply clearly had to account for the increase rather than decrease in the wage differential by 1991. Various studies that analyze these other factors, including trade and immigration effects, are examined in chapter 2.

Table 1.4 reports the fraction of the prime college age groups that were enrolled in school over the past three decades. The table shows that the first big surge in college enrollment occurred in the mid-1960s and early 1970s, when the rate jumped from 21 percent to 30 percent. Then from 1970 to 1985 the enrollment rate stayed about constant. The baby boom, combined with a rise in the percentage of the college-aged population enrolled, meant that the absolute number of college-aged students rose by 150 percent from 1960 to 1975. In contrast, from 1975 to 1985 this increase amounted to only 7.7 percent. Allowing for the lag for college completion and workforce entry, the enrollment data reinforce the picture of a rapidly growing college-educated labor supply through the 1970s, followed by a sharp slowdown in this supply growth in the 1980s.

Table 1.4 also suggests that by the late 1980s college enrollment had entered a new phase of expansion. By 1992 enrollment had jumped to almost 40 percent. The baby-boom cohorts had already passed through college years, and the absolute number of college-aged persons fell from about 28 million to 24 million. Nonetheless, the higher plateau of the fraction enrolled meant that the absolute number enrolled rose by 13 percent from 1985 to 1992, about twice the rate of the previous decade. This upsurge in college enrollment suggests that the next few years could see a slowdown or, conceivably, even a modest reversal of the widening wage differential between the college and high school educated.

The general upgrading of the population's educational status evident in tables 1.3 and 1.4 provides an important antidote to what otherwise would be the uniform gloom imparted by Mishel and Bernstein's wage data shown in table 1.2. Those data show that for every specific educational category, real wages fell from 1973 to 1993, and that this decline was severe for those with a high school education or less. Yet the median and average wages did not plummet, because there was a general shift in the workforce toward higher educational categories.

CPS data compiled by Burtless show even more specifically the important trend toward educational upgrading of the US labor force (table 1.5). For full-time, year-round workers of both sexes, the fraction with less

Table 1.4 Enrollment of college-aged population, 1960-92 (thousands and percentages)

	1960	1965	1970	1975	1980	1985	1990	1992
Population (thousands)								
18–19	4,732	6,328	6,964	8,028	8,164	7,202	7,058	6,534
20–21	4,211	4,993	6,110	7,670	8,113	7,671	7,184	6,880
22–24	6,126	7,439	9,463	10,667	11,847	12,237	10,624	10,873
Total	15,070	18,760	22,537	26,364	28,123	27,110	24,865	24,287
Enrolled (thousands)								
18–19	1,817	2,930	3,322	3,765	3,788	3,716	4,044	4,012
20–21	817	1,378	1,949	2,393	2,515	2,708	2,852	3,027
22–24	533	982	1,410	1,728	1,931	2,068	2,231	2,577
Total	3,167	5,290	6,681	7,886	8,234	8,492	9,127	9,616
Percentage enrolled								
18–19	38.4	46.3	47.7	46.9	46.4	51.6	57.3	61.4
20–21	19.4	27.6	31.9	31.2	31.0	35.3	39.7	44.0
22–24	8.7	13.2	14.9	16.2	16.3	16.9	21.0	23.7
Total	21.0	28.2	29.6	29.9	29.3	31.3	36.7	39.6

Source: Calculated from *DOC* (1982-83, 140; 1994, 155).

Table 1.5 Educational distribution of the US labor force[a]

	High school dropout	High school graduate	Some college	College graduate	Post college	Total
Population (millions)						
1969	21.5	22.3	9.7	4.3	3.5	61.4
1973	19.3	25.0	12.2	5.5	4.8	66.8
1979	16.7	29.4	17.1	8.0	6.9	78.2
1989	13.4	34.5	23.3	12.6	10.2	93.9
1993	11.3	32.6	27.9	16.8	8.0	96.6
Percentage						
1969	35.1	36.3	15.8	7.1	5.7	100
1973	28.9	37.4	18.3	8.3	7.1	100
1979	21.4	37.6	21.9	10.2	8.9	100
1989	14.2	36.7	24.8	13.4	10.9	100
1993	11.7	33.7	28.9	17.4	8.3	100

a. Full-time, year-round worker equivalents.

Source: Burtless (1995b).

than high school education fell from 35 percent in 1969 to 21 percent in 1979 and about 12 percent by 1993. This decline is dramatic and substantially assuages the sharp fall in the real wages of high school dropouts (figure 1.10).

High school graduates have retained an approximately constant share of slightly over one-third of the labor force over the past 25 years. The share of workers with at least some college in the labor force has increased from about 29 percent in 1969 to 41 percent in 1979 and 55 percent in 1993.[24] The share of workers with a college degree or more increased from 19.1 percent of the full-time labor force in 1979 to 25.7 percent in 1993 (see the Burtless estimates in table 1.5).[25] The educational upgrading made possible a modest rise in real average wages and approximate constancy or only slight decline in real median wages despite an absolute decline within each educational category (Bosworth and Perry 1994; Juhn, Murphy, and Pierce 1993).

Experience and Unexplained Variation

Two other stylized facts are dominant in the wage differential literature. First, in both the 1970s and 1980s there was a rise in the experience

---

24. It is unclear whether the reversal of the rising share of postcollege educated from 1989 to 1993 in table 1.5 is meaningful or instead is merely an artifact of the Burtless sample.

25. Gottschalk (1997, 30) places this estimate at 22 percent for 1979 and 29 percent for 1994.

Figure 1.10 Hourly wages by education, 1973-93

Index (1973 = 100)

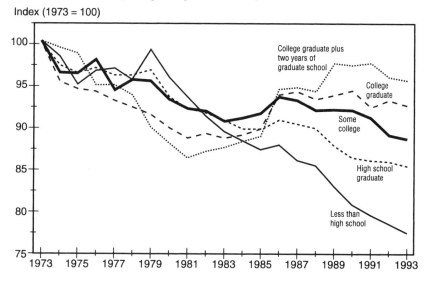

Source: Mishel and Bernstein (1994).

differential. For males, the ratio of wages for age groups 45-64 to 25-34 rose from 1.08 in 1971 to 1.33 by 1987 for high school graduates and from 1.36 to 1.45 for college graduates. In the 1970s, the skill educational differential moderated as the supply of college-educated workers grew. This rapidly offset the rising experience differential, leaving the overall distribution about constant. In contrast, in the 1980s the educational differential widened again, so that the education and experience trends toward concentration were reinforcing rather than offsetting (Levy and Murnane 1992).

The other stylized fact during the 1980s was an increase in wage dispersion even within given educational-experience groups. This rise in inequality within groups suggests the presence of influences not explained by the usual factors (Levy and Murnane 1992; Kosters 1994). As much as one-third of the increase in within-group dispersion may be attributable to a rise in wage fluctuations and, thus, may reflect only transitory dispersion that would not be present in multiyear average wages (Gottschalk 1997).

Productivity and Wage Levels

US postwar growth divides into two broad periods. Until 1973 there was rapid growth in real GDP and in worker productivity. Most of the period since 1973 has been characterized by much slower productivity growth. Thus, from 1963 to 1972, real production per hour of labor input in the private nonfarm business sector grew at 2.8 percent annually. From 1972 to 1978 the rate slowed to 1.7 percent and from 1978 to 1994 it slowed further, to only 1.0 percent. The number of hours worked grew about 1.5 percent annually both before and after 1973, with the overall result that GDP growth fell from 4.1 percent in 1963-72 to 2.5 percent in 1972-94 (CEA 1995, 99).[26]

With a slowdown in productivity growth, it is not surprising that real wage growth slowed down as well. Thus, for men in the 45-54 year age group, real wages grew at 3.0 percent for the 15 years preceding 1973 but at only 0.2 percent for the following 15 years. Adjustment of the CPS data to include fringe benefits and social insurance do not alter this picture by much, as the corresponding annual growth rates fall from 3.2 percent in 1958-73 to 0.35 percent in 1973-88 (calculated from Levy and Murnane 1992, 1337).

For workers in the nonfarm business sector, Bosworth and Perry (1994, 319) calculate that productivity growth fell from 2.5 percent annually in 1960-73 to 0.9 percent in 1973-93. Deflating by the GDP deflator for consumer expenditures (to avoid the bias from the unadjusted CPI as discussed above), real hourly wages grew at 2.0 percent annually in 1960-73 and only 0.4 percent in 1973-93. Growth in real compensation, including fringe benefits, similarly slowed down, from 2.4 percent to 0.6 percent.

Thus, the bulk of the slowdown in real wage and compensation growth is directly consistent with the decline in productivity growth. Even so, there was a puzzle in the latter part of this period, because productivity growth improved moderately from 0.6 percent in 1973-83 to 1.2 percent in 1983-93, while real compensation growth fell from 0.9 percent to 0.3 percent. Bosworth and Perry (1994) conclude that the bulk of the apparent gap between compensation and productivity growth in the most recent decade was attributable to a shift in the "terms of trade" between consumer goods on the one hand, and investment and government goods and services on the other hand.

Thus, workers produced investment goods (especially computers) and services (including government) that had falling relative prices, but consumed goods and services (especially housing) that had rising relative prices. Whereas the consumer expenditure deflator rose more slowly than the overall GDP deflator for nonfarm business in 1973-83, at 7.3 percent versus 8.1 percent annually, the reverse was true in 1983-93, when the

---

26. In 1996, US national accounts statistics shifted from a fixed-weight to a chained index for the GDP deflator, which further reduced measured productivity growth (in considerable part because of the previous distortions caused by rapidly falling prices imputed for computers). This shift does not qualitatively affect the trends and analysis reviewed in this section.

consumption deflator rose at 4.0 percent and the GDP deflator at only 3.3 percent (Bosworth and Perry 1994, 319).

This explanation does leave open the question of who captured the difference between real wage and real output growth. Alternatively, it would raise the question of whether GDP reflects economic welfare accurately as compared with some other measure heavily weighting ultimate real consumption rather than including such a large weight on investment—which, in some sense, can be seen as merely intermediary to the objective of future consumption.

Assuming that GDP, conventionally deflated, is the more appropriate measure, the implication is that households gained in the real value of their assets what they lost in the real slowdown in their consumption. Because the distribution of assets is more concentrated than that of income and wages (discussed above), the story on changing terms of trade between consumer and producer goods would tend to point to another source of widening income inequality, working through the induced effects on assets.[27]

Bosworth and Perry (1994) further argue that the usual source of wage data, the current population survey (CPS) of the Census, is less reliable than wages reported in the "employment cost index" (ECI) of the Bureau of Labor Statistics' survey of business establishments. Even when the census wage data are deflated by the consumption expenditure deflator rather than various versions of the CPI, the real wage for production and nonsupervisory workers shows a decline of 0.6 percent per year from 1976 to 1993, whereas the ECI source shows a decline of only 0.1 percent per year. The two authors conclude that "real wages have stagnated over the past two decades, but claims of a large decline in the average real wage are exaggerated" (328).

International Patterns

Most studies of wage inequality in other industrial countries find several common patterns. First, only the United Kingdom has experienced an increase in wage inequality comparable to that in the United States. Second, a broad group of other industrial countries did experience widening wage inequality, but to a lesser degree than in the United States and United Kingdom. These include the Nordic countries, the Netherlands, France, Italy, and Japan. Only Germany appears to have avoided rising wage inequality over the past 25 years. Third, rising wage inequality began later in the United Kingdom and continental Europe than in the

---

27. Even so, the seeming constancy of the share of compensation in GDP (figure 1.5) suggests only limited scope for what would amount to rising concentration in the functional distribution of income between capital and labor.

United States. Fourth, the increase in wage inequality tended to be greater where wage setting was institutionally more decentralized (the United States and United Kingdom) than where it was more centralized (Germany, Sweden, and the Netherlands) (Gottschalk 1997; Davis 1992; Organization for Economic Cooperation and Development [OECD] 1995; IMF 1997).

Blau and Kahn (1996) examine the level of wage inequality for several industrial countries in the late 1980s. They find US wages were much more concentrated than those in other industrial countries, but the difference was primarily attributable to greater dispersion at the lower end of the US wage distribution. Thus, the $50^{th}/10^{th}$ percentile wage ratio was about 2.7:1 for US workers, while the average of this ratio for other industrial counties was only about 1.6:1 (Blau and Kahn 1996, 7). In contrast, the $90^{th}/50^{th}$ percentile wage ratio was approximately 2.2:1 for the United States, closer to the average of about 1.7:1 for other industrial countries.

The authors attribute the lesser dispersion of below-median wages in most other industrial countries to government wage policies that are more interventionist than in the United States. In particular, they identify centralized collective bargaining or arrangements that extend union contracts to nonunion workers. They also note, however, that continental Europe has greater difficulties with high unemployment than does the United States (as discussed in appendix A of this study).

Overview

Various measures of US inequality—for family income, poverty, wealth, and wages—point to the same broad pattern of widening disparity over recent years. For educationally based skill groups, there was some lessening of inequality in the 1970s as baby-boom college graduates flooded the labor market. Other wage measures, however, such as the $90^{th}/10^{th}$ percentile ratio, show rising inequality even during the 1970s. The pattern of increasing inequality during the past quarter century contrasts sharply with the trend toward greater equality during the first 25 years following World War II.

The past quarter century has also been marked by a sharp increase in the role of international trade in the US economy. Trade turnover (exports plus imports of goods and nonfactor services) has risen from 8.9 percent of GDP in 1960 to 10.7 percent in 1970, 20.8 percent in 1980, and 22.3 percent in 1994. In part because of the coexistence of rising wage inequality and rising trade penetration, many have argued that open trade has adverse consequences on unskilled US workers.

As noted there seems to have been a similar but less pronounced trend toward rising inequality in other industrial countries. Such simultaneous

**Figure 1.11 Deindustrialization and developing-country import
penetration for OECD countries, 1970-90**

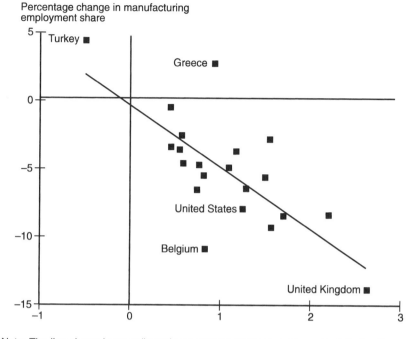

Percentage change in manufacturing
employment share

Note: The line shown is an ordinary least squares regression. To avoid cluttering the
graph, only the United States and a few outliers are labeled.
Source: Saeger (1995) as cited in Wood (1995).

trends could reflect an international influence, although it might be argued
that rapid technological change is just as good a candidate as trade for
international status. As for the US trend toward inequality in comparison
to other industrial countries, an emerging stylized fact is that the explanation lies in labor market flexibility. With high flexibility in the United
States, low-end wages have fallen in real terms. In Europe, where labor
markets and wages are more rigid (and unemployment benefits relatively
more generous), increased pressure on unskilled labor has shown up
primarily as rising unemployment rather than rising wage inequality
(Krugman 1995a; appendix A of this study).

As shown in figure 1.11 from Wood (1995), in a comparison across
OECD countries there is a striking coincidence between the degree of
increased import penetration of manufactures from developing countries
and reductions in domestic employment in the manufacturing sector.
Such circumstantial evidence and the broader correlation of rising trade
and rising inequality has led some, including public figures such as H.
Ross Perot in the United States and Sir James Goldsmith in Europe, to

call for an end to (or reversal of) trade liberalization, to avoid downward wage pressures and a loss of jobs to developing countries (the "giant sucking sound").

This chapter has documented that there has indeed been rising wage inequality in the United States and has shown that there have been increases in inequality in other dimensions that are likely to have been caused importantly by rising wage inequality. Determining the causes of the trend toward inequality and diagnosing a possible causal role of trade and other international forces (immigration, direct investment) is an extremely elusive task that requires great care at both the theoretical and empirical levels. The following chapter surveys the recent efforts of economists to carry out this task.

2

A Critical Review of the Literature

Growing income and wage inequality in the 1980s have prompted a flowering of economics literature seeking to explain the causes. One of the most contentious debates within this literature has been about the role of foreign trade. Some initial studies, primarily by labor economists, showed that trade made a substantial contribution to rising inequality (e.g., Borjas, Freeman, and Katz 1992). Soon, trade economists (especially Lawrence and Slaughter 1993) mounted a critical attack, maintaining that the authors of these studies had misunderstood (or simply omitted) trade theory and that, when properly measured, the role of trade had been minimal. Subsequently, a major study by a development economist (Wood 1994) seemed to provide more credibility to the case for sizable trade impacts on wage distribution.

This chapter summarizes this literature and provides a critical assessment of its most important studies. Much of the literature concerns domestic influences (especially technological change) and will be addressed only briefly here. The principal focus, instead, is on the controversy over the distributional influences of trade and immigration.

Stolper-Samuelson and Factor-Price Equalization

Economists, especially trade economists, tend to be sensitive to the notion that free trade might cause a worsening of the domestic income distribution. Since the publication of Adam Smith's *Wealth of Nations* more than two centuries ago, a cardinal tenet of economics has been that, in general, free trade is more desirable than protection. Yet the Stolper-Samuelson theorem, a famous analysis of the economics literature from the 1940s, has the uncomfortable conclusion that protection increases the real wage of the "scarce factor," unskilled labor in the case of industrial countries. The related "factor-price equalization" theorem has the even more troubling (for industrial-country workers) implication that free trade would cause wages of unskilled labor to converge to a common international level in absolute terms. That is, the strong implication of such a convergence would be some absolute reduction in the wages of unskilled labor in industrial countries.[1]

Although there have been occasional theoretical excursions counter to free trade (e.g., the "optimal tariff" to maximize terms of trade, "infant industry" protection for dynamic efficiency gains, and, more recently, "strategic trade" to capture oligopoly rents), it has been a triumph of economic theory to install as the dominant public policy precept the somewhat counterintuitive notion that the nation will be better off under free trade than under protection.[2] To keep this policy achievement intact, the most convenient attitude toward the Stolper-Samuelson and factor price equalization theorems was that their necessary assumptions were so unrealistic as to turn the theorems into mere curiosities (a position Stolper and Samuelson themselves seemed to take to their articles at the time). An alternative approach, however, would have been to interpret the theorems as meaningful long-run tendencies and, therefore, important grounds for formulating trade policy with key side measures to ensure equitable distribution of the gains from free trade.[3]

The core of the general free-trade precept has always been that it is more efficient for each country to produce the goods it is more adept at producing, whether because of unique natural resources or a different mix in the domestic endowment of labor, skills, and capital from that of its trading partners. With more efficiency, there would be more total

---

1. This implication stems not only from the implausibility of a felicitous jump in real wages to industrial-country levels in such countries as India and China. In addition, the analytical framework of FPE—static equilibrium with fully employed factors—requires a reduction in the industrial-country wage and a rise in the developing-country wage to achieve absolute convergence, because there would not be enough extra output to pay for the shift of income to capital in the industrial country and to boost the developing-country wage to industrial-country levels.

2. The risk of retaliation undermines both optimal tariff and strategic trade arguments, and dismal historical experience (for example, in Latin America) does so for the infant industry argument.

3. Stolper and Samuelson (1941, 73) concluded that their article provided no case for protection, because "it is always possible to bribe the suffering factor by subsidy or other redistributive devices so as to leave all factors better off as a result of trade."

output. With more to go around, all would benefit. Less clear, however, was whether everyone within the home country would share the benefits, or whether some groups would lose.

Adam Smith's formulation emphasized economies of scale (e.g., in his example of the pin factory), gains from specialization, and, thus, the logic of free trade. In the early 19th century David Ricardo's *Principles of Political Economy and Taxation* demonstrated the counterintuitive point that it was advantageous for a nation to trade with another nation even if the first nation was more efficient in the production of all goods in absolute terms (e.g., yards of cloth or bottles of wine per worker hour). All that was required was, instead, that one country be relatively more efficient in one product or have a "comparative advantage" in that product. By concentrating production of each good in the country with the lower relative cost, there would be more total production for the two countries, and the excess could be traded to mutual advantage.

Ricardo's analysis used the abstraction of a single factor of production: labor. If it took relatively more labor hours to produce a yard of cloth than a bottle of wine in Portugal as compared with England, then it was mutually beneficial for Portugal to produce wine, England to produce cloth, and for the two countries to trade. An important but implicit feature of Ricardo's single-factor treatment was that it circumvented the question of distribution among factors (Deardorff 1993a).

In the early twentieth century, the dominant trade theory was that of Heckscher (1919) and Ohlin (1933), two Swedish economists. Their framework extended the Ricardian notion of comparative advantage to two factors (labor and capital) and contributed the important principle that a country would tend to have a comparative advantage in the product that intensively used the production factor that was relatively abundant in the country's factor endowment. That is, the abundant factor would tend to be cheaper relative to the scarce factor, so the goods requiring intensive use of the abundant factor would tend to be relatively cheap and hence would enjoy comparative advantage in foreign trade.

The Stolper-Samuelson (SS) theorem was formulated within the framework of Heckscher-Ohlin (HO) trade. The theorem focused attention on the consequences of free trade for the country's relatively scarce factor of production, unskilled labor in the case of the United States. As Deardorff points out (1993b, 1), before the SS theorem the general presumption of economists was "to expect labor to gain from trade, along with the rest of the economy" and that "even if trade were to lower wages relative to the prices of some goods, it was expected to raise them relative to others," creating an empirical "index number" issue.

Instead, Stolper and Samuelson showed theoretically that, under a list of restrictive assumptions, freeing trade caused an unambiguous reduction in the real wage of the scarce factor (labor). This result was driven by the induced general equilibrium responses of the prices of goods and of the scarce and abundant factors when the economy moved to free trade.

Stolper and Samuelson used equations and general equilibrium analysis to demonstrate their theorem. However, the logic of their theorem can be summarized as follows (Deardorff 1993b):

1. In a small country, the tariff will raise the price of the imported good—relative to the export good, which we take as numeraire—by the amount of the tariff.
2. With homogeneous goods, the rise in the price of the import good will be matched by an equal rise in the price of the import-competing good.
3. The rise in the relative price of the import-competing good will cause the economy's resources to shift towards it and away from the export good.
4. This shift of resources will raise demand for, and hence the relative price of, the factor used intensively in the import-competing industry, relative to the factor used less intensively.
5. From the Heckscher-Ohlin Theorem, import-competing goods will make intensive use of the country's scarce factor. Therefore, the factor whose relative price has risen must be the scarce factor.
6. With free entry into the import-competing sector, zero profit requires that the average prices of all factors employed there rise (relative to the price of the numeraire export good) by the same amount as the rise in the price of the import-competing good.
7. If the scarce factor is not the only factor employed in the import competing sector, the rise in its relative factor price means that its price must also rise relative to this average, and hence relative to the price of the import competing good.
8. Since the prices of imports and import-competing goods are equal and have both risen relative to all other prices, this rise in the scarce factor price is therefore an increase relative to *all* goods, and therefore is an increase in real terms.

Figure 2.1 shows the graphical demonstration of the SS theorem developed by Lerner and Pearce (see Deardorff 1993b). Capital (K) is on the vertical axis and labor (L) on the horizontal axis. The initial wage rate for labor is w^0, and the initial capital cost ("capital rental") rate is r^0. The heavy line shows combinations of labor and capital that represent a single unit of value. At one extreme, if only labor is used, $1/w^0$ units of labor will be employed (so that $1/w^0$ units of labor times w^0 will equal one unit of value). This line is also the "factor-price line," because its slope shows how many units of capital equate in value with how many units of labor. A steeper slope means more units of capital have the same value as fewer units of labor, signifying that the relative price of labor has risen.

Curve X is a production "isovalue curve" showing alternative combinations of labor and capital that will produce one unit of value of good X.[4]

---

4. From "iso" for "same," the isovalue curve equals the corresponding isoquant multiplied by the price (the isoquant is a curve showing alternative combinations of labor and capital that produce the same physical quantity of the good).

Figure 2.1 The Lerner-Pearce diagram of the Stolper-Samuelson theorem

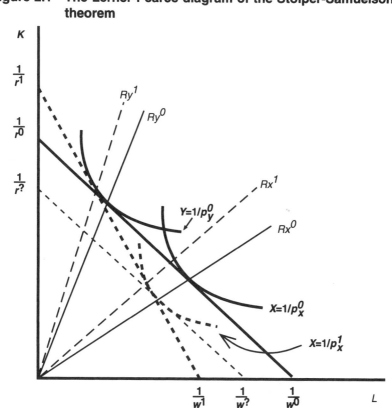

Source: Deardorff (1993).

Curve Y shows the same for product Y. Profit maximization drives firms to select the factor combination where the isovalue curve is just tangent to the factor price line.[5] This occurs at a combination of more labor and less capital for good X and vice versa for good Y. Good X is "labor intensive" and good Y "capital intensive."

The differing factor intensity of the two goods is illustrated by the steeper slope of the ray from the origin to the tangency point of optimal factor combination for good Y (R_y) than that of the corresponding ray for good X (R_x). The slope of the ray from the origin is the ratio of capital to labor employed in the production of each good, respectively. Good Y is

5. Consider a point on curve X below and to the right of the tangency with the factor price line. Such a point yields only one unit of output value for good X but costs more than one unit of value in factor payments—because it lies along a higher-value factor price line that is parallel to and to the right of the original factor price line.

the capital-intensive good and good X the labor-intensive good, because ray R_y is steeper than ray R_x.

Suppose a tariff is imposed on the labor-intensive good. The price of this good increases, and, thus, the unit isovalue curve for good X moves toward the origin of the diagram (to $X = 1/p_x^1$). That is, with a dollar's worth of a good comprising fewer units, it requires proportionately less labor and capital to produce a dollar's worth of output in this sector.

The rise in the price of the import-competing good X calls forth increased demand for labor, the factor used intensively in producing that good. This demand pressure will tend to force up the price of labor relative to that for capital. This process will continue until the new, steeper factor price line (bold dashes) is tangent to both the new unit isovalue curve for good X and the unchanged unit isovalue curve for good Y.

The resulting rise in the relative price of labor causes a reduction in the labor/capital ratio in each product. Thus, the ray from the origin to the new equilibrium point for each good (R_y^1 and R_x^1) will be steeper (more capital per unit of labor) than at the original equilibrium. Only in this way will enough labor be released in the capital-intensive sector (Y) and enough labor economized in the labor-intensive sector (X) for the composition of output to shift away from good Y and toward good X. As discussed below, trade theorists have seized on this implication of changing factor ratios to attack the empirical validity of studies purporting to show that trade had caused rising wage inequality in the 1980s.

The SS theorem demonstrated not only that protection would raise the price of the scarce factor, but that it would do so by a proportion that exceeds the protection itself. Jones (1965) called this the "magnification" effect: any change in relative product prices will cause a magnified change in relative factor prices. Magnification simply sharpens the policy bite of the SS theorem, because it means even greater wage loss for the scarce factor from free trade than might be expected by the preexisting level of protection.

In figure 2.1, the magnification effect may be seen by considering what would happen if the wage increased only in the same proportion as the import price, to w' where $w'/w^0 = p_x^1/p_x^0$ (with the light-dashes isocost line parallel to the original line). At this point there would not be enough labor and capital to produce the original level of good Y (as the dotted isocost line lies inside the unit isovalue curve for good Y). Instead, the wage must rise more than proportionately, to w^1, to induce producers of good Y to free up labor for use in labor-intensive good X.

Samuelson (1948, 1949) extended the original SS analysis to show that, under the same assumptions, trade would equalize factor incomes across nations in absolute terms. That is, real wages of labor in developed and developing countries would converge to some intermediate point. The policy implications of factor-price equalization (FPE) were even more provocative than those of the SS theorem regarding the wage-increasing effect of protection. Samuelson (1949, 59) recapitulates the FPE analysis as follows:

My hypotheses are as follows:

1. There are but two countries, America and Europe.[6]
2. They produce but two commodities, food and clothing.
3. Each commodity is produced with two factors of production, land and labour. The production functions of each commodity show "constant returns to scale," in the sense that changing all inputs in the same proportion changes output in that same proportion. . . .
4. The law of diminishing marginal productivity holds: as any one input is increased relative to other inputs, its marginal productivity diminishes.
5. The commodities differ in their "labour and land intensities." Thus, food is relatively "land using" or "land-intensive" while clothing is relatively "labour intensive." This means that whatever the prevailing ratio of wages to rents, the optimal proportion of labour to land is greater in clothing than in food.
6. Land and labour are assumed to be qualitatively identical inputs in the two countries and the technological production functions are assumed to be the same for the two countries.
7. All commodities move perfectly freely in international trade, without encountering tariffs or transport costs, and with competition effectively equalising the market price-ratio of food and clothing. No factors of production can move between the countries.
8. Something is being produced in both countries of both commodities with both factors of production. Each country may have moved in the direction of specialising on the commodity for which it has a comparative advantage, but it has not moved so far as to be specialising completely on one commodity. . . . Under these conditions, *real factor prices must be exactly the same* in the two countries (and indeed the proportion of inputs used in food production in America must equal that in Europe, and similarly for clothing production) [emphasis added].

The essence of the FPE proof was as follows. First, trade equates commodity prices everywhere. Second, because technology and factor qualities are identical, there is a unique mapping from the commodity price ratio to factor combinations and the factor-price ratio. Third, with a unique factor-price ratio everywhere and a corresponding unique factor combination in each good, the uniformity of technology assures that equal factor price ratios translate into equal factor-price levels in absolute terms.

Samuelson (1949) presented his proof first with a simple diagram and then mathematically. Figure 2.2 shows his two-part diagram. On the right side of the diagram, the wage/rental factor-price ratio (W/R) (e.g., $10 per hour/$100 per acre per year) is shown on the vertical axis and the corresponding ratio of labor, L, to land, T (e.g., 500 hours per year/one

---

6. Today, the corresponding assumption would be an industrial country and a less-developed country. It is interesting to speculate whether Samuelson would have been as comfortable postulating wage equalization between China and the United States as between the then lesser-developed region, Europe, and the United States.

Figure 2.2 Samuelson's diagram for factor-price equalization

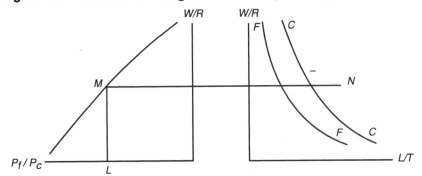

Source: Samuelson (1949).

acre per year) on the horizontal axis. The *CC* curve shows the alternative labor/land ratios that will be selected in the production of a unit of value in cloth at alternative factor-price ratios. Curve *FF* shows the same thing for production of a unit of value in food. Because food production requires relatively more land and less labor, curve *FF* is always to the left of *CC*. For any given wage/land rental rate ratio, food production will employ relatively less labor and more land than will cloth production.[7]

Samuelson then added the left side relating the commodity price ratio to the factor price ratio. Under his assumptions, there had to be a unique mapping from the equilibrium factor-price ratio to a corresponding product-price ratio. A higher price of labor relative to the price of land, for example (upward movement in both diagrams), would only be consistent with a lower relative price of food to the price of cloth (rightward movement along the curve in the left side of the diagram). Moreover, with identical production functions everywhere, the unique equilibrium factor-price ratio applicable to both countries also meant unique absolute factor-price levels and, thus, "factor price equalization."

The crux of both the FPE theorem and the associated SS effect (whereby higher protection raised the real wage of the scarce factor) was the unique correspondence between product price and factor price. This meant that "[a]n increase in the relative price of a good increases the real wage of the factor used intensively in producing that good, and lowers the real wage of the other factor" (Deardorff 1993b, 6). As discussed below, the absence of a clear drop in the relative price of labor-intensive import

7. Note that this conclusion is independent of the product price. Note also that curves *FF* and *CC* are independent of scale. Nor are they isovalue curves (as in figure 2.1) or isoquants. Instead, they are perimeters relating the factor combination on the horizontal axis to the factor price ratio (and thus the ratio of the marginal product of labor to the marginal product of land) on the vertical axis.

goods is one of the key arguments that some trade economists have advanced to reject the idea that international trade has contributed to growing US wage inequality in the 1980s.

From the start, the SS and FPE theorems faced the major problem that they seemed radically divorced from reality. The world comprised more than two goods and more than two factors. Transport costs, tariffs, and other protective barriers patently were not zero. There were cases of complete specialization (Brazil produced coffee, the United States did not). Products were not necessarily homogeneous (precision German engineering might not be matched in Bolivia). Factors were not necessarily homogeneous (an "unskilled" worker with a high school education in the United States might provide higher quality labor hours than an unschooled recruit from the Brazilian countryside). Factors were not necessarily mobile across industries, but could be "specific" to one sector (e.g., capital in the form of existing open-hearth furnaces). Production could have increasing rather than constant returns to scale. "Factor reversal" might occur: goods produced labor intensively in one country (fabric in India) might be produced capital intensively in another (fabric in the United States). Technology was not necessarily, or perhaps not even usually, the same in different countries. Moreover, the largest present-day sector of all, nontradable services, did not fit directly into a world of only two goods, both of which were tradable.

Perhaps for reasons such as these, but also, apparently, because of concern that the article could be read as a sellout to protectionism, the original article by Stolper and Samuelson was rejected for publication in the *American Economic Review*, whose editors acknowledged that it was "a brilliant theoretical performance," but judged that "[i]t does not . . . have anything to say about any of the real situations with which the theory of international trade has to concern itself" (Deardorff and Stern 1993).

As discussed below, some trade economists have stressed that even today the assumptions of the SS and FPE theorems remain so "extraordinarily demanding" that they cannot be "taken seriously" as the "major theoretical construct" justifying fears in industrial countries that trade with developing countries will undermine the wages of unskilled labor (Bhagwati and Dehejia 1994, 39, 42). Even so, there is no doubt an element of truth to the view that the collapse of transportation costs and protective barriers, and the development of modern communications, could mean that "a theory that may have appeared ludicrous in the 1960s is on the brink of reflecting reality today" (Bluestone 1994, 336).

Perhaps more relevantly, half a century of research concerning possible generalization of the SS and FPE theorems has yielded analyses suggesting that the central thrust of the theorems need not collapse as their restrictive assumptions are replaced by more realistic ones. Thus, one key question was whether the theorems foundered on the fact that there are more than two goods and more than two factors ("higher dimensionality").[8] Ethier (1984) showed that when there were the same number of goods as factors ("even" technology), it could be demonstrated that every good is a "friend" to some factor and an "enemy" to some other factor (in that a rise in the price of the good would raise the price of the factor to which it was friendly and lower that of the factor to which it was unfriendly).

Deardorff (1993b, 23) considers that the most vulnerable assumption of the SS and FPE theorems was the requirement of the underlying HO framework that factors be mobile across sectors. This assumption meant that "it was the identity of the factor, not the industry in which it is employed, that determines whether it gains or loses." In the 1970s, authors dissatisfied with this assumption (including Samuelson himself) revived the "specific factors" model associated with Jacob Viner and, earlier, David Ricardo, in which at least some factors are used only in certain industries.

The specific-factors model at first seemed to contradict the conclusions of the SS and FPE theorems. Indeed, when Magee (1980) showed that protectionist lobbying united capital and labor in the industry in question, rather than pitting them against each other, it seemed that the specific-factors model was the more relevant. However, subsequent research showed that if capital were sector specific and labor were mobile across sectors, then at least the weaker "friends and enemies" versions of the SS and FPE theorems would still hold. Each good would be a friend to the specific capital in its sector, explaining the observed lobbying correlations while at the same time maintaining the "weakest but most general versions of Stolper-Samuelson" (Deardorff 1993b, 24).

Consideration of a related, seminal article by Rybczynski (1955) will complete this brief review of the SS and FPE theorems. Using the same HO assumptions about factors and production characteristics (but referring for convenience solely to a closed economy), Rybczynski examined the effects of an increase in one of the two factors of production (for example, through capital accumulation without labor expansion). He first showed that if the commodity price ratio were constant, the factor increase had to lead to an absolute increase in the production of the commodity that intensively used that factor and to an absolute decline in the other commodity (the Rybczynski theorem). He then showed that after changing commodity prices were taken into account (because of the interaction between rising relative output just mentioned and the structure of consumer demand),

---

8. A general problem with higher dimensionality is that when there are more than two factors, which factor is "relatively abundant" and which factor is used relatively "intensively" in a given sector becomes ambiguous. A related problem is that extensions of the SS and FPE theorems require that the number of goods exceed the number of factors. Yet each of these "numbers" is in a sense wholly arbitrary. Labor skill categories can be defined more broadly or more narrowly, as can product categories.

"an increase in the quantity of one factor will always lead to a worsening in the terms of trade, or the relative price of the commodity using relatively much of that factor" (76).

One implication of the Rybczynski theorem was that it served as a proof of the HO proposition that the country would have comparative advantage in the good that intensively used its abundant factor (Bhagwati and Srinivasan 1983, 74).[9] However, in the context of the present study, the theorem is also useful as a way to think about the impact of incorporating labor-abundant countries into the international economy. Such an incorporation resembles an otherwise unchanged world economy in which one factor expands (unskilled labor), with constant amounts of the other (capital, or more relevantly to this study, skilled labor). By the Rybczynski theorem, this expansion of the labor factor in the relevant global economy should worsen the terms of trade of the labor-intensive good. When this proposition is combined with the unique mapping of product to factor prices within the SS framework, the implication would be that the incorporation of the labor-abundant countries into the international economy would tend to drive down the real wages of unskilled labor in industrial countries even without any change in protection.

SS-type results are thus implied from changing factor supply rather than from elimination of protection. This framework is perhaps the more realistic in the present international economy, in which protection has generally been reduced to relatively low levels, but the process of internationalization of the economy and incorporation of labor-abundant countries remains incomplete.

As will be shown in the general equilibrium model developed in chapter 4 of this study, a key to future pressure on unskilled wages in industrial countries from developing-country trade competition is the trade-off between two opposing forces. One is further global integration, that is, the incorporation of labor-abundant countries into the world economy. The other, however, is the faster pace of growth in the endowment of skilled relative to unskilled labor in the developing countries, where the skilled labor base begins from a much lower relative level than in industrial countries. With a constant degree of global integration (e.g., constant transportation and protection costs), this differential evolution of relative skill endowments should reduce downward pressure on the relative wages of unskilled labor in industrial countries.

In summary, the SS and FPE theorems are important theoretical constructs that tend to support the notion that at least in the longer term,

---

9. Thus, comparison of one country with 100 units of capital and 100 of labor against another with 100 of capital and 500 of labor is analogous to comparison of a single country with the same differences at two points of time. The country (period) with the higher endowment of labor will have an absolutely higher level of output for the labor-intensive good and absolutely lower level of output for the capital-intensive good, confirming HO specialization.

integration of the world economy would be expected to tend to reduce the real wage of unskilled labor in industrial countries and raise it in developing countries. It is a matter of continuing debate whether the assumptions of these theorems are so restrictive as to make them useless or whether, instead, their central insights remain meaningful, especially weaker versions of their conclusions.

One undebated precept of these theorems, however, and of the underlying HO model, is that the way trade affects unskilled wages is through an adverse change in the relative price of the commodity that is labor intensive. As developed below, the working of this mechanism is at best opaque in the data for US wage concentration in the 1980s and, at worst, controverted by experience. As also developed below, the noise level in price data may be sufficient to mask changes consistent with significant factor price effects. In addition, other model formulations, in particular the specific-factors model, can be consistent with an adverse influence of trade on relative wages of unskilled labor even without the presence of falling relative prices of labor-intensive goods.

Development Economists 1

A relatively early phase of empirical literature focused on trade's effects on employment in import-competing industries, rather than on wage distribution or distribution between capital and labor. By the mid-1970s, development economists had examined whether imports from less-developed countries (LDCs) were causing major job dislocations. The policy context was one in which the labor-business consensus favoring the pursuit of export opportunities through free trade was breaking down. For example, in the Kennedy Round of trade negotiations in the 1960s, US auto workers had seen it advantageous to reduce the European Economic Community's tariff wall through reciprocal liberalization. By the early 1970s, in contrast, the AFL-CIO was denouncing an alleged loss of nearly one million jobs to imports (Frank 1977, 23). About the same time, the highly protective Multi-Fiber Arrangement (MFA) for textiles and apparel was being assembled (Cline 1987). The new protectionist pressures in part reflected high unemployment from the global recession of 1974-75. Trade and development economists sought to clarify whether the rising fears about job losses to imports were justified.

Frank (1977) presented estimates suggesting that they were not. He used the following accounting approximation: the growth rate of employment equals the weighted sum of the growth rates of domestic demand, exports, imports (negatively), and labor productivity (negatively), where the weights are ratios of each respective aggregate to domestic output, for the first three, and unity for labor productivity. Conducted for about 20 import-competing industries at the two-digit Standard Industrial Classification (SIC) level, his estimates indicated that for the period 1963-71, employment, indeed, had grown much more slowly (0.7 percent annually) than domestic demand (4.0 percent). However, the great bulk of the divergence was attributable to labor productivity growth (-2.9 percent) rather than the adverse effect of imports (-0.9 percent). Moreover, the employment contribution of export growth (0.4 percent) meant that the net impact of trade (-0.5 percent) was only about one-sixth as large as the influence of productivity growth (Frank 1977, 30).

Frank estimated that about 600,000 US manufacturing jobs had been displaced by imports from 1963 to 1971, of which about half were associated with rising imports from developing countries. This loss was about 0.2 percent of the manufacturing labor force annually, and the net loss after considering exports was even smaller (36).

Various other studies used this same general accounting approach to identify the impact of trade with LDCs on employment in industrial countries (e.g., Krueger 1978). Alternatively, studies applied direct and indirect labor coefficients (working through input-output tables) to trade flows with LDCs to determine the net impact on industrial-country employment (e.g., Grinols and Thorbecke 1978).[10] Typically, the results of these various studies confirmed that the impact was small. However, it became clear that results depended on the specific formulation, level of aggregation, and time period. For example, Martin and Evans (1981) argued that the results of the accounting decomposition method were unstable, because they ignored interaction terms that disappeared for instantaneous changes but could be important over discrete time periods. They noted that this was a classic index number problem.

More fundamentally, Martin and Evans (1981) stressed that the all-important rate of labor productivity growth might itself depend on import pressure from developing countries. They cited one study for UK industry that showed a statistically significant role of import penetration in explaining productivity growth. If labor productivity growth was endogenous and lagged with respect to import pressure, then the accounting method could seriously understate the employment impact of imports. Cline (1987) analyzed adjustment in the US textile industry, strongly suggesting that this process was at work in that sector.[11]

---

10. For a survey of these studies, see OECD (1979).

11. During 1961-85, the US textile fabric sector had higher growth in output per worker than did US manufacturing as a whole. In the second half of this period, its labor force shrank 3 percent per year. Import pressure was about the same for textiles and apparel in the 1960s (6 percent of domestic consumption). However, apparel proved difficult to mechanize—its labor productivity growth consistently lagged the manufacturing average—and by the 1980s its import penetration was about 30 percent, compared to about 9 percent for textiles. The accounting method would show a much greater impact of imports in apparel, but the true influence of imports on employment would probably be more similar

Another class of literature sought to examine the implication of future trade trends for the political economy of North-South trade. Cline (1984) estimated statistical (logit) "protection functions" relating the presence of nontariff barriers to economic variables, including the import penetration ratio and the absolute size of employment in the sector (as an indicator of political clout). The study then applied these functions to projected future levels of import penetration by LDC exports into the markets of the United States, Canada, and the United Kingdom to determine whether the model of export-led growth was likely to generate a protective response. The conclusion was that relatively brisk real growth rates (on the order of 12 percent per year) for exports of manufactures from developing countries should prove feasible without provoking major protective response. But there were speed limits, and the rates approaching the range of 30 percent that had been achieved by the East Asian "gang of four" (South Korea, Taiwan, Hong Kong, and Singapore) were unlikely to survive this test if generalized to more numerous and larger LDCs (Cline 1982; 1984, 129).

Estimates by Balassa (1986, 381) were implicitly even more optimistic. He first examined the direct labor coefficients for manufactures trade of 40 industrial and developing countries for the 21 three-digit International Standard Industrial Classification (ISIC) categories. Labor coefficients declined monotonically as per capita income rose, with a median elasticity of about -0.6 (that is, a 10 percent rise in per capita income was associated with a 6 percent reduction in labor per unit of output value). On average, the labor intensity of industrial-country import-competing sectors (15.33 workers per million dollars of output value) was only marginally larger than that of export sectors (14.95). For LDCs, the labor intensities were much higher, but again differed only marginally between their import sectors (57.3) and export sectors (58.5).

Balassa then calculated the impact of three scenarios. A strictly balanced change in absolute values of North-South trade in manufactures would cause a slight decrease in net industrial-country employment (only 2.5 percent of the gross loss of employment that would occur in the import-competing industries). The second scenario, a proportionate growth of trade, would instead cause net job gains in the North, with two new export jobs for each import job lost. However, that scenario was premised on the large trade surplus of industrial countries vis-à-vis developing countries in the base year, 1983. In his third and preferred scenario, Balassa assumed imports from LDCs would continue to grow faster than exports to them, at the pace of 1973-83. In this extrapolation, changes in manufactured trade would generate about 1.2 new export jobs in the North for each job lost to increased imports. Net employment changes would amount to

---

between the two sectors because of the likely impact of import pressure on technological change in the textile sector (Cline 1987, 49, 99).

a loss of about 600,000 jobs in the United States but gains of about 1.2 million jobs in the rest of the countries of the Organization for Economic Development and Cooperation (OECD), along with net job losses of 2.5 million in LDCs.[12]

As discussed below, the razor-thin difference between the Balassa labor coefficients for imports as opposed to exports raises the type of questions explored by Wood (1994) concerning whether the proper factor content measure is being applied and, thus, whether the calculated impact of North-South trade on employment is understated. Moreover, the preferred scenario forecast in Balassa (1986) implied a widening trade surplus for the North in North-South manufactures trade, whereas the more relevant comparison might be for a trade balance that is either unchanged or that is consistent with plausible LDC debt and industrial-country capital flow prospects.[13] More balanced trade would have meant less net-export job creation for the OECD as a whole and larger net job losses for the United States.

More broadly, from the vantage point of the 1990s, the principal question about the various studies of the development economists in the 1970s and early 1980s is whether their generally small estimates of the existing and prospective impact of North-South trade on employment in industrial countries may have been understatements. It is also important to note that the studies in this period typically did not distinguish between effects on unskilled and skilled workers and, hence, did not directly address possible effects on wage inequality.

Labor Economists 1

By the early 1990s, labor economists were poring over US data to diagnose the cause of the increase in wage inequality in the 1980s. The majority view that seemed to be emerging, which we may label group 1 of labor economists, was that the principal cause had been skill-biased technical change that had increased the relative demand for more educated and experienced workers and decreased that for others. If this diagnosis proved correct, it would mean there was little basis for concern about the influences of international trade and migration, because their impacts were too small to make much difference.

---

12. The differential impact for the United States reflected the much higher initial ratio of manufactured imports from LDCs to US exports to these countries than in other OECD countries.

13. For the LDCs in Balassa's sample, the export/import ratio in manufactured trade with the North was 0.35. Exports had grown at 10.5 percent and imports at 7.3 percent. In contrast, given the initial trade "gap factor" (import/export ratio), the trade projections would have to have set LDC export growth at 21 percent (= 7.3/0.35) to avoid a further widening in the LDC deficit in manufactured trade with industrial countries.

The econometric study by Bound and Johnson (1992) is one of the more important in this school. The authors use data from the CPS on weekly earnings, which provides a sample set of about 70,000 in 1973-74 and 150,000 in 1979 and 1988. They define four educational groups (less than high school, high school graduate, some college, and college graduate or more) and four experience groups (0-9 years, 10-14, 20-29, and 30 or more years). With a male-female classification, 32 demographic categories result (4 × 4 × 2). The data further distinguish among 17 industries, of which all but two are in the services sectors. The authors deflate by the CPI to obtain real wages. This deflator potentially exaggerates the reductions in real wages, as discussed in chapter 1 (but not addressed by Bound and Johnson).

The authors first regress the logarithm of wage on dummy variables for the demographic categories. They then compare the estimated mean real wages by category and find their first striking result: a preponderance of falling real wages over time. Thus, for males, 9 of the 16 demographic cells showed reductions in real wages from 1979 to 1988 (although for females, only 4 of 16 groups show reductions). The overall fixed-weight rates of real wage growth are −0.4 percent annually in 1973-79 and −0.7 percent in 1979-88 (including an adjustment for fringe benefits). The actual average real wage (not reported by the authors) performed more favorably (growing at 0.4 percent annually from 1973 to 1993, according to Bosworth and Perry 1994), because of educational upgrading (see chapter 1). That is, the employment weights of the 32 cells did not stay at their 1973 composition, so the fixed-weight wage trend understates the average trend. Nonetheless, these detailed estimates confirm the general picture shown in table 1.2: real wages are generally falling for constant skill-experience categories, with the exceptions of college-educated males and a wider educational range of females.

Most American workers, thus, had to run faster to stay in place. This was especially so for males with less than 10 years experience. For this group, real wages (relative to the overall average for the three periods) fell by 19.2 percent for high school dropouts, 13.4 percent for high school graduates, and 8 percent for those with only some college—but rose by 13.6 percent for those with college or more education, confirming the picture of sharpening wage inequality (e.g., figures 1.8 and 1.9).

The core findings of Bound and Johnson are in their decomposition analysis of the causes of changing relative wages. The conceptual framework for this decomposition is expressed in their equation:

$$dY_i = \left(1 - \frac{1}{\sigma}\right)d \ln b_i - \left(\frac{1}{\sigma}\right)d \ln N_i + \left(\frac{1}{\sigma}\right)d \ln D_i \qquad (2.1)$$
$$+ \sum_{j=1}^{I} (\phi_{ij}dM_{ij} + M_{ij}d\phi_{ij})$$

where d refers to change; σ is the (uniform) elasticity of substitution among labor categories (estimated by the authors at $\sigma = 1.7$); and for each labor category i, Y is the relative log wage, b is the technological efficiency parameter, N is the factor supply, D is an index of industry-wide demand, ϕ_{ij} is the fraction of group i workers employed in industry j, and M_{ij} is the logarithm of the noncompetitive (rental) wage multiple of group i labor in industry j. The authors further divide the technical change parameter b into a sector-specific component and a general component.

The authors stress that increasing relative wages of the college educated along with an increase in their relative supply in the 1980s meant that the demand curve for these workers was shifting out faster than the supply curve, and equation 2.1 seeks to decompose the sources of the demand shift (the first, third, and fourth elements of the equation). By regressing the 32 × 17 demographic-industry wage averages on labor type and industry dummy variables, the authors can measure the final expression in equation 2.1 (the contribution of changes in average industry wage rents).[14] The "product-demand-shift" index, D_i, is calculated as a function of the relative share of output in each sector, the neutral technical efficiency parameter of each sector, and the labor-type technological efficiency parameter (general and sector specific).

The contribution of the change in supply is calculated directly from the change in the number of workers in each education-experience subcategory, as applied to the inverse of the elasticity of substitution. That leaves technological change. Here, the authors directly acknowledge that they face the same classic problem as in the "sources of growth" literature: technological change inherits, by default, whatever cannot be explained by the other, direct influences.[15] As in the sources of growth literature, in the case of relative wage determination this "unexplained residual" is the lion's share of the change.

Table 2.1 reports the Bound-Johnson findings for the period 1979-88. For males, the wage ratio for college- to high school-educated workers rose by the proportion 0.163. Of this amount, 0.036 was explained by the

14. Thus, the male college/high school wage ratio rose by the proportion 0.163 from 1979 to 1988, of which an increase of 0.016 was due to "differential movements between high- and low-wage industries," and 0.022 was attributable to "changes in industry wage effects [rents]," for a total of about one-fifth of the change.

15. The authors do have a tactic to separate directly at least the sector-specific component of technological change. They identify four sectors (durable and nondurable manufactures, transportation, and public utilities) where there was a particularly large drop in employment of younger and unskilled workers relative to college-educated workers in the 1980s. They then estimate differential trends for the composite of these four sectors as the basis for determining sector-specific technological change. However, this component turns out to be relatively small too, once again leaving the pure residual—general technological change— with the bulk of causation.

Table 2.1 Decomposition of estimated sources of relative wage changes, 1979-88

		Relative wage change	Rents	Supply	Demand	Technical change		Unexplained
						Specific	General	
College/ high school	Men	0.163	0.036	-0.100	0.013	0.019	0.196	-0.001
	Women	0.118	0.015	-0.191	-0.047	0.009	0.270	0.062
High school/ dropout (X < 30)	Men	0.072	0.002	-0.193	-0.003	0.018	0.267	-0.019
	Women	0.060	0.011	-0.177	0.027	0.035	0.202	-0.038
Old/young (noncollege)	Men	0.107	0.015	0.062	-0.022	0.062	-0.023	0.013
	Women	0.043	0.013	-0.007	-0.016	0.030	-0.006	0.029
Women/men		0.076	0.005	-0.094	0.026	-0.021	0.145	0.015

X = experience (years).
Source: Bound and Johnson (1992, table 6).

shifting composition and extent of industry-specific wage differentials (rents). However, there was a negative contribution of 0.10 from shifting supply. That is, when the rise in the relative supply of college educated compared with high school educated is considered jointly with the elasticity of substitution, the wage ratio should have fallen by 10 percent (rather than rising by 16.3 percent). The shifting composition of product demand and productivity (D_i) contributed 0.013. Sector-specific technological change contributed 0.019. However, general technological change applicable to all industries contributed 0.196, more than the total net rise in the college/high school relative wage.

The authors conclude that "the principal cause of the significant wage-structure changes of the past decade was a shift in the structure of the $b_i's$ [general technical efficiency parameters] favorable to certain groups, especially women and the highly educated" (Bound and Johnson 1992, 386). They cite Krueger (1992) on the impact of computers as a prime example of skill-biased technological change.[16] However, the authors recognize that the explanation of technological change "involves the residuals" rather than "directly observable phenomena" (383), and for this reason they acknowledge that their conclusion on the primacy of technological change is subject to "other interpretations" (386), particularly "the effect of seniority systems in the face of declining unemployment" (384).

Bound and Johnson never explicitly identify the role of trade. The closest they come is to judge that "the major wage-change phenomena are *not* adequately accounted for by . . . institutional factors or changes in the structure of product demand" and ". . . demand shifts were on balance slightly unfavorable to highly educated labor . . ." (383). Because trade effects work through changes in demand for domestic output, the implication is that trade had minimal impact.

Nevertheless, the Bound-Johnson results would seem to leave open the possibility that trade and immigration could be among the factors relevant in "other interpretations,"[17] particularly because only two broad sectors, out of their 17-sector economy, are for traded goods (durables/mining and nondurables). Such broad sectoral aggregates should be expected to

---

16. Krueger (1992) uses supplementary CPS data on computer use to calculate that, other things being equal, workers using computers had wages higher by about 18 percent than other workers in the late 1980s. From 1984 to 1989, the incidence of computer use rose from 25 to 37 percent of workers. In 1989, 43 percent of women used computers, compared to 32 percent of men. Computer use was associated with education, with 8 percent, 29 percent, and 59 percent incidence of computer use among high school dropouts, high school graduates, and college graduates, respectively, in 1989.

17. The authors note in a footnote (388) that for illegal aliens to have accounted for the full relative wage deterioration for young, low-educated workers in the 1980s, there would have to have been about 27 million undocumented immigrants, compared against usual estimates of about 3 million (and against a native labor supply of 19 million in this group).

fail to capture the impact of intensified HO specialization of manufactures in skilled-labor-intensive exports and unskilled-labor-intensive imports. This reconfiguration, central to the usual trade and income distribution nexus, could simply be disguised as technological change biased against unskilled and in favor of skilled labor for each of the two aggregated tradable sectors. Thus, the Bound-Johnson (1992) study might seem to be a meticulous, exhaustive demonstration that biased technological change has been the main source of growing wage inequality, but there remains considerable room for doubt, because this conclusion rests on attributing unexplained sources to technical change.[18]

Mincer (1991) has provided a simpler[19] but, in at least one way, more satisfying econometric study that similarly focuses on the role of skill-biased technological change. The somewhat more satisfying aspect of this study is its use of direct measures of this technological change, rather than attribution to technological change of the otherwise unexplained residual.

Mincer first notes that, historically, the college wage differential has held up better than might be expected given the rapid increase in the supply of college graduates. He cites two likely reasons. First, physical capital may be less substitutable for (or more complementary to) skilled (educated) labor than for unskilled labor. He cites previous studies that obtain this finding. It implies that physical capital accumulation shifts out the demand for skilled labor relative to that for unskilled labor. Second, technical change tends to be skill biased. Mincer cites findings by Bartel and Lichtenberg (1987) who use cross-section census data to show that relatively more educated workers are employed in those manufacturing sectors with newer capital equipment and more intensive spending on research and development (R&D).

Mincer's most successful variable for skill-biased technical change is R&D spending per worker. Figure 2.3 shows the close relationship between the education differential and this measure of the pace of technical change in Mincer's data. The right axis reports the wage difference per year of additional education between college and high school graduates with equal (6-10 years) work experience. This difference should be multiplied by four to obtain the actual wage difference.[20] On the left axis is real R&D expenditure per worker (economywide, 1982 dollars), with a two-year lag (for example, the observation on R&D displayed as 1965 in figure 2.3 refers to R&D expenditure in 1963).

18. See, for example, Leamer's (1995) critique.

19. Thus, rather than over 100,000 observations, Mincer uses only about 25 (annual data at the aggregate level from the early 1960s through the late 1980s).

20. Mincer's approach is that the education differentials represent returns to investment in education (although without counting costs other than time-opportunity cost) and that there are natural cycles in the rate of college education as the college-age population responds to higher and lower rates of return by increasing and decreasing enrollment rates.

Figure 2.3   R&D per worker versus wage differentials for college and high school workers, 1963-88 (1982 dollars)

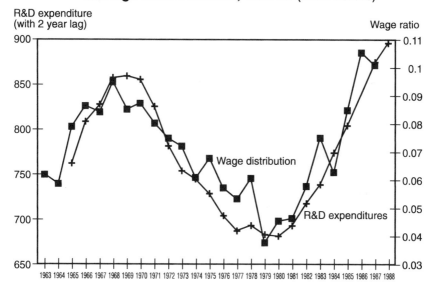

Source: Mincer (1991).

In his regression analysis, Mincer allows several economic influences to compete in explaining the wage differential. On the supply side, he uses the fraction of college graduates in the 20-29 year age group to measure the relative supply of educated (skilled) labor. The drop in the wage differential in the 1970s evident in figure 2.3 occurred in part because of the large rise in the college-educated fraction from the early 1960s up through 1976, associated with the demographics of the baby boom, public subsidies to education beginning in the 1960s, and the Vietnam draft.[21]

On the demand side, technical change is the first variable. One variant for technological change is the amount of R&D spending per worker. An alternative is Jorgenson's estimate of total factor productivity (TFP). Both show a collapse in the 1970s, in part (according to Mincer) because of the oil price shock. Another demand variable is the ratio of the merchandise trade balance to GNP. Mincer includes this trade effect in view of the "growth of world trade hence of international competition." He notes that as "first pointed out by Murphy and Welch (1988)," in the 1980s the loss of exports and increase of imports in such goods as automobiles and electronics put downward pressure on wages and employment in these sectors, which are "generally less education intensive than other sectors

---

21. In one test, Mincer also includes a variable for experience: the ratio of young to total population.

(such as services, finance and insurance, etc.)" (6).[22] The final variable on the demand side is the ratio of employment in services to that in the goods sector, which to some extent is a variant of the trade variable.

All of Mincer's tests find the relative supply variable significant. The trade variable is significant when included in a regression that uses Jorgenson's TFP as the technical change variable, but the highest overall explanation is achieved in an equation in which R&D is the technological change variable, the trade variable is omitted, and, instead, the services/goods employment ratio is included. Mincer recognizes that the latter is related to trade performance, so the results broadly show a role for trade, although the author strongly emphasizes technological change as the primary influence shifting relative demand for skilled workers.[23]

Overall, the Mincer study supports the idea that technological change has a central, if not demonstrably dominant, role in determining the wage differential. Nonetheless, his alternative variables for (skill-biased) technological change are at best imperfect proxies. Moreover, as will be seen in the discussion of Borjas and Ramey (1994a) below, pictures just as impressive as figure 2.3 can be drawn showing close adherence between the wage differential and trade balance variables (see figure 2.5).

The use of the trade balance as an explanatory variable raises another fundamental question. SS effects concern pressures on factoral distribution even with balanced trade. They work through the different factor intensities of exports and imports. They are thus more germane to long-term structural trends, if we make the reasonable assumption that large trade deficits are corrected eventually. In contrast, Mincer's trade measure is for the trade balance, not factor composition. Much the same can be said of other studies by labor economists (as discussed below), as they typically mix the effects of the trade balance in the 1980s with trade factor content.

Unlike Mincer (1991), but like Bound and Johnson (1992), a study by Juhn, Murphy, and Pierce (1993) works with detailed sample survey data (about 50,000 observations for each period) from the CPS. Neither of the two latter studies cites the other, and their apparently independent results show important nuances in interpretation. In particular, Juhn, Murphy, and Pierce are willing only to say that wage inequality rose because "the demand for skill rose" (410). Unlike Bound and Johnson (or Mincer), they do not attribute this shift to skill-biased technological change.

Juhn, Murphy, and Pierce (1993) first screen their data to limit their examination to wages of males working full time and earning above half

---

22. Note that this formulation is close to the specific-factors, noncompetitive, Ricardian model (as opposed to the homogeneous-factors, competitive, Heckscher-Ohlin model) suggested by Sachs and Shatz (1995).

23. Mincer does not conduct counterfactual simulations or otherwise decompose the relative contribution of each of the variables.

the minimum wage. They also deflate by the consumption expenditure deflator of the national accounts, a better deflator than the CPI (used by Bound and Johnson), as discussed in chapter 1. A key finding for their data set is that there was little change in inequality from 1963 to 1969, but thereafter there was a nearly monotonic secular increase in wage inequality over two decades. The distribution widened because of an absolute reduction at the bottom, increase at the top, and stagnation at the middle. Thus, from 1970 to 1989 workers at the 10th percentile lost 25 percent in real wages, those at the median had a decline of about 5 percent, and those at the 90th percentile gained by 15 percent (Juhn, Murphy, and Pierce 1993, 415-16). Moreover, this process was a uniform fanning out rather than widening only at the extremes (as discussed below).

Persistent widening of the distribution in both the 1970s and the 1980s is somewhat at odds with the impression given by the studies that focus heavily on education-based wage differentials. The latter (e.g., Mincer 1991) stress an equalizing trend during the 1970s followed by increased dispersion in the 1980s. That pattern does not seem to apply to the wage distribution itself—leaving somewhat of a puzzle as to what offsetting influence in the 1970s kept the distribution widening during a period when the educational differential was narrowing.

Continuous widening for the past two decades is also an important finding from the standpoint of trade considerations, because more open trade is a phenomenon of this entire period (which marked the implementation of Kennedy Round liberalization as well as the advent of the export drives of the newly industrializing countries [NICs]). Thus, the Juhn-Murphy-Pierce pattern is somewhat more compatible with a role for fundamental globalization and possible HO considerations, whereas the notion of equalizing educational differentials in the 1970s followed by their widening in the 1980s points, more narrowly, toward a role for the large US trade deficits of the 1980s.

The authors find that inequality has widened both within and between educational and experience groups. Figure 2.4 presents a stylized version of their wage growth lines.[24] The figure refers to workers with little (1-10 years) and much (20-30 years) experience and with college and only high school education. The vertical axis shows the proportionate change in the real wage from 1964 to 1988. The horizontal axis shows the percentile location in the distribution for the group in question. A positive slope on the wage growth line means increasing within-group inequality, because real wages are rising proportionately more at the higher percentiles. A vertical gap between two lines of the same type (e.g., education) means

---

24. The original lines have individual plots at each unit-spaced percentile. However, these points adhere closely to the summary lines portrayed here. Note also that the original diagrams refer to the change in the natural logarithm of the real wage. For changes on the order that occurred, this is approximately equal to the change expressed as a proportion.

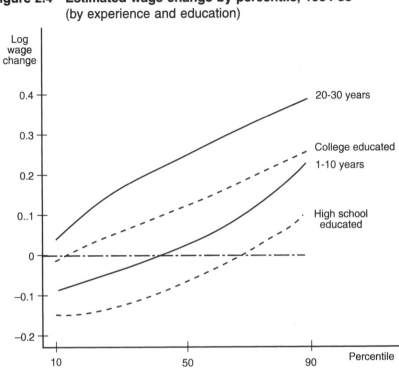

Figure 2.4 Estimated wage change by percentile, 1964-88
(by experience and education)

Source: Juhn, Murphy, and Pierce (1993).

rising intergroup inequality if the higher line refers to the higher-wage group, because it indicates that at each comparable part of the distribution in each group, wage growth was faster in the higher-wage group. The median height of the wage growth line shows how much real growth there has been over the period for workers at the midpoint of the distribution. In a world of constant wage inequality, all of the wage lines would be horizontal and lying at the vertical height corresponding to median real wage growth throughout the economy.

Several sobering trends stand out in figure 2.4. First, for 70 percent of high school (only) graduates, real wages in 1988 were lower than in 1964. That is, the wage line for this group crosses the zero point on the vertical axis at the 70th percentile. Second, for 40 percent of young workers, real wages were lower in 1988 than for young workers in 1964. Third, there was a nearly linear widening of inequality for the distribution within each subgroup, with real wages for the 90th percentile rising by about 20 to 30 percent relative to real wages for the 10th percentile in each of the subgroups. This linearity meant that growing within-group inequality was widespread and not merely the consequence of concentrated movements at each end of the distribution.[25] Fourth, there was growing inequality between the relevant pairs of subgroups. Measured at the 50th percentile, the real wage for college graduates rose over the period by about 20 percent relative to that for high school graduates (i.e., +12 percent − [−8 percent]) and that for workers with 20-30 years experience also rose by about 20 percent (the vertical gap between the respective pairs of wage growth lines). Juhn, Murphy, and Pierce (1993) interpret the widening within-group wage differentials as a trend toward higher prices for skills. They first test for the contrary hypothesis of widening dispersion in "unobservable ability within recent entry cohorts." They reject this possibility because the dispersion of "older cohorts leaving the data" is equal to that of newer cohorts. However, there might be a natural tendency for within-cohort inequality to widen as each cohort ages.[26] If so, then equal dispersion between the oldest and youngest cohort would seem to indicate growing rather than constant dispersion of unmeasurable abilities.

The authors then conduct a decomposition analysis of rising wage inequality. They find that very little of the increase is attributable to a change in the quantity distribution of workers by experience and educational type at fixed (period average) wages for each type, so that "changes in age and education composition of the workforce have not had a direct effect on the level of inequality" (429). Instead, the bulk of the change in inequality is attributable to changes in the "prices" (wages) of each category, and, even more importantly, changes in other "unobservable" influences.

---

25. It is useful to ask whether there is an inherent bias toward measuring an increase in within-group inequality. Such a bias would exist if the sample referred to a fixed set of individuals and defined their position in the distribution strictly by terminal period location. In that case, purely random processes would tend to generate an observed increase in concentration. Random income swings would push some at the top of the original distribution toward higher incomes and some at the bottom toward lower incomes. Similar random shifts would tend to cancel each other out across most of the distribution. As a result, the right tail of the wage growth curve would flare up, the left tail would flare down, and most of the curve would be flat. The measurement problem would be analogous to an index number problem, because use of terminal period sequencing of incomes would tend to show rising inequality, whereas use of initial period sequencing would show the reverse. However, the comparisons here are not for income change of specified individuals arrayed by terminal percentile, but rather for 1988 income of the person at a given percentile compared with the 1964 income of the individual at the corresponding percentile in 1964. There are, thus, changing populations as well as no strict choice of sequencing by terminal or initial period, so there should be no inherent bias toward measured increases in inequality (i.e., toward a positive slope in the wage growth curve).

26. For example, lawyers and doctors at the peak of their careers would seem likely to show greater dispersion (e.g., between super-lawyer partners in large private firms and their contemporaries in government service) than at their entry-level jobs when they emerged from professional school.

The authors divide skills into three dimensions: education, experience, and unobservable skill differentials within education-experience groups. They find that the "price" of unobservable skill rose steadily from the late 1960s to the late 1980s, by a cumulative 50 percent above the 1963 base. The price of experience was flat through 1975 and then rose steadily to the late 1980s, to about 25 percent above the base. The price of educational skill rose in the late 1960s and early 1970s, collapsed below its base level by the late 1970s, and then soared to about 25 percent above the base level by the late 1980s (confirming the changing returns to education reviewed above).

Juhn, Murphy, and Pierce (1993) conclude their analysis by examining the role of changing demand structure by industry and occupation. For each cell in a matrix of 12 sectors by 11 occupational groups, they identify the number of workers by location at each of the 100 percentiles in the overall wage distribution. They then calculate that over the past three decades, the changing structure of output has rather steadily increased the demand for higher skills (i.e., higher positions in the distribution) and correspondingly reduced that for lower-skilled (distributional order) workers. The only exception to the steady pace is some acceleration for the highest skill (distributional) levels. The results refute the popular notion that the changing structure of demand has increased the relative number of low-wage jobs (e.g., by shifting demand from manufacturing to low-wage service sectors as proposed by Bluestone and Harris 1988). They show, instead, that there was a reduction in relative demand in sectors characterized by such jobs. Nonetheless, the compositional demand analysis does not explain why the times series for skill prices differ so much for experience, education, and unobserved skill.

Overall, the authors consider the data to show clearly that "the demand for skill has risen." However, they state that further research is required to determine the sources of this demand shift and conclude that "likely but untested candidates are biased rates of technological progress and changes in the world economy" (438). Thus, they remain agnostic on the crucial distinction from the standpoint of this study. On the evidence, this more noncommittal position would seem more appropriate than the Bound-Johnson (1992) judgment that skill-biased technical change is the principal causal factor.

In contrast, Berman, Bound, and Griliches (1994) argue vigorously that skill-biased technological change is the principal force behind widening skill-wage differentials in the 1980s, and that two other candidate influences—international trade and the defense buildup—were relatively unimportant. The authors use data from the Annual Survey of Manufacturers (ASM) and from the National Bureau of Economic Research database on trade and production, not the often-used CPS.

The ASM data distinguish between "production" workers (up through foreman level, "engaged in fabricating, processing, assembling, inspecting, and other manufacturing") and "nonproduction" workers (those, including supervisors, "engaged in . . . installation and servicing . . . sales, delivery, professional, technological, administrative, etc.") (Berman, Bound, and Griliches 1994, 369). Berman, Bound, and Griliches take pains to show that there is a close correlation between the nonproduction/ production dichotomy of the ASM and the white collar/blue collar distinction of the CPS. The two approaches both identify about 28 percent of the manufacturing workforce as being nonproduction (white collar) in 1973, with the fraction rising to 35-37 percent by 1987.

Burtless (1995a, 810) has criticized the use of production versus nonproduction workers in analysis of skill differentials. Citing estimates by Sachs and Shatz (1994) and Kosters (1994), he notes that the wage premium of nonproduction workers rose by only 4 percent from 1979 to 1986 (from 53 to 55 percent excess above the wage for nonproduction workers), while the corresponding premium for white male college graduates rose by 53 percent (from 36 percent to 55 percent above high school graduates).

Subject to this caveat, the results of Berman, Bound, and Griliches (1994) provide one of the stronger cases to date that the central influence is technical change.[27] The core of their analysis is a decomposition of rising employment (or wage bill) shares of nonproduction workers in manufacturing into between-sector changes (from lower- to higher-nonproduction worker industries) and within-sector changes. They argue that both trade and the defense buildup should show up primarily in between-sector shifts, whereas technological change would be manifest in within-sector shifts. Their decomposition is:

$$\Delta P_n = \sum_{i=1}^{N} \Delta S_i \overline{P}_{n_i} + \sum_{i=1}^{N} \Delta P_{n_i} \overline{S}_i \qquad (2.2)$$

where $P_{ni} = E_{ni}/E_i$ is the proportion of nonproduction workers for sector i, $S_i = E_i/E$ is the share of employment in sector i, Δ refers to change, and the overbar refers to the period average. The first right-side term measures between-industry shifts in the nonproduction worker density, and the second measures the contribution of shifts within industries to the overall change in nonproduction workers as a share of employment.

For 450 US manufacturing industries at the four-digit SIC level, the authors calculate that the total share of nonproduction workers in employment rose 0.3 percentage point per year in 1973-79 and 0.55 percentage point per year in 1979-87. They find that in the first period, between-sector change contributed 0.11 percentage point and within-sector change 0.19 point. The dominance of within-sector change increased in the second

---

27. However, note the Baldwin and Cain (1994) critique that not all trade effects need be between-industry and the Bernard and Jensen (1994) finding that "between" variation is much greater when the data set is for plants. Both studies are discussed below.

period, when the breakdown was 0.16 percentage point per year from between-sector change and 0.39 percentage point from within-sector change. The authors argue that the large share of within-sector change is "not consistent with a dominant role for factors that shift product demand such as trade" (Berman, Bound, and Griliches 1994, 378). Even so, their decomposition further allows for a role of trade even for within-sector change.[28]

The authors further estimate that in 1979-87, exports and imports contributed less than one-third of between-sector change, whereas two-fifths was attributable to the defense industry buildup, and the remainder occurred in production for domestic consumption. The role of trade was practically zero for within-sector change. Considering that between-sector change represented less than one-third of total change, these results lead the authors to conclude that trade played relatively little role in the rising demand for skills. They acknowledge, however, that they do not test for indirect influences of trade pressures that could either shift overall demand from manufacturing toward nontradables or motivate technological change.

The authors then conduct cross-section regressions that show a strong correlation between a rising nonproduction employment share and two alternative indicators of technological change: R&D expenditures relative to sales and investments in computers relative to total investment. They invoke Bureau of Labor Statistics survey results to highlight that in the 1980s there were pervasive computer-related technological changes that shifted demand toward skilled workers.[29]

The study by Berman, Bound, and Griliches (1994) is unable to escape the deficiency of other studies emphasizing technological change—they essentially must attribute an unexplained residual to that change. Nonetheless, their analysis adds weight to the earlier findings of Bound and Johnson (1992). The Berman-Bound-Griliches study works at a more disaggregated level, and high aggregation is inherently biased toward finding within- rather than between-industry causation. They also add some regression and qualitative evidence implicating computerization

---

28. The export, import, defense, and domestic consumption effects are calculated analogously to the full-sector effects. Thus, the between-sector contribution of imports is $-\Sigma_i \Delta S_i^M (P_{ni} - P_n^C)$, where superscript M refers to imports and C to domestic consumption (the implicit "residual pool of labor"), and the within-sector contribution of imports is $-\Sigma_i (\Delta P_{ni} - \Delta P_n^C) S_i^C$. There are corresponding terms for exports, defense, and domestic consumption.

29. Such as a shift from typesetting to electronic composition in printing and toward numerically controlled machines and robots in aerospace. The authors also note that the sectors found by the Bureau of Labor Statistics to have been unamenable to computer-based automation, such as meat packing, tires, and bakery products, are also sectors where there was no shift toward nonproduction workers.

(although they note that labor-saving technological change was also important in the 1950s, so the role of computers in the 1980s experience should not be exaggerated).

Greater sectoral detail helps reduce the bias against finding trade effects. Nevertheless, intraindustry trade is a well-known phenomenon that persists even at relatively fine levels of disaggregation. As a result, the underlying perspective that trade effects will only occur in the form of between-industry changes is subject to doubt. Correspondingly, some portion of the within-sector demand shift could be attributed to trade.[30]

Moreover, Berman, Bound, and Griliches' measurements for exports and imports seem to understate their role (1994, 381). They weigh "domestic consumption" in demand (as opposed to defense or trade related) as 93 percent of demand for manufactures, leaving only 7 percent to be divided among defense, exports, and (the negative of) imports. Yet, against the manufacturing base, external trade would seem to be far more important.[31] For both of these reasons (and for the technical reason in note 30), the study may understate the role of trade in shifting demand for skilled labor.

Freeman (1991) has examined another relatively traditional dimension of the causes of growing wage inequality: the influence of declining worker unionization. The fraction of unionized workers in the nonagricultural work force fell from 29 percent in 1969 to 25 percent in 1978 and just 16 percent by 1989 (when the rate for private-sector workers was only 12 percent, about the level of the 1920s).

Freeman notes that, theoretically, unionization can cause greater or lesser inequality. A union premium on average widens the wage gap between unionized and nonunion blue-collar workers, but narrows that between white-collar workers and blue-collar workers (including unionized). Unionization also tends to narrow the dispersion of wages among the unionized. Freeman (1991, 7) states that by now there is a "general consensus that unionism is associated with lower rather than greater wage inequality." Declining union density in the United States would thus be

30. There would appear to be a bias against identifying trade (or defense) contributions to within-sector change. The decomposition calculation for this change is driven by the difference between the change in the nonproduction employment proportion in the sector in question and the change in that proportion for domestic consumption overall, multiplied by the export (import, defense) share in demand for the sector in question. But in this calculation (Berman, Bound, and Griliches 1994, 394, equation 4), if there were an identical increase in the proportion of nonproduction workers throughout the entire economy, the specification of the equation would attribute the entire within-sector change to change in the domestic consumption component of demand, with zero estimates for exports, imports, and defense.

31. Thus, in 1987 manufactured exports amounted to $200 billion, and imports to $325 billion (Lenz 1992, 31). These magnitudes represented 11.1 percent and 18.1 percent, respectively, of manufacturing GDP (CEA 1995, 284).

expected to have contributed to widening inequality. The question is, by how much?

Freeman uses CPS data for males in 1978 and 1988 to answer this question. His sample ranges in size from about 7,000 to 70,000 observations, with the lower figure a subsample for younger workers in 1978. He estimates a regression of the logarithm of earnings on a series of dummy variables, including for union membership, age, race, industrial sector, and education or occupation. In 1978, the union dummy increased blue-collar wages by 26 percent and white-collar wages by 1 percent. The corresponding union differentials are 16 percent for high school graduates and -2 percent (presumably spurious) for college graduates.

The author then combines the change in union density from 1978 to 1988 with the 1978 union wage differential to calculate the change in the relative wage attributable to falling unionization. Thus, for blue-collar workers, union density fell from 47 percent to 33 percent; the 14 percentage point difference, applied to the 0.26 proportionate wage differential, means that declining unionization caused (or at least was associated with) a reduction of 3.6 percent in the blue-collar wage from ceteris paribus levels. Considering that the white-/blue-collar differential rose by 7 percent over the period, Freeman concludes that deunionization was responsible for half of the widening intercollar inequality. Adding similar calculations for different age and educational groups, he concludes that falling union density was responsible for 40 to 50 percent of the rise in the white-collar premium, 15 to 40 percent of the rise in the college premium over high school graduates, and 20 percent of the rise in the standard deviation of the logarithm of earnings.[32]

Aside from possible selectivity bias, there is the classic question of causation versus correlation in interpreting Freeman's results. It is possible and perhaps likely that other exogenous forces contributed to both declining unionization and widening wage inequality. For example, if technological change and trade eroded the bargaining strength and relative wages of unskilled workers, they might have become more cautious about joining unions for fear of risking their jobs during strikes. If so, even mandatory unionization would not necessarily have rolled back the relative wage erosion attributable to exogenous nonunion influences.

Even within the framework of the Freeman calculation, others have arrived at smaller estimates of the impact of deunionization. Bound and

---

32. Freeman also attempts a longitudinal analysis for individually identified workers using 1987 and 1988 data, as a way to control for the problem of selectivity—unions may recruit the more able candidates, thereby biasing upward the union premium for constant-ability workers. The results show considerably lower union premiums, but data difficulties (including the brevity of the period examined) make the longitudinal test less than satisfactory. Freeman argues, instead, that selectivity is not much of a problem and cites as evidence the persistence of a nearly constant union differential between 1978 and 1988 despite the

Johnson (1992, 379-80) cite Lewis (1986), who found that the upper-bound estimate of the union premium is 15 percent. They estimate that from 1979 to 1988, union density for males fell from 38.5 percent to 27 percent for high school graduates (with no college) and from 17.4 percent to 14.6 percent for college graduates. Thus, they calculate that the college-high school wage ratio should have risen by only 1.3 percent (0.15 × [{17.4 − 14.6} − {38.5 − 27}]) as a consequence of deunionization, less than one-tenth of the total increase of 16.3 percent in the wage differential (as compared with Freeman's range of 15 to 40 percent of the change in the educational premium).

Labor Economists 2

It is probably fair to say that the majority opinion among labor economists has been that growing wage inequality has been primarily due to skill-biased technological change and shifting sectoral composition on the demand side, with the added influence during the 1980s of a slowdown in the formation of new college graduates and consequential upward pressure on college wages from the supply side.[33] The majority view would probably allow some modest additional contribution from declining unionization. However, there is also a group of labor economists that has placed more emphasis on the role of trade and immigration. And some authors have a foot in each camp.

Katz and Murphy (1992) conduct decomposition analysis similar to that of Bound and Johnson (1992) and Juhn, Murphy, and Pierce (1993) but add an explicit calculation of the impact of trade. Nonetheless, they find that "rapid secular growth in the relative demand for more-skilled workers" over the past 25 years has driven rising wage inequality. Their summary conclusion does not mention trade specifically:

> Although much of this shift in relative demand can be accounted for by observed shifts in the industrial and occupational composition of employment toward relatively skill-intensive sectors, the majority reflects shifts in relative labor demand occurring within detailed sectors. These within-sector shifts are likely to reflect skill-biased technological changes. . . . [F]luctuations in the rate of growth of the relative supply of college graduates combined with smooth trend demand growth in favor of more-educated workers can largely explain fluctuations in the college/high school differential over the 1963-1987 period. (87)

The two authors use a sample from the CPS (which covers some 1.4 million workers over the 25-year period) to examine wages of workers

---

falling union density. If unions were selective, the premium would be inversely related to the density of union coverage.

33. See, for example, the survey by Kosters (1994).

divided by sex, education, and experience. They first test the hypothesis that the profile of labor demand has been stable and changing wages have been attributable solely to changing relative supply. This hypothesis would require a strictly negative relationship between the wage change and supply change for each of the demographic-skill categories.[34]

For 64 demographic categories (2 genders × 4 educational groups × 8 experience groups), Katz and Murphy examine the vector product: $[W_t - W_\tau] \cdot [X_t - X_\tau]$, where W is the vector of relative wages across the categories, X is the vector of relative labor supply, t is the current year, and τ is the base year for comparison. If this product is negative, then the dominant result of multiplying wage change by category supply change is negative, tending to confirm the hypothesis of stable demand.[35]

The vector-product test shows results consistent with stable demand during 1965-80. However, it shows unstable demand in the 1980s, when the vector product is positive. Thus, in the 1980s there were increasing relative wages for females and for college graduates, even though the relative supply of each of these groups was rising (positive covariance of wage and supply change), and there was a decline in the relative wages of younger workers even as the share of younger workers in the labor force was declining again as the baby-boom cohort aged (a positive correlation).

The authors then examine demand shifts. For twelve broad sectoral categories available in the CPS data, as well as three occupational groups, they show a shift from 1967 to 1987 "out of 'low tech' and 'basic' manufacturing and into professional and business services," which "is suggestive of a trend demand shift in favor of college graduates and of women and against less-educated males" (55). They also point out that if the within-sector demand for labor is stable, then within each industry the employment shares should have fallen for groups whose relative wages have risen (as each industry substitutes away from the factors with rising relative price). Instead, they find that the employment shares of women and college graduates have increased in almost every two-digit industry. They conclude that there must have been within-industry labor demand shifts as well as cross-industry shifts.

Katz and Murphy (1992) measure overall demand shift for labor type k among the 150 sector-occupation cells as $\Delta X_k = [\Sigma_j \alpha_{jk} \Delta E_j]/E_k$, where α_{jk}

---

34. The test is specified in relative terms (the wage relative to the average wage and the labor supply in a given category relative to the total labor supply); otherwise changing the economic and labor force scale would confound the unambiguous negative correlation between wage change and supply change (the latter of which could be positive even for a category with shrinking relative supply). The authors treat each category's share in labor supply in terms of "efficiency units," which weight the number of workers by the wage relative to the overall average wage.

35. Since the product of vectors **A** and **B** equals the sum of the products of their corresponding elements $(\Sigma_i a_i b_i)$, a negative product will mean the predominance of negative correlations

is demographic group k's share of total employment (in efficiency units) in sector j in the base year, ΔE_j is the change in employment in sector-occupation cell j, and E_k is base year employment in labor type k (in efficiency units). Between-industry demand shift is measured by the same calculation but as applied to the 50 industries. Within-industry demand shifts are then obtained residually as the difference between total demand shift and between-industry shift.

The results indicate substantial between-industry demand shifts. Thus, in 1979-87 between-industry shifts reduced demand for male high school dropouts by 6 percent and increased that for male college graduates by 2.9 percent. For the whole period of 1967-87 the corresponding changes were -14.1 percent and $+10.7$ percent for males and -11.1 percent and $+17.7$ percent for females.

These between-industry shifts seem more important than indicated in the decomposition analysis by Bound and Johnson (1992). One likely reason is that Katz and Murphy work at a more detailed sectoral level (50 industries rather than 17). Another reason may be that Katz and Murphy work in efficiency units, whereas Bound and Johnson consider absolute employment levels. If there were a systematic shift of low-skilled workers out of industries such as unionized steel and automobile plants where there are high labor rents (i.e., wages in excess of market levels for comparable skills elsewhere in the economy) and into sectors without such labor rents, the Katz-Murphy method would show larger sectoral demand shifts than would the Bound-Johnson method.[36]

Within-industry demand shifts are also present, but turn out to be less important for the two decades as a whole.[37] The principal exception is for male college graduates in the 1980s, when the within-sector shift is $+4.3$ percent and between-sector shift 2.9 percent.

The important role found for between-industry demand shift would seem to undermine the heavy emphasis on technological change running through much of the literature by labor economists. Thus, if Bound and Johnson (1992) had measured a higher explanation from between-industry shifts in demand, they would have had a smaller unexplained residual

---

between wage change and labor category change, taking account of the relative importance of each sector.

36. Suppose sector A pays 200 dollars for an unskilled worker whereas industry B—and the economy overall on a weighted basis—pays 100 dollars. A demand shift of one worker from sector A to sector B would show a reduction of one-half of one unskilled job in the approach using efficiency units (Katz and Murphy 1992), but no change whatsoever in the approach using absolute numbers of workers (Bound and Johnson 1992).

37. Thus, within-industry shifts reduce demand for male high school dropouts by 4.7 percent, about one-third the reduction from between-industry shifts, and increase demand for male college graduates by 5.8 percent, about half the increase from between-industry shifts. The within relative to between shift comparisons are similar or even smaller for females.

to attribute to technological change. In this regard, it is somewhat surprising that Katz and Murphy nonetheless stress technological change in their summary.

Katz and Murphy (1992) then estimate the impact of trade on factor demand. Focusing on direct labor effects and ignoring induced input-output effects, they calculate the "implicit supply of labor" of a given demographic group contained in net imports in year t across all industries i, as $\Sigma_i e_i^k E_{it}[I_{it}/Y_{it}]$, where e_i^k is the fraction of efficiency-unit employment in industry i composed of type k workers, E_i is the share of total efficiency-unit employment in sector i, I is net imports, and Y is domestic output. The effect of trade on relative demand for the demographic group k is then

$$T_t^k = -\frac{1}{E^k} \sum_{i=1}^{m} \left[e_i^k E_{it} \left(\frac{I_{it}}{Y_{it}} \right) \right] + \sum_{i=1}^{m} E_{it} \left(\frac{I_{it}}{Y_{it}} \right) \tag{2.3}$$

where E^k is the average share of group k in efficiency-unit employment for all industries in 1967-87. The first term on the right is labor contained in net imports as normalized by the average share of this type of labor in overall employment. The second term effectively normalizes for the level of the trade balance, to leave the trade impact calculus strictly one of relative factor composition.

This second term on the right is important because it greatly reduces the vulnerability of the Katz-Murphy measure to the critique that the results reflect the large but arguably transitory US trade deficit of the mid-1980s rather than any structural labor bias of trade.[38] The measure turns out to be unaffected by the trade balance if there is no difference among sectors in factor propensities.

Thus, suppose demographic group k refers to unskilled labor (e.g., a male high school dropout with 10 years experience). Suppose the fraction of employment comprising this group is identical across sectors: $e_i = \beta$. Equation 2.3 becomes

$$T_t^k = -\frac{\beta}{E^u} \sum_{i=1}^{m} E_{it} \left(\frac{I_{it}}{Y_{it}} \right) + \sum_{i=1}^{m} E_{it} \left(\frac{I_{it}}{Y_{it}} \right)$$

$$= \left(1 - \frac{\beta}{E^u} \right) \sum_{i=1}^{m} E_{it} \left(\frac{I_{it}}{Y_{it}} \right). \tag{2.3'}$$

From the definition here of β, it follows that $\beta = E^u$. The first term in parentheses in the final row of equation 2.3' is thus zero. The Katz-Murphy measure thus identifies zero trade impact when there is no differential factor intensity among sectors, regardless of whether the trade balance is in large deficit ($\Sigma_i E_i[I_i/Y_i] >> 0$) or in surplus ($\Sigma_i E_i[I_i/Y_i] < 0$).

---

38. In 1987, the US external balance on goods and nonfactor services reached a peak of 3.5 percent of GDP (IMF 1994a).

When factor intensities differ between imports and exports, there is an interaction between factor intensity and the size of imports and exports. Appendix 2A shows that the Katz-Murphy index is actually likely to show that a higher trade surplus has a negative impact on the relative demand for unskilled labor, if importables are more unskilled intensive than exportables, as seems likely. Essentially, the index is for relative rather than absolute demand for a given labor category, and as the economy shifts from more unskilled-intensive nontradables to more skilled-intensive exportables, the relative demand for unskilled labor should decline. US experience in the 1980s is consistent with this alternative interpretation, because there was a boom in nontradables (i.e., the construction industry) that kept US employment high despite the rising trade deficit. The Katz-Murphy index indirectly picks up this phenomenon, but their discussion of their results makes no mention of it.

Appendix 2A also shows that under the assumption of unskilled-intensive importables and skilled-intensive exportables, and when trade is in balance, the relative size of trade in the economy is negatively related to the relative demand for unskilled labor. That is, increased unskilled jobs for a given extra value of exports fall short of the reduction in unskilled jobs for the same value of increased imports. Overall, the analysis of appendix 2A suggests that the interpretation of Katz and Murphy, that their results implicate the growing US trade deficit of the mid-1980s as the culprit responsible for declining relative demand for unskilled labor, may be incorrect. Correspondingly, the alternative interpretation would be that it was the rising relative importance of trade overall in the 1980s (as opposed to the rising trade deficit) that drove the declining relative demand for unskilled labor.

This alternative interpretation would be less sanguine, because it would imply that the trend was secular and structural rather than subject to conjunctural reversal as the temporarily large trade deficit reverted to more normal levels. If valid, this alternative interpretation would also mean that the Katz-Murphy measure of the impact of trade on the relative demand for unskilled labor would be unlikely to have reverted to a more favorable trend by the early 1990s, when the US trade deficit fell relative to GDP.

Subject to these caveats, Katz and Murphy (1992, 65) find that

> the effects on relative labor demands of trade were quite moderate until substantial trade deficits developed in the 1980s. The adverse effects of trade . . . are concentrated on high school dropouts. Female dropouts who have traditionally been employed intensively as production workers in import-competing industries such as apparel and textiles are the group most affected by trade. In fact, demand changes from trade are larger for female high school dropouts in the 1980s than are domestic sources of between-sector demand shifts.

For the period 1979-85, the authors estimate that changes in trade caused a reduction of 0.63 to 1.48 percent in the demand for male high school dropouts and a reduction of 2.22 to 4.00 percent for female high school dropouts. The larger figure in each case assumes that the trade effect is strictly concentrated on production workers rather than spread evenly across production and nonproduction workers. For the same period, trade increased the demand for college graduates by 0.55 to 1.50 percent for males and by 1.26 to 1.50 percent for females. These relatively large positive effects suggest that even for this period of a large US trade deficit, sectoral factor differentials and the rising role of trade in the economy were the principal influence, not the rising US trade deficit.[39]

Katz and Murphy (1992, 69) conclude their study with estimates that require specific assumptions about the substitutability of college- and high school-educated workers (with all other workers converted to "equivalents" of one or the other). They calculate that there was a steady annual rise of 4.5 percent in the relative demand for college-equivalent workers during the period 1963-87. The rise in the college wage differential in the 1960s, fall in the 1970s, and rebound to new highs in the 1980s are estimated as the result of the interaction between steadily rising demand for the college educated and slow, then rapid, and finally slow growth in the number of college graduates in these three respective periods.

As for observed experience differentials, the authors do not find a similar neat fit and instead conclude that the "active labor market hypothesis" of Freeman (1975) is the most plausible explanation. By this hypothesis, major changes in the labor market disproportionately affect young workers without seniority and with little firm-specific training. The "collapse of new employment opportunities for less-educated workers in the manufacturing sector in the 1980s is likely to have had its most severe impact on young less-educated males" for this reason (Katz and Murphy 1992, 73).

Overall, the authors find that international influences only began to be significant "with the appearance of the large trade deficits in the 1980s" (76) and that, in any event, the bulk of the relative shift in demand for more-educated workers occurred within rather than between sectors. They invoke the popular idea of skill-biased technological change as a possible explanation, but do not directly test it. Thus, the study gives only a mild, but provocative, nod to the importance of trade. Because of this acknowledgment, and the explicit measurement of trade effects, the study is placed here among "labor economists 2" who emphasize trade, although in terms of the authors' own qualitative interpretation of their results the study probably belongs in the camp of the "labor economists 1" who emphasize technological change instead. It should be noted, none-

---

39. If exports are skill intensive, a reduction in the trade balance would tend to reduce the relative demand for college graduates rather than increase it.

theless, that the authors' own tests tend to limit any bias introduced by the trade deficit as opposed to structural factor propensities combined with rising trade integration (as discussed above). Moreover, even with disaggregation at the level of 50 sectors, the number of traded-goods sectors remains sufficiently limited that changes attributed to "within-sector" influences such as technology could instead reflect increased import and export propensities at more disaggregated levels. Finally, the authors' own estimates do suggest that trade has a substantial impact for the lowest-skilled workers.

Murphy and Welch (1991) provided an early estimate of the impact of trade on trends in US wage inequality. They found that traded-goods sectors tended to employ relatively more workers with lower educational levels, and relatively more males, than did nontradables. Their calculations suggested that because of this pattern, the shift of US trade from balance to large deficit in the 1980s constituted an important dislocation in relative demand by worker type. Moreover, these shifts were consistent with observed shifts in relative wages. However, they explicitly recognized that "[t]o the extent that trade deficits are transitory, wage shifts may also be transitory. . ." (43), so their analysis consciously focused on the conjunctural rather than structural-secular impact of trade.

The Murphy-Welch study works with CPS survey data. The authors aggregate their sample (covering tens of thousands of workers) into four broad industry groups: traded durable goods (including mining); traded nondurables (including agriculture, forestry, and fisheries); traded services (including financial, insurance, real estate, brokerage, legal, and accounting); and a large residual category of nontraded goods.

Table 2.2 shows the Murphy-Welch average allocation of workers across these four broad sectors for 1967-86. It is evident that more highly educated workers tend to be in the nontraded sector. Thus, slightly over half of workers with less than high school education are in this sector, but for college graduates the figure reaches about 65 percent for males and 86 percent for females. Conversely, for traded goods the share of the work force is inversely related to educational level. For male workers this concentration is heavier in durable goods (such as autos and steel); for females, the relative concentration of unskilled workers is greater in nondurables (such as textiles and apparel). Traded services are the exception to the trade-unskilled connection, as the share of more highly educated workers present in these services exceeds the share of lesser educated workers.

It should be stressed that by treating tradables as a block rather than distinguishing between exportables and importables, Murphy and Welch are not able to examine the HO considerations of differential factor impact as the role of trade (as opposed to the trade balance) increases. Nevertheless, their approach provides insight into the labor demand shifts associated with the trade deficit of the 1980s.

Table 2.2 Trends in employment and wages by broad sector and years of education, 1967-86 (percentages)

	A. Employment shares 1967-86				B. Predicted impact of trade on demand and actual wage change, 1979-86 (all sectors)	
	Nontraded goods	Durable goods	Nondurable goods	Traded services	Demand	Wage
Men						
8–11	53.4	28.1	16.9	1.6	−1.97	−10.21
12	58.0	25.0	14.1	3.0	−1.25	−7.85
13–15	62.0	20.7	10.6	6.6	−0.36	−0.33
16+	64.9	15.2	9.3	10.7	0.66	7.80
Women						
8–11	54.2	18.3	24.2	3.3	−0.60	−0.80
12	61.8	12.6	11.6	14.0	0.91	4.03
13	69.9	8.2	6.7	15.2	1.99	8.47
16+	85.5	3.3	3.8	7.3	3.31	12.70

C. Changes in industry employment share, 1979-86

	Nontraded goods	Durable goods	Nondurable goods	Traded services
Predicted	4.1	−14.7	−1.8	1.4
Observed	4.3	−17.1	−8.8	18.7

Source: Murphy and Welch (1991).

Murphy and Welch calculate the "effect of changes in international trade" from 1979 to 1986 using the following equation:

$$\frac{dN_j}{N_j} = \sum_{k=1}^{4} \frac{N_{jk}}{N_j} \left(\frac{\Delta I}{Y} - \frac{dI_k}{Y_k} \right)$$ (2.4)

where N is employment, j is the labor type, k is one of the four aggregated sectors, d and Δ refer to change, I is net imports (with $\Delta I = \Sigma_k dI_k$), and Y is output. On the left is the proportionate change in demand for a given labor type resulting from a change in trade. On the right, the initial quotient shows the relative share of each sector j in question in the allocation of labor of the type in question. The first term in the final bracketed expression shows the total increase in the trade deficit as a fraction of GDP, and the final term inside the brackets shows the change in the sector's trade deficit as a fraction of output in the sector.

The authors estimate that the move from trade balance to large deficit over the period amounted to 4.1 percent of GDP. They reason that this increment was equivalent to an overall increase in US demand unmatched by increased US production. They distribute this component of increased demand uniformly across sectors and labor types (in the term $\Delta I/Y$). They then deduct the reduction in demand for sector k represented by the increased trade deficit in the sector (the effect of the term $-dI_k/Y_k$). As Deardorff and Hakura (1994, 93-94) emphasize, this approach has the important advantage of taking into account the induced demand for labor in the nontraded sector, which was associated with the overall demand expansion under Reaganomics. It thereby avoids exaggeration of job losses attributed to "trade" in studies that do not net out the influence of the widening trade deficit (especially Borjas, Freeman, and Katz 1992, as discussed below).

Table 2.2 shows the predicted change in sectoral employment ($\Delta I/Y - dI_k/Y_k$) as well as the actual change over the period. For nontradables, the term involving sectoral imports drops out, and the overall expansion of demand by 4.1 percent of GDP is applied directly to the sector. The actual change is close to this prediction. The largest adverse effect is in durable goods. There, the reduction in demand from increased net imports amounts to 18.8 percent of sectoral output. After the moderating effect of the overall increase of demand by 4.1 percent, the net effect of "trade changes" amounts to a predicted reduction of sectoral employment by 14.7 percent, relatively close to the actual reduction of 17.1 percent. For nondurables and traded services there is greater divergence between predicted and actual outcomes, although the signs are correct.[40]

After combining the sectoral labor-type propensities (part A of table 2.2) with the sectoral demand shifts (part B), the authors predict the impact

---

40. The authors consider the large difference for traded services to be "not surprising" given the strong trend in services and the crudeness in matching industrial categories.

of trade change on the demand for labor by type (equation 2.4). As shown in table 2.2, in every case the predicted change in demand is consistent with the observed change in real wage. The largest adverse effects are for males with high school education or less (for whom demand falls by 1 to 2 percent). Demand falls for all males except college educated, whereas for females demand declines only for high school dropouts. The greater relative adverse effect of the widening trade deficit on males stems from the greater concentration of males in traded goods (for all but high school dropouts, for whom female concentration is comparable).

Table 2.2 also shows a positive trade balance effect on college graduates for both men and women. The preponderance of the nontraded sector in employment of college graduates means that the overall demand expansion in that sector swamps the adverse effects in traded sectors for these workers.

There are many shortcuts and simplifications in the Murphy-Welch calculation, as the authors recognize. Most fundamentally, it is closer to a calculation of what happens when there is a macroeconomic expansion of absorption relative to production than to an analysis of the secular forces imposed by international trade. Nonetheless, the study is an important benchmark in the trade impact analysis among labor economists. More-over, it highlights the important role of nondurable traded goods, as subsequently developed by others.

One of the most concrete and provocative estimates of the impact of trade and immigration on US wage inequality is that by Borjas, Freeman, and Katz (1992). As discussed below, this study proved to be a lightning rod for criticism by some trade economists, on the grounds that it sought to identify wage effects without explicitly linking them to the SS and HO framework (in which, as discussed above, the indispensable mechanism for reducing low-skilled wages is a reduction in the relative price of the unskilled-intensive product in international trade). As examined below, that critique would seem too narrow to warrant out-of-hand dismissal of the Borjas-Freeman-Katz study. A more serious problem is probably that the trade impact on wages in this study stems mainly from the mid-1980s US trade deficit, a misleading effect both because the deficit can be reversed and because the deficit finances expansion of demand and employment in the nontradables sector that is left out of the analysis.

Using CPS data for 64 skill groups and 22 manufacturing sectors, Borjas, Freeman, and Katz (1992) calculate the "direct labor embodied in trade"[41] as

$$L_t = \sum_{i=1}^{m} L_{it}(T_{it}/O_{it})$$

$$L_{jt} = \sum_{i=1}^{m} a_{ij} L_{ij}(T_{it}/O_{it}) \qquad (2.5)$$

---

41. The authors ignore the input-output requirements of indirect labor.

where L_t is aggregate labor embodied in trade in year t, L_{it} is total employment in sector i (for each of 21 broad manufacturing categories), O is domestic output, T_i is net imports in the sector in question, L_{ij} is direct labor embodied in trade in skill category j, and a_{ij} is the share of skill group j in employment in sector i.[42] Because T_i is negative when the sector is a net exporter, exports have the effect of subtracting off workers from the effective labor supply. The basic notion is that imports add to the domestic labor supply and tend to depress wages, whereas exports subtract from available domestic labor and tend to push up wages.

Parallel equations provide corresponding estimates in terms of labor efficiency units, weighting the proportion of persons in each of 64 subgroups (2 sex × 4 education × 8 experience) by the average wage in each group (1963-87). A variant of the estimates assumes that all import effects are concentrated solely on production (as opposed to nonproduction) workers, because of the possibility that sales, finance, and other nonproduction jobs "may be relatively complementary with production workers overseas" (Borjas, Freeman, and Katz 1992, 216). This variant would seem to exaggerate the relative impact on nonproduction workers, because it implicitly assumes that all increases in imports are associated with outsourcing by US multinationals, whereas the bulk of import increases would seem more likely to originate from foreign firms.

The estimates find that in 1979-81, the net effect of trade was to reduce net US labor availability by 0.3 percent. However, by 1985 this effect had shifted to a net addition to effective labor availability of 1.63 percent, composed of a 3.69 percent addition from imports and a 2.06 percent subtraction from exports. When calculated in efficiency units, the addition from imports was 3.49 percent and the export subtraction 2.15 percent, for a net addition of 1.34 percent (about one-fifth smaller than for absolute person-hours). The efficiency-unit estimate amounted to a 6.36 percent net addition to labor supply in the manufacturing sector. The differences between the calculations confirm the view that imports are relatively unskilled intensive (1 percent fewer efficiency units than person-hours) and exports skilled intensive (4 percent more efficiency units than person-hours).

The calculations with skill detail show that trade effects were "quite modest" up through 1980, when US trade was in balance. However, by 1985 the implicit supply of male high school dropouts embodied in trade added 4 to 8 percent (the higher figure calculated with complete allocation of imports to production workers), with the corresponding figure reaching 8 to 13 percent for female dropouts. The shares were about three times as high when compared with employment in manufacturing alone. In

---

42. The authors use CPS data for skill-demographic information and the NBER Immigration, Trade, and Labor Markets Data Files (Abowd 1991) for data on production, trade, and sectoral employment by production and nonproduction workers.

contrast, the relative supply effects were much smaller for college graduates. Nor do the results show much relationship between trade and experience levels.

Borjas, Freeman, and Katz then examine the labor-supply effect of immigrants. The estimated stock of immigrants (including uncounted illegal entrants) in the labor force stood at about 7 million in 1980 and 10 million in 1988 (rising from about 7 percent to about 9 percent of the labor force). The authors note that in recent decades immigration has been concentrated in workers with low education. Thus, whereas the fraction of high school dropouts fell from 22.7 percent to 15.3 percent for native males from 1980 to 1988, this fraction was considerably higher, at 39.6 percent in 1980, for immigrants (including an estimate of uncounted illegal immigrants) and the gap had widened by 1988 (when the figure for immigrants stood at 36 percent). The immigrant contribution to the male high school-dropout labor supply rose from 13 percent in 1980 to 23 percent in 1985 and 26 percent by 1988. In a U-shaped educational curve, the corresponding contribution in 1985 was only 7 percent for workers with high school or some college education, and 10 percent for college graduates.

The authors combine the trade and immigration estimates to conclude that these influences "have been skewed toward increasing the workforce with less than a high school education." In 1985-86, the two sources increased the nation's effective supply of high school-dropout workers by about 27 percent (and 33 percent under the second variant). In contrast, the increment was only about 9 percent for college graduates and solely from immigration. The authors interpret the finding that both trade and immigration increase the relative supply of unskilled workers as consistent with the HO trade model (232-33).

Borjas, Freeman, and Katz (1992) then calculate the wage-differential impact of trade and immigration. They use a weighting scheme to divide all workers into either high school or college-graduate equivalents. They then apply their estimates of changes in relative supply from trade and immigration (an effective increase of about 12 percent for high school equivalent workers but only 8 percent for college equivalents) to alternative assumptions about the elasticity of substitution between the two types of labor.[43] Under their central estimate, the rise of 4.4 percent in high school graduate equivalents relative to college caused by trade and immigration

---

43. On this procedure, Deardorff and Hakura (1994, 92) protest that "[o]nly in the most extreme specific-factors model, where *all* factors are immobile, can factor prices be inferred in a simple way from factor supplies. Therefore we would not place too much credence in the Borjas, Freeman, and Katz estimates of effects on relative wages." However, they then cite the theoretical model of Deardorff and Staiger (1988) as showing that the factor content of change in trade is correlated with change in factor prices. Thus, they accept at least the qualitative findings of Borjas, Freeman, and Katz as "incidental" evidence that relative wage changes were associated with trade changes.

meant a rise of 2 percent in the relative wage of college graduates. Because the overall rise in the college/high school wage differential from 1980 to 1985-86 was about 11 percent,[44] the authors conclude that trade and immigration were responsible for nearly 20 percent of the increase.

The wage impact was much more dramatic for high school dropouts. The authors again dichotomize the labor force by weighting, this time between dropouts and all other workers. The log wage ratio for all other workers to dropouts rose from 0.39 in 1980 to 0.47 in 1985-86, and 40 percent of this increment can be attributed to the increased relative supply of dropouts from trade and immigration.[45]

The authors conclude with a discussion of the apparent contradiction between their results and those of other studies on immigration that tend to find little impact on wages in destination areas. They contend that the US labor market is relatively well integrated, so wage pressure would not be expected primarily at the level of local labor markets.

The Borjas-Freeman-Katz (1992) study provides seemingly strong evidence that trade and immigration had a major impact on wage inequality, with a particularly severe effect on those at the lowest end of the educational spectrum. Quite apart from the controversy over whether this analysis is consistent with trade theory (see the discussion of Lawrence and Slaughter 1993, below), however, there is an important limitation of the study. Its trade estimates are heavily driven by the US trade deficit of the mid-1980s (and the authors' own estimates show some moderation for their extrapolations through 1988).

Yet there are two problems with this diagnosis. First, the US trade deficit is likely to be much more modest on a sustained basis, relative to the overall economy, than it was in 1985. For longer-term purposes, it is the skill bias inherent in balanced expansion of trade relative to the economy that is of more interest.

Second, even for 1985, the estimates fail to take into account the induced employment in nontradables. The United States was running large fiscal deficits in the mid-1980s. Reaganomics was premised on high interest rates to offset inflationary pressures from fiscal deficits. The high interest rates bid up the dollar, causing the large trade deficit. But without the foreign capital resources that financed the trade deficits, interest rates would have been even higher to avoid the inflationary consequences of excess demand. With higher interest rates, there would have been less

---

44. The log wage ratio was 0.391 in 1980 and 0.498 in 1985-86, meaning that college wages stood about 48 percent and 65 percent above high school wages in the two respective periods.

45. The increment would be even higher if the authors had used a higher elasticity of relative wage with respect to relative labor supply, which they place at only 0.32 for this dichotomy of the labor force. This is the inverse of the elasticity of substitution between the different classes of labor, which chapter 3 argues should be on the order of 0.7 to 1.0 for skilled versus unskilled labor (rather than about 3).

domestic activity in nontradables, particularly in construction, which is interest-rate sensitive. Construction tends to be unskilled-labor intensive, so a proper analysis of the counterfactual would have to count the number of extra high school-dropout jobs in construction (for example) that went along with the reduction of jobs implicit in the rising trade deficit. Borjas, Freeman, and Katz calculate the second effect but not the first.

For these reasons, the principal direction of bias in the estimates seems to be an overstatement of the impact of trade on US labor demand and wages. In contrast, the estimates of immigration's impact seem much more robust. Because the negative wage impact on high school dropouts stems primarily from the immigration estimates, this part of the findings remains intact as sobering evidence on the pressure of this influence on US (but not international!) wage inequality.

For the trade estimates, the aggregation level goes in the opposite direction from the downgrading that might be appropriate after consideration of longer-term patterns as well as correction for the macroeconomic counterfactual. It seems likely that results from data at the level of 21 manufacturing sectors will tend to understate the divergences between skill intensities of net-import and net-export sectors and, therefore, understate the role of trade in adding effective labor supply at low skill levels and subtracting it at high skill levels.

In updating their estimates, Borjas, Freeman, and Katz (1997) consider the period from 1980 to 1995. They estimate that during this period the ratio of college to high school wages rose by 21 percent in the United States (0.19 log points) and the ratio of high school to high school-dropout wages, by 11.5 percent. These increases are consistent with the central estimate used in the present study, that the ratio of skilled to unskilled US wages, defining skilled as some college or more and unskilled as high school or less, rose by 18 percent from 1973 to 1993 (figure 1.7).

Applying the same basic methodology as in their 1992 study, the authors estimate that for this period immigration and LDC trade together contributed one-tenth of the rise in the college/high school wage ratio (a central estimate, one-seventh if the elasticity of substitution between the two types of labor is 1.0 instead of 1.4). However, immigration contributed 40 to 50 percent of the rise in the high school/dropout wage ratio, and LDC trade contributed approximately an additional 10 percent. The impacts of trade and immigration were evenly divided for the college/high school differential, but immigration accounted for about four-fifths of the combined impact in the case of the high school/dropout differential. Thus, they conclude that when the period considered goes well beyond the 1980s (when the US trade deficit was high), immigration and LDC trade do "not explain much" of the rising college wage premium or overall US wage inequality, but do explain an "important part of the decline in the relative wage of high school dropouts" (Borjas, Freeman, and Katz 1997,

52). Chapter 5 further considers the new results of the authors and compares them with the simulation results of chapters 3 and 4.

Within the group of labor economists emphasizing trade causes of rising wage inequality, Borjas and Ramey (1994a; 1994b) have proposed one of the most sharply stated views, supported by statistical tests. The Borjas-Ramey thesis is that the existence of market concentration in the durable goods manufacturing sector—which includes automobiles, primary metals (e.g., steel), and machinery—tends to lead to wage rents, as firms share some of the oligopoly rents with workers. Increased import competition in these industries tends to reduce wages in two ways: by eroding the sharable monopoly rents and by dislocating sectoral workers toward other sectors where wages are lower.

The authors support their thesis with an empirical contest among competing explanations for the trend in the wage differential by skill level (either log wage difference between college graduate and high school dropout, or that between college and high school graduate). The candidate influences include the relative supplies of college, high school, and high school-dropout workers; the unemployment rate; the percent of the workforce not in unions; immigrants as a percent of the workforce; female participation; R&D per person in the labor force; nondurables trade deficit as a percentage of GDP; and durables trade deficit as a percentage of GDP. The authors test for cointegration between each of these influences and each of the two wage-differential variables.[46] They find that, for the period 1963-88, the only variable that is cointegrated with the wage differential(s) is the ratio of durable trade balance as a percentage of GDP. Figure 2.5 shows the close relationships between the durable goods trade balance and the college/high school dropout and college/high school graduate wage differentials.[47]

To explain this finding, Borjas (1995, 6) argues that

> Durable goods in the United States are typically produced by industries that not only employ a relatively large number of unskilled workers, but that are also highly concentrated and unionized, and pay relatively high wages. In 1976, for example, 78 percent of all workers employed in the set of trade-impacted highly concentrated industries (such as automobiles and steel) were high school graduates or dropouts. Moreover, workers in the automobile industry earn about 24 percent

---

46. Two nonstationary time series (i.e., series that do not systematically revert to entire-period averages) are cointegrated if they share a common stochastic trend. If so, there is a linear combination of them that is stationary. The cointegration test involves regressing one variable on the other and then testing whether the residual is stationary (i.e., whether one can reject the unit-root hypothesis that this residual behaves as a random walk with a drift).

47. Note that, visually, the fit is not particularly better than that between R&D spending and the wage differential given by Mincer (1991) and shown in figure 2.3. One wonders whether Borjas and Ramey would have found cointegration for R&D spending if they had used a two-year lag as in figure 2.3.

Figure 2.5 Durable goods trade deficit and the return to skills, 1949-90

Log wage ratio   Deficit as percent of GDP

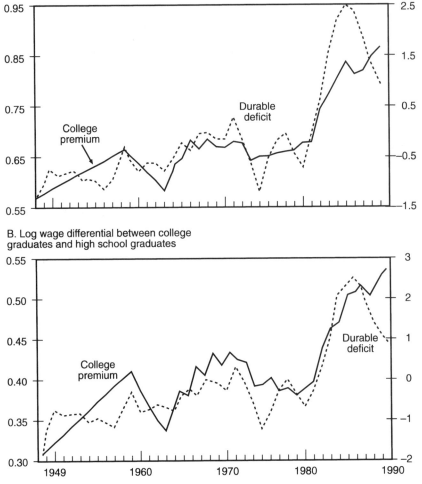

A. Log wage differential between college graduates and high school dropouts

B. Log wage differential between college graduates and high school graduates

Source: Borjas and Ramey (1994a).

more than equally skilled workers [elsewhere] . . . while the wage advantage . . . in the steel industry is about 16 percent.

Similarly, Borjas and Ramey (1994a, 235) show that there is a strong inverse correlation between the logarithm of the ratio of the average college graduate wage to the high school-dropout wage for males and compensation in durable goods as a percentage of aggregate employee compensation.[48]

When Borjas and Ramey (1994b) further explore durable goods trade by regressing the log wage differential on both the import/GDP and export/GDP ratios, they find that the coefficient on imports is larger (in absolute value) than that on exports, so that the adverse effect of import competition on wage equality is greater than the favorable effect of improved export performance. They further argue that because the residuals in these regressions show no pattern over time, they "do not look like technology levels," and on this basis they "doubt the importance of technological change . . . on relative wages" (14). Thus, Borjas and Ramey directly confront the mainstream view among labor economists, which emphasizes technological change rather than trade.

The authors' conclusion faces at least three possible inconveniences. First, there is a growing divergence between the durable deficit line and the wage differential line after 1986 (as also remarked by Burtless 1995a, 814). The two lines begin to move in the opposite direction in 1987-90 (see figure 2.5). Second, the monocausal role of durables trade leaves no room for immigration, which, however, Borjas stresses elsewhere (Borjas, Freeman, and Katz 1992). Third, as the authors are aware, their thesis turns on the somewhat implausible premise that "such a small set of industries could have such a tremendous impact" (Borjas and Ramey 1993, 27).[49] On this last point, they invoke significant size in the sectors themselves, plus spillover effects. Even so, this sector size problem seems serious to the extent that the authors seek to crown the effect of the trade balance in concentrated durable goods as the principal determinant of wage inequality.

In subsequent research, Borjas and Ramey (1993) somewhat downgrade the singular role of this influence (though retaining its importance) and incorporate other forces as well. This study applies pooled time-series and cross-section data for 44 US metropolitan areas (CPS data), under the assumption that there is at least some labor immobility that permits differential influences to show up in divergent relative wage patterns. Using multivariate regression (rather than single-variable cointegration), they relate the college/high school-dropout wage differential to the fraction of employment in each of four manufacturing groups (high- and low-concentration import industries, other durables, and other manufactures) and other variables (the fraction of population foreign born, fraction of women in the labor force, unemployment rate, and unionization).

---

48. The former rises from 0.58 in 1964 to 0.80 in 1988, while the latter falls from 20.6 percent in 1966 to 13.8 percent in 1988. However, "aggregate employee compensation" is undefined and seems to refer to an aggregate far more narrow than the overall economy.

49. Thus, in Borjas and Ramey (1993, 20), high-concentration import sectors account for only 9 percent of high school dropouts and 5 percent of college graduates.

In this test, the high-concentration-import variable is significant and has the right (negative) sign. However, this variable explains only about 10 percent of the decline in the relative wage of unskilled workers. For the college/high school dropout ratio, the immigrant population is even more important (explaining about 20 percent of the decline).[50] The female proportion and unemployment do not explain relative wage trends. Overall, this study somewhat more moderately supports the Borjas-Ramey thesis while admitting a relatively greater role for immigration.

Revenga (1992) examines the impact of the overvaluation of the dollar in the mid-1980s on employment and wages in US manufacturing. Her study does not examine skill differentials and, thus, is only indirectly relevant to the question of the impact of trade on wage inequality. Using import price data series for a panel of 38 manufacturing sectors (comprising 72 percent of imports and 35 percent of employment in manufacturing overall), she applies instrumental variable techniques to estimate that the elasticity of employment with respect to import price is in the range of 0.24 to 0.39 and the elasticity of real wages is 0.06 to 0.09.[51] Given the 19 percent real appreciation of the dollar that she estimates for the period, Revenga suggests that dollar overvaluation from 1980 to 1985 reduced employment in the trade-impacted industries examined by 4.5 to 7.5 percent and reduced real wages by 1 to 2 percent.

When the author groups the sampled industries by import penetration (imports as a percentage of output plus imports), she finds a clear pattern relating import penetration and employment reduction. For industries with import penetration above 20 percent in 1984, employment fell by 24.3 percent from 1980 to 1987; for 10-20 percent penetration, by 13 percent; and for less than 10 percent penetration, by only 7.5 percent (267).[52] In contrast, wage changes were much smaller (about 0.5 percent overall), and in fact wages declined the most in the lowest-penetration sectors (1.7 percent). These results and the regression estimates suggest that the principal adjustment to rising import competition during the period of dollar overvaluation was in the form of employment reduction rather than wage reduction.

The Revenga estimates are qualitatively similar to the estimates by Branson and Love (1987), who estimated that the dollar's rise from 1980

---

50. The authors explain the difference between this cross-sectional finding on immigration and the more usual finding of minimal impact on the grounds that the tests here include a time series. Thus, even with instantaneous diffusion of immigrant effects across cities—which would remove intercity variation in wage differentials in the cross-section data—there will be over-time differences in immigrant effects that are captured by all cities as a pool.

51. The employment elasticity is much lower in ordinary least squares (OLS) estimates. The two-stage least squares (2SLS) estimates apply industry source-weighted exchange rates (and alternative specifications) as instrumental variables for import prices.

52. The original figures are in log changes.

to 1985 caused a reduction of US manufacturing employment by 1.1 million workers, 5.7 percent. However, both sets of estimates raise the question of the macroeconomic *antimonde* (or counterfactual), as discussed above. Moreover, for the purposes of the present study, the principal question is the influence of secular trends in globalization on the domestic distribution of wages. The Revenga estimate addresses neither, because it only captures the effects of the temporary dollar overvaluation and does not consider even these effects in terms of wage differentials by skill category.[53]

More direct evidence on the role of trade in rising inequality is given in a study by Karoly and Klerman (1994). The authors use CPS data at the regional and state level to conduct shift-shares and regression analysis of trends in wage inequality. The regional detail not only increases the number of observations but also brings out such effects as rust-belt decline in manufacturing.

Karoly and Klerman first conduct a shift-shares, decomposition analysis. They use the variance of the logarithm of real wage as their measure of inequality. This measure has the convenient property that it can be decomposed into the following:

$$\theta = \theta\,(\mu_1,\ \mu_2,\ ...\ \mu_G) + \sum_{g=1}^{G} n_g\,\theta_g \qquad (2.6)$$

where θ refers to variance of the logarithm of wages, μ is the mean of the group in question, n is the fraction of employment in the group, and θ_g is log variance within group g. Overall log variance breaks down into between-group variance across group means (the first term on the right) and compositionally weighted within-group variance (the second term).

The authors first find that the changing age composition of the work force actually tended to moderate rising inequality from 1979 to 1988. Their shift-shares analysis freezes a given dimension at its base period profile, calculates the hypothetical terminal period distribution under this assumption, and compares that against the actual terminal period distribution to detect the effect of actual change in the dimension in question. For men, log variance rose from 0.201 to 0.288 in this period and would have risen to 0.297 (about a 10 percent greater increase) if age composition had remained unchanged. The passage of the baby-boom cohorts into the prime working-age category (25-44 years) was a net

---

53. Note further that Revenga uses an incorrect formulation of the real exchange rate. She takes the nominal exchange rate against a given trade partner and deflates by the US producer price index. Instead, the proper measure is the nominal exchange rate, deflated by the foreign producer price index and multiplied by the US producer price index. The distortion can be large for high-inflation countries, as is evident in her graph of the real exchange rate against Korea (268).

equalizing influence. There was little corresponding impact for women, despite equally dramatic age composition shifts.[54]

Karoly and Klerman then examine the effects of shifts in industrial composition. Their prior expectation is that the shift from manufacturing to the services sector should have contributed to widening wage inequality, because "[t]he services sector, on average, pays lower wages and exhibits greater wage dispersion than the goods-producing sector" (184). From 1979 to 1988, the absolute level of employment in manufacturing fell by 8 percent for durable goods and 4 percent for nondurables, and these reductions reached as high as one-fourth in the New England, middle Atlantic, and east north central regions. The shift-shares analysis finds that shifts in industrial composition explain 13 percent of the rise in wage inequality for men from 1979 to 1988, and this contribution reaches 23 percent for the east north central region (the rust belt).[55]

It is informative to compare these results with the Borjas-Ramey emphasis on durable goods manufactures. The Karoly-Klerman shift-shares analysis has the advantage that it does not leave out the other (service) sectors, where jobs were being gained. In broad terms, the Karoly-Klerman results are consistent with the later, less monocausal version of Borjas and Ramey (1993), where the durable goods import effect is responsible for about 10 percent of widening skill differentials.

Karoly and Klerman (1994) also conduct regression analysis on their data set, with results even more reminiscent of the Borjas-Ramey thesis.[56] In pooled time-series, cross-section tests, the authors include a variable for manufactured imports relative to GDP, either for durable goods (in one variant) or for all manufactures. For males, these tests find that, depending on the geographic region, between 55 and 141 percent of the increase in wage inequality between 1979 and 1988 was attributable to an increase in the durable goods import variable. However, the authors are cautious about interpreting this finding. They note that because this variable is economywide, it varies only in the time series (not cross-sectionally). As a result, it might be standing in for some other systematic time trend. Moreover, the data set does not include the period after the late 1980s, when the ratio of durable goods imports to GDP started falling again even as inequality kept rising (figure 2.5).

The regression analysis, somewhat disconcertingly, does not find important effects for industrial composition or for age structure and, thus,

---

54. The authors' suggested explanation, that wage distribution was flatter among women, seems inconsistent with the fact that the log variance measures are close to those for men: 0.183 in 1979 and 0.266 in 1988 (193).

55. Once again, for women the analysis shows little impact.

56. Curiously, Karoly and Klerman (1994) do not mention the Borjas-Ramey studies (1993, 1994a, 1994b).

tends to contradict the shift-shares analysis.[57] The regression results do confirm an important effect of changing unionization (reaching as high as 17 percent contribution to increased inequality for the east south central region, but only 4 percent for the west south central).

Overall, the Karoly-Klerman study would seem to suggest that changing sectoral composition played a significant role in widening (male) wage inequality and that the collapse in the trade balance in durable goods was probably a key element (either separately or because of its role in this changing composition). Yet the point estimate that trade's impact on widening wage inequality was some 50 to 140 percent of the total almost surely overstates the role of this factor, as the authors implicitly suggest.

The group of labor economists focusing on international factors includes authors who have examined two other influences beyond trade: the impact of immigration and the effects of multinational competition and outsourcing. Borjas (1994) provides an extensive survey of the literature on immigration effects, literature that contains a subcomponent narrowly oriented toward wage differential effects. First, though, a synopsis of other salient themes in this literature follows, drawing on the Borjas review.

The magnitude of US immigration rose in the 1980s to a total of 7.3 million over the decade. This entry accounted for 33.1 percent of population growth, compared with 21 percent in the 1970s and 14 percent in the 1960s—higher than the 25 percent of the 1920s before immigration collapsed to a trickle under national-origin quotas and in the face of depression. By 1990 the foreign-born share in the US population stock was up to 7.9 percent, compared with 4.7 percent in 1970. By 1993, annual legal immigration amounted to about 800,000, about the same in absolute numbers as in the peak decade of 1901-10. Illegal immigration added perhaps another 200,000 to 300,000 to the annual flow.

Rising immigration has been associated with liberalization and a shift of the admissions screen from country quotas to family ties in 1965, an amnesty to three million illegal aliens under the 1986 Immigration Reform and Control Act (IRCA), and a major quota increase in the 1990 Immigration Act. These changes facilitated a shift of country origin from about two-thirds European (or Canadian) in the 1950s to nearly half from other countries of the Western Hemisphere and more than one-third from Asia by the 1980s.

The economics literature on immigration initially seemed to show that immigrants had a negative wage intercept relative to natives upon entry but a sufficiently strong time gradient that their wages overtook those of natives within about 15 years (Chiswick 1978; Carliner 1980). Subsequent research suggested more pessimistically that after correction for compositional differences associated with the decade of entry, the time gradient was much flatter. On average, immigrants earn 15 percent less than

---

57. Nor, once again, do the tests explain much for trends in female wage inequality.

natives, and recent arrivals (1985-89) earn 32 percent less. Borjas (1994, 1674) judges not only that "more recent immigrants waves are relatively less skilled" but also that "[i]t is extremely unlikely that the earnings of more recent cohorts will ever reach parity with . . . the earnings of natives."

Falling relative education is one trend for immigrants. The number of US-born high school dropouts fell from 39.6 percent in 1970 to 14.6 percent in 1990, while the immigrant dropout rate fell only from 48.2 percent to 36.9 percent. As noted earlier in this chapter, immigrants tend to be concentrated at the educational extremes, but their slight advantage over natives in incidence of college educated in 1970 (18.9 percent versus 15.4 percent) disappeared by 1990 (26.6 percent for both groups). As much as 90 percent of the declining relative educational attainment of immigrants can be explained by the shift in source nationality (for example, away from Europe, with education typically at 11 to 14 years, and toward Mexico and Central America, with levels of 8 to 9 years).

Borjas (1994) reviews the controversial literature on the link between immigration and the welfare burden, on the one hand, and the "net fiscal burden," on the other. Whereas about 6 percent of both immigrant and native households were welfare recipients in 1970, by 1990 the rate was about one-fourth higher for immigrants (9.1 percent) than for natives (7.4 percent). Welfare incidence for the immigrant cohorts of 1965-69 was 5.5 percent in 1970 but 10 percent in 1980 and 1990, indicating a "perverse" assimilation "*into* welfare" (Borjas 1994, 1702). Welfare rates are 12 percent for Mexican immigrants and nearly 50 percent for those from Laos and Cambodia, in part because of special programs for refugees.

Borjas (1994) makes a back-of-the-envelope calculation of net fiscal effects. He notes that immigrants comprise 13.1 percent of welfare benefits but only 8.3 percent of nonwelfare income. Assuming the same (13 percent) share for all means-tested entitlements, he calculates that in 1992 immigrants received $23.8 billion in benefits. Their tax payments amounted to an estimated $85.4 billion. However, Borjas also estimates that their share in non-means-tested public goods (schools, roads) amounted to 91 percent of their tax payments, leaving a net fiscal burden of $16 billion imposed on natives. He shows that radically differing results of various other authors stem from their inclusion or exclusion of such elements as share in non-means-tested benefits and shakily hypothesized losses of tax payments by displaced native employees.

Borjas reviews the literature on the impact of immigration on native wages. Many studies show an extremely small impact, based on cross-city data (e.g., the minimal impact in Miami of the Mariel inflow of Cuban refugees). He criticizes this literature for its failure to recognize that dispersion of workers would tend to equalize wages across cities.[58]

---

58. Borjas, Freeman, and Katz (1997) have subsequently argued compellingly that interspatial analyses are a misleading basis for examining the wage effects of immigration. They find a striking inverse correlation between changes in real wages at the state level between

Instead, he cites the labor-supply estimate in Borjas, Freeman, and Katz (1992) of one-third as the fraction of the relative wage decline for high school dropouts attributable to immigration.

Overall, Borjas's (1994) review is a sobering picture of relative lags in educational attainment and income growth prospects among recent waves of immigrants and of a corresponding potential net burden upon the United States as host country—in contrast to the more traditional neoclassical view of immigration as largely a positive sum game for natives and high-achiever immigrants. The shift toward family ties and away from regional or skills quotas in US immigration policy has played a role in this outcome. The results may be more equitable among immigrants but less equitable with respect to the distributional impact among natives. For example, a more severe preference for highly skilled immigrants would tend to equalize US wage distribution by boosting the relative supply of college-educated skilled workers and reducing that of high school dropouts. However, this would mean even fewer opportunities for unskilled workers in such source countries as Mexico.[59]

As for the effects of technological catch-up and outsourcing, recent literature includes a provocative line of analysis by a team (Johnson and Stafford 1992, 1993, 1995) that includes one of the labor economists that attributed most of the increase in wage dispersion to skill-biased technological change (Johnson). However, this alternative approach more properly belongs in the section of this study on trade theorists who believe there may be something to the notion that globalization has been an important cause of widening domestic inequality (see Trade Economists 2).

The final entry in this group of labor economists is not a direct analysis of trade, immigration, or outsourcing. Instead, it revisits the decompositional analysis seeking to determine whether technology or demand factors such as trade have driven widening inequality. Because this study, by Bernard and Jensen (1994), reaches conclusions far more compatible with the notion of trade demand impacts, it is appropriately grouped with the labor economists sympathetic to a relatively large trade role.

Bernard and Jensen work with plant-level data for more than 50,000 plants. They are thus able to capture effects that are masked in the more aggregate 450 industry categories examined in earlier studies, especially

---

1970-80 and 1980-90. This means that analyses linking concentration of immigration to changes in state wages would find directly opposite results depending on the period in question, considering that the principal immigration states (including California, New York, Florida, and Texas) remained unchanged. The decadal inversion of state wage change rankings would seem to show a strong tendency for labor mobility within the United States to dampen any temporary shocks to regional wage differences.

59. Any tightening of immigration policies in the direction of higher skill requirements would presumably face some, and perhaps considerable, leakage through higher induced illegal immigration.

Berman, Bound, and Griliches (BBG) (1994). Bernard and Jensen examine concepts similar to those in the earlier studies. They focus on the employment shares and wage shares of nonproduction versus production workers in US manufacturing. They use a decomposition formula for between-plant (or industry) versus within-plant (or industry) changes that is identical to the BBG measure (equation 2.2 above).

For manufacturing overall, the authors estimate that the employment share of nonproduction workers rose by 0.32 percent annually in 1973-79 and jumped to a rate of 0.55 percent annually in 1979-87. The wage share of nonproduction workers accelerated even more, from an annual increase of 0.33 percent in the first period to 0.72 percent in the second. The difference between the wage and employment share trends is a measure of trend in relative wage, and, thus, these data confirm relative stability in the 1970s followed by substantial increases in the second.

When the authors repeat the industry-group tests for between and within decomposition, they find results similar to those of BBG. However, when they conduct the decomposition at the plant level, they find a much stronger influence of the between-plant change. For wage shares, between-plant changes accounted for a 0.14 percent increase per year in 1973-79 and a within-plant 0.13 percent. In 1979-87 both changes accelerated, but the between influence did so the most. Between-plant changes accounted for a 0.32 percent annual increase in nonproduction wage shares, and within-plant, 0.22 percent.

The authors are cautious to avoid an automatic reversal of the BBG policy conclusion—that technological change was far more important than demand change—because technological change may broadly be identified with within change and demand change with between change. Yet the successive analyses in Bernard and Jensen point increasingly in the direction of such a policy inference reversal. When they divide their sample into exporters and nonexporters, they find that in 1980-87 there is a sharp difference between nonproduction wage share change for exporters (+ 0.36 percent per year) and nonexporters (− 0.09 percent). They note that "unlike" BBG, "who attribute only 6 percent of the increase in the aggregate employment and wage ratios to exports," in their plant-level data "shifts of employment to exporting industries account for more than 59% of the aggregate change . . . [and] results for the wage ratio are even stronger" (13).

Similarly, when the authors conduct regressions using technology variables (e.g., R&D), they find that "[t]echnology, while significantly related to changes in within-plant wage inequality in the 1980's, does not contribute to the between movements" (21). This finding warrants relaxation of their initial caution that technological change rather than demand shifts (such as trade) could be playing a major role in the between-industry as well as within-industry shifts. They further find that export-related demand shifts are particularly important. Their final conclusion is that from the 1970s to the 1980s, . . . the increase in the relative employment of nonproduction workers and the associated increase in the wage gap between high-skilled and low-skilled workers can be attributed substantially to changes at exporting establishments. . . . [M]ost of the change occurred between plants rather than within plants. This result raises anew the possibility that product demand changes are responsible for a larger portion of the relative demand increase for high-skilled employees than previously thought. (25)

This verdict confirms the suspicion raised above about the BBG results: even at the 450 industry level, sufficient variation remains within the industry that it is misleading to dismiss trade effects from the decomposition finding that most change is within industry.[60] Thus, the Bernard-Jensen study casts doubt on the seeming dominance of the technological change explanation and on a minimal role for trade changes in the industrial decomposition analysis of the labor economists.

Trade Economists 1

The debate on the relationship between trade and domestic wage inequality has been divided between two groups of labor economists, with the predominant view favoring a technology explanation but a vigorous minority view placing greater stress on trade and globalization. In addition, trade and labor economists have been divided (so have trade economists, as discussed below). Perhaps the most trenchant and at first glance devastating attack on the minority view of labor economists who find significant measures of trade impact is that by Lawrence and Slaughter (1993). They emphasize that when trade theory is properly applied to the task, trade stands exculpated rather than convicted of responsibility for widening inequality.

Lawrence and Slaughter first critique the Ross Perot populists rather than the labor economists. The authors consider and reject the populist proposition that US real wages have fallen absolutely or at least from levels that would have been reached under past growth trends because of trade and globalization (the "giant sucking sound"). They stress that real wages (deflated by production prices) have kept pace with productivity, which actually grew rapidly in the past two decades for manufacturing. Instead, the real culprits are, first, the collapse in productivity growth in the services sector and, second, the decline in the terms of trade between what workers produce (with falling computer and investment good prices) and what they consume (with rising housing prices) as discussed in chapter 1.

---

60. As discussed below, Baldwin and Cain (1994) further point out that trade theory would not justify this rigid dichotomy.

Next, the authors consider and reject what might be called the straw-man version of the SS theorem: trade has shifted income shares away from labor toward capital.[61] As also noted in chapter 1, the data show constant capital-labor shares in the economy, rather than a falling labor share.

Lawrence and Slaughter then focus their critique on the labor economists enamored of trade explanations.[62] They make two central arguments, one theoretical and the other empirical. The theoretical critique is that the SS theorem requires that trade's adverse impact on the relative wages of unskilled versus skilled labor operate through a decline in the relative price of the traded good intensively using unskilled labor, a point already stressed in this debate by Bhagwati (1991). In contrast, the factor content approach used by some labor economists, especially the trade balance version, fails to recognize this point. The empirical critique is twofold: relative prices of unskilled-intensive goods did not fall, and factor ratios of skilled to unskilled workers rose instead of falling. The authors argue that both patterns would have had to be present for SS forces to widen wage inequality.

Within the SS framework, the Lawrence-Slaughter critique is appealing in theoretical terms (but see the critique of Leamer [1994] discussed below). Returning to figure 2.2, there is a one-to-one mapping of the relative product price to the relative factor price. Turning to figure 2.1, when there is a reduction in the world price of the unskilled-intensive good, there is a shift toward greater production of the skilled-intensive good, and the relative wage of unskilled workers must fall so that in both sectors the skilled/unskilled factor ratio can fall to free up more skilled workers for expansion of the relatively skilled sector. So the ratio of skilled to unskilled labor in each sector should fall if SS effects are driving a reduction in the relative wages of unskilled workers.

The authors' critique raises several questions. The first is whether its exclusive focus on the Stolper-Samuelson framework is appropriate. Labor economists can rightly point out that trade economists have argued that the bulk of trade is not HO (the requisite type for SS results), but instead

---

61. Straw man because the recent economics literature has not purported this, and the more popular public discussions are unfamiliar with the SS theorem.

62. Before doing so, however, they cite one prominent study within this group—Borjas, Freeman, and Katz (1992)—to the effect that the maximum impact of trade on the college/high school wage differential by 1988 was 15 percent of the 12.4 percent increase from 1980, or 1.9 percentage points. They then argue that because the trade deficit fell from $106 billion in 1988 to $47 billion in 1991, the impact must have been down to less than 1 percentage point by 1991. This extrapolation is incorrect, because the Borjas-Freeman-Katz measure incorporates not only trade balance effects but also factor intensity effects of imports versus exports (see equation 2.5 above). Also, as noted above, the impact is much greater for the high school-dropout differential from other wages, especially including immigration effects.

is intraindustry trade based on product differentiation and economies of scale (Linder 1961; Krugman 1980, 1992). Trade economists can reasonably reply, however, that the HO framework does largely apply to North-South trade in manufactures, and it is this component of trade that is the most relevant for downward pressure on the wages of unskilled workers.

Even so, the theoretical framework need not be limited to the HO theorem. Ricardian trade theory implies the notion of sector-specific factors, and this approach was revived by Jones (1971) and Samuelson (1971). As discussed below, Sachs and Shatz (1995) invoke the specific-factors model in considering how trade may have affected wages without having reduced the relative prices of unskilled-labor-intensive goods.

A second question concerns the evidence that sectoral ratios of skilled to unskilled workers rose instead of falling. Lawrence and Slaughter stress that from 1979 to 1989, the ratio of nonproduction to production workers in manufacturing rose from 35 to 44 percent, which, they argue, was the wrong direction for consistency with SS effects. They also show that at the levels of two-, three-, and four-digit SIC industries, scatter diagrams of the percent change in the relative wages of nonproduction to production workers on the vertical axis against the percent change in the ratio of nonproduction to production employment (1979 to 1989) show at least half of industries in the Northeast quadrant (rising skill differential, rising skill composition), rather than in the Northwest (rising skill differential, falling skill composition) as the SS theorem would require.

However, this analysis stumbles on the classic problem of ceteris paribus, that is, other things held constant. The problem is that all else was not held constant. As reviewed in chapter 1 and in the survey of the labor economists above, it is a stylized fact that in the 1970s the US economy experienced a rapid outward shift in the college educated relative to the high school educated (or less); although this trend slowed down in the 1980s, it began to accelerate again by the early 1990s. If there was a generalized rise in the relative supply of skilled workers, then trade could have reduced the skilled to unskilled factor ratios across the relevant sectors from levels they otherwise would have reached, while, nonetheless, leaving the terminal-period levels higher than the initial-period levels.[63]

This chapter concludes with a discussion of this point and shows graphically (figure 2.9) that if trade effects (or technological change or other

---

63. On the Lawrence-Slaughter evidence of rising rather than falling skill intensity across sectors, Hall (1993) judges that "that finding tells us nothing, given the big positive change in the skill composition of the labor force." He suggests that a more appropriate test would be whether "the skill intensity of most [manufacturing] industries fell relative to the national average" (212-3). Similarly, Leamer (1994) argues that Lawrence and Slaughter "improperly leap to the conclusion" of minimal trade effects. His reason is that the Heckscher-Ohlin model "takes the technology as fixed, and is therefore materially at odds with Lawrence

sources) cause a steady outward shift in the relative demand for skilled labor, and if there is a slowdown in the outward shift in the supply of skilled relative to unskilled labor, one would expect to observe precisely the combination of rising relative skilled factor ratios and rising relative skilled/unskilled wage ratio that Lawrence and Slaughter cite. Thus, one of the two pillars of their argumentation falls.

There is also the question of the data set used by Lawrence and Slaughter and, in particular, whether its identification of "nonproduction" with "skilled" workers is meaningful. Hall (1993) points out that many nonproduction workers are low-skilled (clerical, janitors, security guards), while many production workers have problem-solving skills and relatively few are in routine assembly operations. As noted above, Burtless (1995a) points out that skill differentials widened much less if measured under the production/nonproduction worker distinction than if measured by educational differentials, so that the Lawrence-Slaughter tests would have had less variation to diagnose.

Then there is the question of the empirical test of falling relative prices of traded goods intensive in unskilled labor. Using Bureau of Labor Statistics indexes of prices for exports and imports over the period 1979-89, Lawrence and Slaughter show that for two- or three-digit SIC industries these traded-goods prices either showed no systematic relationship to skill intensity or actually showed lower relative increases for higher-skilled sectors.[64] As discussed below, however, Leamer (1992), using a different aggregation of industries, found the correlation of falling trade prices with unskilled-intensive sectors as required for SS effects. As also discussed below, Krugman (1995b) has suggested that because of the magnification effect, a plausible relative wage change from trade could have been associated with a product price change that was present but too small to be detected from background noise in view of other forces influencing prices.

Nor is the alternative price test used by Lawrence and Slaughter necessarily persuasive. The authors show that fixed-weight terms of trade for the United States fell from 100 in 1979 to 92 in 1980, rose steadily to 107 in 1986, and then declined to a plateau of 102 in 1987-89. They argue that because US exports are skilled intensive and imports unskilled intensive, the terms of trade provide a direct test of whether skilled-intensive prices are falling in relative terms. They regard the trends in the 1980s as "basically flat" and, moreover, note that the US terms of trade fell in the 1970s. Therefore, they consider this test a negative finding for SS effects. Actually, the test could be regarded as support for the SS theorem, because the

---

and Slaughter's observation concerning the large decrease in the ratio of production to nonproduction workers" (4).

64. The authors use scatter diagrams with 1979-89 price increases on the vertical axis and the 1980 ratio of nonproduction to production workers on the horizontal axis.

terms of trade fell in the 1970s (when there was a narrowing of skilled-wage differentials) and rose in the 1980s (when there was a widening of the differentials). However, it would be misleading to consider overall terms of trade to be a valid price test, because the price of oil (and other commodities) has dominated this variable, and it is instead the price of unskilled- versus skilled-intensive manufactures that is relevant.[65]

In sum, despite its analytical rigor and important contribution in sharpening the debate, the Lawrence-Slaughter study (1993) falls short of providing a definitive refutation of the notion that trade has played an important role in widening US wage differentials.

Krugman and Lawrence (1994) provide a well-argued statement of the case against blaming trade for either stagnating wages or widening wage differentials. They first note that the relative decline of manufacturing output and employment in the economy is a secular trend, not merely or principally a reflection of declining competitiveness in the 1980s. The sector's share of GDP fell from 29.6 percent in 1950 to 25.0 percent in 1970 and 18.4 percent by 1990. The corresponding shares in employment fell from 34.2 percent to 27.3 percent and 17.4 percent, respectively. The authors do not point out the acceleration in this trend, however (as the changes are greater, especially proportionately, in the second 20 years than the first).[66] They attribute falling manufacturing shares to the difference between high productivity growth in goods and low productivity growth in services and the consequential rise in relative prices (and hence GDP shares) in services.

The authors acknowledge the rapid rise of imports, from 11.4 percent of manufacturing output in 1970 to 38.2 percent in 1990. However, they point out the parallel rise in exports, from 12.6 percent to 31.0 percent of manufactured output. The manufacturing trade balance shifted from +0.2 percent of GDP to −1.3 percent for the same period, having reached −3.1 percent in 1986. The net decline of 1.5 percent of GDP was less than one-fourth of the 6.6 percent reduction in manufacturing's share in GDP. After accounting for intermediate inputs (a 40 percent share of gross sales, so that one dollar of trade balance shift represents only 60 cents in changed value added and GDP), they conclude that if there had been no change in the trade balance, the 1990 manufacturing share of GDP would have been 19.2 percent instead of 18.4 percent, so six-sevenths of the decline in manufacturing's share would have occurred even without a decline in the trade balance.

---

65. It is no accident that the terms of trade reach a trough in 1980 when oil prices were at their peak and reach a peak in 1986 when oil was at its trough.

66. Sachs and Shatz (1994, 6) similarly note that the Krugman-Lawrence analysis "glosses over the particularly sharp decline" in the manufacturing labor share in the 1970s and 1980s.

Similarly, Krugman and Lawrence calculate that the $73 billion trade deficit in manufactures in 1990, which corresponded to $42 billion in value added, translated to about 700,000 jobs (at $60,000 value added per manufacturing employee). Noting that the average manufacturing worker earns about $5,000 more than nonmanufacturing workers, they infer that the "loss of 'good jobs' in manufacturing as a result of international competition" represented a wage loss of $3.5 billion, just 0.07 percent of national income (Krugman and Lawrence 1994, 47).

Addressing possible losses from the increased ability of LDCs to produce manufactures previously dominated by industrial countries (Hicksian convergence, discussed below), Krugman and Lawrence acknowledge that a 20 percent decline in US terms of trade from 1970 to 1990 represented an income loss of about 2 percent. However, they point out that because real wages rose by just 6 percent over this period, and the increase would have been only 8 percent without terms-of-trade loss, increased foreign competition cannot account for the stagnation of US wages.

The authors then explicitly address the distribution, as opposed to level, of wages. They state that "[e]conomists have generally been quite sympathetic to the argument that increased integration of global markets has pushed down the real wages of less educated US workers" (48), primarily because of the SS tradition. They then refer implicitly to the Lawrence-Slaughter results to report that "[s]urprisingly, . . . increased wage inequality . . . is overwhelmingly the consequence of domestic causes," despite the "rapid growth of exports from nations such as China and Indonesia" (48).

Krugman and Lawrence (1994) add a nuance to the analysis, noting that by the SS theorem, trade should not only reduce the ratio of skilled to unskilled workers in all industries, but also "employment should increase more rapidly in skilled-intensive industries than in those that employ more unskilled labor." This result presumably stems from the reallocation of output toward the skilled-intensive sectors where relative product prices are rising (under the SS theorem). They note that the difference between employment growth in the two sectors was only "slight . . . at best" (48). However, if overall labor productivity were rising faster in high-skilled sectors (as is certainly the case between higher-skilled textiles and lower-skilled apparel, for example), the employee-count test would be misleading, because output could be shifting toward the high-skilled sectors with little observable corresponding shift in overall employment shares.

Krugman and Lawrence conclude that while "no one can say with certainty what has reduced the relative demand for less skilled workers . . . globalization cannot have played the dominant role" (49). As further support, they invoke the fact that the bulk of US trade is with high-wage countries in any case, so that the weighted average of manufacturing-sector wages for US trading partners is 88 percent of the US wage. Similarly, nonoil imports from countries with wages less than half the US average are only 2.8 percent of US GDP. Krugman and Lawrence's overall message is that the US economy does suffer from problems, but they are primarily slow productivity growth outside manufacturing and shrinking relative demand for unskilled labor in a high-technology economy, not a lack of international competitiveness in manufactures as politicians and elites seem to think.

The Krugman-Lawrence analysis is subject to the same limitations as the Lawrence-Slaughter study discussed above. Moreover, neither study directly considers immigration effects or effects on high school dropouts (which Borjas, Freeman, and Katz [1992] suggest are important). Overall, the two studies seem more effective in debunking Perot populism and beltway competitiveness angst than in exonerating globalization as an influence on widening wage disparities.[67]

Jagdish Bhagwati has entered into the trade and wage distribution debate at the theoretical level (Bhagwati 1991; Bhagwati and Dehejia 1994). He argues that trade, particularly through SS and factor-price-equalization dynamics, has played no significant role in widening wage inequality. His principal target is the work of "Labor Economists 2" and, in particular, the influential study of Borjas, Freeman, and Katz (1992).

Toward this end, Bhagwati adopts two central arguments, which to outsiders (perhaps including some labor economists) might seem mutually contradictory. The first is that the FPE theorem is hopelessly divorced from reality. The second is that the empirical labor research has been flawed because it has not respected, or perhaps been cognizant of, the required mechanisms of the SS and FPE theorems. Yet to some readers, each telling argument Bhagwati makes against FPE might seem to be an additional reason why empirical analysis need not be confined to the assumptions of this framework (the HO, SS, and FPE theorems).

The problems with FPE are numerous, according to Bhagwati and Dehejia (1994). They state that "the assumptions that underlie the FPE theorem . . . are extraordinarily demanding . . . [such that] the iron hand of the FPE theorem on real wages of the US unskilled cannot be taken seriously" (42). They begin with the observation that Samuelson's FPE was initially considered only a curiosus. They note that considerable analytical work was later devoted to showing why FPE seemed to be frustrated in reality, with much of this work stimulated by the finding

---

67. Moreover, as discussed below, Krugman (1995b) has subsequently shown that the initial Lawrence-Slaughter and Krugman-Lawrence critique of the labor economists' "factor content of trade" approach as theoretically without basis turns out to have been unfair, because when a general equilibrium approach is taken and the trade changes are small, this method provides a close approximation to the correct answer.

of Leontief (1953) that US exports were labor-intensive rather than capital-intensive as HO theory predicted (the Leontief paradox).

Factor reversal was one candidate explanation. The SS and FPE theorems require that technology be identical across countries, but analytical work on production functions with constant elasticity of substitution (CES) showed that in the face of a sufficiently large shift in relative factor prices, goods could switch over from being intensive in one factor to being intensive in the other. Uniform technology could also diverge because "[k]nowhow manifestly differs across North and South" (43). Scale economies could be another reason for de facto differences in technology and, in particular, could "invalidate the SS theorem, causing both factors' real wages to rise" (44) as scale efficiencies from trade swamp adverse effects on the scarce factor.

The authors cite complete product specialization as another way that the SS and FPE theorems can break down, as both require incomplete specialization. Thus, "once specialization is achieved it follows that any further rise in that good's (relative) price will mean that both factors will gain from it" (44). Moreover, each factor's gains from trade will depend on the propensity of the factor to consume the cheaper imported goods. The authors cite my work on textiles (Cline 1990), which shows that the share of income spent on apparel varies inversely with a household's position in the income distribution. They also cite Deardorff and Haveman (1991) for evidence that administered protection is not oriented toward sectors with workers in poverty.

Bhagwati and Dehejia (1994) cite the efficiency-provoking role of competitive pressure from imports (X-efficiency) as another reason why free trade could raise the real wages of unskilled workers. Furthermore, they argue that even if the FPE theorem were correct in direction, for at least the North American Free Trade Agreement (NAFTA) the large relative size of the US economy would probably pull Mexican wages up rather than US wages down, because "goods prices will gravitate toward US prices" (46). This interpretation rests heavily on the rigid mapping of goods prices to factor prices, however. An alternative view might be less certain, because of the sizable pool of unskilled Mexican labor relative to the unskilled US workforce.

The authors then turn to their second task, a critique of the early labor studies on trade and wage inequality. Here, their principal critique is that "nowhere do they build on the essential fact that trade should affect goods prices in the desired direction before anything can be inferred concerning the trade-induced effects on factor rewards" (47). At this point the skeptical reader may ask, if SS and especially its FPE extreme are irrelevant, why must the labor economists adhere to its mechanisms? For example, if factor reversal is as real a possibility as Bhagwati and Dehejia stress, then the unique mapping of relative goods prices to relative factor prices simply collapses.

Figure 2.6 Trade and factor prices

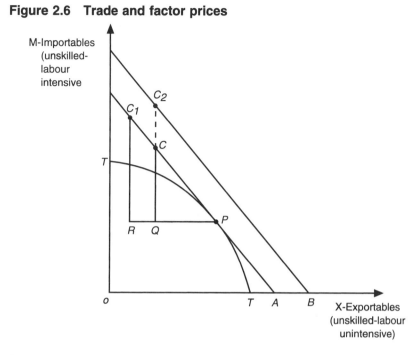

Source: Bhagwati (1991).

At the outset, the authors clarify their frame of reference: "[I]s integration into the world economy through the reduction of trade barriers the cause of decline in the real wage of the unskilled?" (47) Yet surely this is too narrow a formulation. The more interesting question for the future is whether secular integration such as more outward oriented development strategies in countries such as China and India and falling transport and communications prices might have such an effect even at unchanged levels of protection.[68]

Bhagwati (1991) illustrates the required link between goods prices and factor prices with a diagram reproduced here as figure 2.6. The production

68. Similarly, Bhagwati (1991) may overstate the role of trade liberalization per se when he observes that the timing of widening US wage inequality is incompatible with a trade explanation, because US protection was increasing rather than decreasing in the 1980s. Actually, the extra protection was in automobiles (not an LDC sector), whereas protection in television sets and footwear was allowed to lapse, and increased textile-apparel protection occurred both in the mid-1970s and mid-1980s. The more fundamental point is that secular integration forces drove rising trade and swamped variations in protection. Thus, North American (excluding Mexican) imports of manufactures from non-OECD countries grew at a real rate of 11 percent from 1980 to 1991, far in excess of growth in the US economy. (Calculated from General Agreement on Tariffs and Trade [GATT] 1993, 34, deflating by US producer prices.)

possibility curve between importables and exportables is shown as curve *TT*. The international price line between the two goods is shown by line *CP* (a steeper negative slope would mean cheaper imports, as a greater quantity of importables would equate in value with a smaller quantity of exportables). For efficiency, the economy produces at point *P*, where the production possibility frontier is tangent to the highest international price line possible. Domestic consumption is at point *C*. The home country thus exports amount *QP* in return for amount *QC* of imports.

Now suppose that trade intensifies with no change in relative prices. There is simply a proportionate magnification of both exports (to *RP*) and imports (to RC_1). Because importables are more unskilled-intensive than exportables, the Borjas-Freeman-Katz method will conclude that there has been an adverse effect on unskilled wages. That is, the "effective supply" of unskilled workers, in their estimates, will have risen (because in relative terms highly skilled workers are being diverted to more exports and unskilled workers displaced by more imports). Yet the international price line *CP* has not changed, so by SS (and Bhagwati) there can have been no change in the skilled/unskilled wage ratio.

Similarly, suppose the country goes on a private or public spending spree and enters into a large trade deficit. The consumption point would shift out to C_2, at a higher (but parallel) international price line (with unchanged slope). The Borjas-Freeman-Katz method will identify an increase in the effective supply of unskilled workers through higher imports; yet, the SS theorem (and Bhagwati) hold that there can be no change in relative wages because the goods price line has not changed in slope.

The fundamental question, however, is whether it is axiomatic that there must be a shift in relative product prices for there to be a shift in relative wages. Under the SS theorem (which, otherwise, Bhagwati readily criticizes) there must be, but in other frameworks, such as the specific-factors trade model, there need not be. The question then arises as to whether the labor economists had really signed on to the SS and FPE theorems. Borjas, Freeman, and Katz (1992) do make one statement in passing that their findings are "consistent with Heckscher-Ohlin models of trade and factor endowments" (233), but that is all.

Bhagwati and Dehejia (1994) cite Lawrence and Slaughter (1993) as providing evidence rejecting a reduction in the price of unskilled-labor-intensive goods (or imports) relative to skilled-intensive (or exports). They do not mention Leamer's (1991) contrary evidence. On the strength of the combined SS mapping from relative goods prices to relative factor prices and the supposed evidence against falling relative prices for unskilled goods, Bhagwati and Dehejia conclude that "[t]he Borjas-Freeman-Katz conclusion that trade has adversely affected wages may well be right, but their analysis does not show this, and we can be quite confident that the FPE-SS explanation has been a red herring in the story" (52).

The core issue is essentially whether the international marketplace, with its supposedly fixed relative prices of unskilled relative to skilled goods, provides an open-ended vent for a surplus of unskilled labor from a country as large as the United States. Are there more unskilled immigrants? If so, the SS theorem says produce more unskilled-intensive goods and place them on the world market (or produce fewer exportables and purchase fewer importables and more domestic import substitutes). As Bhagwati and Dehejia state, in reference to the bulge of immigrants in Miami following the Mariel boat lift from Cuba, "as the Rybczynski (1955) theorem underlines, the added labor may have been absorbed at constant goods and factor prices by relative expansion of labor-intensive activities" (70).

Similarly, does Congress cut off student loans? If so, there is no problem for wage distribution, because the SS and Rybczynski theorems assure us that as long as trade remains incompletely specialized, the resulting squeeze on the skilled labor supply and the surfeit of high school graduates can easily be accommodated with no change in relative wage. How? By "relative expansion of labor-intensive activities." The heart of this debate is simply that the labor economists do not consider this world very realistic and instead think it is likely that relative US wages will be affected by relative US supplies of skilled and unskilled workers.

Such an alternative world is not difficult to envision. It is one, for example, in which there are differentiated products (rather than homogeneous goods as in the SS and HO theorems), and the United States is not marginally sized, so that fixed goods prices in trade cannot be assured.[69] Even more importantly, it is a world in which the great bulk of labor is in the untraded services sector. In this real world, it is unconvincing that virtually any shock of excess unskilled labor can be vented smoothly through international trade at fixed prices and wages.[70] In light of such divergences from the SS theorem, it is not surprising that the Lawrence-

---

69. Bhagwati and Dehejia (1994) explore an alternative model that can yield rising wage differentials as a consequence of greater trade volatility. They call it the "rolling stone gathers no moss" model. High-skilled and low-skilled labor would augment skills proportionately over time under certainty. However, high-skilled labor is assumed to augment skills regardless of whether it changes sectors, whereas low-skill labor loses its sector-specific skills when it moves between sectors. The effect of greater trade (and hence sectoral) volatility is thus to raise skill augmentation for the high skilled relative to the low skilled, widening the wage differential. Note further that the authors consider a sectoral wage-rent model (but make no mention of Borjas-Ramey 1994a), but cast doubt on the importance of the model by noting that recent research has tended to downgrade the unexplained sectoral wage rents estimated earlier by Katz and Summers (1984).

70. Note that Bhagwati (1991) extends the analysis of figure 2.6 by adding a nontradables sector. However, he assumes that services are more unskilled intensive than importables. Yet as shown in table 2.2 above, nontradable services are actually more skill intensive (education intensive) than tradable goods.

Slaughter-Krugman-Bhagwati (LSKB) attack on the labor economists who identify trade as a factor in growing wage inequality can seem severe even to sympathetic observers. Thus, Deardorff and Hakura (1994, 99) conclude of the LSKB phalanx:

> We find these arguments ingenious and compelling. . . . [But] even for trade economists, this much reliance on the strong implications of the two sector, H-O model leaves us somewhat uncomfortable.

Sachs and Shatz (1994) have provided useful additional empirical evidence on the influence of trade on the relative demand for unskilled labor. The overall tone of their study is much more sympathetic to the viewpoint that trade has a substantial impact than are those of Lawrence and Slaughter (1993) and Krugman and Lawrence (1994). Nonetheless, in terms of quantitative magnitudes, the Sachs-Shatz findings also suggest only modest trade effects. Their study thus fits with the majority group of trade economists.

The authors work with a more detailed data set than those of most previous studies, a data set comprising 131 manufacturing sectors (three-digit SIC) and 150 trading partners. Their central finding is that "increased net imports between 1978 and 1990 are associated with a decline of 7.2 percent in production-worker jobs in manufacturing, and a decline of 2.1 percent in nonproduction-worker jobs in manufacturing" (3). In one dimension, these estimates are more refined than those in Borjas, Freeman, and Katz (1992), because they incorporate input-output effects and are calculated at a much finer level of product and country detail. In another dimension, however, they are less refined, because they use the production-nonproduction worker distinction rather than educational levels as the indicator of skill. As discussed above, the production worker approach tends to give a much smaller estimate of increased wage inequality and is conceptually less meaningful. Moreover, the Sachs-Shatz analysis suffers from the same potential distortion associated with macroeconomic trade balance effects as in Borjas, Freeman, and Katz, albeit to a lesser degree because there was a smaller relative external imbalance in the Sachs-Shatz terminal period (1990) than in the mid-1980s.

In qualitative terms, Sachs and Shatz (1994) acknowledge that "we agree with K-L [Krugman and Lawrence] and L-S [Lawrence and Slaughter] that increased internationalization cannot, by itself, account for most of the observed labor market trends" (4). They do not calculate the wage impact of their estimated labor demand effects, but in discussion of the paper, Katz notes (Sachs and Shatz 1994, 77) that under normal assumptions about labor elasticities, the Sachs-Shatz estimates would be too small to account for much of the widening wage differential between skilled and unskilled workers.

In the Sachs-Shatz database from the Annual Survey of Manufactures, the average of nonproduction worker wages stands 56.4 percent above the average for production workers in the 1960s, 54.5 percent above in the 1970s, and 57.9 percent above in the 1980s. These trends fit the stylized facts of narrowing dispersion in the 1970s, followed by widening to new heights in the 1980s; however, the proportionate changes are very small. By 1989-90 the divergence reached 64.8 percent, so by the end of the 1980s the relative wage stood 6.6 percent higher than in the 1970s (i.e., 1.648/1.545). In contrast, the college/high school differential rose by 16 percent for men and 11 percent for women from 1979 to 1988 (table 2.1). The contrast suggests that analysis based on production/nonproduction workers will understate the basic phenomenon being examined: widening wage inequality. In some broad sense this comparison suggests that the production worker definition understates widening skill differentials by about one-half.

In this paper, Sachs and Shatz (1994) adopt the SS framework, whereas in their 1995 paper they depart from it. In the 1994 paper, they state that "[e]ven large changes in the factor content of trade . . . will have little effect on relative wages unless output prices also change as a result of trade" (9), a condition of the SS and FPE theorems. Accordingly, they reexamine the price issue. They note that the Lawrence-Slaughter price tests use varying starting points and cover a minority of sectors. Sachs and Shatz instead examine domestic price deflators for three-digit SIC sectors. When they regress price change during 1978-89 on unskilled intensity (ratio of production to total workers) and include a dummy variable for computers (because of the problematic price measure in that sector), they obtain a statistically significant negative relationship between change in goods price and unskilled intensity. So, as often seems to be the case with US price data, removing computers can substantially change the results. However, they caution that the magnitude of the coefficient is too small to account for a significant widening of wage inequalities (Sachs and Shatz 1994, 40).

Sachs and Shatz (1994) array their data on 131 manufacturing sectors in ascending order by unskilled/skilled (production/total worker) ratios. They present summary data for the category (not employment or output) deciles. In the first, production workers are 41.2 percent of the total; in the 10th, the ratio rises to 86.7 percent. It becomes obvious from the analysis that much of the action regarding trade impacts on unskilled workers is taking place solely within this last decile, which includes footwear and most apparel. This decile comprises 8.7 percent of production workers, only 3 percent of nonproduction workers, 6 percent of imports, and only 3.4 percent of value added.

The decile averages confirm HO expectations for US trade. The ratio of exports to imports falls from 1.2 in the most-skill-intensive 1st decile to 0.8 for the average of the 5th and 6th deciles and to 0.4 for the 10th decile (Sachs and Shatz 1994, 17). However, this pattern disappears when only trade with industrial countries is considered—confirming the stylized fact that whereas North-South trade is HO, North-North trade is driven by other influences (product differentiation and scale economies). Correspondingly, the authors calculate the Grubel-Lloyd index of intraindustry trade and find that it is much higher for trade with industrial countries than with developing countries. They note that when trade is intraindustry, increased trade should not affect the relative demand for skilled versus unskilled workers, although this would seem to miss the possibility of different products and factor combinations within statistically defined sectors (as suggested by the Bernard-Jensen results discussed above).

The authors provide estimates of protection, composed of both tariffs and tariff equivalents of nontariff barriers. The structure of US protection is clearly related to factor intensity. For the eight most-skill-category deciles, total protection fell from an average of 5.6 percent in 1978 to 3.0 percent in 1991. By contrast, for the 9th and 10th deciles (heavily influenced by apparel), protection was much higher and edged further upward, from 18.8 percent to 21.4 percent (22). This dichotomy further implies that effective protection (i.e., on value added) is especially high for unskilled-intensive goods.

The authors show that for the two most unskilled category deciles, from 1978 to 1990 there was a major erosion of both employment of production workers (−25.5 percent average) and of the trade balance with developing countries (from a deficit of 15.2 percent of value added to a deficit of 43 percent). Conversely, there was much less employment decline in sectors at the skill-intensive end of the distribution.

The core of the Sachs-Shatz analysis is a calculation of the impact of trade changes on labor demand. They take 1978 ratios of net imports to final demand as their counterfactual. When they calculate the vector of total output for 1990 that would have occurred if this trade counterfactual had prevailed and compare the estimate with actual 1990 output, they find that changes in trade have reduced demand for production workers by 7.2 percent and for nonproduction workers by 2.1 percent. The reductions are heavily concentrated in the 10th (most unskilled) decile. Thus, the simple average employment reduction for the first through ninth deciles is 2.7 percent (and still only 3.4 percent by the ninth decile). In contrast, the reduction amounts to 23.5 percent for the 10th decile (29). This result crystallizes the fact that any adverse impact of trade on US unskilled workers seems to have been exceedingly concentrated in the familiar problem sectors of footwear and apparel.[71]

---

71. The authors also show a close adherence of the counterfactual labor demand impacts with the actual employment changes. Large percentage reductions in both are concentrated in four out of 20 two-digit SIC industries: textiles (22), apparel (23), leather goods (31), and miscellaneous manufactures (39). Note that there is also a large actual decline in primary metals (33) that is not identified in the counterfactual calculation.

There is a corresponding concentration of reduced employment demand on trade with developing countries. Trade pattern changes with industrial countries reduced demand for unskilled manufacturing workers by only 1 percent and increased demand for skilled workers (concentrated in export sectors) by 2.2 percent, for an overall net reduction of only 0.2 percent. Thus, virtually all of the net reduction in labor demand was attributable to trade with developing countries.

The authors then consider qualitatively what their findings might imply for wages. They note that because manufacturing employment is only a fraction of total employment, even a 10 percent reduction in demand for unskilled manufacturing workers would have "only a very small effect on the overall demand for unskilled workers" (34). However, their subsequent work, which explicitly recognizes factor intensity and substitutability in the nontradables sector, suggests the possibility of somewhat larger impact (as discussed below). They do note that the timing of the trade impact was right to be associated with widening US wage inequality, as import competition from low-wage countries rose in the late 1970s and early 1980s.

Sachs and Shatz (1994) further include statistical regressions of a "gravity" trade model incorporating a variable for transnational corporations. They find near-unitary elasticities of trade with respect to population size and distance, somewhat greater than unitary elasticity with respect to per capita income, and an elasticity of about three with respect to the share of trade conducted among transnational company affiliates. They speculate that future trade pressure from China could be high because of intensive direct foreign investment by transnational companies in that country.

Overall, the Sachs-Shatz (1994) study opens the door a bit to the view that trade has had a significant impact on unskilled workers.[72] It clearly demonstrates the concentration of effects in trade with developing countries and in the extremes of the unskilled-intensive sectors.

Cooper's heuristic analysis (1994) takes advantage of this sectoral concentration to focus attention on a limited set of relevant sectors. His study gives an interesting ballpark estimate of the relative importance of trade in explaining unskilled wage reductions. Methodologically, it opens the theoretical door yet another few inches to the possibility that non-SS mechanisms mean trade could be having an effect even if the relative prices of unskilled-intensive manufactures are not observed to be falling.

---

72. The authors explicitly reject the Lawrence-Slaughter test of rising skilled/unskilled labor ratios as evidence contrary to a trade impact and seek with a numerical example to establish that ongoing technological change could account for the coexistence of rising skilled/unskilled ratios for both factor inputs and wages. Their example depends on a coterminous decline in the relative price of unskilled goods in international trade.

Cooper first suggests a focus on unskilled labor rather than "production" workers, because the latter include many skilled. He notes that unskilled workers are concentrated in a few manufacturing sectors and cites average hourly wages of production workers in early 1993 as evidence: apparel, $7.05; leather-working, $7.49; and textiles, $8.81. The manufacturing average was $11.62. He uses these three sectors as a proxy for all unskilled workers and traces the trade impact through them. While this strategy is somewhat supported by the Sachs-Shatz finding of concentration of effects in these same sectors, it runs considerable risk of minimizing the problem by assuming away much of its potential dimension. Cooper notes that the three sectors (plus nontradable meatpacking) constitute 15 percent of the 12.3 million US production workers in manufacturing. Thus, by shifting "unskilled" from "production" to "apparel-footwear-textiles," he runs the risk of understating the problem by as much as five-sixths.

What he gets for taking this risk is a crisp, back-of-the-envelope calculation of the contribution of trade to the decline in unskilled wages. First, however, he enumerates several facts pointing toward such an influence. In the 1980s, the value of US textiles and apparel imports grew, respectively, at 10 and 14 percent annually. By 1992, imports from developing countries amounted to 6 percent of US apparent consumption in textiles and 28 percent in apparel. From 1980 to 1990, overall US manufacturing employment fell by 1.2 million jobs; a remarkable 40 percent of this reduction was in textiles, apparel, and leather (TAL), whereas this group's employment share had been only 14 percent in 1980. For benchmarks, he estimates that over the decade the real wage of US unskilled workers fell by 10 percent,[73] and he notes that whereas TAL accounts for about 1.5 million jobs, the primarily unskilled retail services sector (where wages are in the range of $6 per hour) has 17 million workers.

Cooper next tries yet another test for falling unskilled-goods prices. This one simply uses value-added deflators in textiles and apparel, which turn out to have risen by about one-seventh relative to other manufactured-goods deflators over the decade. However, rather than declaring the case closed against import effects because they violated the SS theorem, Cooper loosens the vise of the theoretical framework (though without explicitly stating a specific-factors or other alternative).

In his more flexible view, domestic producers respond to import competition by quality upgrading. As a result, one cannot observe the falling prices that the SS theorem would otherwise predict. In this approach,

> Foreign trade sectors such as textiles and apparel contribute to . . . demand [for unskilled workers] and thus influence the wage without however determining it,

---

73. He notes that this is deflating by the CPI. Otherwise his measure is undefined. Note that the CPI overstates the real erosion, as discussed in chapter 1.

as in the Stolper Samuelson framework. Cheap foreign goods (e.g., shoes, clothing) appeal to some consumers . . . But other consumers prefer the higher quality, higher priced domestic goods . . . Such goods are not homogeneous, as required by the Stolper Samuelson theorem. Firms under increased pressures from imports have an incentive to cut their production costs, but also to improve the quality of their output . . . Domestic output will fall but domestic prices may not fall . . . The released labor gets absorbed into the general economy, albeit perhaps at lower wages. If this is so, the release of unskilled workers from textile and apparel production during the 1980s surely put downward pressure on the wage, regardless of what happened to domestic prices of textiles and apparel, by reducing overall demand for unskilled labor . . . (Cooper 1994, 16-17)

Cooper now has the back of his envelope ready for calculations. As his counterfactual, he postulates employment reduction in TAL from 1980 to 1990 of only 3.9 percent, the figure for overall manufacturing. That decline would have released 90,000 production workers. Instead, the actual TAL release was 478,000, for an "excess" decline of 387,000. In contrast, employment of production workers in retail trade, hotels, and restaurants rose from 21.4 million to 27.5 million. The "excess" displaced TAL workers thus represented an increase in supply of 1.4 percent of terminal-period unskilled labor.

Citing Katz and Murphy (1992), Cooper uses an elasticity of 1.41 for substitution between college and high school graduates. He adds another 0.25 to capture induced demand increases from falling prices in unskilled-labor-intensive services as the unskilled wage falls. With an overall elasticity of 1.66, and a 1.4 percent shift in supply from excess TAL workers, Cooper calculates that trade would have depressed unskilled wages by 0.8 percent. On this basis, he concludes that "increased import competition from low wage countries can account for 10 percent of the relative decline in wages of US unskilled workers during the 1980s. . . . [M]ost of the explanation lies elsewhere" (8).

Although Cooper resides comfortably in the company of trade economists who conclude that trade has had only a minor impact on wage inequality, his short article opens a Pandora's box. He sanctions a non-SS trade model in which displaced workers from traded sectors must find jobs in the nontradables sector and resultingly depress unskilled wages there—in a fashion that cannot be denied simply by pointing to an absence of falling prices for unskilled goods. This framework is very close to what the labor economists who identify trade as an important cause of rising wage inequality seem to have in mind, and it can become a vehicle for estimates of more severe effects by trade economists with parallel views (see "Trade Economists 2," most relevantly, Sachs and Shatz 1995).

As for the point estimate that trade has contributed only 10 percent of the erosion of unskilled wages, Cooper's calculation would seem useful primarily in establishing a lower bound. As noted above, his TAL subset represents only one-sixth of production workers in manufacturing. Even acknowledging the Sachs-Shatz concentration of trade effects in these subsectors, that leaves considerable room for expansion of his estimate under more comprehensive sectoral inclusion.

Baldwin and Cain (1994) get high marks in a survey by Richardson (1995, 37) as representing a second generation in the trade and wage distribution literature that uses improved modeling, specification, or data. The two authors use 13 years of education or more as their definition of skilled, improving on the common nonproduction definition. Using the 79 two-digit sectors of the US input-output table, they document that US exports are significantly more skilled intensive than US imports. By their definition, the ratio of skilled to unskilled workers directly or indirectly embodied in exports rose from 36.4 percent in 1967 to 54.7 percent in 1977 and 75.3 percent in 1987. The corresponding ratios for labor embodied in imports were 33.2 percent, 46 percent, and 61.5 percent, respectively. The greater skill intensity of exports thus rose from 9.6 percent (36.4/33.2) in 1967 to 22.4 percent by 1987. It is likely that the skill differential is even greater in US trade with developing countries.[74]

Although Baldwin and Cain are sympathetic to the role of technological change, they maintain that Berman, Bound, and Griliches (1994) are inconsistent with trade theory when they seek to identify trade effects strictly with between-industry as opposed to within-industry changes in employment and wage shares.[75] Similarly, they are sympathetic to the Lawrence-Slaughter (1993) and Krugman-Lawrence (1993) diagnoses reviewed above. However, they judge that

> [I]t is not enough to state that unskilled labor-saving technological change is the dominant cause . . . [Such change] in all sectors coupled with the observed more rapid increase in the supply of skilled labor . . . is likely to worsen the terms of trade [given that US exports are skill intensive], whereas the terms of trade improved slightly over the decade. Introducing increased foreign competition can explain the improved terms of trade, but this then gives a role for increased foreign competition in explaining the observed changes in the wage gap . . . that may not be quantitatively minor, as Krugman and Lawrence claim . . . [N]either the evidence they present nor the analysis here support such a strong statement. (30)

Baldwin and Cain carry out two empirical analyses. The first applies regressions somewhat similar in spirit to Leamer (1992) to detect the

---

74. This picture is qualitatively the opposite and intuitively more plausible than that given by the minimal difference between labor coefficients of OECD imports and exports reported by Balassa (1986), discussed above. The Balassa coefficients do not distinguish by skill level. An important implication is that US comparative advantage is driven more by the endowment of human capital relative to raw labor than by the endowment of physical capital relative to all labor.

75. As one example, reciprocal trade liberalization will raise the domestic price of the skill-intensive export good. If coefficients are fixed, there will be no change in the quantities of skilled and unskilled labor either between or within industries, but the relative wage of skilled workers will rise (from the SS theorem). Similarly, technological change can give rise to shifts in labor demand between as well as within industries.

sources of changing factor prices. The second applies the Deardorff-Staiger (1988) model to obtain order of magnitude estimates for the impact of trade on US skill differentials.

The first analysis starts from the zero profit condition that the proportionate change in real price equals the sum of factor shares times proportionate changes in real factor prices ($\dot{p}_j = \Sigma_i \theta_{ij} \dot{w}_i$, where p is product price, w is wage, i is skill level, j is sector, and the overdot indicates proportionate change). From the SS theorem (and its weak version that each of multiple products is a "friend" to a given factor), they argue that changes in product prices should be associated with corresponding changes in relative factor prices. They regress changes in relative product prices for 79 input-output sectors on sectoral value-added shares of skilled labor (≥ 13 years education), unskilled labor (≤ 12), and a composite capital-land factor. This analysis essentially takes product prices and sectoral factor shares as given and infers changes in factor prices ($\dot{w}_i$).

The authors reason that if the changes in factor prices predicted by product price changes are consistent with observed factor price trends, the trends would be consistent with changing factor endowments. If, instead, the predicted and observed factor price trends diverge, differential technological change may have occurred. Their tests for 1967-77 show positive estimates for unskilled labor and capital-land, and negative coefficients for skilled labor. These results are consistent with a changing factor endowment in this period, when the stock of workers with above high school education was rising rapidly. Thus, by their definition, the relative supply of skilled labor rose by 43 percent in this period.[76] Their results coincide with the usual diagnosis of dominant supply-side influences in this period. For the period after 1977, the same estimated signs on factor prices persist, yet the observed relative factor prices moved in the opposite direction, as the skill differential rose sharply. The authors infer that technological change may have been dominant in the second period, again a finding consistent with much of the labor economics literature (e.g., Katz and Murphy 1992).

Baldwin and Cain then reason that price differences across countries at points in time under autarky should similarly reflect different factor endowments. Because trade will respond to these different potential

---

76. Baldwin and Cain (1994, table 6) estimate that skilled-worker supply rose by 58.8 percent and unskilled supply by 8.2 percent from 1967 to 1977. In contrast, skilled-worker supply rose by 64.3 percent and unskilled supply by 22.2 percent in 1977-87. By this measure, the relative increase for skilled was 46.8 percent in the first period but only 34.5 percent in the second period. Although the authors do not focus on this point, these data seem rather eloquent evidence in support of a steady technological shift over the whole period in favor of skilled labor. This shift would have moderated the severity of the decline of relative skilled wages in the 1970s. Then, when relative growth of skilled-labor supply decelerated in the second decade, the continuing (steady) demand shift was sufficient to cause a reversal in skill differential trends. See figure 2.9 below.

autarky prices, they argue that measures of observed comparative advantage (e.g., the logarithm of the ratio of exports to imports for the sector) should similarly bear a systematic relationship to sectoral factor shares. The notion is to regress such trade ratios on factor shares at different points in time and then observe changes in the coefficients—which are implicit factor price differences between the US and the rest of world—on factor shares to determine whether trends are consistent with changes in relative factor endowments.

These estimates find the highest coefficient on skilled labor, the lowest (typically negative) on unskilled labor, and an intermediate coefficient on capital-land. Thus, under autarky the United States would have a factor-price advantage in skilled labor and disadvantage in unskilled labor. (This is another indirect demonstration that US trade obeys comparative advantage for the two types of labor.) Once again, the pattern of changes over time is consistent with a rising relative supply of US skilled labor in the 1970s; however, it shows ambiguous results in the 1980s.

They interpret their results to imply one of two cases. First, there was generalized skill-biased technological change that reduced the return to unskilled labor, combined with increased foreign competition that more than offset any resulting tendency for US terms of trade (in skill-intensive exports) to decline. Or, second, skill-biased technological change was not generalized but greater in skill-intensive sectors, causing a rise in the skilled wage differential without any change in product price.[77]

The second principal estimate of Baldwin and Cain (1994) employs the Deardorff-Staiger result that changes in relative product prices and, thus, relative factor prices can be inferred from changes in the factor content of trade. Deardorff and Staiger use Cobb-Douglas production and expenditure functions, meaning that factor and product shares are constant regardless of factor and product prices. Payments of wages (w_i) to factors (L_i) are equal to constant fraction (c_i) of expenditure (E): $w_i L_i = c_i E$.

Let L be the vector of the country's endowments. Let S be the vector of its factors embodied in net exports. For a given factor i, if the amount of the factor embodied in exports exceeds (is less than) that embodied in imports, S_i is positive (negative), reducing (augmenting) the domestic availability of this factor. The effective factor endowment under autarky is thus $L - S$. It follows that the wage for factor i in autarky would be

$$w_i = \frac{c_i E}{L_i - S_i} \qquad (2.7)$$

By normalizing prices, total expenditure can be defined to equal unity, so E drops out of the equation.

---

77. Always observing the SS-HO framework, whereby factor prices cannot change if product prices do not do so.

The authors then use this relationship to obtain the following equation for calculating the impact of the change in factor trade on relative factor prices from base year a to terminal year b:

$$\frac{w_h^{b'} - w_u^{b'}}{w_u^{b'}} = \frac{[1 + (S_h^a - S_h^b)/B_h^{b'}]w_h^b}{[1 + (S_u^a - S_u^b)/B_u^{b'}]w_u^b} - 1 \qquad (2.8)$$

where subscripts h and u refer to skilled and unskilled workers, respectively, the prime designates the hypothetical value that would have obtained without a change of trade-embodied factors, and $B = L - S$.

Baldwin and Cain use this equation to calculate that if factors embodied in US trade had remained unchanged at 1977 levels, then by 1987 the hypothetical skilled/unskilled wage gap would have been 50.0 instead of 52.3 percent of the base period unskilled wage. Thus, the change in trade contributed 4.2 percent of the terminal period gap. They interpret this to mean that "changes in trade play only a small role in explaining the wage gap" (34). However, since the gap rose from 35.4 percent in 1977 to 52.3 percent in 1987, 16.9 percentage points, the 2.3 percentage points contributed by trade changes comprised 13.6 percent of the increase in the wage gap. This is about half again as large as the 9 percent contribution to the widening wage gap that the authors report for another experiment.[78]

The authors do not comment on a sobering estimate reported in their tables: the change in the factor content of trade from 1977 to 1987 amounted to a loss of 1.8 million unskilled jobs and 440,000 skilled jobs, about 10 percent of the manufacturing labor force. This finding of negative job trends associated with trade in the 1980s is also obtained by other authors, especially Sachs and Shatz (1994). The seeming contradiction between the large job effect and small relative wage effect apparently stems from the fact that in applying equations 2.7 and 2.8, the authors are using economy-wide wage shares, so that the proportionate changes in B are much smaller than implied when gauged against the manufacturing base alone.

The overall finding of Baldwin and Cain (1994) is that trade changes can only explain a small part of rising wage differentials. However, they acknowledge that their result might be sensitive to the Cobb-Douglas assumptions. Analytically, an important feature of the Baldwin-Cain approach is that it comes very close to the labor economists' factor content

---

78. In the second experiment, wage changes from trade with labor supply held constant are -4 percent for unskilled and -2.9 percent for skilled from 1977-87, for an increase of 1.1 percent in the relative skilled wage. In the same period, wage changes from labor supply change with trade held constant are -18.3 percent for unskilled and -39.4 percent for skilled, so that in the absence of other considerations, labor supply changes in this period should have reduced the relative wage of skilled labor by 25.8 percent! Instead, the actual wage change was -4.8 percent for unskilled and $+7.1$ percent for skilled, for 12.5 percent increase in the relative wage of skilled labor.

of trade approach. The principal difference is that in the Baldwin-Cain approach, there is an underlying HO framework requiring product price changes, whereas the labor economists apply the change in factor content of trade to estimated wage-supply elasticities to judge wage impacts. As discussed below, Krugman (1995b) has reinstated the theoretical consistency of the factor content calculation for the economy that is large relative to trade, so the more recent work by the trade economists seems to be moving toward accommodation with the factor content approach in the earlier labor economics literature.

Trade Economists 2

Just as labor economists have been divided between one group that considers international influences relatively unimportant in explaining widening US wage inequality ("Labor Economists 1") and another that gives considerable weight to trade and immigration ("Labor Economists 2"), there has been a similar division among trade economists. Those just reviewed ("Trade Economists 1") argue that trade has not been a major influence. A smaller group ("Trade Economists 2") contends that trade has been important. Among these, one prominent trade economist (Leamer, 1992, 1994, 1995) fully shares the theoretical framework of SS-FPE invoked in the Bhagwati-Krugman-Lawrence-Slaughter critique of the labor economists, but arrives at different conclusions because of different empirical findings. Others in this second group of trade economists instead approach the problem from different theoretical frameworks as well (Sachs and Shatz 1995; Feenstra and Hanson 1995; Johnson and Stafford 1992, 1993, 1995).

Leamer (1992) states in stark terms just the kind of FPE-based pessimism that Bhagwati and Dehejia (1994, 40) decry as overdone among economists ("FPE . . . as an inescapable destiny," 40). Thus, according to Leamer,

> Relatively free international trade has produced and will continue to produce substantial changes in the relative earnings of skilled and unskilled workers. This redistribution will surely fuel the fires of protectionism. . . . [I]n countries like the United States with heterogeneous populations, weak private social insurance networks, and democratic political systems, trade protection is an important instrument for income redistribution . . . The assumption on which this paper is founded is that the U.S. will have relatively high rates of protection against labor-intensive imports. . . . [We] cannot have a free trade agreement with Mexico and also maintain the wages of low-skilled workers with other forms of protection since Mexico will become a platform for entering the U.S. market . . . What other kind of life boat are we going to offer our low skilled workers, if any? The most appealing answer is education and training. If that is not enough, a commitment to redistribute through changes in the income tax might sensibly be exchanged for the commitment to free trade. (2-5)

Leamer (1992) uses past US trade experience as a metaphor for what could happen under NAFTA liberalization. His method is as follows:

The component of the historical change in commodity prices that is associated with the commodity's labor intensity is extended into the future. Then these predicted relative price declines of labor-intensive products are mapped into the corresponding changes in factor earnings. One calculation of this type indicates that the annual earnings of $1000 of capital would increase by $13, that the annual earnings of professional and technical workers would increase by $6,000 and the annual earnings of other workers would decline by $1,900. (5)

In other words, Leamer accepts the SS-FPE rule emphasized in "Trade Economists 1": factor price changes must occur through product price changes. However, Leamer's reading of the data finds such changes and, thus, reaches the conclusion that major unskilled wage erosion has been linked with trade, opposite from Lawrence and Slaughter's conclusion (1993).

The key difference is that Leamer eschews normal SIC groupings as his observational groups, because many two-digit categories contain three-digit subgroups that are disparate in factor intensity. Instead, he creates nine cells in a three-factor matrix and sorts each three-digit industry into one of these cells. The three factors are capital, skilled labor, and unskilled labor. The three rows in the matrix distinguish by capital per worker (<$15,000, intermediate, and >$24,000). The three columns distinguish by skill level (scientists, engineers, and managers comprise <11 percent, intermediate, and >17 percent of labor). The upper-left cell (1,1) is thus the most unskilled intensive; the bottom right (3,3), the most unskilled nonintensive.

The unskilled-intensive sectors are familiar candidates: apparel, food, furniture, and footwear in cell 1,1; textiles, paperboard, and appliances in cell 2,1 (which has little skilled labor but an intermediate capital/labor ratio); and steel, sawmills, and planning mills in cell 3,1 (low skill but high capital/labor ratios). The average price increase from 1972 to 1985 is 140 percent. The increase for cell 1,1 is only 96 percent and for cell 2,1 only 120 percent. Over the same period, the trade balance relative to domestic production fell by 13 percentage points in cell 1,1 and 14 points in cell 2,1. Similarly, employment fell by disproportionately large amounts in the sector cells using little human capital. Leamer concludes that the data support the proposition that product price changes have been consistent with downward pressure on unskilled wages as a consequence of rising international competition.[79]

Leamer does not mention that his technique faces the classic problem of identifying factor intensity when there are more than two factors. Implicitly, he appeals to the "higher dimensionality" literature (Ethier 1984) and its somewhat weaker form of the normal SS conclusions: "every

---

79. The results are more ambiguous on the export side, as they do not similarly show a rising share of net exports in output for skill-intensive goods. Note also that Leamer separates out computers into a tenth sector to avoid misleading price trends.

good is a friend to some factor and an enemy to some other factor" (Deardorff 1993b).

Like Lawrence and Slaughter (1993), Leamer (1992) criticizes those labor economists who focus on the trade deficit, which is only "a temporary phenomenon," for being unclear about their counterfactual and for the fact that their "calculations have no clear theoretical foundation." Similarly, he invokes the SS theorem to call for a two-step test that the labor economists should have used: first, mapping from falling relative product prices to falling relative unskilled wages and, second, attributing product price changes to international market influences (35-36). Correspondingly, he questions the studies calculating immigration's wage effects, because "[t]he potential effect on wages of an increase in the labor force may be fully dissipated by a shift in the product mix in favor of commodities that use labor intensively" (35). Thus, Leamer seems to subscribe to the school of infinite vent-for-surplus for unskilled labor portrayed above, except where product price changes can be demonstrated. His theoretical framework is more SS-rigid than that of Cooper (1994), also discussed above.

The core of Leamer's (1992) analysis is a regression-based examination of the impact of trade trends on factor prices. He notes that a direct test would simply relate changes in factor prices to changes in product prices. However, he argues that such a test is likely to be econometrically difficult. Cross-sector tests within a country at a point in time will by definition not capture factor price variation, because factors are mobile within a country. Cross-country tests are likely to confront too little internal price and wage variation relative to data noise. Time series tests face the problem of changing technology.

Leamer's solution is to invoke the Rybczynski (1955) theorem as the "dual" to the SS theorem.[80] Whereas the SS theorem states that the change in the vector of relative factor prices is a function of the change in relative product prices ($\partial w = A'_h - 1 \, \partial p$), Rybczynski states that the change in the vector of product quantities is a function of the change in the vector of factor endowments ($\partial q = A_h^{-1} \, \partial v$).[81]

This relationship provides the theoretical basis for Leamer's regression estimates, which relate levels of manufacturing production to factor supplies. The data refer to 13 OECD countries, for the years 1972 and 1985. For each of 37 three- or four-digit ISIC (International Standard Industrial Classification) sectors, the cross-country regressions relate the level of

---

80. The dual of a quantity change is a price change, and vice versa.

81. Where A is an $m \times n$ matrix of requirements of each of the m factors for the production of a unit of each of the n products, q is the production vector, $\mathbf{w}$ the factor wage vector, p the price vector, and $\mathbf{v}$ the factor supply vector. Full factor use implies $Aq = \mathbf{v}$; zero profit implies $A'w = p$.

production as the dependent variable to the country's endowment of capital, professional labor, and "other" (unskilled) labor.[82]

Leamer finds the results mixed. Reassuringly, textiles, iron, and steel are located in countries abundant in capital and nonprofessional workers and motor vehicles in countries with abundant capital and professional workers. The results are also consistent with expectations for the unskilled-intensive sectors of footwear, leather products, textiles, and apparel. However, numerous sectors have positive coefficients on all three factors, whereas the Rybczynski theorem indicates a negative coefficient for at least one factor. Several of these have a low degree of explanation.

Leamer then estimates regressions relating sectoral price changes for 1972-85 to sectoral capital/labor ratios. He assumes that "the component of variability of price that is correlated with capital intensity is associated with foreign competition" (46). He then uses this relationship to predict the future under NAFTA-influenced free trade, assuming, alternatively, once-fold further price change, half the past price change, or fivefold the past change. With predicted product prices, he then applies the Rybczynski regression parameters to infer relative factor price changes.[83] In the central case (once-fold replication of past trends), he obtains the factor price changes cited at the outset of this section.

Overall, Leamer's conclusions about a substantial role for globalization seem reasonable. However, his estimation method is circuitous (necessarily so, he seems to say). Moreover, his theoretical framework seems unduly wedded to the SS theorem and, hence, vulnerable to his particular shuffling of data into a nine-celled product breakdown.

82. Lawrence and Slaughter (1993) consider Leamer's technique "debatable" because "Rybczynski partial derivatives are not well defined when the number of goods exceeds the number of factors" (189). The Leamer test uses 3 factors and 37 goods. However, the theoretical emphasis on "evenness" between the number of goods and factors itself would seem rather arbitrary, as changes in breadth of definitions can always increase or decrease the "number" of either goods or factors. Leamer himself (1994) has replied to Lawrence and Slaughter that "[i]n a model with more goods than factors, price variability is limited in dimension to the number of factors, and the economy (after aggregation) behaves as if it had equal numbers of factors and commodities" (21).

83. Thus, Leamer first estimates: $Q_i = \alpha + \beta_1 K + \beta_2 S + \beta_3 U + \epsilon K$, where K is capital, S skilled labor, and U unskilled labor. A z percent change in the price of good i will then cause an expected change of $\beta_j z_i$ percent in the price of factor j from the standpoint of this sector's influence. Second, for 1972 to 1985 he estimates the regression: $\%\Delta p_i = a_i + b_i (K/N)_i$, where p is the relative price and $N = S + U$. It is unclear why there should be a monotonic relationship between relative price change and capital intensity; moreover, this procedure does not distinguish between skilled and unskilled labor, arguably more important for US comparative advantage than labor versus capital. In any event, the scenario for future price change is determined by the sector's capital/labor ratio. For example, the relative price of apparel (low K/L) is projected in the central case to fall by 23 percent, whereas that of plastics (high) rises by 47 percent. There is a corresponding set of sectorally estimated factor price changes. The overall estimate of factor price change is a weighted average of the sectoral estimates.

The next of Leamer's studies in his recent trilogy (Leamer 1994) concentrates on refuting Lawrence and Slaughter (1993) and Krugman and Lawrence (1993). Leamer first criticizes the proposition in both studies that the SS theorem requires a reduction in all sectoral skilled/unskilled employment ratios in response to a fall in relative unskilled wages caused by a reduction in the relative price of the unskilled-intensive product. Instead, Leamer argues that "[t]his lowering of wages can occur without any change in output levels or any change in factor input ratios, completely contrary to Krugman and Lawrence's (1993) assertion" (Leamer 1994, 8). This critique essentially says that a lack of substitutability in fixed-coefficient sectoral factor combinations could prevent the shift in factor ratios expected by Lawrence and Slaughter, without controverting the SS theorem or preventing the decline in relative unskilled wages. Leamer elaborates a simple fixed-coefficients model to make the point.

Leamer then criticizes the Lawrence-Slaughter-Krugman conclusion that technology rather than trade is the cause of widening wage inequality. Leamer (1994 9, 5) maintains that

> in elementary trade theory . . . innovation in the skill-intensive sector causes reductions in wages of unskilled, but technological change in the unskilled-intensive sector causes an *increase* in wages of the unskilled. The data [in Lawrence-Slaughter-Krugman] look pretty neutral, and seem initially compatible with the notion that technological change has had no impact on income inequality. This makes globalization seem more important . . . completely contrary to the conclusions of Lawrence and Slaughter (1993) and Krugman and Lawrence (1993).

Using a two-sector, two-factor model with fixed coefficients, Leamer (1994) confirms that unskilled wages fall if the technological change is concentrated in the skill-intensive sector. He also finds that the amount of wage reduction is greater the more similar are the technologies in the two sectors and that globalization and technological change interact multiplicatively to affect income inequality but have separate effects on it.

Leamer then reworks the same National Bureau of Economic Research data set used by Lawrence and Slaughter (1993). He finds that from 1976 to 1986, there was an 18 percent rise in average capital per unit of value added, in contrast to a 9 percent reduction in nonproduction workers and 21 percent reduction in production workers per unit of value added. This seeming fall in relative demand for production workers is inconsistent, however, with an observed 96 percent increase in production worker wages and an 89 percent increase for nonproduction workers (seemingly controverting the overall assumption of widening wage inequality). This anomaly highlights the sensitivity of the trends to the end points, as much of the Lawrence-Slaughter decline in relative unskilled wages occurs between 1986 and 1989.

Leamer principally concludes that the distinction between production and nonproduction workers is a misleading criterion for skills, and he cites truck delivery drivers, routine office workers, and cafeteria employees as examples of unskilled workers who are nonetheless classified as nonproduction workers. In any event, when he conducts regressions specified to capture technology effects, he finds that "[i]n every case, technology has led to a larger increase in wages for the production . . . than for the nonproduction [workers] . . . completely the opposite of the [Lawrence-Slaughter-Krugman] conclusions" (20).[84]

Leamer (1994, 4) provides an important calculation almost as an aside. He notes that his earlier (1993) estimate of the impact of price declines for labor-intensive products translated into a wage impact that was "about 20 percent of the total amount of income redistributed." He bases this figure on an estimated $60 billion transfer away from low-skilled workers, compared to "Heckman's $300b (sic) total transfer." Leamer does not provide the Heckman citation or describe his method. He finds "globalization" effects on wage inequality ("lower prices for labor-intensive products, less market power in autos and steel, and increased international mobility of physical capital and technology") to have been important, alongside the other two major influences: changes in relative factor supply ("education and migration") and ongoing technological change ("computers").

What is revealing about Leamer's 20 percent calculation is that it suggests that Leamer too places rather modest limits on the relative influence of trade in explaining widening wage disparity. Considering that Krugman (1995a) places the impact of North-South trade in manufactures on OECD wage disparity at 10 percent of the increase (as discussed below), Leamer's 20 percent figure would seem to make the range of the debate much narrower than the rhetoric would suggest.

A closer look suggests, however, that Leamer's calculations really imply a much larger share of influence for trade. His estimate of a $1,000 reduction for unskilled wages corresponds to 5 percent of the 1985 wage for production workers, and the $6,000 increase for skilled workers amounts to 20 percent of the nonproduction worker's average wage (from Sachs and Shatz 1994, 8). The implication is a 25 percent increase in the skilled/unskilled wage ratio. Considering that the increase in the 1980s amounted to about 15 percent (chapter 1, figure 1.7), comparisons suggest that Leamer's point estimate of wage impact explains more than 100 percent of past trends in the wage differential, rather than the 20 percent figure he notes as an aside.

The third recent Leamer (1995) study seeks to statistically test the role of technological change as opposed to "globalization" effects. Leamer

84. Leamer's regression is far from transparent. The left side is payroll savings on unskilled workers divided by skilled input intensity. The right side has the unskilled/skilled input ratio times "a coefficient equal to the increase in the wages of the unskilled workers plus a constant equal to the increase in unskilled wages."

argues that product price change should equal factor cost change, less the rise in total factor productivity:

$$\hat{p}_i = \theta'_i \hat{w} - \hat{TFP} \qquad (2.9)$$

where the circumflex denotes proportionate change, i refers to the product sector, $\hat{TFP}$ is total factor productivity, θ_i is the vector of factor shares in sector i, and $\hat{w}$ is the vector of factor price changes. He emphasizes that because product prices drive factor price changes, and technological change affects product prices through changes in total factor productivity, "the factor bias of technological change is entirely irrelevant. What matters is only the sectoral distribution of TFP growth" (Leamer 1995, 32). However, this proposition would seem incorrect except in the small-country case and within the rigid SS framework. Certainly for a large closed economy, wage differentials by skill class are bound to be affected by the skill bias of technological change.

Next, Leamer stands the usual analysis of technological change on its head. He measures technological change $(\hat{TFP})$ directly and then finds factor price change associated with all other influences—called "globalization"—as the residual. To do this, he first divides the product price change into that caused by technological change and that from other (globalization) influences: $\hat{p}_i = \hat{p}_i(t) + \hat{p}_i(g)$. Assuming a uniform pass-through ratio of λ from total factor productivity change to product price change, $\hat{p}_i(t) = -\lambda \hat{TFP}$. Price change from globalization is total price change less the technological change component, yielding $\hat{p}_i(g) = \hat{p}_i + \lambda \hat{TFP}$.

Leamer then uses this measure of globalization price impact to estimate a regression of the form

$$\hat{p}_i + \lambda \hat{TFP}_i = \theta'_i \hat{w}(g). \qquad (2.10)$$

The variables on the right are sectoral factor shares (capital, skilled, and unskilled labor) in the base period. The regression coefficients are the respective factor price changes implied by the product price changes net of the influence of technological change (all on the left).

The average factor shares in manufacturing are surprisingly high for capital (rising from 48 percent in 1961 to 60 percent in 1991), low for skilled labor (falling from 23 percent to 17 percent), and especially low for unskilled labor (from 13 percent to 8 percent), suggesting possible data problems. Total factor productivity growth was about 8 percent in the 1960s, close to zero in the 1970s, and 4 percent in the 1980s. Although the results vary depending on the assumed $\hat{TFP}$ pass-through (λ), Leamer's overall qualitative result is that in explaining inequality trends, "most of the action comes from globalization, not from technological change" (36). However, it is difficult to extract a summary fraction for attribution globalization, and, of course, in this method the residual overattribution problem is shifted to globalization rather than technological change.

The Leamer (1995) study is replete with other important stylized facts and analytical demonstrations. For example, Leamer notes that in the initial postwar decades, Europe, the United States, Japan, and the Asian NICs opted for integrated development, whereas other LDCs chose isolation. The failure of inward-oriented development subsequently caused the other LDCs to shift toward integration, thereby imposing a major task of absorbing these countries into the international economy in a manner that does not aggravate wage inequality in industrial countries. At the same time, the average per capita income of US trading partners relative to that of the United States has risen rather than fallen, as income convergence within the OECD has swamped the rising trade shares of the LDCs. Another secular trend has been the US shift from a unique position at the upper perimeter of high-capital and skilled-labor abundance in factor endowments to a merely ordinary position among industrial countries.

A significant empirical finding is that Leamer's earlier demonstration of falling prices for textiles and apparel was driven mainly by price reductions in the period 1972-83, earlier than the period examined in Lawrence and Slaughter (1993). As Cline (1990, 26-7, 44) notes, there was a massive shift from cotton to lower-cost synthetic fibers in the 1960s and 1970s. Falling prices in the period identified by Leamer could reflect this phenomenon rather than SS pressures.[85]

Considering the scope for withstanding wage pressure from LDC trade, Leamer (1995) invokes the version of the HO model in which there are more goods than factors to emphasize that the outcome for an industrial country will depend on whether it is in a "specialization cone" that includes or excludes the simplest unskilled-labor-intensive goods. Typifying such products as "apparel" and distinguishing them from intermediate "textiles" (with more capital) and "machinery" (with more capital and skilled labor), Leamer remarks that if the United States makes enough investment in capital and education, it will bid up the price of unskilled labor so that the US cone of specialization excludes the most unskilled good ("apparel"). Under these circumstances, an inundation of the world market by such goods from the large new LDC entrants would tend to reduce the price of such goods, rather than depress unskilled wages in

---

85. The decline was mainly in textile fabric. The US textile shipments price index, relative to the overall manufacturing GDP deflator, fell from 138 in 1960-61 to 109 in 1970-71. It spiked with oil prices in 1974 to 127, but then fell to 101 by 1982-86. In contrast, the relative apparel price index rose from 100 in 1960-61 to 117 in 1970-71 and then fell again to 101 by 1980-86 (Cline 1990, 45). Yet there has been far greater increase in import penetration in apparel (from 6 percent of apparent consumption in 1970 to 25 percent in 1986), primarily from developing countries, than in textiles (from 5 percent to 8 percent) (Cline 1990, 35-44). Nonetheless, product upgrading in response to import pressure has probably disguised constant-quality price declines, as suggested by Cooper (1994).

the United States. This perspective to some extent has the globally perverse implication that capital would not be flowing from the rich country to the poor country. It does, however, stress that the US problem is not so much with trade as with a low rate of investment.

The study also stresses that the outcome depends critically on which margin it is that sets the unskilled wage. Thus,

> If the marginal demand for unskilled workers comes from labor-intensive manu-
> factures such as apparel, then competition with Chinese apparel production inevi-
> tably forces wages down. If, on the other hand, the marginal demand for unskilled
> workers comes from the nontraded goods sector and if traded goods manufactur-
> ing is concentrated in the more capital intensive goods, then declining apparel
> prices mean cheaper goods for consumers but not lower wage rates. (1995, 12)

Leamer introduces his study with a review of the unfinished research task. He mentions the need to consider other theoretical frameworks, including the Ricardo-Viner specific-factors model, and to consider the implications of unskilled wage determination on the internal rather than external margin. Overall, the study broadens Leamer's framework in the debate while chipping away at, if not fully undermining, the majority view of both labor and trade economists that technological change is the principal culprit.

The 1994 study of Sachs and Shatz was sympathetic to the argument of trade effects, but it found only modestly different results from those of Lawrence and Slaughter (1993), and it remained within the confines of the SS model. Their 1995 study not only shifted the model but at least implicitly obtained larger estimates of trade effects.

In this later study, the theoretical framework is Ricardo-Viner specific-factors trade, rather than HO trade. Factor prices are determined at the internal margin rather than the external margin. The crux of the model is a phenomenon of labor shedding by manufacturing, which places workers onto the market in the nontradables sector where unskilled labor is relatively less useful and poorly substitutable for skilled labor. The result is a falling unskilled wage, determined at the internal margin in the nontradables sector.

The authors first note that manufacturing employs relatively more unskilled workers than nonmanufacturing.[86] The respective employment shares of high school or less-educated workers were 70 percent versus 54 percent in 1979, falling to 60 percent versus 46 percent in 1990. A decline in manufacturing thus disgorges unskilled workers in a greater proportion than the existing average in the nonmanufacturing sector where they must seek work.

---

86. The authors divide manufacturing into a high-skill sector and a low-skill, low-wage, footloose sector.

Production is noncompetitive, and when trade places pressure on importables production, firms respond not by reducing prices but by reducing quantity. There is, accordingly, a labor-shedding effect, but no relative price decline observable for identification of SS international pressures on factor prices.

Sachs and Shatz (1995) examine sectoral data on manufacturing wages for the period 1979-90 and show that the change in the skill differential is systematically related to trade. Sectors with high import growth have a disproportionately large drop in the high school/college wage ratio.

The authors then propose simple examples to show that within their framework, trade's relative wage effects can be large. With an economy composed of 20 million manufacturing workers and 80 million nonmanufacturing workers, they postulate a 10 percent reduction in manufacturing attributable to trade.[87] For the base period, the share in manufacturing employment is 70 percent unskilled and 30 percent skilled, whereas the breakdown is approximately 50-50 in nonmanufacturing. A proportional manufacturing cutback would impose onto the nonmanufacturing sector extra unskilled (high school) workers, who represent 3.5 percent of unskilled workers present there. In contrast, the skilled (college) workers imposed on nonmanufacturing amount to only 1.5 percent of skilled workers already present in nonmanufacturing.[88]

If the elasticity of substitution between high school and college workers is 0.5 in nonmanufacturing, the 2 percent (3.5-1.5) increase in the relative supply of unskilled workers will reduce unskilled wages relative to skilled by 4 percent (2 percent/0.5). When the same exercise is rerun concentrating all manufacturing job loss on the unskilled, the calculation yields a rise in the wage gap by 10 percent (5 percent/0.5).

The Sachs and Shatz (1995) formulation is appealing. It more closely approximates an implicit model that could lie behind the thinking of the studies described in "Labor Economists 2" and suggests that trade economists appear to be moving away from SS and product-price tests and toward specific-factors models incorporating nontradables. These specific-factors models can be consistent with greater trade impact on wage inequality than previously thought.

An important recent study is that by Feenstra and Hanson (1995). The authors' theoretical framework leads them to contradict the Lawrence-Slaughter conclusion despite using the same data. Similarly, the authors conduct further tests with the same data used by Berman, Bound, and

---

87. This experiment is curious, because with an unchanged trade balance there should be increased exports to offset increased imports (unless there is a disproportionate rise in services exports).

88. That is, there are 1.4 million unskilled workers displaced from manufacturing (20 million × 10 percent × 70 percent), compared to 40 million present in nonmanufacturing (80 million × 50 percent). Similarly, $20 \times 0.1 \times 0.3 = 0.6$; $0.6/40 = 0.015$.

Griliches (1994) and find a much greater influence of trade on rising wage inequality than do those authors.

Feenstra and Hanson (1995) postulate a world with only a single final manufactured good, but a continuum of possible intermediate goods that may be used to produce the final good. This continuum is indexed by z, ranging from 0 to 1. Production of the input requires $a_H(z)$ units of skilled labor and $a_L(z)$ units of unskilled labor. The index is constructed such that $a_H(z)/a_L(z)$ is strictly rising in z. The production function is Cobb-Douglas in capital and labor, with the labor input being a fixed-coefficient (right-angle isoquant) combination of skilled and unskilled labor.[89]

The authors posit that technologies and factor endowments are sufficiently different that factor prices are not equated. The return on capital is lower in the North than the South ($r_N < r_S$), whereas the ratio of skilled wage (q) to unskilled wage (w) is lower in the North than the South ($q_N/w_N < q_S/w_S$). Capital flows from North to South once the South liberalizes direct investment.

Figure 2.7 shows the locus of minimum costs for inputs produced in the North and the South, along the continuum z. At the left side of the diagram, where techniques are unskilled intensive, the cost function for the South lies below that for the North. At the right side of the diagram, where $a_H(z)/a_L(z)$—relative skill intensity—reaches its maximum, the cost function for the South lies above that for the North. Initially the two functions intersect at z^*. All activities $z > z^*$ will take place in the North, and all activities $z < z^*$ will take place in the South.

Now let capital flow from the North to the South. This reduces the return on capital in the South and raises it in the North. As a result, unit costs rise in the North and decline in the South. The Northern cost curve shifts upward to C'_N, and the Southern cost curve shifts downward to C'_S. They now intersect at z'. Over the range of activities from z^* to z', production now shifts from the North to the South. The authors then reach their first striking conclusion:

> The activities in the range (z^*, z') are more skilled-labor-intensive than any that formerly occurred in the South, but less skilled than any that now occur in the North. Thus, at unchanged wages, this will increase the relative demand for skilled labor in *both* countries. . . . The result is that the relative wage (q_i/w_i) in *both* countries increases. Of course, these factor price changes feed back into figure [2.7], shifting both the cost loci. (8-10)

Here, then, we have just the opposite of the test postulated by Lawrence and Slaughter (1993). According to Lawrence and Slaughter, SS effects should show up in a falling skilled/unskilled ratio in all activities. Leamer

---

89. That is, the labor input is min {$L(z)/a_L(z)$, $H(z)/a_H(z)$}, where L is unskilled and H skilled labor.

Figure 2.7 Locus of minimum costs for inputs produced in the North and South

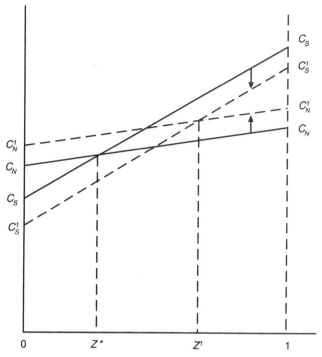

Source: Feenstra and Hanson 1995.

(1994) disputed that proposition on grounds that the SS theorem could hold even if technologies were fixed-coefficient (Leontief). Now Feenstra and Hanson suggest an even stronger proposition: globalization and trade should show up in a rising skilled/unskilled ratio in activities in the North. Moreover, the Feenstra-Hanson model turns on its head the HO property emphasized by Wood (1994): trade should widen wage differentials in the North but should narrow them in the South. Feenstra-Hanson widens wage inequality in the South, because the relative skilled-unskilled demand and, thus, the relative wage rise in both North and South.

There are at least two important shifts in the framework that bring about these seeming reversals. First, Feenstra and Hanson examine the impact of a capital flow, with free trade both before and after. This is globalization, rather than a movement toward free trade. In contrast, the SS theorem examines what happens when free trade is introduced and capital remains immobile. Second, Feenstra and Hanson have dispensed with the two-good world. There is either one good (the final product) or an infinite number of goods (any point along continuum z for intermediate products). Thus, it is not surprising that it is no longer possible to adopt the broad Stolper-Samuelson outcome that every good is a "friend" to a particular factor or, correspondingly, to test for factoral impacts through observing product price trends.

Feenstra and Hanson (1995) further show that the capital flow reduces the factor share of labor in the North but increases it in the South. Nonetheless, even in the North the flow can cause a real increase in the wages of all labor. There is a terms-of-trade improvement relative to the South, and all workers can gain in real terms "if the change in z^* is sufficiently small" (13).

With this simple, powerful, and surprising construct in hand, Feenstra and Hanson then conduct empirical tests that challenge earlier findings of the studies in "Labor Economists 1" and "Trade Economists 1." They reexamine the Lawrence-Slaughter (1993) data and confirm the earlier finding that relative prices of imports intensive in production workers did not fall relative to prices of imports intensive in nonproduction workers (and may have actually risen slightly). However, the authors point out that for the United States, Germany, and Japan, domestic manufacturing prices (whether weighted by production or nonproduction workers) rose faster than import prices, as predicted by their model.[90] They infer:

> This modified Stolper-Samuelson result recognizes that the factor-intensities of Northern production and imports from the South within the same industry are likely to differ, with the domestic industry employing a higher ratio of nonproduction workers. Thus, the increase in the price of domestic production relative to imports is fully consistent with increase in the relative wage of these workers. (18)

Feenstra and Hanson then conduct regressions similar to those of Berman, Bound, and Griliches (1994) for 450 SIC manufacturing industries in 1973-87. They regress the annual percent change in nonproduction workers' share in the wage bill against changes in capital per unit of output (with alternative measures of capital). The authors add the change in the import share (imports relative to domestic shipments plus imports) as a further variable. Although the results depend on the capital variant employed, the overall finding is that "the growth of imports over 1979-87 explains 15-33% of the increase in the share of nonproduction labor" (22).

This finding is highly provocative. It seems to refute the Berman-Bound-Griliches finding of "no room for trade influences" using the same data set. It is not fully clear whether the Feenstra-Hanson regressions pass the model coherence test of Deardorff and Hakura (1994), who bristle at the hint of ad hoc insertion of trade variables into relative wage equations without proper specification (such as identifying what is changing the trade).

---

90. For the United States, they report that manufacturing prices rose by about 33 percent from 1980 to 1989 for domestic goods and only about 27 percent for imports (37).

Perhaps more importantly, Feenstra and Hanson are not sufficiently explicit in interpreting their results in terms of the relative wage debate. Even if their 15 to 33 percent role is accurate, the composition of the changing wage share of nonproduction workers matters. Is the share rising because of higher relative wages, higher relative factor quantities, or both? Rising nonproduction wage shares could be consistent with constant relative wages given the rising relative quantity of nonproduction workers.

Even if the authors had fully distinguished between rising relative wages and relative skill quantity in the rising skilled wage shares, there would still be another step required to interpret the meaning of their fraction of causation attributable to imports. Because the relative supply of skilled labor was rising rapidly in this period, attribution of m percent of relative wage change to the influence of imports could easily be consistent with less than m percent of the composite of effects raising relative skilled wages. Thus, the relative wage for nonproduction workers rose by 8 percent from 1982 to 1990 in the Feenstra-Hanson data (their figure 1).[91] Suppose that the general rise in education and skills would have reduced the skilled/unskilled wage ratio in the absence of trade and other forces (e.g., technological change). Then the total impact of these inequality-widening forces was greater than the 8 percent relative wage increase, and the fraction of the unequalizing forces attributable to trade (accepting the 2 percent impact) was smaller than one-fourth.[92]

The final set of tests in Feenstra and Hanson (1995) concerns US-Mexico trade and investment. The authors stress the large inflows of capital to Mexico in the late 1980s, especially to border maquiladora assembly plants. Mexican industrial data show a rising ratio of skilled to unskilled wages after 1985, especially in border areas. The authors interpret this evidence as supportive of their model (as outlined above, the relative skilled wage rises in both the North and South).[93] However, it seems likely that a major influence on the skill differential in Mexico in this period was the economic dislocation associated with the debt crisis. The authors are cognizant that the real minimum wage fell sharply, but argue that it applied to a minuscule fraction of the labor force. Nonetheless, the macroeconomic crisis almost certainly contributed to low-end wage ero-

---

91. From 1.525 to 1.65.

92. This comment, however, also applies to virtually all of the studies reviewed here. As shown in chapter 5, rising relative supply of skilled labor should have sharply reduced the skilled/unskilled wage ratio over the past two decades, so the sum of all components working in the direction of an increase in this ratio greatly exceeded the net increase in the wage ratio.

93. The authors also find a widening of the variance of skill intensity in Mexico, another implication of their model for the South.

sion. Data for healthy economies such as South Korea and Taiwan would provide a stiffer test of their model.

Overall, nonetheless, the Feenstra-Hanson analysis supports the contention that trade and globalization have substantially contributed to rising wage inequality. Unfortunately, their data set distinguishes between production and nonproduction workers, as most studies do. The 8 percent rise in relative nonproduction wages is much smaller than the rise of about 20 percent in relative college/high school wages over the same period (figure 1.7). As a result, attributing even one-third of the trend to trade and investment generates a small effect, on the order of 2 percent— without assurance that if the proper measure of skills were used (and the larger widening of the differential), the fraction of overall effects attributable to trade would remain the same.

The final entry in this section takes yet another tack. Whereas most of the debate on globalization has focused at least implicitly on whether SS effects are finally playing a significant role in eroding the relative wages of unskilled labor in the United States and other industrial countries, another line of analysis is potentially even more disturbing. This is the notion that as other countries catch up in technological proficiency, the terms of trade for the United States and other leader countries will be depressed because their manufactured exports will face increased competition. The implication is slow growth of real wages and, if the goods with new competition are unskilled intensive, rising skill/wage differentials.

Johnson and Stafford (1992, 1993, 1995) have pressed this theory. They trace it to Hicks (1953), who argued that part of Britain's growth slowdown in the postwar period stemmed from its loss of exports to North America in the face of import-substitute-biased technological change in North America. They also point out that Krugman (1979) analytically modeled essentially the same theory, even though more recently, Krugman (1994) has concentrated on debunking the notion and importance of international competitiveness. It may be added that the Feenstra-Hanson (1995) model is similar in spirit to the Hicks approach, because it emphasizes the consequences of rising capacity of the South to produce the goods previously dominated by the North.

The essence of Johnson and Stafford's work is a two-country, four-sector model in which the follower country (2) gradually becomes competitive in production of a shared tradable good, worsening the terms of trade of the lead country (1). Good A is produced solely by the leader (say, US wide-body aircraft). Good B starts out as the strong preserve of the leader (say, US electronics) but can also be produced by the follower (say, South Korea).[94] Good C is produced only by the follower (say, South Korean apparel). Good D is the domestic nontradable in each country.

---

94. Johnson and Stafford use Britain for the leader and the United States as the follower in the early postwar period, but a US-South Korea variant seems more natural now.

The authors define the expenditure shares on goods A, B, C, and D as, respectively, α, β, γ, and δ. Good C is the price numeraire. All price and income elasticities are unitary. With Cobb-Douglas production functions relating output to labor (N) and capital (K), and an exogenous technological productivity parameter m, they show that there will be three distinct zones of production and trade. In the first zone, only country 1 will produce good B. In the second zone, the technical productivity parameter in country 2 for good B (i.e., m_{B2}) will have risen sufficiently that country 2 also produces good B. In the third zone, this technological improvement will have proceeded further and country 1 will shut down production of good B.

In the simple Stafford-Johnson world, these three zones will correspond to the following:

$$\frac{\alpha + \beta}{\gamma} > \frac{m_{B1}N_1^{\theta}K_1^{1-\theta}}{m_{B2}N_2^{\theta}K_2^{1-\theta}} > \frac{\alpha}{\beta + \gamma}. \tag{2.11}$$

If the first inequality is not satisfied, only country 1 produces good B (zone I in figure 2.8); if, instead, the second is not satisfied, only country 2 produces good B (zone III).

Figure 2.8 summarizes the Johnson-Stafford framework. The vertical axis shows the real income of lead country 1. The horizontal axis shows the technological productivity parameter for follower country 2 in commonly produced tradable good B. The authors conclude the following:

1. Productivity increases in the production of tradables produced exclusively in one country (goods A and C) increase the real wage rates of both countries proportionately;
2. Productivity increases in the production of nontradables in one country increase the real wage in that country but have no effect on the real wage in the other country; and
3. A productivity increase in the tradable sector of one will increase the real wage rate in that country but reduce the real wage rate in other countries that produce that good (Johnson and Stafford 1992, 21).

Thus, in figure 2.8, once country 2 has high enough productivity in good B to begin producing it (at m^1), further increases in its productivity in good B raise the real income of country 2 but reduce the real income of country 1. When country 1 completely phases out of production of good B at the even higher country-2 productivity (m^2), then further increases in country-2 productivity in the good raise real income in both countries.

This overall line of analysis might be called "Hicksian regressive wage convergence." Ironically, it has similar implications to the FPE theorem, yet it has a different theoretical framework, because it explicitly incorporates complete specialization (goods A and C), and, in the first instance, it is about intercountry differences in single-factor prices rather than relative factor prices.

Figure 2.8 Real income in countries 1 and 2 as a function of the efficiency of country 2 in the production of good *B*

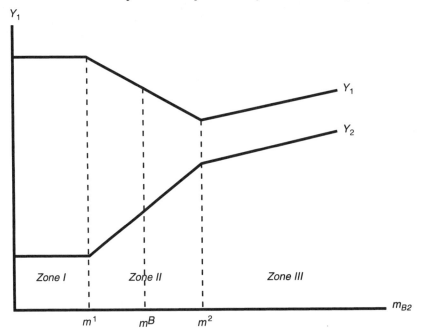

Source: Johnson and Stafford (1995).

As elaborated by Stafford and Johnson, Hicksian regressive wage convergence has pessimistic implications for industrial-country real incomes, under the reasonable assumption that because of technological catch-up, there has been higher productivity growth in traded manufactures in the follower countries (first Japan and now the NICs). The authors argue that the model is consistent with the lag of real wage growth behind productivity growth in the United States. The model identifies the culprit as the ongoing loss in terms of trade as new competitors capture what were formerly lead-country gains from trade.

The authors also suggest that the model can be extended to the process of outsourcing and can thereby help explain rising wage skill differentials. In this formulation of the model,

$$Q_A = m_A S_A^\omega (U_{A1} + b U_{A2})^{1-\omega} \tag{2.12}$$

where Q is output, A refers to the product sector, S is skilled labor (which is available only in country 1), and U is unskilled labor. The latter can be hired at home (U_{A1}) or, through outsourcing, abroad (U_{A2}). As the productivity parameter b of foreign unskilled labor increases, home production of good *A* declines in a manner analogous to the lead country's falling output of good *B* as the follower country catches up (figure 2.8). The falling demand for domestic unskilled labor will increase the wage-skill differential.

Johnson and Stafford do not really test their model (except for a broad-brush characterization of postwar Britain). Thus, Hicksian regressive wage convergence remains more of a specter than a demonstrated source of widening US wage inequality. As the authors note, the model stands in considerable tension with the more usual view that what is good for the developing countries is also good for industrial countries, as growth spillovers tend to be positive.[95]

Development Economists 2

Wood (1994) has conducted the most comprehensive review to date of the impact of North-South trade on wage inequality in the two regions. His point of departure is the literature on the factor content of trade. This approach has essentially asked: What is the composition of factors (skilled labor, *E*; unskilled labor, *L*; and capital, *K*) per unit of exports to LDCs and per unit of imports from LDCs. The conventional approach then estimates the net impact of North-South trade on the demand for each factor by applying the difference in the two skill profiles to the scale of North-South trade. In Wood's terms:

$$\mathbf{Z}_N = X_S(\mathbf{z}_{xN} - \mathbf{z}_{mN}) \tag{2.13}$$

where $\mathbf{Z}_N$ is a vector of net factor demands (in this case, 3×1 for *E*, *L*, and *K*); X_S is the total value of manufactured exports from South to North; and $\mathbf{z}_{xN}$, $\mathbf{z}_{mN}$ are vectors (3×1) of trade-weighted average factor coefficients (*E*, *L*, and *K*) for the exports and imports of the North, respectively.[96]

This formulation abstracts from any imbalance in manufactured trade by implicitly assuming that the exports of manufactures from North to South equal those in the reverse direction (X_S). The presumption is that in vector $\mathbf{Z}_N$, the first entry, *E*, will be positive; the second, *L*, negative;

---

95. In the 1970s when there was greater concern about resource limitations on growth, some worried that growth in the North would preempt future growth opportunities in the South. The usual analytical response was to demonstrate that higher growth in the North widened export market opportunities and stimulated rather than deterred growth prospects for the South. Hicksian convergences constitute a different, non-resource-based reason why growth in the two regions might be substitutes rather than complements.

96. Wood calculates a corresponding net factor impact for the South, with all *N* subscripts on Z correspondingly replaced by *S*, but still scaled by X_S.

and the third, K, of ambiguous sign, because exports from the North are skill intensive, those from the South are intensive in unskilled labor, and the two regions have comparable capital costs because of identical international technology and mobile capital. The last assumption especially is questionable, but it is not the principal focus here.

Wood's principal critique of the conventional approach is that it is mistaken to apply the North's factor coefficients when evaluating the impact of imports from the South (i.e., z_{mN}). He argues that the bulk of manufactured imports from LDCs comprise goods that have been phased out of production in industrial countries, because their labor-intensive nature makes them too expensive to produce where labor is costly.

Under the strong assumption that all imports from LDCs are "noncompeting" goods, the author asks what would be their factor-displacing impact when measured not at the North's coefficients but instead at appropriate counterfactual coefficients. The counterfactual is based in the first instance on the actual coefficients observed in the South, but makes allowance for the likely substitutions that would occur if the South faced the same relative factor prices as does the North. This adjustment makes the counterfactual coefficient profile for imports from the South more skill intensive and less unskilled intensive than the actual coefficients in the South. Even so, the profile remains less skill intensive and much more unskilled intensive than the exports from the North, essentially because the influence of "different products" is far greater than the difference induced by factor prices.

Wood (1994) thus proposes that the estimated factor content of trade be revised to:

$$Z_N = X_S(z_{xN} - z_{xS}^*). \qquad (2.14)$$

This time the coefficient of factor requirements to be subtracted off to account for imports from LDCs is estimated not by sectoral coefficients in the North but by those characterizing export sectors in the South, after adjustment to the counterfactual profile at Northern relative factor prices.

Wood's central estimate is that each $1,000 of exports of manufactures from the North contains 21 hours of skilled labor, 20.8 hours of unskilled labor, and $582 in capital. In contrast, $1,000 of exports from the South contains 31.7 hours of skilled labor, 207.5 hours of unskilled labor, and $426 in capital (at Southern prices). The disparity is the most extreme in the case of unskilled labor.

Wood first adjusts the South's coefficients to Northern quality (for skilled labor) and prices (for capital), which change the coefficients to 15.8 hours of skilled labor and $709 in capital (but leaves unskilled labor unchanged). He then applies his relative factor price adjustment and winds up with the following counterfactual coefficients for Southern exports, per $1,000: 23 hours of skilled labor, 139.7 hours of unskilled labor, and $1,137 in capital.[97] Thus, despite the adjustment for substitution in response to the different relative factor prices, his factor requirement profile remains not much different between North and South for either skilled labor or capital, but exceedingly different for unskilled labor.

Even after adjustment to Northern factor price ratios, Wood's total labor coefficients for the South's manufactured exports are 162.7 person-hours per $1,000, compared with only 41.8 hours for exports from the North. This fourfold divergence is the driving force in his results, which sharply differ from the finding of small employment effects usually encountered in the literature on North-South trade (as reviewed above). In comparison, the Balassa (1986) study placed the North's import labor coefficient at only 2.5 percent higher than its export labor coefficient.[98]

The central question about the Wood study is whether the strong assumption of noncompeting goods and the corresponding logic of using adjusted Southern rather than straightforward Northern labor coefficients to calculate the impact of imports make sense. The answer might be no for two reasons.

First, Wood's key assumption that all manufactured imports from the South are noncompeting goods seems extreme. In a large US sample survey of retail products in 1978, enumerators had no difficulty finding comparable products produced domestically and imported from developing countries (Cline 1979). It is possible that over the last decade specialization has increased, but it seems nonetheless likely that for such key products as apparel, textiles, footwear, and electronic goods, at least half of LDC exports are in competing rather than noncompeting goods.

Second, even for noncompeting goods we must ask whether Wood has properly taken account of international differences in efficiency— essentially the question of whether the production function or factor quality differs between North and South. By Wood's estimates it takes four times as much labor and almost twice as much capital to produce a given value of output in the South's export sector as in that of the North (1994, 136). It seems likely that although some of this difference might be attributable to different products, much of it could be caused by lower

---

97. Wood uses a two-stage CES production function methodology in which capital and skilled labor form a composite factor, which is then combined with unskilled labor. This function is used to calculate the counterfactual Southern factor ratio at Northern relative factor prices. For example, there is an eightfold multiple between the ratio of the unskilled wage to the price of capital in the North and that ratio in the South. With Wood's elasticity of substitution of 0.5 between composite skills-capital and unskilled labor, the shift to Northern factor prices would imply cutting the Southern unskilled/skilled factor ratio to $\frac{1}{8}^{1/2} = 0.35$ of its actual value, close to the 58 percent cut specifically estimated by Wood.

98. Note that at least the coefficients for Northern exports are comparable. Balassa's 15 workers per million dollars is not radically different from the 21 workers implied by the Wood estimate (assuming 2,000 hours per year).

quality factors in the South and a different, inferior production technology.[99]

Wood's first calculation contrasts the unadjusted with the adjusted factor-content-of-trade estimate (equation 2.13 versus 2.14). Using a 1985 trade base, he finds that LDC exports of manufactures displace 1.1 million jobs in the North using the usual, unadjusted method, but that the figure rises to 12.7 million jobs using the adjusted method. This radical difference is to be expected given the 4-fold multiplication of the labor coefficient for Northern imports in the adjusted method (with this difference mushrooming to 12-fold because one is dealing with differences between import and export levels, rather than with the levels themselves).

Wood then refines the estimates. These are based on a counterfactual experiment in which the primary exports of the South remain unchanged, the trade balance of the South drops from a $56 billion surplus to zero, and the North not only increases its manufactured exports by enough to reach a zero trade balance but its exports of unskilled-labor-intensive manufactures constitute half of the new total.[100] The counterfactual makes adjustments for induced effects (such as the reduction in the North's estimates of skill-intensive exports that formerly went as inputs into the South's manufactured exports). It also is careful in translating trade effects into output effects.[101] The elaborate counterfactual does not change the overall result much, however. The net job loss for the North attributable to manufactured imports from the South drops to nine million workers, qualitatively a result similar to that from simply applying adjusted factor-content-of-trade coefficients to the base volume of this trade (equation 2.14).

The counterfactual experiment does, however, provide additional detail on skilled versus unskilled labor. It turns out that the employment effect for the North is almost wholly from a loss in unskilled jobs (9.2 million),

---

99. Wood does attempt to convert Southern units to Northern norms. He sets a Southern skilled worker at half the quality of the Northern counterpart and adjusts capital requirements for the fact that constant quality capital goods cost only 60 percent as much to construct in the South as in the North. But he makes no adjustment for unskilled labor quality nor any further adjustment for difference in the production function (technology).

100. A more natural formulation would have been to examine changes in labor-intensive import substitutes in the domestic market, rather than assume that the North would be able to export these goods to the South.

101. One of the more telling adjustments is Wood's calculation that cutting off manufactured imports from the South would triple the price Northern consumers would have to pay for domestic substitutes (because of their high unskilled labor content and the high price of unskilled labor in the North). Thus, Wood adjusts the volume by applying a price elasticity of demand to the increase in unit price. The resultantly lower volume of the import substitute, rather than the actual volume of imports, then forms the base to which the counterfactual factor coefficient is applied to calculate the change in factor demand that would occur from producing the manufactures in the North rather than importing them from LDCs.

countered by an almost negligible increase in skilled jobs (0.1 million). The key result is Wood's estimate that manufactured imports from LDCs reduce the demand for unskilled labor in the North by 5.3 percent (and by 12 percent of employment in manufacturing) (1994, 149).

Wood then extrapolates his estimate dramatically. He adopts two sweeping assumptions that each double his calculated labor impact. First, there are labor-saving technological changes induced in the North in response to import pressure from the South, and these effects are at least as large in reducing Northern demand for unskilled labor as are the trade effects themselves. As Burtless (1995a) has pointed out, however, Wood is trying to have it both ways here. He argues that the manufactured imports from the South are solely in noncompeting goods. But if that is true, these goods have no Northern domestic counterpart production sector to be subjected to pressure for labor-saving biased technological change. So Wood can have either noncompeting goods and no induced technical change, or competing goods and induced technological change, but not both as he desires.

Wood's second meta-assumption superimposed on the counterfactual estimates is that the calculations for merchandise trade should be expanded by 50 percent to take account of trade in services and by 40 percent to take account of induced intermediate effects in nontraded services. These adjustments too seem to be seriously exaggerated.

Consider LDC exports of nonfactor services (i.e., excluding capital income and worker remittances). Wood's ratio of 50 percent to merchandise trade seems overstated. Cline (1989, 143, 245) places the ratio of these service exports to merchandise exports at a weighted average of 14 percent. Wood (1994, 139) estimates that manufactures accounted for 34.3 percent of LDC merchandise exports in 1985, with primary goods representing 46 percent and processed primary goods 19.6 percent. On this basis, nonfactor services exports should be 41 percent of manufactured exports (14/34.3). Moreover, of nonfactor services exports, about one-third are earned in tourism.[102] It makes no sense to postulate that foreign tourists visiting South Korea, for example, are doing so at the expense of an expansion of industrial-country exports of tourist services to South Korea through greater South Korean visits to industrial countries. So Wood's 50 percent expansion from merchandise trade should be reduced to two-thirds of 41 percent, 27 percent.

For nontraded services that are used as inputs into traded goods, the problem is more fundamental. There is no reason to suppose that the factor intensities of intermediate inputs should be correlated with those of the input-using sectors. Wood postulates high unskilled-labor-intensive

---

102. For 1990, the weighted average is 35 percent for Argentina, Brazil, Mexico, South Korea, Singapore, and India (calculated from IMF 1994a; 1994b).

output replacing imports from LDCs in his counterfactual, but presumably the intermediate inputs into these products would be no more unskilled-labor-intensive than is generally true for the Northern economy. The application of Wood's fourfold labor ratio would surely be inappropriate for the intermediate inputs, including those from nontraded services.

In sum, Wood identifies a 5.3 percent reduction in demand for unskilled labor in the North as a consequence of manufactured trade with developing countries. He doubles this estimate to account for induced labor-saving innovation and doubles it once again for consideration of traded and nontraded services. His resulting estimate is that imports of manufactures from LDCs depress the demand for unskilled labor in the North by 22 percent of the unskilled labor force. He concludes that this shift in demand can account for 100 percent of the observed changes in relative wages (Wood 1994, 261). Of the total shift, 70 percent is likely to have occurred in the 1980s.

However, a "corrected" estimate might start by defining a series of fractional estimates, λ, that shrink Wood's estimates to more plausible values. Let λ_1 be the fraction of manufactured imports from LDCs that are noncompeting. Let λ_2 be the ratio of the unskilled-labor displacement effect that would be expected on competing imports relative to those on noncompeting imports. Let λ_3 be a fraction to be applied to the employment estimates to take account of differences in underlying factor quality and production functions not already captured by Wood. Let λ_{4n} be the fraction of Wood's doubling for induced innovation that should be allowed for noncompeting goods and λ_{4c} the corresponding fraction for competing goods. Let λ_5 be the fraction that should be allowed of Wood's expansion multiple of 1.5 to include traded services and λ_6 the corresponding fraction for his expansion for intermediate nontraded services.

Wood's unskilled-labor impact as a percent of the Northern unskilled labor force is estimated as $5.3 \times E_T \times E_{ts} \times E_{nts}$, where E is the expansion factor, and subscripts T, ts, and nts refer to induced technological change, traded services, and nontraded services. Thus, his estimate is 22.3 percent ($5.3 \times 2 \times 1.5 \times 1.4$). The adjusted estimate applying the factors just enumerated would then be $[\lambda_1 \times (5.3 \times \lambda_3 \times \lambda_{4n} \times 2) \times (\lambda_5 \times 1.5) \times (\lambda_6 \times 1.4)] + [(1 - \lambda_1) \times (\lambda_2 \times 5.3) \times (\lambda_{4c} \times 2) \times (\lambda_5 \times 1.5) \times (\lambda_6 \times 1.4)]$. Reasonable adjustment factors might be as follows. Only 40 percent of LDC manufactured imports are noncompeting ($\lambda_1 = 0.4$). Labor displacement on competing versus noncompeting goods is only one-third as large ($\lambda_2 = 0.33$).[103] Shrinkage for different technology and factor quality is 20 percent ($\lambda_3 = 0.8$). Induced technological change for noncompeting goods is nonexistent ($\lambda_{4n} = 0.5$).[104] The same concept for competing goods

103. The fraction might be as small as one-twelfth, given the difference between Wood's unadjusted and adjusted FCT estimates (equations 2.1 and 2.2).

104. This shrinkage factor is against $E_T = 2$.

is two-thirds of the doubling used by Wood ($\lambda_{4c} = 0.83$). Expansion for traded services is cut from 50 percent to 27 percent ($\lambda_5 = 0.85$). And expansion for nontraded intermediate inputs of services is cut from 40 percent to 10 percent ($\lambda_6 = 0.79$).

These adjustment factors cut Wood's 22 percent reduction in demand for unskilled labor in the North to 4.9 percent. Of this amount, 2.7 percent represents the direct effects (corresponding to Wood's 5.3 percent) and the remaining 2.2 percent represents the expansion for induced technological change and for traded and nontraded services (as contrasted with Wood's extra 16.9 percent for these influences).

Overall, Wood's study is a major contribution to the literature on the labor impact of North-South trade in manufactures, but its estimate of this impact would seem seriously overstated (especially the final estimate with the expansion factors overlaid on the direct estimate from counterfactual labor requirements).

Trade Economists 1 Revisited

Krugman (1995a, 1995b) has fired the latest volleys in the debate. They are pointed toward the studies in "Trade Economists 2" and, curiously, come to the aid of the studies in "Labor Economists 2," previously a target area for Krugman's fire. The crux of Krugman's refocused analysis is (1) because LDC trade remains small, it cannot have had major effects on industrial-country factor prices (an argument he had made before); (2) the trade-theoretic propositions to the contrary from studies in "Trade Economists 2" are misleading; and (3) Krugman's mea culpa, the factor content of trade analysis of the studies in "Labor Economists 2" was theoretically acceptable after all, and the important thing to realize is that it is consistent with the small effects expected from the small relative magnitude of LDC trade.

Krugman (1995a) drives home the "small trade, small effect" argument by setting forth a simple general equilibrium model of OECD trade with LDCs (as set forth in detail in chapter 3 below). There are two factors (skilled and unskilled labor) and two goods (the OECD skill-intensive export and unskilled-intensive import). He dispenses with capital, because the constant capital-labor shares in western economies make it a neutral actor for purposes of the important distributional trends.

Factor inputs in each sector depend on the relative wage. In the "American" model there is full employment and wage flexibility. All elasticities (production and consumption) are unitary (Cobb-Douglas). The initial ratio of skilled to unskilled wages is 2, the sectoral ratios of skilled to unskilled workers are 0.5 in good 1 (export) and 0.2 in good 2 (import), and skilled workers are 40 percent of the labor force. LDC entry into manufactured trade from virtually zero in 1970 to present levels is simulated by imposition of an external offer curve of imports amounting to 2.2 percent of OECD output, about the present level. This impact is only enough to raise the relative price of the skilled (export) good by 1 percent. Because of the magnification effect, the relative wage for skilled labor rises by 3 percent.

Thus, Krugman finds support in his simple general equilibrium model for his earlier view that LDC trade has been too small to have been a primary source of widening wage inequality. Specifically, he interprets his results to mean that the advent of LDC manufactured trade has contributed only about one-tenth of the erosion of relative unskilled wages for the United States (implying 30 percent as his estimate of the increase in the skilled/unskilled wage ratio, somewhat higher than the estimates suggested in chapter 1 above). He also shows that when the wage ratio is set rigidly, as in the "European" model, the result of new LDC supply is an increase in unemployment. For the American model, an important inference he draws is that the relative price change is too small (1 percent) to pick out from the statistical noise. Thus, there could have been a trade impact on relative wages despite the absence of an observed relative product price change consistent with the SS theorem.

Krugman further maintains that in his model, larger future North-South trade does not pose much threat. It requires only a 50 percent rise in the skilled/unskilled wage ratio from OECD autarky levels (and a corresponding 14.5 percent rise in the relative price of good 1) to cause complete specialization in the skill-intensive good and, thus, a halt to any possibility for still further relative wage change as a consequence of trade. Yet, this point is far beyond likely prospects, because it occurs when manufactured imports from LDCs have reached 29 percent of OECD GDP.

It is unclear how sensitive these results are to the particular elasticities assumed, and how the outcome might be altered by such important modifications as introducing a nontraded sector.[105] Chapter 3 of this study examines the first question, and chapter 4 examines the second. Nonetheless, the exercise provisionally strengthens Krugman's "small effects," while pointing the way to the need for more thorough general equilibrium modeling of the issue.

The misleading inferences from partial equilibrium analysis are an underlying theme of Krugman (1995b). Krugman first criticizes Leamer's (1994) argument that the small volume of LDC trade is "irrelevant . . . [because] prices are determined on the margin" (Krugman 1995b, 2). Krugman must of course refute this proposition if he is to sustain the principle that "small trade means small effects."[106] For this purpose Krug-

---

105. Discussant T. N. Srinivasan expressed skepticism about the significance of the numerical results (373).

106. My summation, not his.

man needs only invoke his general equilibrium exercise (Krugman 1995a) as counterevidence. In this debate, the intuitive appeal surely lies with Krugman's position. Indeed, my discomfort with the notion of an unlimited vent of home surplus of unskilled labor through trade (discussed above) similarly rests on the point that economic sizes matter. Like Krugman's analysis, this doubt suggests that the essential problem is that some trade theorists have approached the issue by treating the United States (or even the OECD) as a small country and LDC trade as an infinite international market, when for practical purposes the reverse is true. The obvious next volley is for Leamer or someone else to reformulate the analysis with explicit attention to relative economic size (ideally, with product differentiation and even upgrading).

A second broad point in Krugman (1995b) is that the critique of Leamer (1994) dismissing the importance of skill-biased technological change is mistaken because it is premised on the small-country, partial-equilibrium case used in classrooms to illustrate the SS theorem, whereas, in fact, the international spread of technological change makes its effect closer to that in a closed economy. In such a case, the traditional Hicksian effects dominate, rather than the SS product-price straitjacket. Skill-biased technological change raises the relative wage of skilled labor.[107]

In the same article, Krugman revises his earlier grade given to the studies in "Labor Economists 2" on their implicit trade theory. This time, instead of failing, they pass with flying colors, even though they may have only guessed at the right answer. The reason, once again, is relative size: in a world where the OECD essentially moves from autarky to modest trade in manufactures with LDCs, the changes are sufficiently marginal (as in the general equilibrium model just described) that the factor content of trade calculations (in the style of "Labor Economists 2," not Wood 1994) turns out to be a close approximation of the proper estimates.

Krugman reaches this conclusion by starting with a closed (OECD) economy, where it must be true that the proportionate relative wage change looks like

$$\hat{w} = -\frac{\hat{S} - \hat{U}}{\sigma_A} \tag{2.15}$$

where the circumflex is proportionate change, S is the supply of skilled labor, U is the supply of unskilled labor, and σ_A is an aggregate elasticity of substitution. The factor content of trade calculation becomes legitimate because trade is so small that calculus may be used to obtain a linearized

---

107. Krugman first satisfies himself that the admittedly anemic total factor productivity growth has been sufficient over the past two decades for the skill-biased change story to be consistent with the rise in the relative use of skilled workers.

impact on effective labor supply. Trade balances in goods X and Y may be written as $dQ_X - dC_X$ and $dQ_Y - dC_Y$. The change in effective supply for skilled labor is thus $dS^e = (dC_X - dQ_X)(S_X/Q_X) + (dC_Y - dQ_Y)(S_Y/Q_Y)$, and similarly for unskilled labor (dU^e). The eventual result is

$$\hat{w} = \left[\frac{dS^e}{S} - \frac{dU^e}{U} \right] \Big/ \sigma_A.$$

(2.16)

This is parallel to the closed economy version, essentially because marginal trade is small. Thus, "[t]he change in factor prices from trade will, indeed, equal the change in 'effective' factor supplies divided by the aggregate elasticity of substitution, just as the advocates of the factor content approach have claimed" (Krugman 1995b, 26).

Krugman's reading of the estimates in "Labor Economists 2" is that trade has been a minor influence on growing wage inequality. However, as reviewed above, a careful reading of that literature does not necessarily lead to this conclusion. Lawrence and Slaughter (1993, 164) cite the figure from Borjas, Freeman, and Katz (1992) of "at most, 15 percent" as the share of the increase in the college/high school wage differential from 1980 to 1988 attributable to trade. But they, and apparently Krugman, gloss over the fact that the same study finds that trade and immigration were responsible for about 40 percent of the increased wage differential between high school dropouts and all other workers in the same period (as reviewed above). It is unclear whether Krugman is equally comfortable with accepting this estimate, in view of his theoretical resurrection of the labor economists' factor content of trade calculation.

Labor Economists 1 Revisited

The final study to be considered in this survey returns to the original camp: the group of labor economists who think trade and immigration have played only a marginal role in rising wage inequality. Burtless (1995b) introduces new evidence that makes him somewhat less sympathetic than before (Burtless 1995a) to the position of Wood (1994) and others who argue for a major trade impact.

Using CPS data, Burtless (1995b) classifies workers into three groups: most trade affected, intermediate, and least trade affected. His first point is that trade cannot be of overwhelming importance, because it must work through wages, and wages can only explain part of the trend toward inequality. Thus,

> In sum, increased earnings inequality *among persons who work* is the single most important source of increased U.S. income inequality, but it does not account for even half of the growth in overall income inequality. Changes in family composition, declining male labor force participation, increases in unearned income, and

a sharp rise in the correlation of married partners' earnings account for more than half of the growth in U.S. income inequality. (30)

This emphasis on social structure is similar to that suggested in chapter 1 in consideration of poverty trends. However, such trends do not eliminate grounds for concern about rising wage inequality. Indeed, rising inequality from these other factors might appropriately provide a basis for even greater concern about rising inequality deriving from the economy's changing productive structure, because society has less cushion to absorb the extra pressure on inequality.

The core of Burtless's (1995b) analysis is the argument that if trade is a major factor in rising skill differentials in wages, one should observe contrary trends in skilled/unskilled factor ratios and wage ratios in traded versus nontraded goods sectors. Thus, the trade impact argument "does not provide an obvious explanation for the drop in demand for less-skilled workers outside the traded-goods sector" (31). Instead, as low-skilled workers are shed by the traded goods sector, "employers [elsewhere] . . . can now hire less-skilled workers for lower pay . . . [and] they should move to adopt technologies that rely heavily on workers with limited skill" (31). Accordingly, the factor-content-of-trade analyses of Murphy and Welch (1991), Borjas, Freeman, and Katz (1992), and especially Wood (1994) "would be more persuasive if it could be shown that the intensity of use of less-skilled workers has fallen more sharply in trade-affected than in non-trade-affected industries" (36).

The author accordingly sorts the CPS data files into three sectors: most trade affected (labeled here MTA: manufacturing, mining and agriculture, forestry and fisheries); least trade affected (LTA: construction, retail trade, personal services, professional and related services, and public administration); and intermediate sectors (ITA: transportation, wholesale trade, finance, insurance, real estate, business and repair services, entertainment and recreation). He then examines the trends of male and female wage inequality for each sector. The data refer to full-time, year-round workers.

Using the ratio of the wage at the 90th percentile to the wage at the 10th percentile, Burtless finds that from 1979 to 1993 the proportionate increase of this ratio among male workers was almost identical in the LTA sectors (from 4.14 to 5.36, 29.4 percent) and the MTA sectors (from 3.71 to 4.69, a 26.4 percent increase). He considers this evidence against a trade impact. However, for female workers the increase in the $90^{th}/10^{th}$ percentile ratio was modestly greater in the MTA sectors (from 2.99 to 4.00, 33.8 percent) than in the LTA sectors (from 3.57 to 4.67, 30.8 percent). He acknowledges that this outcome could reflect a trade impact on female workers; a concentrated trade impact on female workers is reminiscent of the Sachs-Shatz findings on concentration in apparel, textiles, and footwear and the above-cited observation of Katz and Murphy (1992) that female high school dropouts have been disproportionately affected by the trade impact on these sectors.

Burtless (1995b) then turns to a second test, based on educational-level wage differentials. He again finds mixed patterns, with no clear differences between MTA and LTA. He then somewhat belatedly acknowledges that in an efficient labor market, wages for a given skill should be identical throughout the economy, so that the trends for wage ratios and skill differentials should not be expected to differ between MTA and LTA. Accordingly, he tries a third test using a quantity indicator rather than the price: the relative number employed. He finds "little evidence that less-skilled workers were shed faster in trade-affected than in non-trade-affected industries" and considers this "hard to square with the claim that earnings inequality has been driven mainly by pressures originating in foreign trade." Arguing that employers in LTA should have had an incentive to hire low-skilled workers if such workers were being displaced by trade, he considers the overall evidence to show that "the proportion of inequality that is attributable to liberalized trade or rising imports from developing countries must be quite small" (44).

A closer look at Burtless's summary table (1995b, 5) seems to show just the opposite, however, using his criterion of the relative number of skilled and unskilled employed. For the period 1979-93, when most of the trade impact is perceived to have occurred, there does seem to be a systematic tendency toward greater shedding of unskilled workers and shift toward skilled workers in MTA than in LTA and ITA, for both males and females. Thus, in LTA the ratio of college graduates to high school or less-educated workers rose by 38.4 percent over this period, compared with increases of 65.4 percent in ITA and 75.6 percent in MTA. The divergence was even more dramatic for females. The ratio of college to high school employees rose by 69 percent in LTA, but soared by 177 percent in ITA and by 212 percent in MTA.

In short, Burtless acknowledges that on two of the three criteria, his test is inappropriate (under efficient wage diffusion across sectors). On the test that is appropriate, his data seem to show a clear pattern consistent with the argument that trade matters: the intensity of the shift from unskilled to skilled workers was strictly and positively related to the degree of trade relevance among the three sectors.

Burtless's alternative interpretation, that the trends are mixed, seems to be based on looking at the absolute levels of the indexes, which have 1969 as a base. All three sectors show reductions of high school workers by about 30 to 40 percent from 1969 to 1993. However, a ceteris paribus test should adjust for a generalized shift in the economy toward skilled and away from unskilled labor. To do this it is necessary to look not at the absolute decline in unskilled workers by sector but instead at the ratio of skilled to unskilled, as done here. On this relative basis and when the focus is on the period 1979-93, the conclusion shifts to supporting the hypothesis of trade impact.

Overview

Table 2.3 summarizes the studies reviewed here. These results may be synthesized as follows.

Extent of Rising Wage Inequality

Most of the studies use one of two definitions for skilled versus unskilled labor: (a) nonproduction versus production workers in manufacturing and (b) educational distinctions (e.g., more than high school versus high school or less). During the 1980s, the increase in the skilled/unskilled ratio was about 8 percent under the first definition and about 15 percent under the second (chapter 1, figure 1.7). The educational definition is usually considered superior.

Proportion of Rising Inequality Attributable to Trade

The final column of table 2.3 reports the central estimate for each study of the fraction of the increase in the skilled/unskilled wage ratio attributable to trade, immigration, and/or globalization (and, in one case, to deunionization). There is a concentration in the distribution of estimates somewhere in the range of 10 to 15 percent of causation. However, there are important extremes as well. The most obvious extreme is that of Wood (1994), who places 100 percent of the causation on trade over the past two decades and 70 percent over the 1980s. Leamer (1992) may also be interpreted as attributing 100 percent or more of the widening skill differential to trade (as discussed above), although at one point he translates his results into only 20 percent of the total transfer away from unskilled labor. The other extreme estimate at the high end is that by Karoly and Klerman (1994).

At the other extreme, Berman, Bound, and Griliches (1994), Bound and Johnson (1992), and Lawrence and Slaughter (1993) attribute little if any role to trade, and an overwhelming role to technological change. The Bernard-Jensen (1994) study casts serious doubt on this monocausal allocation to technological change.

The Krugman (1995a) study suggests 10 percent as the contribution of North-South trade to the rising skill differential over the past two decades. This estimate supersedes his earlier diagnosis of minimal impact. However, Krugman's estimate of a 3 percent impact is more appropriately expressed against a central estimate of 18 percent for the increase in the

Table 2.3 Alternative estimates of the impact of trade on rising US wage inequality[a]

Author	Type	Portion of change due to trade[b]	Remarks
Labor Economists 1			
Bound and Johnson 1992	Ed, Ex	T: minimal	Detailed econometric study attributes almost all causation to technological change (residual). Only 2 of 17 aggregate sectors are tradables.
Mincer 1991	Ed, Ex	T: small	Aggregates regressions with research and development and trade balance; finds primary influence is technological change.
Juhn, Murphy, and Pierce 1993	Ed, Ex	T: ?	Finds rising demand for skills as cause, but noncommittal between technological change and changes in the world economy.
Berman, Bound, and Griliches 1994	NPR/PR	T: minimal	Decomposes skills changes into between- and within-sector for 450 manufacturing sectors. Small "between" implies limited trade effect. Main influence is technological change.
Freeman 1991	Ed, Ex	T: ? U: 15-40 percent	Wage regressions on age, education, race, occupation, and union dummy. Coefficient applied to falling union density.
Burtless 1995	90/10	T: small	Divides current population survey (CPS) wage data into high, moderate, and nontradable. Interprets wage and employment trends as showing neutral impact for trade.
Labor Economists 2			
Katz and Murphy 1992	Ed, Ex	T: modest	Decomposition analysis finds trade reduced demand for HSDO by 0.6 to 4 percent and increased demand for CG by 0.6 to 1.5 percent. Overall between-industry effects larger. Cites (incorrectly?) trade deficit. Invokes technological change as main influence.
Murphy and Welch 1991	Ed	T: moderate	Divides CPS data into 3 tradable and 1 nontradable sectors. Shift to large trade deficit reduced unskilled-intensive durables, boosted skilled-nontradable services.

Study	Description	Method	Estimate
Borjas, Freeman, and Katz 1992	Uses CPS data for 22 manufacturing sectors to calculate labor embodied in trade. Finds in mid-1980s trade deficit added 4-13 percent to effective supply of HSDOs and increased immigration added 13 percent. Ignores induced nontradables demand from macroeconomic imbalance. Also, effect diminishes.	Ed	T and I: CG/HS, 20 percent; Othr/HSDO, 40 percent
Borjas and Ramey 1994	Cointegration tests relate wage differential to trade balance in durable manufactures. Wage rent hypothesis.	Ed	T: very high
Borjas and Ramey 1993	Regressions on metropolitan CPS data.	Ed	T: 10 percent; I: 20 percent; c
Revenga 1992	Regresses all manufacturing employment and wages on trade balance. Substantial deficit impact.	c	
Karoly and Klerman 1994	CPS data show 13 percent of inequality rise due to shifts from manufacturing to services. Regional tests show 55-141 percent of inequality rise due to rising durable goods imports.	log-normal	T: 55-141 percent
Borjas 1994	Rising volume of immigrants and rising share with little education.	Ed	I: 1/3 of Othr/HSDO; n.a.
Bernard and Jensen 1994	Uses 50,000 observations at plant level to show that between-plant demand shifts, especially to exporting plants, account for much of rising nonproduction worker share.	NPR/PR	

Trade Economists 1

Study	Description	Method	Estimate
Lawrence and Slaughter 1993	Relative prices of unskilled-intensive imports not falling; skilled/unskilled labor quantities rising; Stolper-Samuelson effects rejected.	NPR/PR	T: none
Krugman and Lawrence 1994	Share of total employment in skill-intensive industries minimal rise; less-developed country (LDC) trade is small.	c	T: minimal
Bhagwati and Dehejia 1994	Stolper-Samuelson assumptions unrealistic; labor studies ignore theory (e.g., goods price test).	c	
Sachs and Shatz 1994	Increased net imports (1978-90) reduced relative unskilled/skilled manufacturing employment by 5 percent.	NPR/PR	T: very small
Cooper 1994	Decline in textile, apparel, and leather manufacturing as impact of trade upon unskilled.	Ed	T: 10 percent

(continued next page)

Table 2.3 Alternative estimates of the impact of trade on rising US wage inequality[a] (continued)

Author	Remarks	Type	Portion of change due to trade[b]
Baldwin and Cain 1994	Sectoral price regressions on factor shares give implicit factor price changes. Supply shifts dominate 1970s; 1980s more ambiguous. Deardorff-Staiger model for wage impact.	Ed	T: 9 percent (14 percent)
Krugman 1995a	General equilibrium approach; LDC imports of 2 percent of Organization for Economic Cooperation and Development GDP cause 1 percent relative price and 3 percent relative wage change against the unskilled.	Hyp	T: 10 percent
Trade Economists 2			
Leamer 1992	Regresses product profile on factor endowments (Rybczynski) as dual to wages on product prices (Stolper-Samuelson). 1972-85 trade reduced US unskilled wages $1,000 and raised skilled wages $6,000.	SEM	T: major
Leamer 1994	Debates Lawrence and Krugman on factor ratio test, technology impact theory, and Rybczynski regressions.	N.S.	T: 20 percent
Leamer 1995	Regression tests on the role of technological change, with globalization as the residual.	N.S.	G: most
Sachs and Shatz 1995	Model of unskilled-manufactures labor shedding onto skill-intensive nontradables. 10 percent cutback in manufacturing raises skill premium 4-10 percent.	Hyp	T: moderate
Feenstra and Hanson 1995	One-good, many-intermediates model. Capital flow to South raises skill differential in both North and South. Regresses skill share on import share.	NPR/PR	G: 15-33 percent
Johnson and Stafford 1992, 1993, 1995	Hicksian technological convergence erodes North's terms of trade on good produced in common with South.	Hyp	c

Development Economists 1

Wood 1994 — Factor content of trade analysis with Northern import impacts using adjusted Southern factor requirements; induced technological changes. LDC manufactured imports have reduced Northern relative demand for unskilled labor by 14-30 percent and 10-21 percent in 1980s. — d — T: implicit, 1/3 to 2/3

a. During the 1980s unless otherwise stated.
b. T: Trade; I: Immigration; G: Globalization; and U: Unionization.
c. Wage differentials not examined.
d. Based on white-collar/blue-collar distinction, and subgroups.

Notes:
Ed, Ex: Education and experience differentials
NPR/PR: Nonproduction/production worker wage differentials
90/10: Ratio of 90th to 10th percentile wages
HSDO: High school dropout; HS: high school; CG: college graduate; Othr: all other
Hyp: hypothetical skilled/unskilled; SEM: scientists, engineers, managers = skilled
N.S.: not specified
n.a.: not available

US skilled/unskilled wage ratio from 1973 to 1993 (chapter 1, figure 1.7). Thus, the Krugman estimate amounts to 17 percent of the rise in the skilled wage ratio rather than 10 percent.

Similarly, Krugman (1995b) refurbishes the theoretical consistency of the labor economists using factor content of trade, thereby nullifying his earlier critique. These estimates, in turn, are typically at the mode of the distribution: about 15 to 20 percent of total causation (e.g., Borjas, Freeman, and Katz 1992). Cooper's (1994) 10 percent estimate seems a reasonable lower bound, considering that he treats only three product sectors.

A reasonable estimate based solely on the literature reviewed in this chapter would be that international influences contributed about 20 percent of the rising wage inequality in the 1980s.[108] This point estimate from the literature for the impact of external influences would be higher as the unskilled category shifts toward lower skills and as the definition widens to include migration. Based on the Borjas, Freeman, and Katz (1992) estimates, perhaps one-third to 40 percent of the decline of the relative wage of high school dropouts can be attributed to international factors, especially migration. Moreover, the Feenstra-Hanson (1995) results suggest about one-fourth for the contribution for outsourcing to rising wage inequality, adding a considerable impact when the widest definition of causes is used, even if the outsourcing component is smaller than they calculate.

I consider the Wood (1994) estimates to be exaggerated, as argued above. The Leamer (1992) estimate is sufficiently indirect that it seems primarily illustrative, and, in any event, Leamer has translated it to only 20 percent of the observed relative factor share loss for unskilled labor.

What, then, caused the other 70 to 80 percent of widening inequality? The review here suggests that the standard answer—technological change—is probably too facile and overstated. It is typically only based on unexplained residuals. Even so, it probably plays a major role. But an also large part of the other 70 to 80 percent of causation seems to be simply unexplained increases in earnings dispersion for seemingly identically

---

108. Rodrik (1997) has adopted this benchmark, in part based on the survey provided in the present study. He suggests a new reason why existing estimates may be understated. By imposing a new potential threat of job loss, globalization (trade, immigration, and outsourcing) may have increased the wage elasticity of the demand for unskilled labor (flattened the demand curve). Workers who in the past could have successfully pressed for higher wages would now face greater fear of job loss. He cites the pervasive invocation of "global competitiveness" as the reason firms (or politicians) give for why they cannot raise wages (or minimum wages and social benefits). In this interpretation, direct measurements based on actual trade and immigration flows would fail to capture the full extent of international influences in holding down low-end wages. It is difficult to see how this hypothesis could be tested, however. It also has the ironic implication that because of the flatter labor demand curve, there was the compensation of an employment boom as real wages in fact declined for unskilled workers.

trained and located workers, associated in part apparently with increasing volatility of incomes (Kosters 1994; Richardson 1995).[109]

The range of about 20 percent for trade to 30 percent for more comprehensively defined international influences as the central estimate of their contribution to widening US wage inequality in the 1980s would mean that these forces should neither be ignored nor exaggerated in diagnosing the problem. Moreover, as Burtless (1995b) emphasizes, wage trends cannot account for more than about half of the widening overall dispersion of incomes in the United States.

As will be developed in chapter 3 and, especially, 4, this study's estimate of the past impact of trade and immigration on US wage inequality is considerably higher than the modal range from the existing literature. The synthesis in chapter 5 finds that about one-third of the net increase in the skilled/unskilled wage ratio from 1973-93 was attributable to trade, and an additional one-ninth was attributable to immigration.

However, the concluding analysis in chapter 5 also emphasizes that there was a massive equalizing effect at work on the supply side: a persistent rise in the availability of skilled relative to unskilled labor. Most studies mention this fact in passing, but then go on to attribute a given fraction of the observed net rise in the skilled wage differential to trade. Clearly, however, if the intent is to detect the relative contribution of trade and immigration to the full set of forces causing a widening of wage inequality, this contribution should be gauged against the gross unequalizing forces rather than just the net outcome. Otherwise, the sum of the attributed shares of various unequalizing forces will far exceed unity.

As set forth in chapter 5, measured against the full set of unequalizing influences (including erosion of the real minimum wage, the decline of unionization, skill-biased technological change, and other unexplained forces), trade and immigration only accounted for about one-tenth of the gross unequalizing pressures over the past two decades. Ironically, then,

---

109. Pryor and Schaffer (1997) have attacked the technological change explanation from another, fundamental standpoint. They argue that college graduates, especially those with relatively low performance (as proxied by functional literacy), have increasingly taken jobs previously held by high school graduates. Examining detailed occupations, they identify numerous cases where educational levels have risen (typically from about 10 years to about 12) since the early 1970s, even though there is little evident basis for inferring skill-biased technological change (taxi and truck drivers, janitors, fire fighting, animal caretakers). They conclude that "downward occupational mobility" rather than "upskilling" has driven rising skill densities. This is essentially a model of screening or queuing, whereby the role of education is more to ration workers across jobs than to provide needed skills. While this interpretation would certainly be consistent with the rise in relative supply of higher-educated workers, a queuing model would seem considerably less capable of explaining why the relative wage of college-educated workers should have increased as the relative supply also increased.

**Figure 2.9 Interaction of supply and demand for skilled and
unskilled labor**

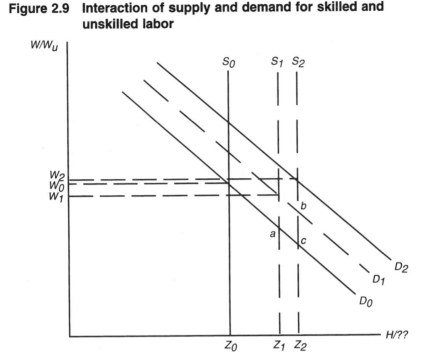

this study places the impact of trade and immigration at about twice the
modal range in the existing literature in terms of direct comparison to
net change in the skilled/unskilled wage ratio, but at somewhat below
the corresponding modal interpretation of the relative importance of trade
and immigration to widening wage inequality because the estimates in
the literature typically fail to calculate against the gross rather than net
unequalizing influences.

Supply-Demand Interaction

Figure 2.9 summarizes the forces affecting US wage inequality in the last
two decades. The horizontal axis shows the ratio (Z) of skilled (H) to
unskilled (U) workers in the labor force. The vertical axis shows the
corresponding wage ratio. The diagram shows the interaction of demand
(D) and supply (S) of skilled relative to unskilled workers, with equilibrium relative wage occurring at the intersection of the demand and supply curves.

At any point in time, it is assumed that the available quantity of
unskilled and skilled workers is fixed, in view of the time lags for training
and education required to transform one into the other. Accordingly, the

supply curve is depicted as vertical, or unresponsive to the relative wage in the current period. The figure shows a large outward shift of this skilled/unskilled supply curve from the base period (representing 1970) to period 1 (1980), but a much more modest outward shift to period 2 (1990). Thus, $Z_2 - Z_1 < Z_1 - Z_0$. This pattern reflects the large cohort of college graduates in the 1970s and the smaller cohort in the 1980s.

In the base period the demand curve for the skill ratio was D_0. At a lower skilled/unskilled wage ratio firms demand a higher skilled/unskilled workforce composition. The market equilibrium occurs at wage ratio w_0 and skills ratio Z_0. Over time, skills deepening shifts the supply curve outward. If demand had remained unchanged along curve D_0, by period 1 the wage ratio would have fallen from w_0 to a, and by period 2, to c. But demand did not remain unchanged. There was a secular increase in the relative demand for skilled labor, shifting the demand curve outward to D_1 and then D_2.

Figure 2.9 demonstrates that even with a steady outward shift in the relative demand for skilled labor (i.e., equal distances between successive demand curves D), there could have been a decrease in the relative skilled wage in the 1970s followed by an increase to new heights in the 1980s. In the diagram, in period 1 (1970s) the outward supply shift dominates, causing the equilibrium wage ratio to fall to w_1, but in period 2 (1980s) the outward shift in the demand curve dominates, causing the equilibrium wage ratio to rise to w_2—higher than in the base period.[110]

The literature reviewed in this chapter may be seen as an attempt to quantify and explain the shifting supply and demand curves depicted in figure 2.9. The overall picture that emerges is that in the 1970s, the skill differential fell because of a surfeit of new college graduates, whereas in the 1980s the differential rose to a new high because of a slowdown in new graduates combined with steady, ongoing increases in relative demand for skilled workers (figure 2.9) or, perhaps, an acceleration in this secular demand shift (placing D_2 further to the right than shown here).

Rising North-South trade contributed to the outward shift in the demand curve. So did technological change. Immigration reduced the pace of outward shift in the supply curve (at least if the denominator of the skills ratio refers to high school dropouts), helping forestall or reverse a decline in the relative wage of skilled labor that otherwise could have occurred. The summary here suggests that the modal estimate in the literature is that the combined effect of trade and immigration in the 1980s was to cause the rise from w_1 to w_2 to be about one-third larger than it would have been otherwise.[111] As noted above, the present study finds a larger impact for the past two decades.

---

110. This interpretation is similar to that given by Katz and Murphy (1992), as quoted above—although the conclusion here leaves more room for trade and immigration effects.

111. Using one-fourth as the share of trade and immigration in the total increase (i.e., $0.25/0.75 = 1/3$).

Figure 2.9 shows that it is not necessary to invoke accelerating techno-logical change in the 1980s to explain a rising skilled wage differential despite an absolute increase in the relative availability of skilled workers. All that is necessary is a constant pace of technological change and shifting demand, combined with the slowdown in the outward shifting supply curve. This is helpful, because the case for accelerating technological change is less than convincing.

Thus, Mishel and Bernstein (1994-95, 180-81) argue against any accelera-tion in technological change in the 1980s. They note that although in manufacturing labor productivity grew faster in the 1980s than in the 1970s, the reverse is true in the larger nonmanufacturing sector. Their estimates relating within-industry shifts toward skilled labor to R&D activity and equipment accumulation show no difference between the two decades, and separate tests for computers show no differential impact compared with other equipment.

These summary inferences conclude this survey of literature. Chapters 3 and 4 examine general equilibrium exercises to shed further light on the past impact of trade and, especially, on prospective future trends. Chapter 5 turns to the policy implications that emerge from the existing research on the relationship between trade and wage inequality.

Appendix 2A

A Note on the Katz-Murphy Measure of Trade Impact

Katz and Murphy (1992) estimate the impact of trade on the relative demand for a demographic labor group k as

$$T_t^k = -\frac{1}{E^k}\sum_{i=1}^{n}\left[e_i^k E_{it}\left(\frac{I_{it}}{Y_{it}}\right)\right] + \sum_{i=1}^{n} E_{it}\left(\frac{I_{it}}{Y_{it}}\right) \qquad (2A.1)$$

where E^k is the economywide share of group k in employment, e_i^k is the fraction of group k in employment in sector i of the n total sectors, E_i is the fraction of economywide employment in the sector, Y_i is output in the sector, and I is net imports in the sector ($I < 0$ for net export sectors).

Consider a simple three-sector economy composed of importables (sector 1), exportables (2), and nontradables (3). In a Heckscher-Ohlin world, importables will be unskilled-labor-intensive, exportables skilled-labor-intensive, and nontradables perhaps somewhere in between. Let e_i^u be the fraction of labor used in sector 1 that is unskilled, and similarly for sectors 2 and 3. Then let $e_2^u = \lambda e_1^u$, where $\lambda < 1$; and let $E^u = \psi e_1^u$, where $1 > \psi > \lambda$, considering that E^u is the economywide fraction of unskilled labor.

For simplicity, assume that the share of all labor (skilled and unskilled) in each sector is equal to the share of the sector in output. Then $E_i \equiv \alpha_i = Y_i/Y$ where Y is total output. Define net exports in the exportables sector as the fraction γ of net imports in the importables sector, so that $I_2 = -\gamma I_1$, and $TB = -I_1(1 - \gamma)$, where TB is the trade balance. Note that $I_3 \equiv 0$.

Equation 2A.1 may then be restated, for unskilled labor, as

$$T^u = -\frac{1}{\psi e_1^u}\left[e_1^u \alpha_1 \frac{I_1}{\alpha_1 Y} - \lambda e_1^u \alpha_2 \frac{\gamma I_1}{\alpha_2 Y}\right] + \left[\alpha_1 \frac{I_1}{\alpha_1 Y} + \alpha_2 \frac{(-\gamma I_1)}{\alpha_2 Y}\right]. \qquad (2A.2)$$

Note that sector 3 disappears from the equation because its net imports (I_3) are zero.

Defining $m \equiv I_1/Y$, and simplifying, we have

$$T^u = -\frac{1}{\psi}(m - \lambda\gamma m) + (m - \gamma m)$$

$$= m\left(\frac{\lambda\gamma}{\psi} - \frac{1}{\psi} + 1 - \gamma\right). \qquad (2A.3)$$

From 2A.3, the derivative of T^u with respect to m is

$$\frac{\partial T^u}{\partial m} = \frac{\lambda \gamma}{\psi} - \frac{1}{\psi} + 1 - \gamma. \qquad (2A.4)$$

When trade is balanced, $\gamma = 1$, and the derivative becomes $\partial T^u / \partial m = (\lambda - 1)/\psi$. Because $\lambda < 1$, this derivative is unambiguously negative. This means that, given balanced trade, a more open economy (higher m) reduces relative demand for unskilled labor. This result makes sense because unskilled jobs displaced by additional imports are not compensated for by the increase in unskilled jobs from additional exports.

Correspondingly, from equation 2A.3 the derivative of T^u with respect to the export/import ratio γ is

$$\frac{\partial T^u}{\partial \gamma} = m\left(\frac{\lambda}{\psi} - 1\right). \qquad (2A.5)$$

Under the assumption that exports are less unskilled-intensive than the economy as a whole ($\lambda < \psi$), the expression in parentheses is negative, $\partial T^u / \partial \gamma < 0$, and a larger trade surplus (higher γ) reduces relative demand for unskilled labor. This result is paradoxical, because the superficial expectation would be that a higher trade surplus increases demand for unskilled labor. However, the demand in question is relative demand, and intuitively it makes sense that as the economy shifts away from production of nontradables (such as construction) toward production of exports that are less intensive in the use of unskilled labor, there will be a reduction in the relative demand for unskilled labor that is associated with a higher trade surplus.

It is of course possible that $\lambda > \psi$, that is, even exports are more unskilled-intensive than nontradables. For example, if the nontradables are primarily professional and business services, their skill intensity might be greater than that of manufactured exports. Considering that λ might thus be either greater or smaller than ψ, the sign of $\partial T^u / \partial \gamma$ might be seen as ambiguous.

The conclusion that the impact of a larger trade deficit on relative demand for unskilled labor is ambiguous (but more probably positive) is in sharp contrast to the Katz and Murphy (1992) interpretation of their results to the effect that a larger trade deficit in the mid-1980s was a major factor in declining relative demand for unskilled labor.

3

Experiments with the Krugman Model

Introduction

As reviewed in chapter 2, most empirical studies to date on the impact of international influences on US income distribution have been econometric decomposition analyses, "factor content" calculations, or specific tests oriented toward consistency with trade theory. These analyses are typically partial equilibrium and retrospective. This chapter and the next extend the analysis in three dimensions. First, they adopt a general equilibrium approach. Second, they attempt not only to understand past trends but also to consider those likely in the future. Third, the model developed in the next chapter directly incorporates the nontraded services sector.

As an initial step toward a general equilibrium analysis of trade's impact on wage dispersion, this chapter uses and extends the simple model suggested by Krugman (1995a). The treatment here first replicates Krugman's results and then explores that model's sensitivity to key assumptions. The analysis then reformulates the Krugman model to account for nonunitary elasticity of substitution and considers future trends with such a reformulation.

The new model developed in the next chapter provides a somewhat more detailed but still highly aggregative general equilibrium analysis. That model uses estimates of actual factor endowments for major countries and regions.

The Krugman Model[1]

Krugman (1995a) examines the OECD as a whole and asks the following question: how much impact should the opening of the OECD to manufactured imports from the newly industrialized countries (NICs) have on the relative wages of skilled and unskilled workers in the OECD? He argues that because there were negligible manufactured imports from the NICs until 1970, the difference between two static equilibria for the OECD—with and without NIC supply—provides an estimate of the impact of the historical entry of these countries into manufactured exports.[2]

In the model, there are two goods. Good 1 is skill intensive and is produced and exported to the NICs by the OECD. Good 2 is unskilled intensive and is produced in the OECD but is also supplied by imports from the NICs. There is no nontradables sector.

The OECD maximizes utility from consumption of the two goods:

$$MaxU = U(C_1, C_2). \tag{3.1}$$

The function is Cobb-Douglas (CD),[3] which means that the elasticity of utility with respect to each good is constant and the expenditure shares are also constant (so that if the price of one good changes, there is an exactly compensating change in the quantity consumed, and expenditure remains unchanged).

Production is a function of the amount of skilled and unskilled labor applied in each good:

$$Q_1 = F(L_{s1}, L_{u1});$$

$$Q_2 = G(L_{s2}, L_{u2}). \tag{3.2}$$

The OECD exports the excess of output over consumption for good 1 and imports the excess of consumption over production for good 2.

$$X_1 = Q_1 - C_1;$$

$$M_2 = C_2 - Q_2. \tag{3.3}$$

There is an "offer curve" depicting various amounts of good 1 that the

---

1. I am indebted to Marcus Miller for extremely helpful comments on this section and the next.

2. Krugman estimates that exports of manufactures from NICs amounted to 0.24 percent of industrial-country GDP in 1970 and 1.61 percent in 1990. For the United States, the increase was from 0.28 percent to 1.91 percent.

3. Of the form $U = kC_1^{\beta}C_2^{(1-\beta)}$.

OECD is prepared to export at alternative price ratios for good 1 relative to good 2. The NICs have a similar offer curve. Where these two offer curves intersect tells the magnitude of trade. Krugman expresses this equilibrium with imports of good 2 being a function of the OECD exports of good 1:

$$M_2 = T(X_1). \tag{3.4}$$

The OECD economy has 60 unskilled workers and 40 skilled workers. The unskilled wage is set by definition to unity. The skilled wage is twice as high, but for convenience the unit for skilled workers is redefined to half a worker, so there are twice as many skilled-worker units (80), each earning unity.

Krugman then uses the duality between production and cost to identify the unit price. His production is CD with constant returns to scale, so the production function is

$$Q_i = B_i L_{si}^{\alpha_i} L_{ui}^{1-\alpha_i} \tag{3.5}$$

where i is the sector and B is a constant.

The unit cost "dual" of the production function may be expressed as[4])

$$c_i(w_s, w_u) = K_i w_s^{\alpha_i} w_u^{1-\alpha_i}, \text{ where}$$

$$K_i = \alpha_i^{-\alpha_i}(1 - \alpha_i)^{\alpha_i - 1} \tag{3.6}$$

With the unskilled wage normalized to unity, $w_u^{1-\alpha_i}$ turns to unity. Krugman also implicitly normalizes the definition of the output unit so that K_i equals unity. With profit maximization (at zero profit under perfect competition), unit price equals unit cost. Defining relative wage $w = w_s/w_u$, the resulting price function is

$$p_i = w^{\alpha_i}. \tag{3.7}$$

Krugman sets $\alpha_1 = 2/3$ and $\alpha_2 = 1/3$, because sector 1 is the more skill intensive and thus has greater elasticity of output with respect to skilled labor. Correspondingly, $p_1 = w^{2/3}$ and $p_2 = w^{1/3}$.

Given unit cost as a function of wage rates, it is possible to determine factor demand per unit of output. With L the vector of labor demand, w the wage vector, and c unit cost, demand for factor j for a unit of a given product equals the derivative of the cost function with respect to

---

4. This unit cost results from minimizing the wage bill subject to the constraint that enough of each type of labor is used to produce one unit of output. See Varian (1978, 15).

the wage vector: $l_j(w) = \partial c(w)/\partial w_j$.[5] Taking the derivative of the unit cost function in equation 3.6 and after considering that $K_i \equiv 1$ and that $w_s^{\alpha_i} w_u^{(1-\alpha_i)} \equiv w^{\alpha_i}$, factor demand per unit of output in sector i is, thus,[6]

$$a_{si} = \alpha_i w^{\alpha_i - 1};$$

$$a_{ui} = (1 - \alpha_i) w^{\alpha_i} \tag{3.8}$$

where a_{si} is the input of skilled labor per unit of output in sector i, and a_{ui} is the corresponding coefficient for unskilled labor.

In isolation, the equilibrium allocation of OECD factors will generate a vector of products that, when applied to the unit factor input coefficients of equation 3.8, will just exhaust factor availability. If we designate A as the matrix of labor coefficients, L as the vector of labor availability, and Q as the vector of output, then[7]

$$L = AQ;$$

$$Q = A^{-1}L \tag{3.9}$$

Krugman first solves this system for the OECD in isolation. That solution generates a base level of production of each of the two goods. With initial product prices at unity, these output levels are also value levels, with corresponding expenditure shares $\phi_1 = [p_1 Q_1]/[p_1 Q_1 + p_2 Q_2]$ for good 1 and $(1 - \phi_1)$ for good 2. Under CD consumption behavior, this expenditure share remains fixed regardless of product prices.

Krugman now shocks his solution by postulating that the relative wage of skilled labor rises by 3 percent. Thus, w rises from 1.0 to 1.03. This generates new prices (equation 3.7), new labor input coefficients (equation 3.8), and new equilibrium output levels (equation 3.9). At the new output levels, production of good 1 will exceed consumption, and the excess will be exported in exchange for imports of good 2. This equilibrium trade will leave the consumption pattern such that product shares in expenditure remain unchanged. Thus,[8]

---

5. Shephard's lemma (Varian 1978, 32). Note that the units are consistent for this result: l is (for example) man hours (mh) per ton (t), c is dollars per ton, and w is dollars per man hour; so $mh/t = (\$/t)/(\$/mh)$.

6. Corresponding to Krugman's equation 11 (1995a).

7. In Krugman's terms for the 2 × 2 case: $L_s = a_{s1}Q_1 + a_{s2}Q_2$; $L_u = a_{u1}Q_1 + a_{u2}Q_2$, for factor exhaustion, and $Q_1 = [1/D][a_{u2}L_s - a_{s2}L_u]$, $Q_2 = (1/D)(-a_{u1}L_s + a_{s1}L_u)$, where $D = a_{s1}a_{u2} - a_{s2}a_{u1}$, for output determination.

8. Krugman's equation 15 (1995a).

$$T = \frac{P_1 Q_1}{P_1 Q_1 + P_2 Q_2} - \phi_1. \qquad (3.10)$$

Krugman tests a base case in which $\alpha_1 = 2/3$, $\alpha_2 = 1/3$, $L_s = 80$, $L_u = 60$, and $w_s = w_u = 1$. This generates a consumption share of $5/7$ for good 1. He then shocks the relative wage rate to 1.03 and finds that the new pattern of production requires exports (T) equal to 2.2 percent of total product value to keep the consumption pattern unchanged with good 1's share at $\phi_1 = 5/7$. He notes that this level of imports is about what the OECD now purchases from the NICs and concludes that North-South trade is only large enough to have caused a 3 percent increase in the ratio of OECD skilled to unskilled wages. The corresponding increase in the relative price of good 1 (equation 3.7) is only 1 percent—too small to be picked up in the statistical noise and, understandably, not detected in various empirical studies.

Table 3.1 presents results of the Krugman model for each of the key variables, under alternative parameter assumptions. The first and second columns report the experiment conducted in Krugman (1995a). The estimates here replicate his findings. The remainder of the table examines the sensitivity of the results to alternative assumptions.

Columns 4 and 5 reduce the skilled labor elasticity in sector 1 to 0.6 and increase that in sector 2 to 0.4. One result is that the closed OECD economy adopts $6/7$ as its consumption share for good 1, higher than in the base case. Another result is that when a relative wage shock of 3 percent is imposed, the resulting trade amounts to 3.6 percent of product value. So trade is more sensitive when the factor elasticities are closer together in value. Correspondingly, if trade is limited to the original 2.2 percent of OECD output, the relative increase in the wage of skilled labor will be smaller than the base case estimate of 3 percent. Similarity of elasticities in the two sectors means it is easy to switch from one good to another, and the economy will more quickly move toward specialization and do so for a moderate change in the relative wage signal.[9]

Column 6 shows that when the elasticities are even closer together, at $\alpha_1 = 0.55$ and $\alpha_2 = 0.45$, the model is so responsive that it breaks down. The system of equations here generates negative output in good 2 so it can allocate more than its available stock of labor to good 1. The implication is that complete specialization in good 1, even in isolation, occurs at an intermediate point as α_1 declines from 0.6 to 0.55 and α_2 rises from 0.4 to 0.45. An important implication of this result is that the model is sensitive to the elasticities and implodes if they are too close in value.

Columns 7 through 10 consider the opposite change in the sectoral elasticities: widening the differences between them. When α_1 is set at 0.8 and α_2 at 0.2, the autarkic product profile is more evenly allocated than

---

9. As emphasized in the general equilibrium study of Kim and Mieszkowski (1995).

Table 3.1 Experiments with the Krugman model

	1	2	3	4	5	6	7	8	9	10	11	12	13
α_1	0.667	0.667	0.667	0.6	0.6	0.55	0.8	0.8	0.8	0.8	0.667	0.6	0.8
α_2	0.333	0.333	0.333	0.4	0.4	0.45	0.2	0.2	0.2	0.2	0.333	0.4	0.2
W_s/W_u	1	1.03	1.25	1	1.03	1	1	1.03	1.25	1.055	1.03	1.03	1.03
P_1	1	1.02	1.16	1	1.018	1	1	1.024	1.195	1.044	1.02	1.018	1.024
P_2	1	1.01	1.08	1	1.012	1	1	1.006	1.046	1.011	1.01	1.012	1.006
S	80	80	80	80	80	80	80	80	80	80	66	66	66
U	60	60	60	60	60	60	60	60	60	60	66	66	66
Q_1	100	102.8	120.6	120	125	170	86.7	87.8	94.8	88.7	68.6	70.7	67
Q_2	40	37.2	18.6	20	15	−30	53.3	52.2	44.6	51.3	63.4	61.3	65
ϕ_1	0.714	0.714	0.714	0.857	0.857	1.214	0.619	0.619	0.619	0.619	0.5	0.5	0.5
θ_1	0.714	0.736	0.875	0.857	0.893	1.214	0.619	0.631	0.708	0.641	0.522	0.537	0.512
Z	0	0.022	0.161	0	0.036	0	0	0.012	0.089	0.022	0.022	0.037	0.012

Notes:

α: Elasticity of output with respect to skilled labor

W_s, W_u: Wage of skilled and unskilled labor ($W_u = 1$)

P: Product price

S, U: Availability of skilled and unskilled labor

Q: Output volume

ϕ_1: Share of good 1 in closed-economy consumption

θ_1: Share of good 1 in production

Z: Exports of good 1 as fraction of total output

before ($\phi_1 = 0.62$ instead of 0.71), but trade is less responsive to factor price changes. Thus, a 3 percent skilled-wage shock only induces trade equal to 1.2 percent of OECD output (instead of 2.2 percent). The factor price change that would be required to induce trade of 2.2 percent of GDP is a 5.5 percent rise in the relative price of skilled labor. This test again suggests that the Krugman results are sensitive to the particular elasticities chosen, as the same North-South trade would be generating almost twice as large a wage-skill differential as under his base case.

The last three columns of table 3.1 examine the impact of a different estimate for OECD factor endowments. Murphy and Welch (1991, 63) report that in the United States, over the past two decades the average share in the workforce of workers with 12 years of education or less has been about 60 percent for whites and 70 percent for blacks. Thus, the unskilled fraction of the labor force might be set at nearly two-thirds. This would mean $L_u = 66$, and (with the unit halved to obtain identical wages) $L_s = 66$.

For equal endowments of skilled and unskilled labor (thus defined), the model evenly splits consumption between the two goods in autarky; otherwise, the trade results are almost identical to those under the disparate factor endowments. Thus, the 3 percent relative wage shock generates almost exactly the same trade as in the prior analogous cases (i.e., trade is equal in the following pairs of cases: 11 and 2, 12 and 5, and 13 and 8). This result is somewhat counterintuitive, as one might have expected that with a greater relative endowment of unskilled labor, opening to trade with the NICs would produce a smaller relative wage shock, because unskilled labor in autarky would be less scarce relatively than in the original base case.

Overall, these tests suggest several points. First, the Krugman model is sensitive to the sectoral factor elasticities. As these elasticities approximate each other, the model breaks down. As they get further apart, the wage impact of the observed North-South trade gets larger. Second, however, the sensitivity tests suggest that if technology is CD, the Krugman estimate is neither severely overstated nor understated. A relatively high sectoral elasticity difference does no more than double the wage differential impact, from 3 percent to 6 percent.

Two important considerations about Krugman's basic conclusion of "small trade, small impact" warrant examination. The first is whether trade is actually small by the relevant gauge. The second has to do with the ease of substitution between skilled and unskilled labor.

With respect to the first issue, in OECD economies about two-thirds of output is in the services sector, so more than half of GDP is nontradable. Is the tradables sector, about half of GDP, the relevant output base for comparison with trade? With the North-South manufactured trade share at say 5 percent of the tradables base, the wage differential impact might arguably be twice as high as otherwise predicted. Thus, in table 3.1 the relationship between trade as a percentage of GDP and the percentage change in the wage differential is approximately linear (for given parameters), so doubling the estimated relevant trade impact would double the wage differential effect.

The basic problem with focusing on the impact relative to the tradables base alone, however, is that implicitly this approach would assume that wages are set at the "external margin." That is, the trade sector would have to set factor prices, which then spread through the rest of the economy. This is essentially the approach of Leamer (1992). However, at least apart from the most rigid confines of the HO framework (which in its traditional formulation does not even consider nontradables), there would seem to be no reason to give primacy to the trade sector as opposed to the rest of the economy as the determinative "margin" where factor prices are set. As Krugman (1995b) points out (and as discussed in chapter 2), sole emphasis on the tradables sector implicitly assumes the small-country case, whereas the OECD economies constitute a "large country" trading with a relatively "small country" comprising the developing nations. In short, Krugman seems right to gauge the labor and, thus, wage impact against the full economy (including nontradables), although if calculated just against the tradables portion, the proportionate effects would all be at least doubled.

The second consideration is that the CD production function used by Krugman affords easy substitution between factors. Specifically, the elasticity of substitution is unity: a 10 percent increase in the relative price of skilled labor calls forth a 10 percent reduction in the ratio of skilled to unskilled labor in production. It is generally thought that manufacturing production has less than unitary elasticity of substitution between factors.[10] With greater difficulty in substituting skilled labor by unskilled labor, one would expect a greater impact on the relative wage skill differential when the effective supply of unskilled labor is increased by opening to NIC trade. Thus, Krugman's choice of production function may have biased his results toward a small impact. The appropriate range for the elasticity of substitution between skilled and unskilled labor is examined below.

Constant-Elasticity-of-Substitution Reformulation

Although the CD production function is convenient, its assumption of the specific value of unity for the elasticity of substitution between skilled

---

10. Thus, Wood (1994) treats skilled labor and capital as a joint factor (with an elasticity of substitution between them of only 0.1), and then sets the elasticity of substitution between capital skills and unskilled labor at 0.5 (136).

and unskilled labor makes it a special case. Over recent decades the literature on production functions has evolved toward greater flexibility. The constant-elasticity-of-substitution (CES) function permits the elasticity to be any value between zero (Leontief fixed-coefficient production) and infinity (linear production function where one factor substitutes for another with a constant rate of transformation). Other production functions, such as the translog function, further relax the assumption that the elasticity of substitution is constant and that it is identical between various pairs of factors in multiple-factor production.

It will be argued below that unitary elasticity of substitution of the CD function overstates the ease of substitution of unskilled for skilled labor. For this reason, this section develops a Krugman-type model based on the CES function. Although the implementation here will assume that the constant elasticity of substitution is less than unity, the formulations that follow could also apply if the elasticity were unity (in which case the CD results obtain) or greater than unity.

In the CES function, still with constant returns to scale, production is of the form

$$Q_i = \tau_i[\delta_{si}L_{si}^{-\rho_i} + \delta_{ui}L_{ui}^{-\rho_i}]^{-\frac{1}{\rho_i}} \tag{3.11}$$

where τ is a technical efficiency parameter (set equal to unity for convenience here), δ is a "distribution parameter" related (but not equal) to the factor share for the factor and sector in question, and ρ_i is a parameter reflecting substitutability between the two factors of production (Chiang 1984, 426; Wood 1994, 134; Varian 1978, 17). Specifically, $\rho = [(1/\sigma) - 1]$ where σ is the absolute value of the elasticity of substitution between the two factors. Whereas this elasticity must be unity (absolute value) in the CD function, it can be below or above unity in the CES function.

The unit cost function corresponding to equation 3.6) then becomes[11]

$$c_i(w_s, w_u) = \frac{1}{A}\left[\delta_{si}^{\frac{1}{1+\rho_i}} w_s^{\frac{\rho_i}{1+\rho_i}} + \delta_{ui}^{\frac{1}{1+\rho_i}} w_u^{\frac{\rho_i}{1+\rho_i}}\right]^{1+1/\rho_i}. \tag{3.12}$$

Similarly, the factor demand for unit output, corresponding to equation 3.8, becomes, for skilled labor,

$$a_{si} = \frac{\partial c_i}{\partial w_s}$$

$$= \frac{1}{A}\frac{1+\rho_i}{\rho_i}\,\delta_{si}^{\frac{1}{1+\rho_i}}\,[\delta_{si}^{\frac{1}{1+\rho_i}} w_s^{\frac{\rho_i}{1+\rho_i}} + \delta_{ui}^{\frac{1}{1+\rho_i}} w_u^{\frac{\rho_i}{1+\rho_i}}]^{\frac{1}{\rho_i}}\, w_s^{-\frac{1}{1+\rho_i}} \tag{3.13}$$

and for unskilled labor,

---

11. See appendix 3A for the derivation.

$$a_{ui} = \frac{\partial c_i}{\partial w_u} = \frac{1}{A} \frac{1 + \rho_i}{\rho_i} \delta_{ui}^{\frac{1}{1+\rho_i}} \left[\delta_{si}^{\frac{1}{1+\rho_i}} w_s^{\frac{\rho_i}{1+\rho_i}} + \delta_{ui}^{\frac{1}{1+\rho_i}} w_u^{\frac{\rho_i}{1+\rho_i}} \right]^{-\frac{1}{\rho_i}} w_u^{-\frac{1}{1+\rho_i}}. \qquad (3.14)$$

To calibrate this CES version of the Krugman model to parameters comparable to his CD version, it is necessary to know the CES distribution parameter δ that corresponds to the CD factor elasticity α. In the CES function, as the elasticity of substitution approaches unity, the distribution parameter for the factor in question approaches the CD factor elasticity. However, for a lower elasticity of substitution, the two diverge.

In the CES function, the chosen factor ratio in the sector depends on the ratio of the factor prices, the distribution parameters, and the elasticity of substitution as follows (Henderson and Quandt 1980, 114):

$$\frac{S}{U} = \left[\frac{\delta_s}{\delta_u} \right]^\sigma \left[\frac{w_u}{w_s} \right]^\sigma. \qquad (3.15)$$

In the special circumstances of the Krugman model, factor units are chosen so that the wage of unskilled labor equals that of skilled labor, so the final term in equation 3.15 becomes unity. Also, with identical factor prices, the ratio of factor amounts will also be the ratio of factor payments and, in a two-factor model, the ratio of factor shares as well. Defining the factor share as ϕ, we have:

$$\frac{\phi_s}{\phi_u} = \left[\frac{\delta_s}{\delta_u} \right]^\sigma. \qquad (3.16)$$

Also, in the CES function, when the two factors have the same units, the sum of the distribution parameters is unity ($\delta_s + \delta_u = 1$) (see e.g., Henderson and Quandt 1980, 111). Taking the power $(1/\sigma)$ of both sides of equation 3.16 and letting $[\phi_s / \phi_u]^{1/\sigma} = k$, we have $\delta_s = k/(1 + k)$ and $\delta_u = 1 - \delta_s$.

By way of illustration, if the factor share of skilled labor is 0.667, and the elasticity of substitution is 0.5, then the CES distribution parameter for skilled labor is 0.716. As the elasticity of substitution approaches unity, this parameter approaches the skilled-labor share, 0.667. The divergence between the factor share and the distribution parameter increases as the elasticity of substitution decreases.[12]

As in the CD version of the Krugman model, the CES version developed here treats sector 1 as the skill-intensive sector with the share of skilled labor greater than 0.5 and sector 2 as the unskilled-intensive sector with the share of unskilled labor greater than 0.5. As before, sector 2 mirrors sector 1, so that $\phi_{s2} = \phi_{u1}$ and $\phi_{u2} = \phi_{s1}$. Once the distribution parameters

---

12. Thus, with $\phi_s = .667$ and $\sigma = 0.4$, $\delta_s = 0.85$.

δ_{s1} and δ_{u1} are calculated from equation 3.16 (with the requirement that their sum equal unity), we know immediately that $\delta_{s2} = \delta_{u1}$ and $\delta_{u2} = \delta_{s1}$. The CES model is now fully calibrated to parallel Krugman's specifications and may be examined under alternative assumptions about the elasticity of substitution (σ) and, thus, ρ, to determine whether the Krugman results are sensitive to the unitary elasticity of substitution in the CD function.

Elasticity of Substitution between Skilled and Unskilled Labor

The empirical literature on the elasticity of substitution between skilled and unskilled labor leaves much to be desired. Because data are readily available, most studies use nonproduction and production labor to represent skilled and unskilled workers; yet, as discussed in chapter 2, this classification is far from satisfactory.[13] Perhaps because the categories do not mean much, the range of estimates of the elasticity of substitution is enormous. Of 18 estimates reported in a survey by Hamermesh (1993, 109), 9 are above unity, 5 are between zero and unity, and 4 are below zero (meaning that the two labor groups are complements rather than substitutes). The maximum estimate is 5.5; the minimum is -0.48.

In the same survey, among 17 studies examining substitution by occupation or education, only two explicitly report the elasticity of substitution by educational class. Both are from aggregate data (in one case, US states; in another, cross-section data among 22 countries), and both are from the 1970s. One shows the elasticity of substitution between college and high school workers at 1.34 (Johnson 1970); the other shows the elasticity between workers with more than eight years of education and those with less at 0.61 (Fallon and Layard 1975).

Hamermesh himself is silent on whether the elasticity of substitution between skilled and unskilled labor is greater or less than unity, suggesting that the empirical literature is inadequate to reach a conclusion. He does conclude that homogeneous labor is a substitute for energy. Moreover, we can be "fairly sure" that capital and skilled labor are complements rather than substitutes (so that a reduction in the price of capital increases rather than decreases the demand for skilled labor) (Hamermesh 1993, 135).

---

13. Hamermesh (1993, 65) judges that "because there is a remarkably large overlap in the earnings of these two groups, [the degree of substitution between them] tells us relatively little about substitution between high- and low-skilled workers." He estimates that in 1980, 49 percent of nonproduction workers earned less than $10,000, not far from the 59 percent figure for production workers, and 25 percent of production workers earned over $25,000, not far from the 35 percent figure for nonproduction workers.

Sachs and Shatz (1995) judge that the existing empirical studies "lack appropriate econometric estimates of the short-run and long-run elasticities of substitution" between skilled and unskilled labor (32). They assume alternative values of one-third and one-half in their analysis, so they distinctly consider the substitutability to be lower than implied by the CD function.

In contrast, Katz and Murphy (1992, 69) provide an indirect estimate that places the elasticity above unity. They convert educational categories to college and high school equivalents. Then they estimate a regression of the logarithm of the wage ratio for the two groups against the logarithm of the corresponding ratio of worker equivalents and a time trend, using aggregate US data for 1963-87. The time trend shows a 3.3 percent annual increase in the skilled/unskilled wage ratio. The coefficient on relative supply is 0.709, meaning that a 1 percent rise in the availability of skilled relative to unskilled workers reduces the skilled/unskilled wage ratio by 0.709 percent. The elasticity of substitution tells the percentage change in the factor ratio for a given percentage change in the factor price ratio, so it is just the inverse of this coefficient, 1.41.

My own inclination is closer to that of Sachs and Shatz (1995) than that of Krugman's unitary elasticity or the Katz-Murphy elasticity of greater than unity. The Katz-Murphy estimate uses aggregate data and a simple two-variable equation (factor ratio and time), so it may be understating the true sensitivity of the wage rate to changes in relative factor availability.[14] For example, if the data were sufficiently bad, one would expect the coefficient estimated to approximate zero: random noise on the left-hand side would be regressed against random noise on the right-hand side. In such an equation, the elasticity of substitution would be the inverse of the estimated coefficient, infinity. If we accept that an aggregate test of the Katz-Murphy type is likely to have a downward bias in the relationship measured, the implication is that the implied substitution elasticity is upward biased.[15]

At a broader level, one suspects the substitutability between skilled and unskilled labor must in some fundamental sense be limited; otherwise, the policy problem that is the subject of this book would disappear. That is, great ease in substituting unskilled for skilled labor would mean there would have been minimal opportunity for wide skill differentials to arise in the wage distribution even in the face of technological, trade, or other shocks.

---

14. The authors themselves state that "We are somewhat skeptical of estimates of σ recovered from 25 nonindependent time series observations" (Katz and Murphy 1992, 69).

15. It is a classic view in the international trade literature that empirical estimates of trade price elasticities have tended to be downward biased because of econometric and data problems (Orcutt 1950).

Table 3.2 Trade response to relative wage increase

	Elasticity of substitution					
	0.5	0.7	0.9	0.5	0.7	0.9
	Percentage change in relative					
Wage		Price		Trade response (percentage of GDP)		
A. $\phi_{s1} = 0.667$						
3	0.99	1.05	1.03	1.18	1.50	1.90
6	1.96	2.07	2.03	2.32	2.95	3.74
10	3.23	3.41	3.35	3.78	4.80	6.10
25	7.72	8.17	8.01	8.71	11.08	14.10
B. $\phi_{s1} = 0.60$						
3	0.80	0.77	0.67	1.42	1.98	2.89
6	1.57	1.53	1.33	2.78	3.89	5.68
10	2.59	2.51	2.18	4.54	6.34	9.25
25	6.16	5.99	5.17	10.45	14.62	21.38
C. $\phi_{s1} = 0.80$						
3	1.48	1.62	1.75	0.92	1.04	1.15
6	2.82	3.22	3.47	1.80	2.05	2.26
10	4.66	5.32	5.74	2.93	3.33	3.69
25	11.24	12.91	13.96	6.76	7.70	8.52

Note: ϕ is factor share for skilled (s) or unskilled (u) labor in sector 1 or 2. Also, $\phi_{s2} = \phi_{u1} = 1 - \phi_{s1}$, and $\phi_{u2} = \phi_{s1}$.

Finally, it should be emphasized that the Katz-Murphy estimate of 1.41 for the elasticity of substitution between college- and high school-equivalent labor applies to the US economy as a whole, and, thus, incorporates substitution among products in consumer demand and producer decisions. As the economy is disaggregated below this single, all-encompassing "sector," the resulting subsectors should be expected each to have lower elasticities of substitution. As the number of sectors becomes increasingly large, the concept of substitution becomes that of direct substitution in production of the single product, rather than an intermixture with product substitution. The Krugman model examined in this chapter has two sectors rather than one and so should have a lower elasticity of substitution in each than would be appropriate at the economywide level.

CES Estimates with Limited Substitutability

For these reasons, the analysis here assumes that the elasticity of substitution between skilled and unskilled labor is less than unity. Table 3.2 reports the results of the CES sensitivity tests on the Krugman model for values of this elasticity. The table shows the OECD's exports to (imports from) the NICs as a percentage of GDP when the OECD moves from autarky to open trade, and the result is a postulated shock in the relative wage of skilled labor. As expected, for each specified relative wage shock, the extent of trade created is greater when the elasticity of substitution is higher. The converse implication is that given the observed level of NIC trade (which Krugman sets at about 2 percent of OECD GDP), a higher elasticity of substitution means that a smaller change in the relative wage is required.

The table shows that for most cases, the relative wage impact from NIC-OECD trade is higher than the 3 percent estimated by Krugman. The most extreme case shown is the combination of a relatively low elasticity of substitution ($\sigma = 0.5$) with a relatively high difference in sectoral factor shares (skilled labor share of 0.8 in sector 1 and 0.2 in sector 2). In this case, NIC-OECD trade of 2 percent of OECD GDP would cause a rise of 6.7 percent in the skilled/unskilled wage ratio.[16] However, if the factor shares are closer between the two sectors, at $\phi_{s1} = 0.60$, the wage shock would actually be somewhat less than Krugman's 3 percent if the elasticity of substitution is relatively high ($\sigma = 0.9$).[17] Perhaps the preferred estimate in table 3.2 would be for factor shares of 2/3 and 1/3 (the same as used by Krugman), but with an elasticity of substitution of 0.7 rather than unity. Interpolating from table 3.2, trade of 2 percent of OECD GDP would be consistent with a relative wage change of 4 percent for this central case. On this basis, the CES reformulation of Krugman's analysis suggests that his estimate may understate the wage impact of North-South trade by about one-fourth. If the appropriate elasticity of substitution is only 0.5, then the Krugman estimate would understate the relative wage impact by almost one-half.[18]

Finally, note that in table 3.2 the relative price impact rises substantially with the difference between sectoral factor shares. The further apart the (mirror image) factor shares, the larger the price impact for a given relative wage change. Thus, a 3 percent relative wage change raises the relative price of good 1 by only 0.8 percent when $\phi_{s1} = 0.60$, but by about 1.4 to 1.8 percent when $\phi_{s1} = 0.8$. Intuitively, as the factor shares tend toward equality, the sectors become indistinguishable with respect to factor intensity, and there is no reason for a relative factor price change to affect relative product prices.

---

16. Interpolating between the table entries a 6 percent relative wage increase associated with a 1.8 percent of GDP trade, and a 10 percent relative wage increase for 2.93 percent of GDP trade.

17. That is, it would require 2.89 percent of GDP trade to generate a relative wage shock of 3 percent (table 3.2).

18. That is, for $\sigma = 0.5$ and $\phi_{s1} = 0.667$, table 3.2 shows a 6 percent relative wage impact resulting from trade of 2.3 percent of OECD GDP.

Decadal Outlook with the CES-Krugman Model

Krugman's (1995a) central result was that North-South trade in manufactures has probably accounted for a 3 percent rise in the skilled-unskilled wage ratio in the OECD, which he places at one-tenth of the total rise over the past two decades. In addition, he argues that the reason Lawrence and Slaughter (1993) did not detect a corresponding decline in the price of unskilled-intensive goods is that this decline would have been expected to be only about 1 percent, small enough to be lost in the statistical noise of other influences in the economy that could be causing larger changes. The CES reformulation suggests instead that the impact may have been on the order of a 4 percent relative wage increase, for a central case with a skilled-labor share of 2/3 in one sector and 1/3 in the other and an elasticity of substitution of 0.7. Thus, trade would account for about one-seventh of the rise in the skilled/unskilled wage ratio if we accept Krugman's stylized fact of a 30 percent relative wage increase over two decades. If instead this benchmark is placed at about 20 percent (as might be suggested by the review in chapter 1 here), then the share attributable to trade would be about one-fifth.

The relative price change corresponding to the 4 percent relative wage change would have been about 2.8 percent.[19] This range could easily have been small enough to be undetected by Lawrence-Slaughter (1993) (or, alternatively, consistent with the contrary finding of relative unskilled product price decline found by Leamer 1992).

Qualitatively this retrospective analysis remains similar to Krugman's: trade has not been the primary cause of relative unskilled wage deterioration. However, the question remains: Is the trade impact on relative wages likely to remain modest in the future?

One way to gauge the future is to consider the past. The ratio of manufactured imports from developing countries to the GDP of industrial countries is the driving force in the model of this chapter. Thus, it is useful to consider past trends in the elements determining this ratio.

Manufactured imports from developing countries as a fraction of industrial-country GDP may be decomposed as follows:

$$m_L \equiv \frac{M_L}{Y} = q m_T \phi_L \tag{3.17}$$

where M_L is the level of imports of manufactures from developing countries, Y is OECD GDP, q is the share of domestic manufacturing value added in OECD GDP, m_T is the ratio of total imports of manufactures to

---

19. From table 3.2, for this case a 1 percent relative price change is associated with a change of about 1.4 percent in the relative wage.

Figure 3.1 Output and imports of manufactures of industrial countries

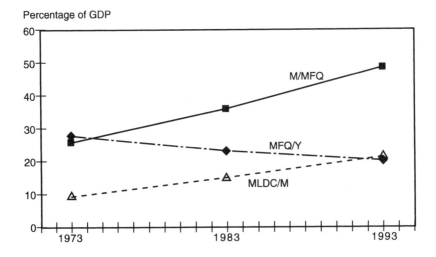

Percentage of GDP

domestic value added in manufacturing, and ϕ_L is the share of developing-country goods in total imports of manufactures. The share of manufacturing in GDP is an approximate measure of OECD demand for manufactured goods. The first right-hand term of equation 3.17 thus determines the magnitude of demand for manufactures. The next two terms are elements in determining whether on the supply side this demand is filled by imports (with higher imports implying higher exports of manufactures and greater specialization) (m_T) and the extent to which these imports are supplied by developing countries (ϕ_L).

Figure 3.1 shows persistent trends in each of the three ratios in equation 3.17. For the industrial countries, value added in manufacturing at current prices has fallen from 27.5 percent of GDP in 1973 to 23 percent in 1983 and 20.5 percent in 1993 (IMF 1997, 50).[20] This decline primarily represents high productivity growth and, consequentially, falling relative prices in manufacturing, especially as compared with the services sector. Taking the deceleration of this declining trend into account, by the year 2013 manufacturing value added could stand at about 19 percent of industrial country GDP.

---

20. For the present purposes, the share of manufacturing in current prices is the appropriate concept. The sector's share at constant prices would overstate relative value of the sector after a long period of time because of falling relative prices for manufactures.

The second ratio is that of total manufactured imports to domestic value added in manufacturing. For industrial countries this ratio has risen from 25.7 percent in 1973 to 48.7 percent in 1993, about 12 percentage points per decade.[21] Because of the unusually rapid pace of increased trade over the past two decades, associated with historic trade liberalization, falling transportation costs, and the process of European integration (intra-European Union imports are included in the manufactured import data used here), it is reasonable to expect a deceleration of the increase in this ratio. If the further increase amounted to 10 percentage points from 1993 to 2003 and an additional 8 percentage points from 2003 to 2013, manufactured imports would reach 67 percent of domestic value added in manufacturing for industrial countries by the latter date.[22]

The third ratio, imports of manufactures from developing countries as a fraction of total manufactured imports, has risen from 9.5 percent in 1973 to 21.5 percent in 1993 (WTO 1997, 17). This increase has accelerated, and at its more recent rate could amount to an additional 7 percentage points over each of the next two decades. This pace would bring the share of developing-country goods in industrial-country imports of manufactures to 35.5 percent by 2013.

Chaining these three ratios, manufactured imports from developing countries have risen from 0.67 percent of industrial-country GDP in 1973 to 1.22 percent in 1983 and 2.15 percent in 1993.[23] Applying the projected values of these three ratios for 2013, manufacturing imports from developing countries would reach 4.5 percent of industrial-country GDP by that date.[24]

Returning to table 3.2, we can determine the implied relative wage change that would be consistent with import penetration of this magnitude. Part A of table 3.2 and 0.7 substitution elasticity imply that the relative wage increase for skilled workers would reach a total of 9.4 percent, of which the first 4 percentage points would have already occur-

---

21. These estimates refer to manufactured imports into the United States, Canada, Western Europe, and Japan (WTO 1997, 17). GDP is calculated from IMF (1996).

22. Note that because imports are gross values whereas domestic value added is net of intermediate inputs, the ratio tends to overstate the relative magnitude of imports.

23. Calculated from WTO (1997) and IMF (1996), as noted above. The comparable figures based on World Bank estimates would be a rise from 0.37 percent of OECD GDP in 1970 to 2.3 percent in 1993. Calculated from World Bank (1995b, 192-3). That source shows that OECD imports of manufactures from low- and middle-income countries plus Hong Kong, Singapore, and Taiwan amounted to $7.7 billion in 1970 and $412 billion in 1993 (Taiwan's figure approximated). The corresponding GDP of high-income countries excluding Hong Kong, Singapore, and Taiwan amounted to $2.07 trillion in 1970 and $17.97 trillion in 1993.

24. That is, $m_L = 0.19 \times 0.67 \times 0.355$.

red between 1970 and 1993 based on the analysis of the previous section.[25] The additional increase in the skilled/unskilled wage ratio by about 5 percent would be comparable in magnitude to that estimated in this exercise as the impact of trade over the past two decades.

It is important to ask whether this rough calculation is consistent with plausible rates of growth for OECD imports of manufactures from developing countries in the future. The economies of the industrial countries seem likely to grow at about 2.5 percent annually in real terms over the next two decades. If imports of manufactures from developing countries rise from 2.15 percent of industrial country GDP to 4.5 percent, as suggested by the analysis based on the three trend lines in figure 3.1, these imports would grow at an annual real rate of 6.5 percent.[26] In contrast, from 1973 to 1993 this rate averaged 10 percent annually.[27]

The projections here thus suggest a significant slowdown in the growth rate of manufactured imports from developing countries into industrial countries. There is some reason to anticipate a slowdown, because Hong Kong, Singapore, Taiwan, and, arguably, South Korea are now high-income countries,[28] and a sizable portion of increased exports of manufactures to the OECD from other developing countries will merely replace labor-intensive manufactures previously imported from these four countries.

Figure 3.2 shows that there has been a reduction in the growth of manufactured imports into the OECD from the gang of four (G4): Hong Kong, Singapore, Taiwan, and South Korea.[29] Although for the decade 1982-83 to 1992-93 the growth of these imports averaged 10 percent annually in real terms, the growth was wholly concentrated in the first half of the decade, and the absolute level has been almost unchanged since 1988.

---

25. Interpolating from table 3.2, which for this case shows a 6 percent relative wage increase for 2.95 percent of GDP trade, and 10 percent relative wage increase for 4.8 percent of GDP trade.

26. That is, $(0.045 \times 1.025^{20})/.0215 \approx 1.065^{20}$.

27. The WTO (1997) data show these imports rising from $22.2 billion in 1973 to $398.5 billion in 1993. Deflating by the US producer price index yields 10 percent real average annual growth.

28. In 1993 per capita income stood at $18,060 for Hong Kong, $19,850 for Singapore, $10,652 for Taiwan, and $7,660 for South Korea (World Bank 1995b, 163; Taiwan 1995). The figure for the United States was $24,700. Note that these estimates are at market, not purchasing parity, exchange rates.

29. The data for figure 3.1 are drawn from OECD (1984) and OECD (1991) for 1970 through 1988 and refer to Standard International Trade Classification groups 5 through 8. The estimates for later years are from the World Bank's World Development Reports for 1990-95. The OECD data give a 1970 figure of $13.1 billion versus the World Bank's estimate of $7.7 billion for that year. The difference seems to be primarily that the World Bank excludes SITC 68, which is mainly copper. Figure 3.1 shows the data in real terms deflating by the US producer price index.

Figure 3.2 OECD manufactured imports from LDCs

billions of 1990 dollars

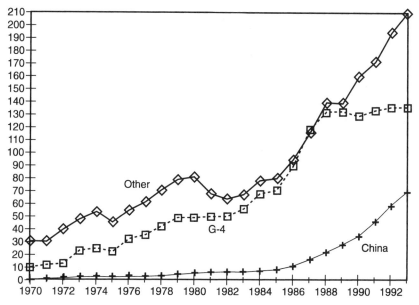

Rapid growth of manufactured exports to the OECD from other developing countries has taken up much of the slack. As shown in the figure, the absolute increase of imports from China alone has approximately equaled the shortfall of imports from the G4 level that would have been reached if this group's trend line had not broken in 1988. For the decade 1982-83 to 1992-93, real manufactured imports into the OECD from China grew at an astounding 27.5 percent per year. Those from other developing countries (excluding the G4) grew at 12 percent per year.

Despite this offset, the overall growth rate of manufactured imports from developing countries into the OECD has slowed. Thus, this rate was 10 percent annually in real terms for 1973 to 1993 as a whole, but 7.4 percent for the period 1988-93 (figure 3.2). This rate is broadly consistent with the projected rate of 6.5 percent for the period 1993-2013, especially if it is considered that a rising portion of imports from the G4 should be subtracted from the base because they increasingly resemble imports from industrial countries rather than unskilled-intensive goods from developing countries.

Another important consideration also suggests some limit on the future unequalizing effect of manufactured imports from developing countries. As noted in chapter 2, Krugman observes that his general equilibrium model sets a ceiling on future relative wage widening, imposed by the point at which the OECD becomes fully specialized in the skill-intensive good. Krugman estimates this ceiling at a 50 percent rise in the skilled/unskilled wage ratio for the OECD, with the import ratio reaching 29 percent of GDP. This ceiling is far above the estimate of this chapter of an increase of 5.4 percent in the skilled/unskilled wage ratio, as the consequence of a rise in developing-country import penetration from 2.15 percent to 4.5 percent of OECD GDP (the latter also far below Krugman's 29 percent ceiling).

Moreover, in a more realistic model a ceiling on the relative wage impact could be lower than this estimate, because of the presence of more tradable goods and because of a nontradable sector. As set forth in the discussion in chapter 2 of Leamer (1995), in a three-good model, sufficient investment in physical and human capital could leave the OECD producing only the skill-intensive and capital-intensive goods, and the unskilled-intensive good would be produced wholly by the developing countries. The unskilled-intensive good would then lie outside the "cone of diversification" of the OECD.[30] As a result, there would be no further downward pressure on OECD unskilled wages relative to skilled wages from further expansion of North-South trade.

Similarly, chapter 4 shows that introduction of a large nontradables sector into a general equilibrium analysis sharply reduces the potential scope for movement toward equal international factor prices. Effectively, nontradables offer a safe haven that cushions unskilled labor from competition through trade.

In summary, this chapter finds that recalculation of the Krugman model to allow for somewhat less substitutability between skilled and unskilled labor boosts the estimate of the impact of North-South trade on the OECD skilled/unskilled wage ratio from a rise of 3 percent to a rise of 4 percent. The simple projection for the next 20 years suggests that there could be an additional increase of about 5 percent in this wage ratio, in view of prospective growth in industrial-country GDP and likely imports of manufactures from developing countries. The model developed in chapter 4 below finds somewhat greater impact over the past two decades, but somewhat less over the next two. Chapter 5 draws overall conclusions based on the literature and the results of the models developed in chapters 3 and 4.

---

30. Referring to figure 2.1 of chapter 2, envision a third product Z with a field of isovalue curves centered around a much flatter ray from the origin. The OECD production point could be such that production was strictly between rays R_y and R_x, and production points between R_x and R_z (not shown in the figure) would lie outside the cone of diversification formed by R_y and R_x.

Appendix 3A

The Cost Function under CES Production[1]

The CES production function is

$$q = A[\delta S^{-\rho} + (1 - \delta)U^{-\rho}]^{-\frac{1}{\rho}} \tag{3A.1}$$

where S is skilled labor, U is unskilled labor, δ is the distribution parameter for skilled labor, and ρ is determined by the elasticity of substitution (see, e.g., Henderson and Quandt, 1980, 111). The latter relationship is: $\rho = 1/\sigma - 1$, where σ is the (positively defined) elasticity of substitution.

The unit cost function and the corresponding labor demand per unit of output are central concepts in the Krugman model set forth in chapter 3. Total cost of a given level of output q is equal to the wage (w) of each factor times the respective amount of each factor applied. Factor combinations are such as to minimize cost for a given level of production. At the optimal factor combination, the wage ratio of the two factors will equal the ratio of their respective marginal products. Canceling common elements of the latter, this gives

$$\frac{w_s}{w_u} = \frac{\delta S^{-\rho-1}}{(1 - \delta)U^{-\rho-1}} . \tag{3A.2}$$

Multiplying both sides by S/U:

$$\frac{w_s S}{w_u U} = \frac{\delta S^{-\rho}}{(1 - \delta)U^{-\rho}} . \tag{3A.3}$$

Adding the equivalent of unity to both sides:

$$\frac{w_s S + w_u U}{w_u U} = \frac{\delta S^{-\rho} + (1 - \delta)U^{-\rho}}{(1 - \delta)U^{-\rho}} . \tag{3A.4}$$

Considering that the numerator of the left side is total cost, and that the numerator of the right side is the expression inside brackets from the production function and considering the result of taking both sides of equation 3A.1 to the power $-\rho$, we have

---

1. This derivation follows Varian (1978, 18-20). However, it follows the more usual specification, whereby the CES exponent is $-\rho$ rather than ρ. Note that, correspondingly, Varian's distribution parameters (his a's) are an inverse function of the more normal distribution parameters (δ's).

$$\frac{C}{w_u U} = \frac{(q/A)^{-\rho}}{(1 - \delta)U^{-\rho}} \qquad (3A.5)$$

where C is total cost.

Solving for U:

$$U = (1 - \delta)^{\frac{1}{1+\rho}} (C)^{\frac{1}{1+\rho}} \left(\frac{1}{w_u}\right)^{\frac{1}{1+\rho}} \left(\frac{1}{q/A}\right)^{-\frac{\rho}{1+\rho}}. \qquad (3A.6)$$

By analogy:

$$S = \delta^{\frac{1}{1+\rho}}(C)^{\frac{1}{1+\rho}} \left(\frac{1}{w_s}\right)^{\frac{1}{1+\rho}} \left(\frac{1}{q/A}\right)^{-\frac{\rho}{1+\rho}} \qquad (3A.7)$$

Multiplying equation 3A.6 by w_u and equation 3A.7 by w_s and adding the two resulting equations, we have an expression for total cost:

$$w_u U + w_s S = C = \left[\delta^{\frac{1}{1+\rho}} w_s^{\frac{\rho}{1+\rho}} + (1 - \delta)^{\frac{\rho}{1+\rho}} w_u^{\frac{\rho}{1+\rho}}\right](C)^{\frac{1}{1+\rho}} (q/A)^{-\frac{\rho}{1+\rho}}. \qquad (3A.8)$$

Dividing both sides by $C^{1/(1+\rho)}$ and then taking the power $(1 + \rho)/\rho$ of both sides, we solve for cost as

$$C = \left[\delta^{\frac{1}{1+\rho}} w_s^{\frac{\rho}{1+\rho}} + (1 - \delta)^{\frac{\rho}{1+\rho}} w_u^{\frac{\rho}{1+\rho}}\right]^{\frac{1+\rho}{\rho}} (q/A). \qquad (3A.9)$$

When the output level is unity, q disappears and the resulting unit cost equation is that shown as equation 3.12 in the main text.

For its part, the labor demanded for each unit of output, for each type of labor, is simply the derivative of the unit cost function with respect to the wage of each type. These derivatives are shown in the main text as equations 3.13 and 3.14.

4

The Trade and Income Distribution Equilibrium (TIDE) Model

The CES version of the Krugman model developed in chapter 3 provides important benchmarks for past and prospective effects of North-South trade on wage inequality in the industrial countries. However, it is useful to supplement the model with further general equilibrium analysis that is somewhat more detailed and empirically grounded. It is desirable that such a model incorporate the nontraded sector explicitly, considering the large size of this sector. This chapter develops a general equilibrium model that divides the world into major countries or regions, estimates trends in factor endowments in each of these, and simulates trends in trade patterns and factor prices. The model is more illustrative than strictly empirical, and its potential contribution is to show parametrically the impact of alternative broad scenarios and hypotheses on the skilled/unskilled wage ratio, rather than to offer a definitive explanation of past trends in this ratio.

Model Structure

The TIDE model divides the world into 13 "countries," or regions: United States, Canada, European Union, Japan, rest of OECD (RO), Mexico, rest of Latin America (RL), China, G4 (Hong Kong, South Korea, Singapore, and Taiwan), India, rest of Asia (RA), Eastern Europe including Russia (EE), and rest of world (RW). There are five product sectors: skill-intensive manufactures (1), unskilled-intensive manufactures (2), capital-intensive manufactures (3), skill-intensive nontradables (4), and unskilled-intensive nontradables (5). There are three factors of production: skilled labor (S), unskilled labor (U), and capital (K).

Production (Q) in a given country (i) and product sector (j) is either a Cobb-Douglas (CD) function (equation 4.1a) or a constant-elasticity-of-substitution (CES) function (equation 4.1b) of factor inputs:

$$Q_{ij} = \tau_{ij}[S_{ij}^{\gamma_{Sj}} U_{ij}^{\gamma_{Uj}} K_{ij}^{\gamma_{Kj}}]; \tag{4.1a}$$

$$Q_{ij} = \tau_{ij}[\delta_{sj} S_{ij}^{-\rho_i} + \delta_{uj} U_{ij}^{-\rho_i} + \delta_{kj} K_{ij}^{-\rho_i}]^{-\frac{1}{\rho_i}} . \tag{4.1b}$$

As discussed below, when the factor units are specified so that they all have a common numeraire (as Krugman does by measuring skilled workers in unskilled-worker equivalents—see chapter 3), the distribution coefficients in the two alternative functions will tend toward identical values (e.g., $\delta_{sj} \rightarrow \gamma_{sj}$) as the elasticity of substitution in the CES function tends toward unity ($\sigma \rightarrow 1$ and $\rho \rightarrow 0$—see chapter 3).

The implementation of the model below simplifies by imposing a single technical efficiency constant across all sectors for a given country. However, the constant is allowed to rise over time to capture technological change. Thus,

$$\tau_i = e^{a_i + b_i t} \tag{4.1c}$$

where e is the base of the natural logarithm, and t is the year (1973 = 1 through 1993 = 21).

The country's consumption (C) of good j is equal to its domestic production plus its effective imports (M^*) minus its exports (X) of the good. For nontradables, consumption merely equals production:

$$C_{ij} = Q_{ij} + M_{ij}^* - X_{ij}, \, j = 1,3;$$

$$= Q_{ij}, \, j = 4,5. \tag{4.2}$$

Effective imports available for consumption are equal to the sum of other countries' exports to the home country for the good in question, less the "leakage" in trade attributable to transport costs (fraction λ) and trade barrier costs (fraction β). Thus,

$$M_{ij}^* = \Sigma_{p=1}^{n} X_{pij}(1 - \lambda_{pij} - \beta_{pij}), \, j = 1,3;$$

$$= 0, \, j = 4,5 \tag{4.3}$$

where p refers to the partner country, and the direction of the trade flow is from the first subscript to the second. (Subscript j refers to the product sector.) By contrast, gross imports—what must be paid to acquire effective imports—are merely the sum of partner exports:

$$M_{ij} = \Sigma_{p=1}^{n} X_{pij}. \tag{4.4}$$

This treatment of protection ignores the tariff revenue of the importing country as well as the quota rents of countries imposing voluntary export quotas. In principle, tariff revenue could be redistributed to households, and quota rents could be incorporated into producer behavior. Instead, here the rents from protection are considered as deadweight losses equivalent to real transportation costs. This simplification should have little effect on the principal question being examined—US wage differentials between skilled and unskilled labor.[1] However, a model more oriented toward estimating gains from trade liberalization, especially for developing countries with higher tariffs, would require a more complete treatment of protection.

Households and, thus, countries maximize their welfare by consuming according to Cobb-Douglas (CD) utility functions. This form has the property that expenditure on a specific product is a constant fraction of total expenditure, because the quantity consumed varies inversely with the price.[2] The outcome of the market process of consumer utility maximization mimics an optimization program from the standpoint of a global planner seeking to maximize multicountry utility with undifferentiated welfare weights (i.e., equal to unity for all countries). Thus, the global market process is simulated by

$$MaxW = \Sigma_{i=1}^{n} W_i;$$

$$W_i = \Pi_{j=1}^{5} C_{ij}^{\phi_{ij}} \tag{4.5}$$

where W_i is utility at the country level, ϕ_{ij} is the expenditure share for good j in country i, and W is utility (or welfare) at the global level.

Maximizing consumption subject to factor availability to produce the goods consumed is the quantity version of a general equilibrium model. In this version, prices of goods and factors emerge as the "dual" and, in particular, are the shadow prices generated by the maximization program.[3] In contrast, in the Krugman model employed in chapter 3, factor

---

1. US tariffs are now generally low, and their revenue is insufficient to comprise significant resources for fiscal redistribution.

2. Consider the form $U = C_1^\alpha C_2^{1-\alpha}$. The price of good 1 is the change in the utility function for unit change in availability, or $P_1 = \partial U/\partial C_1 = \alpha C_1^{\alpha-1} C_2^{1-\alpha}$. Expenditure is price times quantity: $P_1 C_1 = [\alpha C_1^{\alpha-1} C_2^{1-\alpha}][C_1] = \alpha U$. Thus, expenditure on good 1 is the constant share α of total utility.

3. The shadow price is the change in the utility function in response to a unit change in the availability of the good or factor.

and product prices are the direct elements of the general equilibrium problem, and quantities emerge as dual results. Thus, the analysis there shocked factor prices and examined the resulting change in the quantity of domestic production of goods 1 and 2—and, thus, the amount of trade.

Using the quantity formulation of the general equilibrium process is more appropriate for the purposes here. It permits us to apply historical and prospective factor endowments to estimates of production functions and transport and trade barrier leakage and then to calculate expected optimal profiles of trade and production. These optimal solutions will generate shadow prices of factors, permitting us to examine the implications for relative wages of skilled and unskilled labor. Working instead with the price duals as the primary determinants would require specifying arbitrary factor-price shocks and then examining whether the quantity duals appeared reasonable—a considerably more indirect procedure. For example, for each year and scenario it would be likely to take numerous iterative optimization runs of alternative postulated relative factor prices in order to find that set of factor prices generating implied factor endowments acceptably close to actual (or scenario experiment) factor endowments, thereby multiplying severalfold the already extensive calculation task.

The translation of the optimization results into factor prices requires care. Because the variable being maximized in the objective function is welfare-based on a CD function of consumption in the various sectors, the shadow price of a given factor, such as skilled labor, will show the marginal impact of an additional unit of this factor on welfare, not production. In contrast, the factor price is the marginal product of the factor, or its incremental impact on production, not welfare. Thus, the optimization shadow price will not equal the factor price. However, the two vary directly together. More importantly for the analysis here, the ratio of the shadow price of skilled labor to that of unskilled labor (or, for that matter, the shadow price ratio for another pair of factors) is equal to the corresponding ratio of the factors' marginal products or factor prices.[4] Thus, we can use the optimization framework to determine factor/price ratios.

4. Suppose welfare $W = Q_1^\psi Q_2^{1-\psi}$, where there is no trade so consumption is output (Q) for each sector. Let $Q_i = S_i^{\alpha_i} U_i^{1-\alpha_i}$ where i is the sector, S is skilled labor, and U is unskilled labor. General equilibrium means shadow prices are equal across sectors for a given factor and so are factor marginal products, so we need examine only one sector. The shadow price of skilled labor can be told from $\partial W / \partial S = (\partial W / \partial Q_1)(\partial Q_1 / \partial S_1)$. Taking the derivatives of the welfare and production functions with respect to output and skilled labor respectively and simplifying, $\partial W / \partial Q_1 = \psi(W/Q_1)$, and $\partial Q_1 / \partial S_1 = \alpha_1(Q_1/S_1)$. So $\partial W / \partial S_1 = \psi \alpha_1 (W/S_1)$. Similarly, for unskilled labor, $\partial W / \partial U_1 = \psi(1 - \alpha_1)(W/U_1)$. So the ratio of the shadow price of skilled labor to that of unskilled labor is $p_s^*/p_u^* = [\alpha_1/(1 - \alpha_1)][U_1/S_1]$. Since the marginal products (factor prices) of the two factors are $\alpha_1(Q_1/S_1)$ and $(1 - \alpha_1)(Q_1/U_1)$, respectively, the factor price ratio is also $[\alpha_1/(1 - \alpha_1)][U_1/S_1]$; QED. Thus, the shadow price ratio

The maximization problem in equation 4.5 is subject to the restraints of factor availability. Thus,

$$\Sigma_{j=1}^{5} S_{ij} \leq S_i;$$

$$\Sigma_{j=1}^{5} U_{ij} \leq U_i;$$

$$\Sigma_{j=1}^{5} K_{ij} \leq K_i. \tag{4.6}$$

There is also a need to constrain the model so that levels of trade are within reason. One such constraint should concern plausible trade balance outcomes. Another should take account of the level of exports relative to domestic production, and of imports relative to domestic consumption, for the sector in question.

The spirit of the TIDE model is to keep as simple as possible all elements not directly focused on the relative wage of skilled and unskilled labor. The model applies only the most basic trade constraints. First, the trade balance may not be in deficit or surplus by more than 1 percent of GDP (total domestic output in all sectors, i.e., $Q_i = \Sigma_{j=1,5}Q_{ij}$).[5] Second, for a given sector, imports (net of "leakage") may not exceed half of domestic consumption, and exports may not exceed half of domestic output. Thus,

$$-0.01Q_i \leq X_i - M_i \leq 0.01Q_i, \text{ where}$$

$$X_i = \Sigma_{p=1}^{n} \Sigma_{j=1}^{3} X_{ipj},$$

$$M_i = \Sigma_{j=1}^{3} M_{ij} \tag{4.7}$$

and

$$X_{ij} \leq 0.5 \, Q_{ij};$$

$$M_{ij}^* \leq 0.5 \, C_{ij}. \tag{4.8}$$

derived from the optimization of welfare equals the factor price ratio, even though the level of the shadow price differs from that of the factor price. In general, the former will tend to be smaller than the latter, as is found below and as might be suspected from the fact that the coefficients ψ and $1 - \psi$, each of which is less than unity, premultiply what otherwise looks like the factor price (marginal product), but with W replacing Q.

5. An earlier version of the TIDE model set only an upper bound on the trade deficit at 30 percent of the export base. However, this resulted in optimal solutions showing the United States in large trade surplus, especially for 1973, contrary to actual experience. A large trade imbalance intermixes transitory employment-level effects of trade with long-term effects associated with factor intensity of exports and imports, clouding the effect of the latter. Moreover, factor-price equalization and other results of the HO-SS framework (chapter 2) may not hold when the trade imbalance is large. I am indebted to an anonymous reviewer for this observation.

The use of a 50 percent limit on imports as a fraction of sectoral domestic consumption is a simplified way to avoid extreme solutions of complete specialization. Frequently, trade models accomplish the same result by applying imperfect substitution between imports and domestic goods in the consumption function. In particular, the "Armington assumption" specifies a given elasticity of substitution between imports and domestic goods, typically allowing perfect substitution only among alternative foreign sources of the good in question. In contrast, the TIDE model assumes perfect substitution between imports and domestic goods in consumption (equation 4.2). Identifying the proper elasticity of substitution between imports and domestic goods is itself difficult and in the type of exercise here would in any case need to result from experimentation yielding "reasonable" import penetration levels similar to the 50 percent ceiling imposed directly. Once again, the objective of the model is to focus the modeling effort on relative factor prices, rather than other aspects.

Although the TIDE model is general, implicitly it refers principally to trade in manufactured goods. There is no attempt to incorporate natural resource inputs, which would be appropriate if trade in primary goods were to be included explicitly. Similarly, the rough comparisons below of model results to actual trade flows consider only trade in manufactures. Moreover, the oil exporting country group is excluded from the model simulations.

In principle, it would be possible to add trade in oil and other raw materials exogenously. For example, more realistic trade balance constraints could explicitly add the influence of imposed levels of trade in raw materials. Rather than introducing such adjustments, the strategy followed here is to focus on trade in manufactures, where the impact of North-South trade on unskilled wages is most likely to arise. However, in interpreting the results it will occasionally be necessary to keep in mind that a specific country relies heavily on raw materials exports or imports.

Similarly, setting a limit on the trade deficit relative to GDP implicitly limits capital inflows, rather than attempting to optimize them. Adding capital flow optimization would require a much more complicated specification. As structured, the model can be solved for static equilibrium at each of several points in time. Endogenous capital flows would instead require a dynamic specification, whereby capital stock and factor payments in a given period would have to be linked to capital flows in an earlier period.

Finally, implementation of the TIDE model applies the GAMS (General Algebraic Modeling System) optimization methodology developed by Brooke, Kendrick, and Meeraus (1988).

Factor Data

The retrospective analysis using TIDE examines factor endowments and patterns of trade specialization in three benchmark years: 1973, 1984, and

1994. Data on the total labor force for each country or region come from the World Bank (1995a).[6] Estimates of educational attainment compiled by researchers at the World Bank (Nehru, Swanson, and Dubey 1995) provide the point of departure for dividing the labor force into skilled and unskilled workers.[7] These data report the mean years of education of the working-age population (15 to 64 years) in each country for individual years. It is then necessary to translate mean education into skilled versus unskilled.

Wood (1994, 402-03) estimates the manufacturing labor force composition by skilled and unskilled workers for the "North" and the "South." He considers white-collar and blue-collar workers separately. Within the white-collar group, he identifies professional, technical, and managerial workers as skilled, in addition to an assumed portion of clerical and sales workers.[8] In the blue-collar category, he draws upon the limited data available to distinguish between skilled and unskilled manual laborers. He considers the latter data relatively satisfactory for the North, but much less so for the South. Moreover, whereas his estimates for the North are a weighted average of data for industrial countries, his calculations for the South are based on only three countries (South Korea, Hong Kong, and Taiwan).

Wood's resulting estimate is that in 1984-85 50.2 percent of the workforce in the North was skilled and 49.8 percent unskilled, whereas in the South the corresponding shares were 13.25 percent and 86.75 percent.

For its part, the World Bank database shows that in 1984, mean years of schooling stood at 11.3 for the United States. The corresponding manufacturing-employment-weighted figure for industrial countries was 9.4 mean years of schooling. For South Korea, this database shows 7.1 mean years of schooling in 1984 (the World Bank estimates do not include Hong Kong and Taiwan).

We may posit a relationship between the fraction of the workforce that is skilled and the average educational attainment of the working-age

---

6. For countries with data missing for the year in question, the entry for the closest available year is used. For countries not included in the *World Tables*, estimates are derived from US Central Intelligence Agency data and from data on labor force relative to population as reported in the Penn world tables (Penn 1994).

7. These human capital data as well as the physical capital data discussed below are from the World Bank's STARS (Socio-economic Time-series Access and Retrieval System) database. For missing observations, educational attainment is imputed on the basis of a cross-country quadratic regression relating mean education years to purchasing power parity GDP per capita. In the cross-country regressions, the observations for the former Soviet Union and Eastern Europe impute an additional 20 percent to the reported purchasing parity per capita incomes to allow for probable understatement in the international tables, and extreme observations (Kuwait and the United Arab Emirates) are omitted.

8. Wood's basic data source is the International Labour Organisation's *Yearbook of Labour Statistics*.

population. If, for simplicity, this relationship is linear, then the observations for South Korea and the "North" provide two points along this line, and we may interpolate intermediate points. For countries with lower mean educational attainment than that of South Korea, it is simply assumed that the skilled fraction may be linearly interpolated between the zero point (zero education, zero skilled fraction) and the observation for South Korea.[9]

Another World Bank database (Nehru and Dhareshwar 1993) provides the information that lies behind the estimates of capital stock. This source uses series on real investment dating as far back as 1950 to compile capital-stock estimates. The contribution of a given year's investment to current capital stock is based on a geometric decay rate meant to incorporate depreciation and rising productivity from better technology embodied in later vintages.[10]

The capital-stock data are in constant prices but are expressed in local currency. Thus, it is necessary to convert the data into internationally comparable values. Estimates of purchasing power parity (PPP) GDP provide a basis for obtaining capital stock on a PPP basis.[11] The World Bank's capital stock data set also reports GDP in the same units (real domestic currency). Thus, it is possible to obtain the estimate of the capital/output ratio. Multiplying PPP GDP by the capital/output ratio yields an estimate of capital stock in each country, expressed in PPP dollars.

Table 4.1 reports the shares of each of the countries in the TIDE model in global aggregates of skilled labor, unskilled labor, PPP capital stock, and PPP GDP for each of the three benchmark years considered.[12] These

9. The estimate is $s = -49.27 + 8.805N$, where s is the percentage of labor force that is skilled ($1 - s$ is the percentage unskilled) and N is the mean number of years of education, for $N > 7.1$ (the figure for South Korea) and $s = 1.866N$ otherwise.

10. For the important estimate of capital stock in the initial year before data on annual investment are available, the authors use what they call a modified Harberger approach. Under the assumption that capital and output are growing at equal rates in the initial period, the initial capital stock equals the first year's investment flow divided by the sum of the GDP growth rate and the depreciation rate. To abstract from annual fluctuation, the authors impute the first year's investment rate based on a log linear regression of investment on time.

11. PPP GDP per capita in US dollars for 1993 is available from the World Bank (1995a,b). PPP GDP is obtained by multiplying the per capita figure by population (from the same source). For earlier years (1984 and 1973), estimates are taken from Penn (1994). All estimates are converted to 1990 dollars by deflating by the US GDP deflator. In addition, the figures for the earlier years are adjusted by country-specific ratios of World Bank to Penn PPP per capita income for 1992, a year for which estimates are available from both sources. Where data are not available for the specific year in question, the estimate is obtained by extrapolation from the closest year available based on growth rates reported in World Bank (1995a).

12. Note that for the human capital database, 1987 is the most recent year available. The 1993 estimates in table 3.1 are obtained by linear extrapolation from the 1984 and 1987 data

estimates show the developed-country (DC) share of PPP global product as having declined from 64.5 percent in 1973 to 57.7 percent in 1993. Over these two decades, the DC share of the global stock of skilled labor fell from 58.2 percent to 45.2 percent; of unskilled labor, from 15.7 percent to 11.9 percent; and of capital, from 67.2 percent to 59.0 percent.

There was a sharp increase in the global output share of Asian LDCs, which rose from 12.1 percent to 20.5 percent. However, there was a major reduction in the world output share of Eastern Europe (including the former Soviet Union), which fell from 7.9 percent to 4.8 percent.

Table 4.1 reveals certain idiosyncrasies in the measured factor stocks. The United States has shown a considerably higher relative supply of skilled labor than has the European Union (EU). Thus, in 1993 the United States showed 72 million skilled and 53 million unskilled workers, whereas the European Union showed 49 million skilled and 108 million unskilled workers. These estimates reflect the tendency toward longer formal schooling in the United States and appear to overstate the country's true relative availability of skilled labor.

A somewhat surprising estimate in table 4.1 is the substantial presence of skilled labor in the LDCs. They accounted for about 42 percent of world skilled labor in 1973 and 55 percent by 1993. Significant educational bases, combined with the sheer mass of the labor force especially in China and India, mean that the absolute size of the LDC skilled labor force is large. However, the LDCs have a far larger share of world unskilled labor (about 84 percent in 1973 and 88 percent by 1993). Thus, relative factor endowment is strongly skewed toward skilled labor in the industrial countries.

At the same time, the skill intensity of DC labor endowment has declined over time relative to that in developing countries. Thus, skilled labor rose from 46 percent to 68 percent of total labor in the industrial countries from 1973 to 1993, or by a multiple of 1.48, whereas skilled labor rose from 6.2 percent to 11.2 percent of the LDC labor force over the same period, or by a multiple of 1.81.

Table 4.2 shows the absolute factor stocks and PPP GDP corresponding to the global shares in table 4.1. It also shows growth rates for 1973-84 and 1984-93. Growth rates of the stocks of skilled labor tend to be higher than those of unskilled labor. Indeed, for the later period, there is an absolute decline in the stock of unskilled labor in the main industrial countries and in the G4, as the pace of skills upgrading swamped the underlying growth of the labor force. For both periods, growth rates of skilled labor were generally much higher for developing countries than for industrial countries.[13] Growth rates of unskilled labor were also higher

---

on each country or region. The same method is used to update the most recent capital figure estimates (for 1990) to 1993.

13. The rapid decline in the absolute level of skilled workers in Eastern Europe in the second decade would appear to be a data anomaly, representing, in part, the combined

in developing countries, but the difference between the two regions is smaller than for skilled labor.

These patterns suggest two potentially conflicting trends for the skill composition of North-South trade. Because the level of skills is so much higher in all periods in the North, we would expect any process that increases trade over time (such as falling transportation costs and trade barriers) to cause a shift in product specialization toward skill-intensive goods in the North and unskilled-intensive goods in the South. Conversely, however, for a constant degree of international integration (e.g., constant transport costs and trade barriers), one should instead expect some diminution in the skill intensity of production in the North and increase in that of the South over time, because the relative supply of skilled workers in the South is rising, albeit from a low base.

Table 4.2 also shows that growth rates for capital stocks have tended to be higher for developing countries (especially Asian) than for industrial countries. This phenomenon too should reduce the traditional comparative advantage of the North (in this case, in capital-intensive goods) over time.

Finally, the growth rates of real PPP output in table 4.2 warrant comment. One surprising feature is that although the Asian growth rates exceed those of the industrial countries, the difference is not as great as usually measured, especially for the second period. The Asian growth rates were lower than usually reported (e.g., China's growth in this period is typically gauged at about 10 percent annually, versus about 6 percent in table 4.2). The divergence from the more normal patterns is likely due in part to the difference between PPP and domestic measurement of GDP growth. For the developing countries, PPP weights will expand the weight of agriculture and services relative to manufacturing. This reweighting will tend to drag down the measured growth of overall GDP, considering that manufacturing is the fastest-growing sector.

For the industrial countries, second, Europe and Japan show a surprising acceleration in growth from the first decade to the second, whereas direct estimates from national accounts show decelerating growth (see, e.g., Cline 1994c). This idiosyncrasy may reflect the rise in the dollar in the first period and its decline in the second, combined with a tendency for domestic prices to respond less than fully to exchange rate changes.

Trade Data

Whereas the TIDE model applies "country" factor-endowment data directly, it simulates trade outcomes rather than basing them upon directly

---

effect of falling PPP GDP in this period and the method of interpolating missing educational data points from PPP per capita income.

Table 4.1 Country shares in global factor endowments and output, 1973-93 (percentages unless noted)

Country	Skilled labor			Unskilled labor			Capital			PPP output			Memorandum Capital/output ratio		
	1973	1984	1993	1973	1984	1993	1973	1984	1993	1973	1984	1993	1973	1984	1993
United States	23.1	21.3	19.4	3.4	3.1	2.6	27.0	21.3	20.8	25.5	22.8	22.2	2.60	2.72	2.72
Canada	1.4	1.6	1.7	0.5	0.4	0.4	1.7	1.8	2.0	2.0	2.1	2.0	2.11	2.48	2.71
European Union[a]	17.5	14.0	13.3	7.6	6.6	5.3	25.5	21.3	20.7	23.8	20.3	20.2	2.58	3.02	2.99
Japan	13.4	10.2	8.2	2.0	1.7	1.6	7.3	8.6	10.5	8.1	8.0	9.0	2.21	3.13	3.29
RO[b]	2.8	2.7	2.6	2.2	2.1	2.0	5.7	5.2	5.0	5.1	4.7	4.3	2.76	3.25	3.32
Mexico	0.7	0.9	1.2	1.0	1.2	1.4	1.6	2.1	2.3	2.0	2.3	2.1	2.04	2.71	2.95
RL[c]	2.9	3.3	3.7	4.7	5.0	5.3	6.0	6.6	6.4	6.5	6.4	6.1	2.27	2.99	3.03
China	15.4	19.6	21.7	29.0	30.1	30.4	4.4	5.1	8.3	5.4	7.0	9.6	1.99	2.10	2.37
India	5.4	6.4	7.1	15.2	14.8	15.3	2.8	2.8	3.0	2.8	3.3	3.8	2.42	2.49	2.34
G4[d]	1.0	1.4	3.7	1.3	1.3	0.9	0.9	1.7	2.8	1.2	1.9	3.0	1.86	2.62	2.71
RA[e]	3.8	4.4	5.3	8.5	8.8	9.5	1.8	2.8	3.4	2.7	3.3	4.1	1.69	2.40	2.38
EE[f]	8.0	8.1	3.8	9.9	9.0	8.4	9.9	11.5	6.2	7.9	8.7	4.8	2.70	3.27	3.35
OPEC[g]	2.3	3.1	4.4	6.1	6.6	7.1	2.7	6.3	6.2	4.1	6.0	5.9	1.64	3.04	2.98
RW[h]	2.3	2.9	4.0	8.5	9.4	10.0	2.6	3.0	2.5	2.9	3.2	2.8	2.17	2.64	2.60
Total available[i]	184.7	274.0	371.3	1485.5	1827.6	2065.0	33.42	53.63	81.61	13.6	18.4	28.1	2.45	2.91	2.91

a. 1994 definition.
b. Rest of OECD.
c. Rest of Latin America except Venezuela.
d. Hong Kong, South Korea, Taiwan, and Singapore.
e. Rest of Asia.
f. Eastern Europe, including Russia.
g. Organization of Petroleum Exporting Countries (including Venezuela).
h. Rest of world.
i. Millions for labor; trillions of 1990 dollars for capital and PPP output.

Table 4.2 Trends in factor endowments, 1973-93

Country or group	1973	1984	1993	Average annual growth 1973-84	Average annual growth 1984-93
Skilled labor (thousands)					
United States	42,613	58,498	72,134	2.9	2.3
Canada	2,617	4,491	6,243	4.9	3.7
European Union[a]	32,365	38,362	49,200	1.5	2.8
Japan	24,723	27,955	30,456	1.1	1.0
RO[b]	5,162	7,453	9,703	3.3	2.9
Mexico	1,268	2,577	4,370	6.4	5.9
RL[c]	5,414	9,159	13,586	4.8	4.4
China	28,496	53,671	80,652	5.8	4.5
India	9,889	17,531	26,292	5.2	4.5
G4[d]	1,824	3,792	13,721	6.7	14.3
RA[e]	7,049	11,949	19,670	4.8	5.5
EE[f]	14,796	22,119	14,025	3.7	−5.1
OPEC[g]	4,223	8,488	16,211	6.3	7.2
RW[h]	4,287	7,962	15,019	5.6	7.1
Total	184,726	274,007	371,282	3.6	3.4
Unskilled labor (thousands)					
United States	50,837	56,882	52,666	1.0	−0.9
Canada	6,934	8,052	7,448	1.4	−0.9
European Union[a]	113,101	119,948	108,493	0.5	−1.1
Japan	29,974	31,272	32,862	0.4	0.6
RO[b]	32,835	37,585	41,364	1.2	1.1
Mexico	15,196	22,687	28,992	3.6	2.7
RL[c]	69,817	90,866	108,808	2.4	2.0
China	431,124	549,369	626,818	2.2	1.5
India	225,571	269,859	315,168	1.6	1.7
G4[d]	18,649	24,057	19,502	2.3	−2.3
RA[e]	126,639	161,680	196,480	2.2	2.2
EE[f]	147,545	164,154	172,975	1.0	0.6
OPEC[g]	90,602	120,304	147,539	2.6	2.3
RW[h]	126,665	170,912	205,852	2.7	2.1
Total	1,485,489	1,827,627	2,064,967	1.9	1.4
Capital (billions of 1990 dollars)					
United States	9,856.9	13,412.2	16,926.3	2.8	2.6
Canada	627.1	1,112.9	1,612.0	5.2	4.1
European Union[a]	9,319.1	13,411.3	16,831.6	3.3	2.5
Japan	2,655.3	5,423.5	8,553.7	6.5	5.1
RO[b]	2,096.2	3,274.8	4,052.7	4.1	2.4
Mexico	602.7	1,333.1	1,840.1	7.2	3.6
RL[c]	2,206.7	4,147.1	5,226.0	5.7	2.6

Table 4.2 Trends in factor endowments, 1973-93 (continued)

Country or group	1973	1984	1993	Average annual growth 1973-84	Average annual growth 1984-93
China	1,607.6	3,186.4	6,738.1	6.2	8.3
India	1,014.4	1,775.3	2,429.0	5.1	3.5
G4[d]	324.8	1,075.7	2,314.5	10.9	8.5
RA[e]	669.0	1,764.8	2,741.6	8.8	4.9
EE[f]	3,614.1	7,269.0	5,008.9	6.4	−4.1
OPEC[g]	1,001.5	3,979.4	5,050.1	12.5	2.6
RW[h]	944.0	1,861.3	2,048.0	6.2	1.1
Total	36,539.6	63,026.8	81,372.4	5.0	2.8
PPP output (billions of 1990 dollars)					
United States	3,798.5	4,936.9	6,216.3	2.4	2.6
Canada	297.0	448.8	567.8	3.8	2.6
European Union[a]	3,542.4	4,406.7	5,662.5	2.0	2.8
Japan	1,202.0	1,734.7	2,530.1	3.3	4.2
RO[b]	758.9	1,008.8	1,209.0	2.6	2.0
Mexico	295.6	491.9	597.3	4.6	2.2
RL[c]	970.3	1,386.2	1,702.0	3.2	2.3
China	807.9	1,514.7	2,676.2	5.7	6.3
India	419.8	713.0	1,068.0	4.8	4.5
G4[d]	174.5	411.1	830.5	7.8	7.8
RA[e]	395.1	723.2	1,151.4	5.5	5.2
EE[f]	1,178.8	1,889.2	1,353.2	4.3	−3.7
OPEC[g]	610.7	1,310.5	1,644.3	6.9	2.5
RW[h]	435.0	704.6	778.1	4.4	1.1
Total	14,886.4	21,680.2	27,986.6	3.4	2.8

a. 1994 definition.
b. Rest of OECD.
c. Rest of Latin America except Venezuela.
d. Hong Kong, South Korea, Taiwan, and Singapore.
e. Rest of Asia.
f. Eastern Europe, including Russia.
g. Organization of Petroleum Exporting Countries (including Venezuela).
h. Rest of world.

observed data. Nevertheless, it is important to consider the path of actual trade in manufactures as a basis for gauging the broad success or failure of the model in capturing the trend in trade consequences of changing factor endowments.

The TIDE model divides manufactures into three types: skilled intensive, unskilled, and capital intensive. As discussed in chapter 1, although technically it is impossible to classify a product unambiguously as intensive in a given factor once the number of factors exceeds two, it can be shown that any product is a "friend" to a particular factor in the sense that an increase in the price of the good will tend to increase the relative price of the factor in question. For purposes of the TIDE model, the three "products" may be seen as groupings of goods that are "intensive" in the use of skilled labor, unskilled labor, and capital in the broad sense of being "friends" of these three factors, respectively.

Sachs and Shatz (1994) rank 131 three-digit SIC sectors by the ratio of unskilled to skilled workers (production/total workers). The first four deciles provide a grouping of unskilled-intensive sectors and include such sectors as footwear (SIC 314), certain textiles and apparel (223, 236), and iron and steel (332). The final four deciles provide a guide to skill-intensive sectors and include such industries as computers (357), aircraft (372), engines and turbines (351), and industrial inorganic chemicals (281). Thus, these rankings give one basis for distinguishing between skilled- and unskilled-intensive goods.

Leamer (1992) divides US three-digit industries into a 3 × 3 matrix of ascending capital per worker (rows) and skill levels (columns). The upper-left cell is low skill, low capital, and includes such sectors as apparel, food products, furniture, and footwear. The upper-right cell is high skill, low capital, and includes metal structures and measuring devices. Thus, these two cells provide a basis for identifying sectors that are unskilled and skilled intensive, respectively. Similarly, the bottom-middle cell has high capital per worker but an intermediate level of skills, and so provides an indication of capital-intensive goods (including automobiles and paper mills).

Finally, the US input-output table (DOC 1994) reports the division of value added into compensation of employees, indirect taxes, and payment to capital ("other value added"). An ordering of the manufacturing categories by the share of capital in value added provides a further basis for identifying capital-intensive goods. The median point for this share is about 35 percent, and sectors with a higher capital share are candidates for classification as capital intensive.

Table 4A.1 in appendix 4A reports the classification of two-digit SITC (Standard International Trade Classification) categories into skilled-, unskilled-, and capital-intensive groupings on the basis of information from these three sources. On the basis of this allocation of trade categories, table 4.3 reports net trade in each of the three broad manufactured-product groups between the various pairs of the "countries" of the TIDE model, for the benchmark years 1973, 1984, and 1993.[14] The trade data refer only to manufactures, defined as broad sections 5 through 8 of the SITC.

In models capable of explaining two-way (intraindustry) trade (caused, e.g., by economies of scale and product differentiation), it would be neces-

---

14. The estimates are from a compilation prepared especially for this study by the United Nations statistical division from the data in its trade data set reported in *Trade by Commodities* (annual issues).

sary to consider gross flows of exports and imports in each good. However, the approach here deals with homogeneous goods in which in principle a country will be either an exporter or an importer. Net trade in a product is, thus, the relevant concept.

In the table, the entries report the net exports from the country listed at the head of each subblock to the partners listed within the subblock. For example, US exports of skilled goods to Canada minus Canadian exports of skilled goods to the United States amounted to $2.68 billion in 1973 and $14.8 billion in 1993. The table truncates redundant pairs, so that net exports of China to the United States in unskilled goods (for example) must be read as the negative of the entry for US net exports of these goods to China. Thus, Chinese net exports of unskilled goods to the United States rose from $12.7 million in 1973 to $9.9 billion in 1993.

For the United States, the net trade data in table 4.3 show a systematic tendency toward greater comparative advantage in skilled goods than in unskilled goods, as expected. Thus, in each year, net trade aggregated over all partners is (algebraically) much higher in skilled goods than in unskilled goods. It is also evident that the United States systematically has a greater tendency toward comparative advantage in capital-intensive than in unskilled-intensive goods, as once again the net trade aggregate is higher in capital-intensive than in unskilled-intensive goods in all three years.

As also might be expected, however, the pattern is more ambiguous with respect to skilled versus capital-intensive goods. In 1973 and 1984 the United States had a much larger net trade balance in skilled manufactures than in capital-intensive manufactures. However, by 1993 the reverse was true. The implication is that technological catch-up in other countries may have eroded the comparative advantage of the United States in skilled goods relative to capital-intensive goods.

Table 4.3 also reveals a sharp concentration by country for the exceptions to US comparative advantage in skilled goods. In the first period, Japan was the principal country with which the United States had a net trade deficit in skilled goods. However, by 1984 and especially 1993, the G4 was also important. By 1993, net US trade in skilled manufactures was in deficit by $45 billion with Japan and $23 billion with the G4. Surprisingly, the United States also had a deficit with Mexico in skilled goods that was about five times as large as the US deficit with Mexico in unskilled goods.[15] The rest of Asia is the only other area with which the United States had a trade deficit in skilled goods by 1993. Excluding Japan, the G4, Mexico, and the rest of Asia, US net trade in skilled manufactures stood at a surplus of about $37 billion, which included surpluses with Canada, the European Union, and the rest of the OECD.

---

15. These data are thus consistent with the Revenga-Montenegro (1995) finding of substantial skill intensity in Mexican exports of manufactures.

Table 4.3 Actual net trade in manufactures by factor intensity and partner (millions of dollars)

		Skilled-intensive manufactures			Unskilled-intensive manufactures			Capital-intensive manufactures			Total		
		1973	1984	1993	1973	1984	1993	1973	1984	1993	1973	1984	1993
US	Canada	2,677.1	5,472.7	14,768.9	−251.4	−3,383.8	−1,554.5	−805.0	−11,420.8	−14,959.4	1,620.7	−9,332.0	−1,745.0
	EU	1,600.7	4,499.8	673.8	−3,464.1	−10,781.2	−11,306.4	−1,422.4	−7,405.5	−5,884.0	−3,285.8	−13,686.9	−16,516.5
	Japan	−2,088.1	−19,998.7	−45,284.0	−1,903.4	−10,772.3	−4,702.9	−2,005.2	−17,595.5	−26,075.8	−5,996.7	−48,366.5	−76,062.7
	RO	458.5	1,777.6	2,310.0	−244.0	−1,140.5	−1,164.6	291.3	−128.6	−1,172.9	505.7	508.5	2,318.3
	Mexico	752.1	1,443.7	−2,498.1	−52.5	−542.6	−471.6	542.6	1,746.8	1,905.8	1,242.2	2,647.9	−1,063.8
	RL	1,669.5	2,976.5	8,633.8	11.7	−2,113.3	−400.5	1,548.3	2,430.8	7,075.2	3,229.5	3,294.0	15,308.4
	China	9.3	562.9	−722.5	−12.7	−747.1	−9,934.1	52.2	627.4	2,217.5	48.8	443.2	−8,439.0
	India	66.7	448.5	711.1	−56.1	−856.6	−2,445.8	−108.6	344.6	550.1	−98.0	−63.5	−1,184.5
	G4	−310.8	−8,698.7	−23,431.2	−2,321.8	−18,640.0	−33,013.4	354.2	788.1	7,900.1	−2,278.4	−26,550.6	−48,544.5
	RA	388.3	1,155.2	−2,591.1	−175.6	−1,544.3	−8,474.1	400.7	801.4	3,379.9	613.4	412.3	−7,685.2
	EE	284.8	173.6	1,587.1	−236.3	−468.5	−1,355.4	100.9	18.6	496.1	149.4	−276.3	727.8
	OPEC	1,207.1	5,029.1	6,069.6	206.1	79.3	−2,044.4	717.5	2,921.4	5,846.7	2,130.6	8,029.8	9,871.9
	RW	799.4	2,449.3	2,491.2	−105.7	−526.9	−3,072.7	804.4	1,903.5	2,889.1	1,498.0	3,825.9	2,307.6
	Total	7,514.5	−2,708.5	−37,281.4	−8,605.8	−51,437.8	−79,940.3	470.8	−24,967.9	−13,485.5	−620.5	−79,114.3	−130,707.3
Canada	EU	−635.9	−1,008.7	−1,711.2	−16.0	−963.9	−705.0	−195.0	−792.0	−970.5	−846.9	−2,764.6	−3,386.6
	Japan	−347.4	−1,386.2	−2,576.7	−174.4	−822.1	−185.1	−267.9	−1,498.1	−2,228.5	−789.8	−3,706.4	−4,990.3
	RO	−116.6	−113.5	−298.4	−46.7	−129.6	−94.2	−15.5	43.7	−125.3	−178.7	−199.4	−517.9
	Mexico	20.6	−23.0	−347.8	4.9	23.1	34.3	35.7	36.3	−702.8	61.2	36.4	−1,016.3
	RL	92.9	227.7	277.2	55.2	328.9	−101.4	98.5	190.4	336.3	246.7	747.0	512.2
	China	0.7	5.7	131.3	59.5	−47.0	−654.6	−13.3	57.7	104.6	46.9	16.4	−418.7
	India	10.5	31.0	25.0	4.5	−44.1	−90.5	0.1	107.7	18.4	15.1	94.6	−47.1
	G4	−66.8	−647.9	−1,948.7	−231.7	−1,254.8	−2,239.3	−2.4	−125.7	6.7	−300.9	−2,028.4	−4,181.2
	RA	18.3	60.9	−155.6	−4.2	−80.3	−499.0	20.6	72.1	36.5	34.8	52.7	−618.1
	EE	2.6	24.4	211.8	−41.4	−45.8	−121.8	7.5	43.6	34.5	−31.3	22.2	124.5
	OPEC	65.7	203.0	268.8	20.7	91.9	−100.2	75.9	456.3	458.9	162.3	751.1	627.5
	RW	47.0	132.5	78.8	9.0	25.8	2.8	55.0	150.1	164.8	111.0	308.4	246.5
	Total	−3,585.6	−7,966.9	−20,814.2	−109.1	465.8	−3,199.4	604.2	10,163.1	12,093.1	−3,090.5	2,662.0	−11,920.5

EU	Japan	-1,073.8	-8,141.4	-25,131.9	-579.7	-2,223.3	-203.0	-850.5	-3,620.3	-7,614.3	-2,504.1	-13,985.0	-32,949.2
	RO	3,604.2	7,123.7	11,723.6	2,179.7	2,908.1	5,667.3	2,842.4	3,086.2	8,103.8	8,626.3	13,118.0	25,494.6
	Mexico	356.3	678.2	2,447.3	31.6	120.2	630.7	233.4	459.0	1,717.3	621.3	1,257.5	4,795.2
	RL	2,012.3	3,222.7	8,049.2	-41.0	-225.2	-717.6	1,701.0	2,672.6	8,853.2	3,672.3	5,670.1	16,184.8
	China	116.3	833.1	4,930.4	267.5	198.5	-3,682.5	93.3	243.5	1,191.0	477.0	1,275.0	2,438.9
	India	350.5	1,122.6	2,079.7	-2.0	509.0	191.7	86.0	483.8	-281.3	434.4	2,115.4	1,990.1
	G4	447.5	-347.9	-9,528.6	-1,141.4	-3,683.0	-11,446.1	426.6	790.3	5,535.2	-267.3	-3,240.5	-15,439.5
	RA	621.1	1,824.3	3,472.4	-158.3	-694.6	-4,739.2	615.7	1,197.8	2,859.9	1,078.6	2,327.4	1,593.1
	EE	3,125.8	4,893.2	15,240.6	1,187.7	1,375.6	-5,460.7	1,888.4	3,874.7	11,532.1	6,201.9	10,143.5	21,312.0
	OPEC	2,882.2	14,433.1	17,163.8	1,133.5	6,854.2	3,847.1	2,131.3	10,234.0	10,586.4	6,147.0	31,521.3	31,597.3
	RW	3,801.3	10,875.3	14,826.8	303.8	3,805.4	2,784.4	4,487.8	10,562.2	13,760.0	8,592.8	25,242.8	31,371.2
	Total	15,278.9	33,025.7	46,310.6	6,661.5	20,690.1	-1,116.6	15,272.7	38,181.2	63,097.7	37,213.1	91,897.0	108,291.7
Japan	RO	383.2	3,202.7	4,645.7	336.9	496.5	-419.8	1,041.1	3,680.7	6,377.8	1,761.2	7,379.9	10,603.6
	Mexico	106.7	567.7	2,526.2	-17.1	95.0	471.8	27.6	99.5	732.9	117.2	762.2	3,730.9
	RL	582.1	1,282.7	2,510.2	334.1	63.4	-860.0	886.8	4,160.8	7,481.6	1,803.0	5,506.9	9,131.8
	China	112.9	2,122.1	5,789.1	376.6	2,461.0	-2,398.0	178.8	1,176.7	2,440.4	668.3	5,759.7	5,831.5
	India	57.5	511.9	827.3	101.6	122.7	-580.3	80.3	233.9	215.1	239.4	868.5	462.1
	G4	1,695.7	10,257.3	36,347.8	144.0	2,228.8	-28.5	1,319.4	4,487.3	14,699.4	3,159.1	16,973.5	51,018.6
	RA	765.9	3,436.6	12,115.6	305.8	1,037.3	2,084.3	740.6	2,774.7	7,962.0	1,812.2	7,248.5	22,161.9
	EE	398.7	1,162.0	1,038.5	40.9	900.5	-487.8	249.0	766.4	1,023.9	688.5	2,828.9	1,574.6
	OPEC	786.5	6,847.6	7,163.5	708.2	2,553.6	-369.5	831.9	5,061.7	6,606.4	2,326.6	14,462.9	13,400.3
	RW	410.0	2,295.7	2,251.6	-27.2	674.9	-297.3	2,213.7	2,688.2	5,174.6	2,596.6	5,658.9	7,128.9
	Total	8,808.6	61,212.6	148,208.0	4,961.4	24,451.5	2,205.9	10,692.8	47,843.8	88,632.7	24,462.8	133,507.9	239,046.5
RO	Mexico	96.8	145.0	349.9	8.1	-8.0	17.5	27.0	72.3	184.2	131.9	209.3	551.7
	RL	405.9	413.6	993.2	42.4	1.7	-140.0	296.4	633.3	1,653.1	744.7	1,048.6	2,506.2
	China	28.7	212.6	1,188.1	35.0	97.8	-568.8	-53.5	0.1	24.4	10.3	310.5	643.7
	India	46.7	205.7	324.4	0.5	-57.9	-303.7	0.1	3.4	-94.9	47.4	151.3	-74.3
	G4	203.5	-67.0	-1,970.8	-216.9	-1,301.0	-1,382.6	-27.3	-527.9	-71.7	-40.7	-1,895.9	-3,425.0

continued next page

189

Table 4.3 Actual net trade in manufactures by factor intensity and partner (millions of dollars) (continued)

		Skilled-intensive manufactures			Unskilled-intensive manufactures			Capital-intensive manufactures			Total		
		1973	1984	1993	1973	1984	1993	1973	1984	1993	1973	1984	1993
	RA	182.6	572.7	1,855.6	86.0	27.9	155.2	161.8	400.9	517.2	430.3	1,001.5	2,528.1
	EE	683.8	1,521.0	3,648.0	48.7	455.4	-149.3	545.3	1,589.2	1,892.8	1,277.8	3,565.5	5,391.4
	OPEC	350.1	2,099.8	2,709.4	94.3	1,572.2	1,547.6	297.2	1,905.0	1,574.4	741.6	5,577.1	5,831.4
	RW	493.6	1,191.7	1,216.4	34.2	442.6	916.6	1,003.8	1,212.2	1,932.9	1,531.6	2,846.4	4,065.9
	Total	-1,837.6	-5,695.5	-8,066.6	-2,093.5	-903.9	-3,896.2	-1,908.6	-1,393.4	-7,917.0	-5,839.7	-7,992.8	-19,879.8
Mexico	RL	12.7	40.1	196.2	33.1	41.1	-18.8	69.5	171.0	566.1	115.3	252.2	743.5
	China	0.1	1.8	-36.2	-2.0	27.8	-64.4	0.3	35.1	-17.4	-1.6	64.7	-118.0
	India	0.0	0.2	-1.9	0.0	3.7	-20.2	7.7	5.9	-22.9	7.7	9.8	-45.1
	G4	-3.8	-9.1	-711.4	-8.7	-13.2	-406.6	-0.3	36.2	-285.8	-12.8	13.9	-1,403.8
	RA	0.3	3.9	-126.6	0.2	1.4	-178.6	0.5	14.8	-9.8	0.9	20.0	-315.1
	EE	-4.9	20.4	-20.0	-0.4	10.9	-0.3	3.6	31.5	30.4	-1.7	62.8	10.1
	OPEC	20.7	17.4	25.0	7.7	22.5	-44.0	8.7	22.6	96.6	37.2	62.4	77.6
	RW	0.5	-0.3	-19.6	-0.7	2.3	-2.4	-1.9	11.1	-33.3	-2.1	13.1	-55.2
	Total	-1,306.9	-2,737.1	-3,171.9	54.1	408.7	-1,418.2	-778.1	-2,085.8	-3,513.5	-2,030.8	-4,414.3	-8,103.6
RL	China	-2.3	-5.8	-307.8	34.1	312.5	141.9	-3.0	102.3	-342.5	28.8	409.0	-508.4
	India	0.9	6.8	26.2	2.5	30.0	115.4	7.2	58.5	109.8	10.7	95.3	251.5
	G4	46.6	354.9	2,990.8	164.6	573.6	3,831.5	45.8	1,053.0	3,080.3	256.9	1,981.5	9,902.7
	RA	3.1	29.2	238.5	5.4	94.0	902.2	5.1	41.6	221.5	13.6	164.8	1,362.2
	EE	61.9	126.7	138.4	63.0	191.8	168.8	107.3	303.8	513.3	232.2	622.3	820.4
	OPEC	20.2	254.7	499.0	37.3	462.3	1,456.1	50.1	536.2	1,182.4	107.6	1,253.2	3,137.5
	RW	9.1	130.1	365.0	83.9	120.5	334.6	69.4	361.2	637.5	162.4	611.7	1,337.1
	Total	-4,635.8	-7,266.8	-16,709.7	-44.7	3,688.1	9,188.9	-4,318.7	-7,802.3	-20,563.3	-8,999.2	-11,381.0	-28,084.0
China	India	na	7.6	40.3	na	-1.9	-133.1	na	10.4	75.4	na	16.1	-17.5
	G4	57.7	-1,013.7	-16,924.3	245.3	936.4	717.2	309.7	698.6	-16,390.6	612.8	621.2	-32,597.7
	RA	31.8	208.8	968.0	59.4	105.9	161.4	60.3	279.4	905.0	151.5	594.2	2,034.4
	EE	-30.0	-38.4	-264.6	-32.6	-148.5	-1,283.1	-38.8	-184.8	-1,372.8	-101.3	-371.6	-2,920.5
	OPEC	24.9	61.7	643.5	41.7	145.7	310.6	31.9	16.5	425.2	98.6	223.8	1,379.3
	RW	47.8	41.6	451.6	59.0	17.4	330.3	87.8	76.5	438.5	194.5	135.5	1,220.4
	Total	-133.4	-4,464.7	-26,058.1	-385.2	-1,248.5	17,263.7	196.2	-1,346.3	-21,537.2	-322.4	-7,059.4	-30,331.6

India	G4	6.0	−410.1	−1,206.9	36.7	29.3	1,050.1	17.0	−729.2	−753.1	59.8	−1,110.0	−909.9
	RA	29.3	89.5	137.9	12.8	29.3	382.1	79.0	73.5	506.0	121.1	192.3	1,026.1
	EE	−72.7	98.0	6.9	109.9	346.4	278.8	73.5	539.8	247.6	110.6	984.2	533.4
	OPEC	24.0	90.8	281.0	31.2	130.9	620.4	27.0	−97.7	357.6	82.2	124.0	1,259.1
	RW	17.4	64.6	198.0	−39.8	2.7	146.4	59.2	−150.5	−9.3	36.7	−83.2	335.1
	Total	−528.8	−2,401.6	−4,615.2	99.7	833.6	5,744.3	182.8	−1,612.2	−220.8	−246.3	−3,180.2	908.3
G4	RA	260.8	1,941.7	4,337.8	92.3	718.9	707.1	228.9	2,003.3	7,249.4	582.1	4,663.9	12,294.2
	EE	−5.5	30.4	1,500.1	2.2	118.2	−59.4	−4.3	146.1	584.6	−7.6	294.8	2,025.2
	OPEC	101.7	1,097.0	2,732.3	169.8	1,644.4	624.7	161.5	1,172.2	2,121.8	433.0	3,913.6	5,478.8
	RW	46.7	375.2	2,062.4	19.7	373.5	19.6	99.8	724.4	2,237.5	166.2	1,473.1	4,319.6
	Total	−1,672.0	4,026.5	27,015.9	3,613.9	23,978.9	44,209.8	−1,956.7	−2,424.6	−1,527.3	−14.8	25,580.8	69,698.4
RA	EE	−90.1	−151.5	−29.1	7.6	−7.6	94.6	−17.4	−86.2	−244.7	−99.8	−245.3	−179.1
	OPEC	3.7	63.0	606.5	36.0	137.5	727.9	57.2	310.5	114.7	96.9	511.0	1,449.0
	RW	−1.3	−12.2	−123.1	9.0	23.0	339.6	4.4	58.7	222.3	12.1	69.6	438.8
	Total	−2,389.3	−9,423.3	−19,798.2	−171.3	457.4	10,660.6	−2,268.9	−7,376.4	−23,535.3	−4,829.5	−16,342.4	−32,672.8
EE	OPEC	156.2	1,018.9	335.4	90.0	406.6	196.7	52.7	377.2	151.0	298.9	1,802.7	683.0
	RW	108.6	513.0	−140.1	−0.6	290.6	411.6	22.5	318.0	581.1	130.5	1,121.7	852.6
	Total	−4,089.6	−6,327.8	−22,862.4	−1,060.0	−2,031.1	8,984.0	−2,839.8	−6,347.6	−14,005.7	−7,989.4	−14,706.5	−27,884.1
OPEC	RW	−71.0	−154.9	−195.8	−158.8	−354.9	−447.9	−88.7	−361.2	−709.8	−318.5	−871.0	−1,353.4
	Total	−5,714.1	−31,371.0	−38,693.5	−2,735.4	−14,455.9	−7,220.7	−4,531.5	−23,277.0	−30,232.0	−12,981.0	−69,103.9	−76,146.1
RW	Total	−5,709.0	−17,901.6	−23,463.4	−185.7	−4,896.9	−1,465.8	−8,817.2	−17,554.5	−27,286.0	−14,711.9	−40,353.0	−52,215.2

n.a. = not available.

Notes:

RO: Rest of OECD.

RL: Rest of Latin America except Venezuela.

G4: Hong Kong, Korea, Taiwan, and Singapore.

RA: Rest of Asia.

EE: Eastern Europe, including Russia.

OPEC: Organization of Petroleum Exporting Countries (including Venezuela).

RW: Rest of world.

Table 4.4 Revealed comparative advantage by manufactured product group (index)

	Skilled			Unskilled			Capital		
	1973	1984	1993	1973	1984	1993	1973	1984	1993
US	0.23	0.19	0.06	−0.42	−0.43	−0.30	0.03	0.04	0.11
Canada	−0.28	−0.30	−0.25	0.08	0.02	−0.03	0.14	0.16	0.19
EU	0.02	0.01	0.01	−0.05	−0.02	−0.06	0.02	0.01	0.03
Japan	0.07	0.09	0.15	−0.17	−0.15	−0.50	0.08	−0.01	0.07
RO	0.01	−0.05	−0.01	−0.02	0.02	0.01	0.01	0.03	0.00
Mexico	−0.20	−0.05	0.02	0.48	0.35	0.01	−0.04	−0.13	−0.05
RL	−0.30	−0.27	−0.23	0.48	0.51	0.47	−0.11	−0.14	−0.16
China	−0.19	−0.36	−0.25	−0.11	0.12	0.44	0.19	0.11	−0.24
India	−0.60	−0.43	−0.64	0.15	0.40	0.37	0.21	−0.08	−0.04
G4	−0.21	−0.11	−0.03	0.39	0.28	0.14	−0.28	−0.19	−0.11
RA	−0.35	−0.14	−0.05	0.48	0.44	0.40	−0.08	−0.16	−0.33
EE	−0.07	0.01	−0.31	0.12	0.05	0.36	−0.04	−0.06	−0.08
OPEC	−0.08	−0.12	−0.29	0.06	0.14	0.45	0.05	0.03	−0.09
RW	−0.29	−0.13	−0.18	0.61	0.30	0.40	−0.23	−0.04	−0.17

Notes:
RO: Rest of OECD.
RL: Rest of Latin America except Venezuela.
G4: Hong Kong, Korea, Taiwan, and Singapore.
RA: Rest of Asia.
EE: Eastern Europe, including Russia.
OPEC: Organization of Petroleum Exporting Countries (including Venezuela).
RW: Rest of world.

It might seem an anomaly that US trade in skilled manufactures would show revealed comparative disadvantage with Japan and (even more surprisingly) the G4 while demonstrating comparative advantage with the European Union and other industrial countries. However, this pattern is consistent with the factor endowment estimates in table 4.2. Thus, the two countries both have a higher ratio of skilled to unskilled workers (0.93 for Japan, 0.70 for the G4) than does the European Union (0.45).

Another pattern evident in table 4.3 is the concentration of the overall US trade deficit in manufactures in two partners: Japan and the G4. Thus, in 1993 the United States had deficits of $76 billion in manufactures trade with Japan and $49 billion with the G4, but only $16.5 billion with the next largest partner (the European Union). Considering that the next two largest manufactures trade deficits were with China and the rest of Asia (at about $8 billion each), Asia accounts by far for the largest US trade deficit in manufactures.[16]

Table 4.4 presents additional evidence on trends in comparative advantage. The table reports an index of revealed comparative advantage

---

16. This fact may be of relevance in the consideration of free trade within the Asia Pacific Economic Cooperation grouping. For the United States, the larger manufactured import

defined as $z_i = b_i - b$, where i refers to the product category, and b is the ratio of the trade surplus (export minus imports) to trade turnover (exports plus imports).[17] The unsubscripted b refers to aggregate manufactured trade. It sets a normal benchmark against which the sectoral trade balance is compared. If aggregate manufactured trade is in balance, the sectoral revealed comparative advantage indicator is simply the sector's trade balance relative to its trade turnover.

For the United States, table 4.4 shows a strong ranking of comparative advantage in 1973 with skilled goods highest (index at 0.23), capital-intensive goods relatively neutral (0.03), and unskilled goods clearly lowest (-0.42). However, over time this ranking shifts away from skilled goods and toward capital-intensive goods. Indeed, by 1993 the revealed comparative advantage of capital-intensive goods was higher than that of skilled goods. Unskilled goods remained clearly with comparative disadvantage, although not as strongly as in the initial period.

As suggested by the discussion above, the G4 countries showed a strong trend toward increased comparative advantage (reduced disadvantage) in skilled goods (from -0.21 in 1973 to -0.03 in 1993) and capital-intensive goods (-0.28 to -0.11) and a trend toward reduced comparative advantage in unskilled goods (from 0.39 to 0.14). Even so, these countries remained with revealed comparative advantage in unskilled goods and disadvantage in skilled and capital-intensive goods by the end of the period. Other patterns in the table also reinforce the trends noted above, such as the surprising lack of substantial comparative advantage in skilled goods for the European Union and the strongly rising trend in comparative advantage in skilled goods for Japan.

Model Calibration

The experiments that follow implement the TIDE model with production divided into five sectors. There are three tradable sectors: skill intensive (1), unskilled intensive (2), and capital intensive (3). There are two non-tradable sectors: skilled intensive (4) and unskilled intensive (5). All skilled-intensive sectors have the following factor shares: skilled labor, 0.6; unskilled labor, 0.15; capital, 0.25. All unskilled sectors have the same factor shares but with skilled and unskilled reversed (to 0.15 and 0.6, respectively). The capital-intensive tradable has factor shares of 0.25 each for skilled and unskilled labor and 0.5 for capital.

Like the Krugman factor shares considered in chapter 3, these parameters are simply postulated rather than estimated empirically. The assumed

than export base could mean a wider trade deficit in manufactures from reciprocal liberalization even if US protection began from a lower level than that of its APEC partners.

17. That is, $b_i = (X_i - M_i)/(X_i + M_i)$.

sectoral divergences in factor intensity are more likely to be on the high side than on the low side for these broad tradable sectors (and two broad nontradable sectors). The final section of this chapter considers possible implications if the intersectoral factor intensity differences are overstated.

It is assumed that the CD consumption shares (and, thus, CD elasticities in the utility function in equation 4.5) are as follows: 0.133 for each of the tradables sectors and 0.30 for each of the nontradables sectors. Thus, tradables account for 40 percent of consumption, and nontradables 60 percent. In a closed economy where consumption equals output, the resulting weighted factor shares would be 0.35 for skilled labor, 0.35 for unskilled labor, and 0.30 for capital.

As noted, the optimization exercises limit a sector's exports and imports to 50 percent of output and consumption, respectively; limit the country's trade deficit or surplus to 1 percent of aggregate domestic output (across all sectors); and ignore trade of nonmanufactures as well as debt service and other elements of the current account. These simplifications mean that the estimated optimum levels of production and trade are only illustrative. However, the parametric variations of the optimal results (especially those for the important skilled/unskilled wage ratios), in response to the alternative hypothetical scenarios, should be informative even if the calculated optimal levels are less so.

Transport costs are specified as a logarithmic function of distance, with an elasticity of about 0.5 (so that transport cost rises about 1 percent when distance rises by 2 percent). Table 4A.3 in appendix 4A reports the estimated distance in miles between country groupings.[18] The transport cost functions are specified such that the lowest transport cost between the two closest countries (the United States and Canada) falls from 6 percent of product value in 1973 to 4 percent in 1984 and 3 percent in 1993, while the highest transport cost (between most-distant Japan and rest of Latin America) falls from 25 percent of product value in 1973 to 17 percent by 1984 and 10 percent by 1993.[19]

These stylized transport costs are intended to capture both transport itself and other dimensions of economic distance, such as communication costs. Distance tends to show up strongly in gravity models of trade (Frankel 1997). For all elements of economic distance, it is realistic to assume a substantial decline over the past two decades.

Similarly, protection is specified to have fallen over time. Table 4A.4 in appendix 4A reports the assumed levels of tariff equivalents of both

---

18. The rest of the OECD is a weighted average of distances for relevant countries in Europe (centered at Vienna) and Australia-New Zealand (Sydney).

19. The resulting cost functions give the following results for z = natural logarithm of transport cost as a fraction of product value: 1973, $z = -6.2590 + 0.521 \cdot \ln D$; 1984, $z = -6.7118 + 0.528 \cdot \ln D$; and 1993, $z = -6.4131 + 0.4395 \cdot \ln D$, where D is distance in miles.

tariffs and nontariff barriers for the three benchmark years. Once again, these values are simply postulated rather than measured, but they are at levels most experts would consider plausible. Skilled and unskilled goods face tariff equivalents of 12 percent in most industrial markets in 1973, with Japan charging 15 percent.[20] Unskilled goods (e.g., textiles) imported into industrial countries from developing countries face much higher tariffs of 30 percent (35 percent in Japan). All developing countries levy tariffs of 20 percent.

By 1984, the tariff-equivalent range among industrial countries is down to 9 to 12 percent for goods 1 and 3, and for unskilled good 2 the rate imposed on developing-country suppliers is down to 25 percent (30 percent for Japan). Then, by 1993, there are significant reductions that eliminate protection among NAFTA partners and cut industrial-country tariffs to a range of 5 to 8 percent for goods 1 and 3 and 8 to 10 percent for unskilled good 2. By 1993 the wave of trade reform has hit developing countries, and their tariffs are down to 10 to 15 percent. The 1993 protection assumptions are meant to reflect post-Uruguay Round levels.

The real-world inputs into the simulations are the factor endowments in each benchmark year for each country (table 4.2). When these factor endowments are confronted with the assumed production functions, transport costs, and tariff levels—and nonlinear programming maximization is applied to obtain the optimal allocation of factors across sectors to maximize the objective function (equation 4.5)—the resulting optimal solution generates "shadow prices" of each of the factors, showing their marginal impact on the welfare function. The focus of the analysis is on the resulting ratio of the shadow price of skilled labor to that of unskilled labor, which tells the ratio of the marginal product and, thus, the skilled/unskilled wage ratio as shown above.

For the United States, the endowments of unskilled and skilled labor shown in table 4.2, which result from the general method applying the World Bank's educational estimates and the transformation into skilled/unskilled discussed above, diverge somewhat from an alternative approach based on the dichotomy between workers with a high school education or less and those with some college or more. Labor force composition by the latter measure is reported in chapter 1 (table 1.5). The generalized method (table 4.2) tends to overstate skilled workers in 1973 and understate them by 1993. The adjusted labor endowment estimates used for the TIDE model take an average from the two alternative approaches.[21]

---

20. The generally higher rates for Japan are meant to portray the stylized fact of higher de facto protection.

21. The resulting estimates of skilled and unskilled workers in millions are: 1973, 34.5 and 58.9; 1984, 55.1 and 60.3; and 1993, 70.1 and 54.7.

The simulations are conducted in two major sets. The first uses a CD specification of the production function, the second, a CES specification (equations 4.1a and 4.1b respectively). To calibrate the production functions, it is first necessary to obtain the constant term (technical efficiency coefficient, τ) relevant for each country.

For this purpose, the aggregate production function excluding the technical efficiency term is first applied to the factor endowments of the thirteen countries in the three benchmark years to calculate the total hypothetical production in this pool.[22] This hypothetical total production is then divided into actual total (pooled) production (in billions of 1990 dollars—see table 4.2) to obtain a general production function constant. Second, country-specific efficiency levels and trends are obtained. For this purpose, the ratio of actual country output to that which would be calculated from application of the country's factor endowments to the general production function is interpreted as the country's efficiency measure for the year in question. This measure is then regressed on time (log-linear) over the three observations (and 20 years) for the country in question. The resulting technical efficiency parameters are shown in table 4A.5.[23]

For the CES production function experiments, it is further necessary to consider calibration of the distribution parameters (δ) as well as the substitution parameter. The estimates here assume an elasticity of substitution of 0.7 ($\sigma = 0.7$, and $\rho = 0.4286$) for the reasons discussed in chapter 3.

Calibration of the CES distribution parameters is considerably more complex. Because the function involves addition of factor terms rather than multiplication, the scale of each factor affects the distribution parameter. Conversely, in the CD function the scale of a given factor does not affect the elasticity exponents, because scale merely shifts the constant term. However, there is a way to "trick" the CES function so that the distribution parameters are (approximately) simply the same as the factor-share exponents in the CD function. This trick is the same one used by Krugman: all factors must be calculated in units using a common numeraire. Following Krugman, the specification here takes the unskilled worker as the unit factor.

In the CES production function, the rate of technical substitution (RTS) between two factors bears the following relationship to the corresponding factor-price ratio (Henderson and Quandt 1980, 114):

---

22. That is, $Q = S^{.35}U^{.35}K^{.3}$, for the CD case and analogously for the CES case (as discussed below).

23. Note that the resulting technical efficiency term corresponding to τ in equations 4.1a and 4.1b comprises three terms. The general scaling constant resulting from the first step described here is c. The country-specific efficiency terms are a_i and b_i. The country's overall parameter is, thus, $\tau_i = c[\exp(a_i + b_i t)]$, where exp is the exponential function.

$$\frac{F_i}{F_j} = \left[\frac{\delta_i}{\delta_j}\right]^\sigma \left[\frac{w_j}{w_i}\right]^\sigma \qquad (4.9)$$

where F_f is the amount of factor f applied, δ_f is the distribution parameter for this factor, and w_f is the wage or factor price of the factor. Thus, the amount of a factor that will be used in a sector will vary positively with the distribution parameter of that factor relative to the distribution parameter of the other factor and inversely with the price of the factor relative to the price of the other factor. The extent of variation will be dampened, however, as the elasticity of substitution is lower.

When we apply the device of defining units such that there is a single numeraire for all factors, the final term in equation 4.9 turns to unity and may be ignored, because all factors start with an identical price. This device enables us to interpret the left-hand side of equation 4.9 as the ratio of factor shares, because with identical prices the ratio of factor shares will be the same as the ratio of factor quantities.

In the aggregate production function we seek factor shares of 0.35 for skilled labor, 0.35 for unskilled labor, and 0.3 for capital. Applying equation 4.8 to skilled labor and capital; using as a second equation the fact that the sum of the distribution parameters must equal unity (e.g., Layard and Walters 1978, 272; Chiang 1984, 426); and considering that the distribution parameters for skilled and unskilled labor are set to be equal, we have two equations and two unknowns and may solve directly for δ_k and for δ_s ($= \delta_u$). It turns out that when the elasticity of substitution is $\sigma = 0.7$, as assumed here, the resulting estimate of the CES distribution parameters is extremely close to the CD elasticity exponents (which are the distribution parameters, or factor shares, in the CD case).[24]

With respect to the CES distribution parameters in the sectoral production functions, given the closeness with which the distribution parameters approximate the factor shares under the elasticity of substitution used here, it is simply assumed that the distribution parameters equal the corresponding sectoral factor exponents (elasticities) from the CD version of the model.[25]

---

24. Specifically: with factor shares $\phi_s = \phi_u = 0.35$ and $\phi_k = 0.3$, we obtain distribution parameters $\delta_s = \delta_u = 0.3568$ and $\delta_k = 0.2863$. These are the distribution parameters used for the aggregate function, which in turn is used to calculate the general technical efficiency constant in the CES functions used here. Note further that, using L'Hopital's rule, it can be shown that as the elasticity of substitution approaches unity, the CES function becomes a CD function with factor exponents equal to the respective distribution parameters (δ). See Henderson and Quandt (1980, 113).

25. That is, for sectors 1 and 4, $\delta_s = 0.6$, $\delta_u = 0.15$, $\delta_k = 0.25$; for sectors 2 and 5 the skilled and unskilled distribution parameters are reversed; and for sector 3 the parameters are $\delta_s = \delta_u = 0.25$, $\delta_k = 0.5$.

It still remains to clarify how the factor data in table 4.2 are translated into unskilled-worker equivalents. The basic approach is to specify the general production function for industrial-country conditions as characterized by the aggregate of the United States and European Union in 1984 and then to let other-country divergences be picked up in the efficiency term. For labor, the analysis here assumes with Krugman that one skilled worker is the equivalent of two unskilled workers, so the skilled-worker endowments of table 4.2 are merely doubled.

Capital is more complicated. What the production function input represents is really a flow of factor services over one year. Capital is a stock, and the flow concept is a return on this stock. The flow concept then needs to be translated from dollars into unskilled-worker equivalents.

From table 4.2, aggregate US-EU output in 1984 was $9.34 trillion. Assuming a capital share of 0.3, capital services amounted to $2.8 trillion. This amount represents a rate of return of 10.45 percent on the US-EU capital stock of $26.8 trillion in 1984.

Because aggregate unskilled labor (180 million) is about twice skilled labor (93.5 million × 2), the corresponding factor shares of unskilled and skilled workers would be about consistent with the assumption here of 0.35 for each. That means total unskilled-worker payments were $9.34 trillion × 0.35 = $3.27 trillion, giving an average US-EU unskilled wage of $18,150 (in 1990 dollars).

Capital services are then calculated by dividing their dollar amount by the estimated unskilled wage. Thus, the US-EU capital-service aggregate in 1984 represented $2.8 trillion ÷ $18,150 per unskilled worker. Thus, it was equal in value to 155 million unskilled-worker equivalents.

More generally, the CES implementation of the TIDE model converts all capital stocks into unskilled-worker equivalents, using a conversion coefficient that takes account both of the translation of capital stock into capital services and then translation of capital services into unskilled-worker equivalents.[26]

Backcast and Counterfactuals

Baseline

Table 4.5 reports the CD and CES backcast estimates of the TIDE model for each of the 13 countries. These are the factor shadow prices and factor-price ratios that result from applying the model to the actual time path

---

26. The conversion factor is: $k^* = \Omega k = k \times .1045/\$18,150$, where k^* is unskilled-worker equivalents, k is capital stock, and the two final terms are the rate of return on capital and the annual wage for unskilled labor respectively. Since capital stock is in trillions and labor in millions, the final conversion factor is $\Omega = 0.00576$.

of factor endowments shown in table 4.2 (with the adjustment for US labor noted above) and applying the estimated actual levels of protection and transport costs over this period. This case is referred to as the baseline backcast.

The first pattern to note concerns the levels of the shadow prices. In broad terms they are in the right orders of magnitude. Thus, the shadow price for US unskilled labor in 1973 is $5,010 in the CD version and $5,380 in the CES version. The corresponding shadow prices for US skilled labor are $8,650 (CD) and $8,700 (CES) and for capital, 2.4 percent and 2.7 percent, respectively.

As discussed above, these shadow price levels are all lower than the corresponding factor-price levels, which the model does not estimate directly. The reason essentially is that each time the economy is subdivided into a sector, the welfare function applies a smaller exponent to each of the sectors' respective outputs. Whereas the sum of all sectoral outputs remains unchanged, the product of each sector's output raised to its consumption share exponent diminishes.

Thus, consider an economy with one factor (labor) and one sector. Suppose labor, L, is 18; output, Q, is 18; and the welfare function is $W = Q^1$, also 18 (assume no trade, so consumption equals output). Now divide the economy in half, and make the exponent of each sector in the welfare function equal to one-half. Allocate half of labor to each sector. Output in each sector will now be $Q_1 = Q_2 = 9$. The welfare function will now show total welfare of $W = 9^{0.5} \times 9^{0.5} = 9$. Although we have merely drawn an imaginary line halfway across the economy, measured welfare has fallen by half. Correspondingly, further subdivision of the economy, combined with the use of the CD welfare function, will cause a further reduction in welfare for unchanged aggregate factors and output. Because the shadow price shows marginal welfare (or marginal utility), the shadow price of each factor will similarly decline as we disaggregate the economy further.

This algebraic illusion accounts for the fact that the factor shadow prices are only about one-fourth the level one might have expected for the factor prices. Thus, as discussed above, for the United States and European Union, in 1984 the unskilled wage was about $18,000 (in 1990 dollars). Yet the 1984 shadow price of unskilled labor in table 4.5 is an average of about $5,060 for the two countries and models (CD and CES). Similarly, the shadow prices on capital are about 0.025 rather than the 0.1045 return that may be derived from the model's assumptions (as discussed above).

However, as discussed, the factor shadow-price ratios do tell the ratios of the factor marginal products and factor prices. It is these ratios that are at the center of this analysis. The striking and systematic feature of the factor-price ratios is that there is a generalized decline over time in the ratio of the skilled to unskilled wage, not only in the United States,

Table 4.5 Factor shadow prices in the TIDE model (thousands of 1990 dollars per worker and rate of return on capital)

	1973				1984				1993			
	S	U	K	S/U	S	U	K	S/U	S	U	K	S/U
Cobb-Douglas (CD)												
US	8.65	5.01	0.024	1.73	7.90	6.57	0.025	1.20	7.79	8.50	0.024	0.92
CA	9.22	3.50	0.031	2.63	8.27	4.61	0.026	1.79	7.40	6.08	0.024	1.22
EU	8.78	2.52	0.024	3.49	9.72	3.11	0.022	3.13	9.33	4.06	0.022	2.30
JP	4.38	2.95	0.029	1.48	5.85	4.34	0.022	1.35	7.24	5.70	0.019	1.27
RO	11.93	1.89	0.024	6.31	10.36	2.37	0.020	4.38	9.72	2.48	0.020	3.91
MX	18.38	1.69	0.033	10.86	14.26	1.85	0.023	7.72	10.56	2.05	0.021	5.14
RL	14.71	1.14	0.028	12.92	11.86	1.33	0.022	8.93	9.65	1.38	0.021	7.00
CH	2.24	0.17	0.032	12.84	2.33	0.26	0.032	9.09	2.57	0.39	0.026	6.67
G4	8.01	0.78	0.036	10.22	8.84	1.39	0.025	6.35	5.53	3.21	0.024	1.72
IN	3.36	0.17	0.028	20.23	3.25	0.24	0.027	13.34	3.15	0.33	0.028	9.45
RA	4.50	0.27	0.039	16.55	4.87	0.41	0.028	11.93	4.59	0.52	0.028	8.78
EE	6.75	0.68	0.022	9.96	6.64	0.90	0.016	7.42	7.89	0.73	0.019	10.82
RW	8.24	0.31	0.032	26.31	6.58	0.34	0.024	19.14	4.21	0.39	0.025	10.84

Constant elasticity of substitution (CES)

US	8.70	5.38	0.027	1.62	7.37	7.68	0.027	0.96	6.90	10.66	0.025	0.65
CA	9.29	3.20	0.038	2.90	8.09	4.75	0.031	1.70	7.10	6.62	0.027	1.07
EU	9.36	2.20	0.030	4.25	10.56	2.88	0.026	3.66	9.64	4.11	0.024	2.34
JP	3.25	3.13	0.040	1.04	4.98	4.91	0.027	1.02	6.46	6.82	0.021	0.95
RO	13.65	1.46	0.028	9.37	12.33	2.05	0.023	6.01	11.25	2.33	0.023	4.84
MX	20.47	0.95	0.035	21.62	18.73	1.45	0.029	12.95	15.80	1.91	0.031	8.27
RL	16.54	0.65	0.033	25.33	15.67	0.94	0.028	16.67	13.05	1.15	0.030	11.37
CH	2.07	0.07	0.066	31.88	2.06	0.12	0.060	17.93	2.54	0.21	0.046	12.13
G4	8.47	0.46	0.055	18.26	10.00	1.05	0.033	9.52	4.91	3.29	0.030	1.49
IN	3.54	0.06	0.050	57.10	3.47	0.11	0.048	31.24	3.16	0.15	0.052	20.78
RA	4.39	0.11	0.069	41.03	5.30	0.22	0.048	24.41	4.78	0.31	0.045	15.22
EE	7.56	0.42	0.031	17.83	8.03	0.68	0.022	11.75	9.51	0.46	0.025	20.62
RW	8.70	0.11	0.043	78.38	8.07	0.18	0.039	45.11	5.31	0.23	0.052	23.08

Notes:
S: skilled   U: unskilled   K: capital
CA: Canada   RL: rest of Latin America except Venezuela   IN: India
JP: Japan   CH: China   RA: rest of Asia
RO: rest of OECD   G4: Hong Kong, South Korea, Singapore, and   EE: Eastern Europe, including Russia
MX: Mexico   Taiwan   RW: rest of world

but in almost every other country. Thus, for the United States, the ratio of the skilled to unskilled wage falls from 1.73 in 1973 to 0.92 in 1993 in the CD version and from 1.62 to 0.65 over the same period in the CES version.[27] For the European Union, the corresponding trajectory shows a decline from a ratio of about 3.5 to 4.2 at the beginning of the period to about 2.3 by the end.

This systematic trend toward wage equality stems directly from the systematic trend toward a rising ratio of skilled to unskilled labor stocks. In the baseline backcast, there is no factor bias to technological change. Thus, an increase in the supply of skilled relative to unskilled labor must drive down the marginal product of the former relative to the latter (in the absence of other influences). The trend toward higher availability of skilled labor is strong. Thus, in the (adjusted) US data the ratio of skilled to unskilled labor supply surges from 59 percent in 1973 to 128 percent in 1993. For the European Union, the corresponding rise is from 29 percent to 45 percent (table 4.2).

Considering that the motivation for this study is to explain just exactly the opposite trend—rising skilled wage differentials in the 1980s—one might reasonably ask whether the backcasts are very helpful. The answer is yes and no. Yes, the backcasts, when combined with experiments examining the marginal impact of various influences, should potentially provide a meaningful analysis of the plausible magnitudes of alternative economic forces that are candidates for explaining widening skill differentials. And no, the baseline backcasts do not directly explain a rising skill differential. The strategy of this analysis is to examine the parametric response of the skilled-wage differential to such global influences as immigration and the reduction of protection and transport costs, and it is likely that the model should provide a reasonable estimate of this parametric response even if the absolute levels of the model's central trendline estimates do not capture the historical record.

A supplemental answer is that in the variant in which biased technological change is included (discussed below), the skilled-wage differential falls by much less. It would be possible to turn the variant of biased technological change into the baseline and to intensify the bias so the skill differential rises as much as in the record. However, the parametric response of the skilled/unskilled wage ratio to the other forces being examined would remain largely unchanged, so this recalculation is not essential.

---

27. Note that in the CES results reported in table 4.5 the shadow price of skilled labor is twice the raw estimate from the optimization exercise and that for capital is 0.00576 times the raw result. These conversions translate the shadow prices on unskilled-labor-equivalents (UEQ) of these factors back to levels corresponding to the factor amounts prior to translation to UEQ.

Another key pattern in the baseline backcasts is that the skills differential is far higher in the developing countries than in the industrial countries. Thus, in the CD variant, the 1973 ratio of skilled to unskilled wages stands at about 12:1 in Latin America, 13:1 in China, and as high as 26:1 in the rest of the world (which includes Africa). In the CES variant, where there is less ease of substituting unskilled for skilled labor, the ratios are even more extreme.

One implication of these results for developing countries is that, at least for Mexico and the rest of Latin America, there are underlying causes of relative factor availability that help explain the high degree of inequality. Correspondingly, the relatively high predicted ratio of skilled to unskilled wages in Europe (still over 200 percent in 1993, when the US predicted value is below 100 percent) could help explain high unemployment in Europe. That is, if the wage of unskilled workers would be low under free market determination because of their still large relative abundance in Europe and if social practices impose what amounts to a high minimum wage, then one would expect to see high unemployment.[28]

The very high ratios of skilled to unskilled wages in the developing countries fall rapidly, reflecting the rapid rise in relative availability of skilled labor from a low base. The most dramatic case is that of the G4. The skilled/unskilled wage ratio falls from about 10:1 in 1973 (and almost twice this ratio in the CES variant) to only 1.72:1 in 1993, reflecting the enormous increase in skilled labor availability discussed in the earlier review of comparative advantage.

Finally, the baseline backcast shows a surprising uniformity in the shadow price of capital. In broad terms, this result reflects the surprising uniformity in the capital/output ratios in the World Bank database. It also provides some support for the proposition of Wood (1994) that return to capital is relatively uniform across countries.

Trade Matrix

Table 4.6 reports the matrix of optimal trade levels by 1993 in the baseline backcast (CD version) to provide a sense of the proximity of the baseline to reality. The matrix is surprisingly empty, which means that the optimal solution heavily concentrates trade in just a few product and partner combinations. Nonetheless, the magnitudes and trade patterns are not unreasonable. Moreover, it should be recalled that the TIDE model has only HO trade based on differing factor endowments. As a result, much of the trade among industrial countries, usually explained instead by product differentiation and economies of scale, will not be captured by the model.

---

28. The absolute level is of interest in this connection. The shadow price of unskilled labor in Europe by 1993 stands at just one-half that of the United States.

Table 4.6   Optimal trade matrix in the TIDE-CD model, 1993
(billions of 1990 dollars)

Exporter	US	CA	EU	JP	RO	MX	RL	CH	G4	IN	RA	EE	RW	Total
Skilled goods														
US		25.1			65.2	28.7	90			57.6		70.7	41.6	378.9
CA														0
EU														0
JP								142.6						142.6
RO														0
MX														0
RL														0
CH														0
G4											59.4			59.4
IN														0
RA														0
EE														0
RW														0
Total	0	25.1	0	0	65.2	28.7	90	142.6	0	57.6	59.4	70.7	41.6	580.9
Unskilled goods														
US														0
CA														0
EU														0
JP														0
RO														0
MX	109.6													109.6
RL	92.4													92.4
CH	18.6			189.3					0.5					208.4
G4														0
IN	93.3		127.9											221.2
RA									64.7					64.7
EE			98.7											98.7
RW	126	47.7												173.7
Total	439.9	47.7	226.6	189.3	0	0	0	0	65.2	0	0	0	0	968.7
Capital-intensive goods														
US						78.1								78.1
CA													71.8	71.8
EU										152.1		25.9	89.3	267.3
JP								50.8						50.8
RO										55.1				55.1
MX														0
RL														0
CH														0
G4								5.1			1.8			6.9
IN														0
RA														0
EE														0
RW														0
Total	0	0	0	0	0	78.1	0	55.9	0	207.2	1.8	25.9	161.1	530

Notes:
CA: Canada
JP: Japan
RO: rest of OECD
MX: Mexico
RL: rest of Latin America except Venezuela

CH: China
G4: Hong Kong, South Korea, Singapore, and Taiwan
IN: India
RA: rest of Asia
EE: Eastern Europe, including Russia
RW: rest of world

In the 1993 optimal trade matrix, the United States concentrates its exports heavily in skilled goods (about 80 percent) and capital-intensive goods (the rest). Its imports are entirely in unskilled goods, which come from Mexico, the rest of Latin America, China, the rest of Asia, and the rest of the world.

The optimization shows a modest US trade surplus of $17 billion (1990 prices), equal to about 4 percent of the export base in the 1993 base-case optimization and 0.2 percent of aggregate domestic output (including in nontradables). Instead, the United States had a trade deficit of $131 billion in 1993 (IMF 1996). However, the model excludes oil, in which the United States had a deficit of $52 billion in 1993 (Cline 1995, 33). The magnitude of total trade turnover is about right, at approximately $900 billion as compared to actual 1993 turnover of $1.05 trillion.

The optimal trade pattern in table 4.6 also captures some of the important actual trends in trade reviewed earlier in this chapter. Japan and the G4 are the other strong exporters of skill-intensive goods. Japan and the European Union are dominant exporters of capital-intensive goods. Both of these patterns were identified in the actual trade data reviewed above.

Whereas the 1993 trade matrix bears important similarities to the actual levels and patterns of trade, the 1973 matrix is less successful in doing so. For the United States, 1973 exports are calculated at $39 billion (in 1990 dollars) in capital-intensive goods (sector 3) and $16 billion in skill-intensive goods (1). Imports are in labor-intensive goods, but they only amount to $22 billion. Thus, although the pattern of comparative advantage is plausible, the magnitude of trade is substantially understated, especially for imports. Actual US manufactured exports and imports were, instead, about $125 billion each (in 1990 dollars).[29]

In one important regard, the 1973 simulation of low US imports conforms with stylized facts: imports of manufactures from developing countries were low at that time, and, indeed, the analysis of chapter 3 treats them as zero in that base period. More generally, however, the understatement of trade in 1973 may reflect greater sensitivity in the model than in the real world to the impact of relatively high transportation costs and tariffs in this earlier period. Perfect substitution in the model between imports and domestic goods tends to lead to sensitivity of this type.

Rather than adopting special adjustments to force the model closer to the actual outcome in 1973, the strategy here is to accept the raw simulation results as providing an acknowledgedly imperfect backcast baseline and to concentrate the analysis not on the baseline itself but on the changes

---

29. Note that in an earlier version with no ceiling on the trade surplus, the 1973 solution showed the United States in large surplus, with exports of $176 billion and imports of only $11 billion. This result would appear to reflect a high relative US production efficiency in 1973 (see table 4A.5), such that global optimization obtains utility abroad based on large imports from US producers, unless the US trade surplus is constrained.

induced at the margin by each of the counterfactual shocks. Thus, the TIDE model should be seen primarily as an instrument for exploring the parametric impact of alternative scenarios and forces. Other general equilibrium models constructed with the purpose of modeling international trade may do a better job of reproducing actual detailed trade patterns, but they may be less suited than the TIDE model for the type of analysis sought here.[30]

Autarky

Table 4.7 shows the results of several counterfactual backcasts. For each of the 13 countries and three benchmark years, the table reports the percentage deviation from baseline backcast levels for the absolute level of the shadow price of each of the three factors (S for skilled labor, U for unskilled, and K for capital), using the CD variant. The table also shows the percentage deviation from baseline for the skilled/unskilled factor-price ratio. Table 4A.6 in appendix 4A shows the same set of counterfactual simulation results using the CES variant.

The first counterfactual backcast (CF1) considers the overall impact of trade on factor prices by simulating the TIDE model with the constraint that no international trade is allowed.[31] For the United States, in 1973 autarky would have caused an estimated reduction of the skilled/unskilled wage ratio of only 1.1 percent.[32] By 1984 and especially 1993, the factor-price impact is greater, in large part because, with lower transport and protection costs, the role of trade is considerably greater. The change in factor-price ratio is in the right direction: autarky would favor the relatively scarce factor (for the United States, unskilled labor) and disfavor the abundant factor (skilled labor). Thus, by 1993, imposition of zero trade would cause an absolute increase of 6.4 percent in US unskilled wages, an absolute decline of 9.4 percent in skilled wages, and a decrease of about 15 percent in the skilled/unskilled wage ratio.

If valid, these estimates have a profound implication. They mean that the most extreme formulation of the impact of trade—comparing the

---

30. The greater detail of some existing models may help them replicate reality, but could be cumbersome to include in a model oriented toward the type of simulations conducted here. Even with the streamlined TIDE model, each solution of the model requires up to 10 minutes of computing time using a Pentium-based personal computer. The basic set of calculations here requires 72 separate optimization runs.

31. This is done by removing imports and exports from the consumption equation, 4.2, with the result that each country's consumption in a given sector becomes its domestic production in the sector.

32. The small impact in 1973 reflects the small estimated base level of imports, just discussed. The combined influence of transport and protection costs is high enough in 1973 to yield only limited trade in this type of model.

baseline not just against some early benchmark of import penetration but against an absolute embargo on all trade—would alter the skilled/unskilled factor-price ratio by only about 15 percent. This limit would seem to imply that any impact of trade per se within the confines of what might be a more meaningful alternative policy regime is considerably smaller.

The autarky experiment similarly shows the expected direction of changes for most of the other countries (table 4.7). For example, for 1993 the ratio of skilled to unskilled wages falls substantially under autarky in Japan and the G4 and falls moderately in Canada and the European Union. By contrast, the autarky shock imposes increases of about 15 to 30 percent in the skilled/unskilled wage ratio for the developing countries, where skilled labor is the scarce factor.

Comparison of the CD and CES model variants (tables 4.7 and 4A.6, respectively) shows surprisingly similar results, not only for the autarky experiment but for most of the others as well. Thus, a shift to autarky in 1993 causes the US ratio of skilled to unskilled wages to fall by about 15 percent under both the CD and CES models. The more general pattern of similarity in the results of the two models is somewhat of a surprise, because one might have anticipated that for any given shock, the greater rigidity in substitutability would have meant a larger change in factor prices in the CES version (with elasticity of substitution of 0.7) than in the CD version (elasticity of substitution of unity). In the backcast baseline itself, there is a substantial difference between the CD and CES results. As expected, lesser scope for substitution between skilled and unskilled labor means that the backcast estimate of the skilled/unskilled wage ratio falls further in the CES version (by 60 percent) than in the CD version (47 percent) over 20 years as the endowment of skilled labor rises relative to that of unskilled labor.[33]

The absence of a correspondingly marked difference between the CD and CES results for most of the simulated counterfactual changes from baseline (tables 4.7 and 4A.6, respectively) would seem to stem from the fact that these experiments generally apply shocks that work through changing opportunity for trade and pursuit of comparative advantage. As such, they are simulations that depend on relative considerations across countries. There is no change in the relative degree of factor substitutability as between the two variants. In one case, all countries have unitary substitution elasticity, and in the other, an elasticity of 0.7. So, for those counterfactuals that affect countries primarily through broadly comparable changes in scope for exercising comparative advantage, this

---

33. Indeed, the ratio of the two alternative percentage changes in this factor-price ratio is approximately the inverse of the corresponding ratio of the two elasticities of substitution (0.7).

Table 4.7 Percent deviation of factor prices from baseline: backcast counterfactuals, TIDE Cobb-Douglas model (percentages)

	1973				1984				1993			
	S	U	K	S/U	S	U	K	S/U	S	U	K	S/U
CF1: Autarky												
US	-0.51	0.56	0.00	-1.06	-4.69	4.72	-4.00	-8.99	-9.41	6.40	-4.17	-14.86
CA	0.09	0.09	-3.23	0.00	-0.02	-0.04	0.00	0.02	-0.76	1.20	-8.33	-1.93
EU	0.07	0.04	0.00	0.03	-0.04	-0.06	0.00	0.02	-2.03	2.12	-4.55	-4.06
JP	-10.06	9.86	0.00	-18.13	-9.70	8.78	0.00	-16.99	-9.18	6.84	0.00	-14.99
RO	0.08	0.05	-4.17	0.02	7.01	-7.14	0.00	15.24	4.21	-4.39	-5.00	8.99
MX	6.02	-3.72	-3.03	10.12	6.29	-6.76	0.00	14.00	7.59	-16.65	0.00	29.08
RL	0.00	0.00	0.00	0.00	5.42	-5.12	0.00	11.11	5.93	-7.33	0.00	14.32
CH	6.94	-9.20	3.13	17.76	5.12	-6.64	3.13	12.59	6.99	-8.29	0.00	16.66
G4	0.14	0.13	0.00	0.01	0.00	-0.07	0.00	0.07	-9.75	9.21	-4.17	-17.36
IN	6.40	-5.42	0.00	12.50	6.70	-7.38	0.00	15.20	8.04	-14.71	3.57	26.68
RA	4.38	-3.68	0.00	8.36	6.21	-6.37	0.00	13.43	5.38	-7.46	-3.57	13.87
EE	0.04	0.00	0.00	0.04	0.03	0.00	0.00	0.03	3.81	-8.92	-5.26	13.98
RW	6.28	-5.43	-3.13	12.38	4.94	-6.40	-4.17	12.11	7.11	-15.21	4.00	26.32
CF2: Constant transport cost												
US					-2.29	2.10	0.00	-4.30	-1.87	-1.49	-4.17	-0.39
CA					-0.12	-0.13	0.00	0.01	-0.49	1.50	-4.17	-1.95
EU					-0.12	-0.13	0.00	0.01	-1.75	2.46	-4.55	-4.11
JP					-2.84	2.35	0.00	-5.07	-2.81	0.89	0.00	-3.67
RO					2.44	-3.13	0.00	5.75	0.13	-1.21	0.00	1.36
MX					-0.11	-0.16	0.00	0.05	-0.27	4.04	4.76	-4.14
RL					5.42	-5.12	0.00	11.11	-0.74	-0.51	0.00	-0.23
CH					2.92	-1.56	-3.13	4.56	2.80	-2.33	0.00	5.25

G4	−0.10	−0.14	0.00	0.04	0.45	−0.75	0.00	1.21
IN	2.03	−3.28	0.00	5.49	5.47	−10.81	3.57	18.25
RA	−0.31	−0.74	0.00	0.43	−0.63	−0.57	0.00	−0.06
EE	−0.11	−0.11	0.00	0.01	−1.32	0.96	−5.26	−2.26
RW	−0.82	−0.58	0.00	−0.24	1.93	−8.76	8.00	11.72

CF3: Constant protection

US	−1.05	1.25	−4.00	−2.27	−1.62	−1.49	−4.17	−0.13
CA	−0.05	−0.07	0.00	0.02	−0.62	1.35	−4.17	−1.94
EU	−0.05	−0.06	0.00	0.01	−1.89	2.32	−4.55	−4.11
JP	−1.11	−0.35	0.00	−0.77	−8.03	6.29	0.00	−13.47
RO	0.51	−1.14	0.00	1.67	−2.39	3.54	−5.00	−5.73
MX	0.99	−2.22	4.35	3.28	1.25	−11.68	4.76	14.65
RL	2.18	−3.09	0.00	5.44	−0.80	−1.09	0.00	0.29
CH	0.34	−0.39	0.00	0.74	5.48	−6.48	0.00	12.78
G4	−0.05	−0.07	0.00	0.03	−0.40	−0.37	0.00	−0.02
IN	−0.12	0.00	0.00	−0.12	0.48	−5.71	3.57	6.56
RA	−0.08	−0.25	0.00	0.16	−0.94	−0.96	0.00	0.02
EE	−0.05	0.00	0.00	−0.05	−1.34	−2.06	−5.26	0.73
RW	−0.20	0.00	0.00	−0.20	1.43	−8.76	4.00	11.17

CF4: Constant transport and protection cost

US	−3.52	3.58	−4.00	−6.85	−6.85	3.67	−4.17	−10.15
CA	−0.13	−0.15	0.00	0.02	−0.76	1.20	−8.33	−1.93
EU	−0.12	−0.13	0.00	0.01	−2.11	2.02	−4.55	−4.05
JP	−3.61	2.07	0.00	−5.57	−8.93	6.52	0.00	−14.50

continued next page

Table 4.7 Percent deviation of factor prices from baseline: backcast counterfactuals, TIDE Cobb-Douglas model (percentages) (continued)

	1973				1984				1993			
	S	U	K	S/U	S	U	K	S/U	S	U	K	S/U
RO					6.91	-7.23	0.00	15.24	2.27	-2.46	-5.00	-4.85
MX					1.66	-2.81	4.35	4.61	1.68	-11.73	4.76	15.19
RL					5.42	-5.12	0.00	11.11	5.93	-7.33	0.00	14.32
CH					1.68	-1.95	0.00	3.70	6.80	-7.77	0.00	15.80
G4					-0.10	-0.14	0.00	0.04	0.29	-0.34	0.00	0.63
IN					4.18	-5.74	0.00	10.52	6.93	-12.61	3.57	22.36
RA					0.45	-1.47	0.00	1.95	-0.59	-2.49	0.00	1.95
EE					0.03	0.00	0.00	0.03	-2.07	-2.74	-5.26	0.70
RW					-1.05	-0.58	0.00	-0.47	4.45	-13.14	4.00	20.25

CF5: Zero transport and protection cost

	1973				1984				1993			
	S	U	K	S/U	S	U	K	S/U	S	U	K	S/U
US	12.73	-6.16	0.00	20.13	8.81	-2.62	0.00	11.73	5.73	-0.49	0.00	6.25
CA	-0.29	1.03	6.45	-1.31	-0.24	1.24	7.69	-1.46	4.85	-0.67	0.00	5.56
EU	-0.17	0.76	8.33	-0.92	0.38	0.68	9.09	-0.29	-1.66	3.65	4.55	-5.12
JP	7.59	1.83	3.45	5.66	4.07	0.55	0.00	3.50	-1.38	3.35	0.00	-4.58
RO	0.32	0.00	4.17	0.32	8.06	-6.89	5.00	16.06	5.30	-3.70	5.00	9.35
MX	1.73	2.66	0.00	-0.91	5.48	-3.68	4.35	9.51	8.75	-16.80	9.52	30.71
RL	-5.87	13.27	0.00	-16.90	-1.97	10.32	-4.55	-11.14	4.89	-4.58	4.76	9.92
CH	2.77	8.62	6.25	-5.38	0.34	12.50	3.13	-10.81	0.00	9.33	0.00	-8.53
G4	-7.31	17.50	-5.56	-21.11	-0.46	0.36	4.00	-0.82	-2.51	4.73	0.00	-6.92
IN	3.78	13.86	0.00	-8.85	3.13	13.11	3.70	-8.82	3.46	2.40	3.57	1.04
RA	0.47	15.44	2.56	-12.97	1.34	13.48	0.00	-10.70	-0.89	10.71	-3.57	-10.48
EE	-6.72	13.27	-4.55	-17.65	-3.09	6.26	0.00	-8.79	-2.99	9.05	-5.26	-11.04
RW	3.86	14.70	0.00	-9.45	1.90	15.12	0.00	-11.48	2.59	2.32	4.00	0.27

CF6: No nontradables or sectoral trade limits

US	152.95	25.61	191.67	101.38	182.64	23.92	168.00	128.08	181.75	28.07	166.67	119.99
CA	131.19	31.89	151.61	75.29	149.26	25.38	165.38	98.80	161.63	27.14	158.33	105.79
EU	100.24	38.05	175.00	45.05	87.36	43.50	190.91	30.56	95.28	32.54	195.45	47.33
JP	237.92	8.84	100.00	210.47	184.86	20.82	140.91	135.78	142.21	33.26	184.21	81.76
RO	46.79	83.14	175.00	-19.85	57.90	69.53	190.00	-6.86	54.49	78.66	170.00	-13.53
MX	34.06	150.00	130.30	-46.38	30.73	131.39	160.87	-43.50	35.56	106.04	147.62	-34.21
RL	13.01	188.93	121.43	-60.88	21.11	165.29	131.82	-54.35	28.33	165.72	114.29	-51.71
CH	26.53	221.84	109.38	-60.68	38.01	207.81	96.88	-55.17	46.11	188.08	88.46	-49.28
G4	40.44	184.67	77.78	-50.66	53.44	139.12	92.00	-35.83	156.11	30.34	112.50	96.50
IN	11.76	281.33	110.71	-70.69	10.08	260.25	107.41	-69.44	16.11	224.62	114.29	-64.23
RA	10.51	262.13	102.56	-69.48	16.23	240.44	96.43	-65.86	23.53	220.65	92.86	-61.48
EE	40.83	177.43	77.27	-49.24	39.66	154.08	106.25	-45.03	4.94	235.94	89.47	-68.76
RW	21.13	293.29	115.63	-69.20	13.41	285.17	112.50	-70.56	8.80	235.82	120.00	-67.60

CF7: No US immigration

US					0.80	1.25	-4.00	-0.44	0.56	3.42	-4.17	-2.77
CA					0.00	0.00	3.85	0.00	1.46	-0.99	0.00	2.47
EU					0.00	0.03	0.00	-0.03	0.09	-0.12	0.00	0.21
JP					0.02	-0.02	0.00	-0.04	0.00	0.02	0.00	-0.02
RO					0.00	0.00	0.00	0.00	-0.05	0.00	0.00	-0.05
MX					-0.01	0.00	0.00	-0.01	-0.01	-0.24	0.00	0.23
RL					0.31	-0.30	0.00	0.62	-0.04	0.00	0.00	-0.04
CH					0.00	0.00	0.00	0.00	0.00	0.00	0.00	0.00
G4					0.00	0.00	0.00	0.00	0.00	0.00	0.00	0.00

continued next page

Table 4.7 Percent deviation of factor prices from baseline: backcast counterfactuals, TIDE Cobb-Douglas model (percentages) (continued)

	1973				1984				1993			
	S	U	K	S/U	S	U	K	S/U	S	U	K	S/U
IN					-0.03	0.00	0.00	-0.03	-0.06	0.00	0.00	-0.06
RA					0.00	0.00	0.00	0.00	0.00	0.00	0.00	0.00
EE					0.00	0.00	0.00	0.00	0.04	-0.14	0.00	0.18
RW					-0.02	0.00	0.00	-0.02	-0.07	0.00	0.00	-0.07
CF8: No US unskilled immigration												
US					-1.13	2.33	-4.00	-3.38	-2.37	5.24	-4.17	-7.23
CA					0.04	0.02	3.85	0.01	-1.35	0.94	0.00	-2.27
EU					0.01	0.03	0.00	-0.02	0.05	-0.07	0.00	0.13
JP					0.02	-0.12	0.00	0.13	-0.12	0.11	0.00	-0.23
RO					0.09	0.08	0.00	0.00	0.05	0.04	0.00	0.01
MX					0.07	0.05	0.00	0.02	0.09	-0.19	0.00	0.28
RL					-0.81	0.75	0.00	-1.55	0.05	0.07	0.00	-0.02
CH					-0.04	0.00	0.00	-0.04	0.04	0.00	0.00	0.04
G4					0.01	0.00	0.00	0.01	0.00	0.00	0.00	0.00
IN					0.22	-0.41	0.00	0.63	0.03	0.00	0.00	0.03
RA					0.00	0.00	0.00	0.00	0.04	0.00	0.00	0.04
EE					0.02	0.00	0.00	0.02	0.10	-0.14	0.00	0.24
RW					0.06	0.29	0.00	0.02	0.00	0.00	-0.23	0.02

CF9: Skill-biased technological change

US	2.26	−3.51	−4.00	5.99	5.65	−5.47	0.00	11.76
CA	2.08	−3.86	0.00	6.18	3.76	−5.25	0.00	9.51
EU	1.29	−4.60	0.00	6.17	3.55	−6.63	−4.55	10.90
JP	1.35	−3.09	0.00	4.58	4.66	−5.86	0.00	11.17
RO	1.13	−4.95	0.00	6.39	2.85	−8.17	−5.00	12.00
MX	0.56	−5.41	0.00	6.31	2.14	−8.47	0.00	11.59
RL	−0.08	−5.35	−4.55	5.57	1.76	−9.30	0.00	12.19
CH	1.16	−6.25	−3.13	7.90	1.86	−9.07	−3.85	12.02
G4	0.69	−5.17	−4.00	6.18	4.18	−6.53	−4.17	11.46
IN	−0.09	−6.15	−3.70	6.45	0.99	−9.91	−3.57	12.09
RA	−0.02	−6.13	−3.57	6.51	1.02	−9.37	−3.57	11.47
EE	0.39	−5.47	0.00	6.21	0.41	−9.47	−5.26	10.90
RW	−0.56	−6.40	−4.17	6.23	0.71	−10.31	−4.00	12.29

Notes:
S: skilled   U: unskilled   K: capital
CA: Canada   RL: rest of Latin America except Venezuela   RA: rest of Asia
JP: Japan   CH: ChinaG4: Hong Kong, South Korea, Singapore,   EE: Eastern Europe, including Russia
RO: rest of OECD   and Taiwan   RW: rest of world
MX: Mexico   IN: India

identical relative substitutability could imply similar results between the two variants.

The exceptions, moreover, would seem to prove the rule. The only counterfactuals in which there are country-specific changes in factor endowments, rather than generalized international effects such as lower transport costs, are cases 7 and 8, where US immigration is changed from the baseline. In these cases the CD and CES versions differ substantially, as discussed below. More generally, the similarity of the two sets of model results would seem to provide a degree of confidence in the robustness of the results with respect to model specification, if the interpretation regarding expected similarity of comparative advantage effects when relative production parameters remain unchanged is accepted.

Constant Transport Costs

The second counterfactual (CF2) freezes transportation costs at their 1973 level and solves for optimal factor allocation, production, and trade in 1984 and again in 1993. The resulting impact on relative factor prices is generally in the right direction. In both the CD and CES results, by 1984 for the United States the skilled/unskilled wage ratio would have stood about 4 percent lower if transport costs had not fallen. That is, there would have been less scope for maintaining the relative wage of increasingly abundant skilled labor through taking advantage of exports of skill-intensive goods if transport costs had not fallen (but not as much lesser scope as in the counterfactual of a shift to autarky). However, the change by 1993 is much smaller (a decline in the ratio by only 0.4 percent from the baseline level for the CD version, and 1.1 percent in the CES version).

By way of illustration, the transport cost functions described above assume that in 1973 these costs represented 14.7 percent of FOB value for trade between the United States and the European Union and 18.3 percent between the United States and Japan and that by 1993 these costs had fallen to 6.4 percent and 7.7 percent, respectively. Over the two decades, then, for the United States transport costs are postulated to have fallen by 8 to 10 percent of the export value base (or somewhat less given the importance of US trade with neighboring Canada and Mexico).

The greater part of the decline of transport costs had already occurred by 1984. Even so, the specific result for the United States of a larger impact in 1984 than in 1993 is potentially an anomaly considering the larger gap between the counterfactual and actual transport costs for 1993 than for 1984. The explanation would appear to lie in the interaction of transport and protection costs. With both high in 1973 and substantially lower by 1984, the reversion to 1973 transport costs for 1984 appears to be sufficient to suppress certain trade flows and have a substantial effect on relative factor prices. In contrast, with both protection and transport costs low by

1993, reversion of transport costs alone to 1973 levels is insufficient to suppress trade as much, so the counterfactual impact is smaller than for 1984.[34]

Overall, the broad implication of the results for CF2 from the estimates for both benchmark years and both model variants is that the reduction of transportation costs alone would have contributed an increase of about 1 to 4 percent in the US ratio of skilled to unskilled wages. Results for other countries generally adhere to the expected direction in view of factor endowments. Thus, for 1993 the largest impacts in this counterfactual are increased skilled/unskilled wage ratios in countries abundant in unskilled labor: China, India, and the rest of the world.

Constant Protection

The third counterfactual (CF3) freezes protection at the 1973 level but permits transport costs to fall as in the baseline. For the United States, the impact is in the same direction as the counterfactual of constant transport costs. In both the CD and CES results, if protection costs had not fallen (globally), by 1984 the US ratio of skilled to unskilled wages would have been about 2.3 percent lower than it actually was. By 1993 the US deviation from baseline ranges from only -0.1 percent in the CD model to -3.2 percent in the CES model. In broad terms, the US results show the impact of freezing protection at 1973 levels to be a reduction of about 2 percent in the skilled/unskilled wage ratio, slightly smaller than the average US results if transport costs are frozen instead.

Among other countries, the large impact by 1993 for Japan, present in both the CD and CES versions, is of note. Reflecting the relatively high 1973 levels of protection by and against Japan, prevention of the baseline reduction in protection causes a large drop in the skilled wage and some rise in the unskilled wage, for a decrease in the skilled/unskilled wage ratio in the range of 8 to 13 percent. There is also a large impact for Mexico, where by 1993 there is a rise in the skilled/unskilled wage ratio by 8 to 15 percent in the counterfactual. This suggests a strong impact of US-Mexico free trade in the direction predicted by HO theory. This result is at odds with the perception of some that NAFTA may have increased rather than reduced the domestic skill differential in Mexico (e.g., Revenga and Montenegro 1995). Other sizable increases in the skilled/unskilled wage ratio for unskilled-abundant countries as a result of freezing protection at 1973 levels include the cases of China, the rest of Latin America, India, and the rest of the world.

---

34. This is not uniform across countries, however, as there is a relatively even division of countries between those with larger impacts in 1993 than in 1984 and those with the opposite result.

Constant Transport and Protection Costs

In the fourth counterfactual experiment (CF4), both transport and protection costs are frozen at their 1973 levels. In this case, by 1993 the skilled/unskilled wage ratio would have been an estimated 10 percent lower for the United States than in the baseline in both the CD and CES versions (tables 4.7 and 4A.6, respectively). The 1993 results for the United States show a strongly nonlinear impact of the combination of both higher transport costs and higher protection costs, considering that for this year the counterfactuals for the two influences separately (CF2 and CF3, respectively) show much smaller impacts.

The implication of the constant protection and transport cost counterfactual is that increasing integration of the US economy with the world economy through trade, from the combined effects of both policy changes (protection) and changes in transportation costs, may indeed have represented a major element in the observed rise of the skilled/unskilled wage ratio. Japan shows a somewhat larger reduction in the skills differential in this counterfactual (an average of almost 12 percent for the two models), reflecting the longer trade distances and, thus, higher initial transportation costs, as well as higher initial period protection by and against Japan. Canada and the European Union also show sizable reductions.

Conversely, this case generates a large positive shock to the skills differential for most developing countries, typically with half or more of this shock coming from a reduction in unskilled wages as the counterfactual's high transport and protection costs depress opportunities for exports of unskilled-intensive goods.

Zero Transport and Protection Costs

The obverse experiment postulates that instead of freezing transport and protection costs at their relatively high 1973 levels, these costs would have been eliminated over the whole period. In 1973, the complete removal of transport and protection costs would have raised the skilled/unskilled wage ratio by 18 percent (CES) to 20 percent (CD) for the United States, implying much greater trade and, hence, opportunity for abundant skilled labor in the United States to earn higher wages (and substantial erosion of wages for the scarce factor, unskilled labor). Similarly, all of the developing areas show a large percentage increase in unskilled wages in 1973 (and drop in the skilled/unskilled wage ratio) if somehow transport and protection costs could have been zero in that year.

The impact of this counterfactual falls over time, because falling transport and protection costs in the baseline mean that their elimination causes less change from the baseline at later dates. Thus, both model variants show an increase from baseline of about 12 percent in the skilled/unskilled wage ratio in 1984, but increases of only 6 to 7 percent from baseline by 1993.

The much more limited impact of the counterfactual by 1993 suggests that world trade has already moved a long way in enjoying lower physical and policy impediments to trade and that the remaining levels of protection and transport costs have only a moderate impact on relative factor prices. This inference is strengthened by the forward-looking simulations considered below.

Mexico is an interesting exception to these patterns in the fifth counterfactual (CF5). Elimination of transport and protection costs in 1993 removes an important comparative advantage enjoyed by Mexico: low transport costs and free NAFTA entry to the US market. Other suppliers displace Mexico's exports of labor-intensive goods to the US market (Mexico's sole export in the baseline in table 4.6), sharply reducing unskilled wages and raising the skills differential in the CD results (table 4.7). This outcome is also present but much smaller in the CES version (table 4.6).

No Nontradables: Factor-Price Equalization?

The sixth counterfactual (CF6) implements the FPE experiment (see chapter 2) by considering what would happen to factor prices if there were no transport costs, no protection, and the entire economy were in tradable goods. This experiment is implemented by suppressing the consumption elasticity shares for the two nontradable goods (ϕ_4 and ϕ_5 in equation 4.5) to zero and correspondingly increasing this elasticity (share) to 0.33 for each of the three tradable goods. To assure the closest possible approximation to FPE conditions, the constraints limiting sectoral exports to half of output and imports to half of consumption are also removed.

As both the CD (table 4.7) and CES (table 4A.6) results show, this experiment is by far the most dramatic in its impact on factor prices. The experiment more than doubles the US skilled/unskilled wage ratio from the baseline levels for all three benchmark years. In the CD version, it does so while accomplishing an increase of about 25 percent in the absolute level of unskilled wages, meaning that skilled wages rise by about 150 to 180 percent. The absolute return to capital also rises by about 170 to 190 percent in the CD model and about 100 percent in the CES model. In the CES model the changes in the skilled/unskilled wage ratio are about the same as in the CD model, but they result from somewhat smaller increases from baseline in skilled wages (100 to 145 percent) combined with minimal change in unskilled wages (-4 percent to $+4$ percent). The implication is that in a frictionless world of all tradables and no transport or protection costs, the gains from reallocating factors according to specialization are enormous. When substitutability is greater, all factors gain absolutely, but the scarce factor gains the most. When substitutability is more limited, the relatively scarce factor obtains little absolute gain and may have a small absolute loss, while the relatively abundant factor still shows large gains.[35]

There is indeed a trend toward global FPE in CF6. However, it comes from a huge increase in unskilled wages in developing countries, rather than a plunge in unskilled wages in industrial countries. Real unskilled wages in China, India, and the rest of Asia approximately triple.

There are three influences driving the effects of this counterfactual. The first is the elimination of transport costs and protection. This influence was already examined in counterfactual 5, and it showed significant effects but of much smaller magnitude than the FPE test of the sixth counterfactual. The second influence is the opening of the large nontradables sectors to trade. The third influence is the removal of the constraints limiting exports to half of sectoral production and imports to half of consumption.

To decompose the FPE test into these separate influences, CF6 may be reestimated with only one of the new influences operating at a time.[36] When sectoral limits on exports and imports are removed but nontradables remain nontradable, and under zero transport and protection costs, US skilled wages rise 27 percent from the 1993 baseline, unskilled wages fall 12.7 percent, and the skilled/unskilled wage ratio rises by 45.6 percent (CD version).

When, instead, the nontradables become tradable, but sectoral trade remains constrained to half of sectoral output or consumption, and once again transport and protection costs are zero, the skilled wage rises 143 percent from baseline (1993), the unskilled wage rises by 67 percent, and the skilled/unskilled wage ratio rises by 45.2 percent. This means that the two new influences are equally important in the overall FPE results for relative wages.[37] The results also mean that the conversion of the large nontradable block of the economy into tradables has by far the larger contribution to the absolute increase in the levels of US factor prices.

Both of the model changes in this counterfactual may be seen as elements of a "natural cushion" of the domestic factor-price ratio from

---

35. Nor is the result of large overall gains an artifact of reaggregation of the economy, despite the analysis earlier showing that division of the economy into a number of equal parts artificially reduces measured welfare and shadow prices. It turns out that because the original five sectors were not of equal size, their implied welfare actually exceeds rather than falls short of an economy divided into three equal parts. Suppose the economy has output of 100, and there is no trade. In the TIDE structure welfare is: $(13)^{.13}(13)^{.13}(13)^{.13}(40)^4(40)^4$ = 52. In the structure of CF6, welfare would be: $(33.3)^{.333}(33.3)^{.333}(33.3)^{.333}$ = 33. So the gains from wider potential in trade specialization are meaningful rather than a misleading consequence of a smaller number of compartments to the economy.

36. This decomposition was suggested by an anonymous reviewer.

37. The impact by itself of the first of the three influences (zero transport and protection costs) has already been estimated in CF5 and is much smaller.

full international FPE. The fact that the majority of the economy (and employment) is in nontradables provides about half of this cushion. If we interpret the 50 percent limit on sectoral trade relative to output or consumption as a proxy for a natural proclivity in tastes toward home goods, or a natural orientation of producers toward home markets, then this "home orientation" effect provides the other half of the cushion. As noted earlier, a home bias in tastes is often modeled by imposing imperfect substitution between domestic and imported goods in consumption, rather than by the sectoral trade limit.

The results of CF6 are among the most important of this study. They suggest that economists steeped in the SS-FPE tradition may have instinctively exaggerated the expected impact of trade on domestic wage differentials and, hence, income distribution. The reasons are that when the large portion of the economy that is nontradable and the limits of international specialization imposed by home orientation in consumption and production are taken into account, there is much more limited scope for trade to affect relative factor prices.

This might be seen as good news. In a sense, however, it is bittersweet news, because the simulation also shows that if somehow the entire economy were tradable, the absolute gains in efficiency would swamp relative wage effects, and the unskilled workers would gain in absolute terms even though skilled workers would gain much more. Relative income distribution would be more unequal, but absolute wage levels would be higher for those at the bottom of the wage distribution. The potential for absolute gains by all factors diminishes as factor substitutability declines, however.

These CF6 results broadly echo those identified in Krugman's study examined in chapter 3. Krugman essentially concludes that with trade limited compared to the overall economy, the relative wage impact of trade is similarly limited. The experiment here confirms this perception by showing how the large block of the economy that is nontradable (60 percent in the baseline) sharply dampens the potential of trade to affect relative factor prices (i.e., the SS effect).

The experiment also suggests that factor prices would in fact remain far from equalization globally even under the extreme conditions of zero obstacles to trade and complete tradability of the economy. The absolute level of the shadow price of unskilled labor in 1993 under this counterfactual stands at $10,900 for the United States (versus $8,500 in the baseline), whereas the average shadow price for unskilled labor in China and India reaches only $1,100 (compared with only $360 in the baseline).

The FPE experiment does generate international equalization of relative factor prices for most countries. Thus, for 1993 the CD version gives a uniform skilled/unskilled wage ratio of 3.38 for nine of the 13 countries. The only exceptions are the rest of the world (3.51), Japan (2.31), Canada

(2.51), and the United States (2.02). Broad equalization of relative but not absolute factor prices reflects the fact that one of the FPE conditions is missing: identical technology. Instead, the country-specific efficiency parameters (τ_i) remain different across countries.

The lack of complete relative FPE for the United States reflects the absence of another FPE requirement: incomplete specialization (as discussed in chapter 2). The US economy in this experiment specializes completely in the production of skilled- and capital-intensive goods (1 and 3) and imports all of its consumption of the unskilled-intensive good (2).

Finally, the fact that the US and Japanese economies do not converge to international relative FPE tends to support the idea that the underlying forces toward FPE are more likely to push relative factor prices internationally toward those present in the largest industrial economies, rather than driving US relative factor prices toward those of developing countries. This is evident, for example, in the fact that the US unskilled wage either rises substantially (CD version) or holds about constant (CES) in this experiment, whereas unskilled wages in China and India rise about threefold. It is the case, however, that the movement is more symmetrical when expressed in terms of the skilled/unskilled wage ratio. Thus, for 1993 this ratio falls from a baseline value of 6.67 to 3.38 (CD version) for China, while it rises from 0.92 to 2.02 for the United States. In both cases, then, the relative price of the abundant factor approximately doubles.

No Immigration after 1973

The seventh counterfactual (CF7) postulates that there would have been no immigration into the United States after 1973. Estimates by Borjas, Freeman, and Katz (1992, 227-30) indicate that in 1980, immigrants comprised 13 percent of high school dropouts in the US labor force, 4 percent of high school graduates, 6 percent of those with some college, and 8 percent of college graduates. By 1988 these respective shares stood at 26 percent, 7 percent, 7 percent, and 11 percent. Considering those with high school education or less as unskilled and weighting by the shares of each group in the labor force, the implication is that in 1980 the stock of immigrants added 9.8 percent to the unskilled labor force and 7.1 percent to the skilled labor force. By 1988, these respective contributions stood at 18.7 percent and 9.4 percent.

Applying linear interpolation, corresponding estimates for the stock of immigrant workers amount to 2.8 million unskilled workers in 1973, 5.1 million in 1984, and 6.9 million in 1993; there were 1.6 million skilled workers in 1973, 3.4 million in 1984, and 5.0 million by 1993. CF7 reduces the 1984 and 1993 US labor endowments of unskilled and skilled workers by the estimated increments of immigrant workers of each category over the 1973 levels.[38]

Elimination of US immigration after 1973 reduces the US skilled labor force from baseline by 3.3 percent in 1984 and 4.8 percent in 1993. No immigration reduces the US unskilled labor force by 3.8 percent in 1984 and by 7.5 percent in 1993. Thus, the suppression of immigration would have slightly favored skilled wages in 1984 but by 1993 would instead have favored unskilled wages in relative terms. The impact on relative wages should have been minimal in 1984 because of the small difference between proportionate skills availability. However, one would expect more significant change in the relative wage by 1993, because of the substantially greater impact of immigration on unskilled than skilled labor supply by that date.

The CF7 results indicate a small negative effect of immigration on US relative unskilled wages in 1984 and a somewhat larger negative effect by 1993. Thus, in the CD model (table 4.7), in the absence of immigration after 1973 the skilled/unskilled wage ratio would have been 0.4 percent below baseline in 1984 and 2.8 percent below baseline in 1993. In the CES model (table 4A.6), the corresponding reductions from baseline would have been 0.6 percent and 3.7 percent, respectively. The average estimate is that by 1993, immigration over two decades increased the ratio of skilled to unskilled wages by 3.2 percent above the level it would have reached without immigration. This impact is in the right order of magnitude for consistency with the estimates by Borjas, Katz, and Freeman (1992) reviewed in chapter 2, although the estimate here is somewhat higher because it implies a contribution of close to 20 percent to the rise in the skilled/unskilled wage ratio from immigration alone rather than both immigration and trade.

No Unskilled Immigration after 1973

As discussed in chapter 2, US immigration has tended to be bipolar, with a concentration at the extremes of high school dropouts on the one hand and college graduates on the other. The eighth counterfactual (CF8) examines the impact of a freeze on the stock of unskilled immigrant workers at the 1973 level, but no change from baseline for skilled workers. In the CD version of the model (table 4.7), the US skilled/unskilled wage ratio falls by 3.4 percent from the baseline value by 1984 and by 7.2 percent by 1993. In the CES variant (table 4A.6), the reduction is 5 percent by 1984 and 10 percent by 1993.

---

38. Tests indicate negligible differences in results when, in addition, the US immigrant workers suppressed in the counterfactual are allocated across source countries to increase labor endowments there.

As noted above, this case shows substantial divergence between the CD and CES model results, with the CES impact about 40 percent larger than the CD impact. The most likely reason is that this is the one case in which shocks are applied directly to relative factor endowments for the United States, rather than indirectly working through changes in general trade conditions (protection, transport costs, tradability of sectors). For the latter, general, type of shock, there is no difference in relative country adjustment when all countries face either greater (CD) or lesser (CES) factor substitutability. In contrast, the no-immigration experiment is a unique US shock, so relative conditions across countries are not held constant and more limited substitutability shows up directly.

The results of CF8 suggest that if US policy had been to limit immigration of unskilled workers, the result over two decades would have been to increase the relative wage of unskilled workers in the range of 7 to 10 percent compared to the actual outcome, or an average of 8.7 percent for the two models.

Skill-Biased Technological Change

The final counterfactual (CF9) against the backcast baseline examines the impact of skill-biased technological change. The literature surveyed in chapter 2 suggests as a stylized fact that the ratio of skilled to unskilled wages in the United States rose by about 15 percent in the 1980s and that the forces of trade and immigration probably accounted for one-fifth to one-third of this change. The discussion there also suggests that it would probably be an overstatement to attribute all of the rest of the increase solely to biased technological change. Figure 2.9 in chapter 2 illustrates that much of the evolution of the skills differential was likely to have been attributable to the changing pace of growth in the stock of skilled relative to unskilled labor, set against even a constant pace of skill-biased technological change.

Considering these factors, a reasonable inference might be that about half of the observed increase in the skilled/unskilled wage ratio was attributable to skill-biased technological change. If so, that would mean a pace of 7.5 percent per decade for the time trend in the skilled wage relative to the unskilled wage and, thus, in the marginal product of skilled labor relative to that of unskilled labor, as the impact of skill-biased technological change.

The counterfactual thus assumes that half of the increased differential was caused by skill-biased technological change, for an increment of 7.5 percent per decade in the ratio of skilled to unskilled wages. The wage is the factor's marginal product. In the CD production function, this equals the factor's elasticity (in equation 4.1a) multiplied by the average product (ratio of output to amount of the factor). Thus, we may capture technological change by causing the elasticity parameter to rise over time for skilled labor and fall over time for unskilled labor. To obtain a 7.5 percent wedge over a decade, the experiment here increases the skilled labor elasticity by 3.75 percent per decade and decreases the unskilled labor elasticity by the same proportion.[39]

The results of this counterfactual systematically show an increment of the skilled/unskilled wage ratio by about 6 percent from baseline by 1984 and about 12 to 13 percent by 1993, for both the CD and CES models. This result is almost wholly driven by the change in the elasticities just described.[40]

The paths of the absolute levels of shadow prices are of some note for this case. Whereas the CD shadow price on skilled labor falls from $8,650 in 1973 (in 1990 dollars) to $7,790 by 1993 in the baseline, in CF9 the shadow price falls only moderately, to $8,230 by 1993. Correspondingly, the shadow price of unskilled labor, which rises from $5,010 to $8,500 over the same period in the baseline, only reaches $8,035 in the counterfactual for 1993. This still leaves a major decline in the skilled/unskilled wage ratio (from 1.73 in 1973 to 1.02 by 1993, in contrast to 0.92 by 1993 in the backcast baseline). The implication is that it would require a substantially stronger pace of biased technological change than assumed here to yield a rising rather than falling skills differential.

TIDE Model Forecasts

The counterfactual experiments around the backcast baseline suggest that trade and immigration could indeed have had a substantial role in the widening differential between skilled and unskilled wages. The model may also be used to examine possible effects in the future. Several of the studies surveyed in chapter 2 express concern that in the future the impact of global forces on US wage distribution could be greater than in the past, and the experiments with the extended Krugman model in chapter 3 suggest the same possibility. It is important to determine whether the TIDE model points in the same direction.

---

39. For example, in sector 1 the elasticity of 0.6 for skilled labor rises to 0.6 × 1.0375, and that of 0.15 for unskilled labor falls to 0.15 × 0.9625. In addition, these new elasticities must be normalized so the sum of elasticities (including that for capital) is still unity; the increments differ slightly between the two periods (1973-84 and 1984-93) because of their different lengths.

40. There is, nonetheless, sufficient scope in the model for shifting optimal solutions that there are some idiosyncrasies, such as the 18 percent rise in the case of India by 1993 in the CES model (table 4A.6).

Forecast Assumptions

Forecasts using the TIDE model are driven by projections of factor endowments, technological change as represented by the technical efficiency parameter, and prospective transport and production costs. The time horizon for the forecasts is the same as that of the backcasts: two decades.

Capital stocks in every country are projected to grow at the same rate as in 1984-93, but with a ceiling of 7 percent annually (China and the G4 attained rates of 8.5 percent in 1984-93 but seem likely to experience a deceleration). In view of improved prospects of Eastern Europe now that the initial depressive phase of the transition to market economies is largely past, the rate of growth of the real capital stock for this region is forced to 5 percent annually, instead of the rate of virtually zero in the past decade.

The total labor force for each country is assumed to grow at the same rate as in 1984-93 (except for Eastern Europe, where the 1973-84 rate is used). Within the total, the division between skilled and unskilled labor is determined as follows. The ratio of skilled to total labor is assumed to rise at the same rate as during 1984-93, subject to certain ceilings. By 1993 this ratio was already at 56 percent for the United States and had grown at a rate of 1.8 percent annually (from 48 percent in 1984). This pace would seem implausibly high for the next two decades (the skilled share would reach 67 percent in 2003 and 80 percent by 2013). Thus, the projection sets a ceiling of 5 percent of the total labor force as the increase in the skilled portion in the next decade and an additional 4 percent in the subsequent one (bringing the US skilled share of the labor force to 65 percent by 2013). The same ceiling on the decadal increment is applied to Canada.

For its part, the G4 is limited to a future skills fraction that does not exceed that of the United States. Extrapolation of the G4 skills fraction would cause the grouping to leapfrog the United States in relative skills endowment. For Eastern Europe, where the skills fraction fell in the 1980s to a questionably low estimated level of 7.5 percent, the projections arbitrarily boost the fraction to 10 percent by the end of the first decade and 15 percent by the end of the second.

For technological change, the projections assume continuation of the rates of total factor productivity growth used in the backcasts (coefficient on "time" in table 4A.5 in appendix 4A). Once again, the baseline incorporates no skill bias in technological change, as the strategy remains one of considering parametric changes around the baseline rather than focusing primarily on the baseline.

For transport costs, the projections here assume a further reduction by 10 percent (for example, from 6 percent of product value to 5.4 percent) as of 2003 and an additional 5 percent by 2013. For protection, the base case assumes that the Asia Pacific Economic Cooperation (APEC) initiative and the Free Trade Area of the Americas (FTAA) bring free entry for developing-country members into their respective industrial-country partners' markets by 2003 and, reciprocally, that there is free trade within each area by 2013. All other protection remains at 1993 levels.

Forecast Baseline

Table 4.8 reports the baseline forecasts for the TIDE model. For the United States, the model's trend toward a falling ratio of skilled to unskilled wages continues, reducing the calculated ratio from 0.92 in 1993 to 0.66 by 2013 in the CD version and to 0.39 in the CES version. Again, this outcome stems directly from the fact that the skilled labor stock is so high relative to unskilled labor in the future labor force (by 2013, US skilled labor is 187 percent of the unskilled stock), combined with the model's assumption of unchanged sectoral production elasticities for each factor. Skill-biased technological change would instead arrest or conceivably reverse this tendency toward a falling relative wage for skilled labor.[41]

The broad picture in table 4.8 is one of a benign future in which wage disparities diminish because of the strong continued trend toward a greater relative abundance of skilled workers. Even in developing countries, the skilled/unskilled wage ratio is down from its current range of about 6:1 to 10:1 or higher to a range of about 3:1 to 5:1 by the end of two decades (table 4.5). The G4, with even higher relative skills by 2013, resembles the industrial countries in the skilled/unskilled wage ratio.

In another dimension, however, the projections are less encouraging. The absolute levels of the shadow prices of unskilled labor remain quite low in major developing countries (although it must be kept in mind that factor prices and wages are about four times as high as the shadow prices, for the reasons discussed earlier in this chapter). Although the absolute levels of unskilled shadow prices are about three-fourths higher at the end of the period than at the beginning in India, for example, the initial base is so low that by 2013 unskilled workers still have a shadow price (and wage) only about one-tenth the 1973 level for the United States in the CD version. The implication is that extrapolative growth of factor endowments and observed trends in total factor productivity could leave major developing areas with low absolute wages of the unskilled even after two additional decades of economic development. The prospects for unskilled labor in developing countries are even less favorable in the CES variant of the projections (table 4.8).

---

41. Taken literally, the baseline forecast would mean skilled wages substantially below unskilled wages. This proposition is not as bizarre as it might seem, if one considers the possibility that highly educated workers would accept more pleasant but less well paid jobs than would uneducated workers. However, this outlook should not be considered literally but instead is meant only to serve as a benchmark against which to consider the impact of alternative scenarios.

Table 4.8 Factor shadow prices in the TIDE model: forecasts
(thousands of 1990 dollars per worker and rate of return on capital)

	2003				2013			
	S	U	K	S/U	S	U	K	S/U
Cobb-Douglas (CD) model								
US	8.02	10.68	0.022	0.75	8.56	12.96	0.020	0.66
CA	7.59	7.43	0.020	1.02	7.52	9.34	0.016	0.81
EU	8.64	5.55	0.021	1.56	7.81	8.29	0.020	0.94
JP	8.81	7.91	0.017	1.11	10.67	10.98	0.015	0.97
RO	8.75	2.71	0.019	3.22	8.13	2.82	0.019	2.89
MX	7.63	1.95	0.019	3.90	5.88	1.71	0.019	3.44
RL	7.67	1.40	0.020	5.47	6.16	1.43	0.019	4.31
CH	2.89	0.57	0.022	5.09	3.04	0.87	0.020	3.49
G4	4.92	6.41	0.019	0.77	6.12	9.13	0.015	0.67
IN	3.05	0.43	0.031	7.03	2.93	0.57	0.033	5.17
RA	4.18	0.70	0.027	6.01	3.76	0.97	0.026	3.89
EE	7.46	0.94	0.015	7.92	6.41	1.27	0.012	5.04
RW	2.58	0.40	0.018	6.41	1.62	0.41	0.031	3.97
Constant elasticity of substitution (CES) model								
US	6.846	14.08	0.022	0.49	7.02	18.066	0.019	0.39
CA	6.992	8.768	0.020	0.80	6.88	11.453	0.015	0.60
EU	8.568	5.999	0.022	1.43	7.00	9.851	0.019	0.71
JP	8.356	9.537	0.016	0.88	10.14	13.342	0.012	0.76
RO	10.056	2.733	0.022	3.68	9.11	3.027	0.023	3.01
MX	12.288	2.338	0.033	5.26	9.65	2.602	0.037	3.71
RL	10.964	1.348	0.033	8.13	9.16	1.598	0.035	5.73
CH	2.774	0.353	0.036	7.86	2.91	0.599	0.027	4.86
G4	3.590	7.365	0.019	0.49	4.31	10.463	0.011	0.41
IN	2.790	0.214	0.055	13.04	2.51	0.289	0.057	8.68
RA	4.112	0.443	0.040	9.28	3.51	0.63	0.040	5.57
EE	9.432	0.705	0.020	13.38	8.15	1.155	0.014	7.06
RW	3.128	0.272	0.070	11.50	1.90	0.296	0.089	6.41

Notes:
S: skilled   U: unskilled   K: capital
CA: Canada
JP: Japan
RO: rest of OECD
MX: Mexico
RL: rest of Latin America except Venezuela
CH: China
G4: Hong Kong, South Korea, Singapore, and Taiwan
IN: India
RA: rest of Asia
EE: Eastern Europe, including Russia
RW: rest of world

Free Trade

Table 4.9 reports deviations from the forecast baseline under alternative future scenarios for the CD model. The first alternative scenario (FS1) postulates that all protection is eliminated in 2003 and 2013. Free trade boosts US skilled wages by 4 percent from baseline in 2003 and reduces unskilled wages by 1 percent, raising the skilled/unskilled wage ratio by 5 percent. In contrast, by 2013 there is practically no divergence of the free trade results from the baseline estimates. The CES results (not shown) indicate a somewhat smaller rise in the skilled/unskilled wage ratio for 2003 (2.3 percent) and, again, a minimal impact by 2013 (-0.2 percent). In both cases, the difference between the 2003 and 2013 results reflects the full implementation of APEC and FTAA free trade by the latter date in the baseline and the fact that by then the base case is a close approximation of free trade.

Protection Standstill

The second scenario (FS2) assumes that instead of becoming a reality, APEC and FTAA are stillborn. All protection rates remain frozen at their 1993 levels. There is little change from the baseline for the United States in 2003, but by 2013 the skilled/unskilled wage ratio is about 5 percent lower than in the baseline in the CD model (table 4.9) and about 2 percent lower in the CES model. This outcome stems mainly from a drop in the level attained in skilled wages, considering that unskilled wages rise only 0.8 percent from the baseline in the CD model and actually fall by 1.3 percent in the CES version.

This experiment suggests that the foes of APEC and FTAA have an extremely slight case on equity grounds. Unskilled wage gains from freezing 1993 protection would be negligible by 2013 (average of the two models) whereas skilled wages would fall by 2 to 5 percent from baseline levels.

For China, absence of APEC free trade would increase skilled wages by about 5 percent from baseline by 2013, reduce unskilled wages by about 5 percent, and raise the skilled/unskilled wage ratio by about 11 percent in the CD estimates. The impacts would be in the same direction, but somewhat smaller, in the CES version (increase in the skilled/unskilled wage ratio by about 2 percent from baseline by 2013). China would have less opportunity to use its unskilled labor for export production.

Once again, as in the fifth backcast counterfactual, the results for Mexico are pronounced and somewhat counterintuitive. Freezing 1993 protection means less opportunity for most developing countries to export labor-intensive goods, but for Mexico it means a greater opportunity to do so.

Table 4.9 Percent deviation of factor prices from baseline: forecast scenarios, TIDE Cobb-Douglas model
(percentages)

	2003				2013			
	S	U	K	S/U	S	U	K	S/U
FS1: Free trade								
US	3.98	−0.95	0.00	4.97	0.18	−0.15	0.00	0.33
CA	2.73	−0.32	−5.00	3.06	−0.05	−0.20	0.00	0.15
EU	−2.32	4.72	4.76	−6.72	0.37	0.88	0.00	−0.50
JP	0.20	1.20	0.00	−0.98	0.00	−0.02	0.00	0.02
RO	4.57	−4.09	5.26	9.03	1.02	1.28	0.00	−0.25
MX	7.66	−13.15	10.53	23.96	−0.12	−0.18	0.00	0.06
RL	2.72	−3.28	5.00	6.21	0.39	−0.56	5.26	0.96
CH	−5.29	7.39	0.00	−11.81	−0.13	0.80	−5.00	−0.93
G4	4.59	0.14	0.00	4.44	−0.05	−0.03	0.00	−0.02
IN	1.61	0.46	0.00	1.14	2.39	1.24	0.00	1.14
RA	−1.91	6.04	−3.70	−7.50	0.03	0.10	0.00	−0.08
EE	−0.15	−0.64	−6.67	0.49	2.59	−1.65	0.00	4.31
RW	1.20	−0.25	3.57	1.45	−1.60	3.92	3.23	−5.32
FS2: Protection frozen at 1993 level								
US	−0.72	−0.97	0.00	0.25	−3.93	0.81	5.00	−4.70
CA	−2.10	0.11	0.00	−2.20	−0.45	−1.56	0.00	1.13
EU	−0.38	0.11	0.00	−0.49	−1.17	0.02	0.00	−1.19
JP	−0.64	−1.60	−5.88	0.99	4.39	−5.64	−6.67	10.62
RO	−2.37	4.05	0.00	−6.17	−3.24	5.86	−5.26	−8.59
MX	−0.49	5.32	0.00	−5.51	−8.33	17.58	−10.53	−22.04
RL	−0.01	0.07	0.00	−0.08	−1.19	0.14	0.00	−1.32
CH	1.90	−2.11	0.00	4.10	5.07	−5.40	−5.00	11.07
G4	−0.65	0.56	0.00	−1.20	−3.81	0.51	0.00	−4.30
IN	0.16	0.46	0.00	−0.30	0.41	0.71	0.00	−0.29
RA	0.93	−1.87	3.70	2.86	0.64	−4.24	0.00	5.09
EE	−0.05	0.64	0.00	−0.69	−0.08	1.81	0.00	−1.85
RW	0.23	0.25	3.57	−0.02	−1.73	2.70	0.00	−4.31
FS3: Skill-biased technological change								
US	7.93	−8.43	0.00	17.87	11.13	−10.39	5.00	24.02
CA	4.84	−7.31	0.00	13.11	11.20	−11.64	0.00	25.86
EU	6.10	−10.34	0.00	18.34	10.37	−11.76	0.00	25.09
JP	7.21	−9.54	−5.88	18.51	10.78	−11.95	−6.67	25.82
RO	2.79	−9.36	−5.26	13.40	4.12	−12.72	−10.53	19.29
MX	2.92	−9.88	−5.26	14.20	3.20	−13.20	−10.53	18.89
RL	2.91	−13.26	−5.00	18.64	4.43	−16.46	−5.26	25.01
CH	3.18	−12.68	−4.55	18.16	5.20	−15.38	−10.00	24.33
G4	7.76	−7.92	0.00	17.03	11.10	−10.60	0.00	24.28
IN	1.77	−14.52	−6.45	19.05	3.72	−17.84	−9.09	26.25
RA	2.51	−13.67	−3.70	18.74	4.84	−16.03	−7.69	24.85
EE	1.66	−14.35	−6.67	18.69	3.24	−16.51	−8.33	23.66
RW	2.13	−14.39	−3.57	19.30	8.08	−19.12	−6.45	33.63

Table 4.9   Percent deviation of factor prices from baseline: forecast scenarios, TIDE Cobb-Douglas model (percentages)   (continued)

	2003				2013			
	S	U	K	S/U	S	U	K	S/U
FS4: High DC protection on LDC goods								
US	−1.98	−2.47	0.00	0.50	−5.31	−1.10	0.00	−4.25
CA	−4.90	2.96	−5.00	−7.64	−1.48	−3.77	0.00	2.38
EU	−3.79	4.85	0.00	−8.23	−5.48	3.03	−5.00	−8.26
JP	−2.61	−1.42	−5.88	−1.21	0.90	−3.91	−6.67	5.00
RO	−4.86	11.90	−5.26	−14.98	−8.09	19.08	−10.53	−22.81
MX	4.38	−8.14	5.26	13.62	−3.28	5.61	−5.26	−8.42
RL	1.36	−3.71	5.00	5.26	0.39	−3.64	5.26	4.18
CH	2.21	−4.93	4.55	7.51	7.15	−7.69	0.00	16.08
G4	1.93	−0.05	0.00	1.98	−4.45	1.80	0.00	−6.13
IN	0.79	−5.53	0.00	6.69	−0.14	−2.65	−3.03	2.58
RA	0.38	−2.45	0.00	2.90	3.43	−8.58	3.85	13.14
EE	−0.62	−0.96	−6.67	0.34	1.76	−1.89	0.00	3.72
RW	0.31	−4.47	3.57	5.00	0.68	−2.21	0.00	2.95
FS5: Transport and protection cost frozen at 1993 level								
US	−0.97	−1.05	0.00	0.08	−4.76	0.70	5.00	−5.42
CA	−2.13	−0.03	0.00	−2.11	−0.64	−2.11	0.00	1.50
EU	−0.57	0.59	0.00	−1.16	−1.32	−0.47	0.00	−0.85
JP	−0.68	−1.83	−5.88	1.17	4.26	−6.03	−6.67	10.96
RO	−2.38	4.09	0.00	−6.21	−3.94	7.00	−5.26	−10.22
MX	−0.38	5.68	5.26	−5.74	−8.09	19.51	−10.53	−23.09
RL	−0.09	0.07	0.00	−0.16	−1.06	0.35	0.00	−1.40
CH	2.70	−2.64	0.00	5.48	6.09	−5.4	−5.00	12.14
G4	−1.22	0.86	0.00	−2.06	−4.51	0.96	0.00	−5.43
IN	−0.23	−0.46	−3.23	0.23	0.48	0.88	0.00	−0.40
RA	0.91	−1.73	3.70	2.68	2.37	−6.93	3.85	9.99
EE	0.17	0.21	0.00	−0.04	0.16	2.04	0.00	−1.85
RW	−0.12	−0.50	0.00	0.38	−1.48	2.70	0.00	−4.07

Notes:
S: skilled   U: unskilled   K: capital
CA: Canada
JP: Japan
RO: rest of OECD
MX: Mexico
RL: rest of Latin America except Venezuela
CH: China
G4: Hong Kong, South Korea, Singapore, and Taiwan
IN: India
RA: rest of Asia
EE: Eastern Europe, including Russia
RW: rest of world

Mexico's NAFTA advantage remains in place, and the erosion of the "margin of preference" that otherwise would occur through APEC and FTAA in the baseline does not occur under the protection standstill. The result is an increase of almost 18 percent from baseline in the unskilled wage rate for Mexico by 2013 and a drop of about 22 percent in the skilled/unskilled wage ratio as skilled wages decline by about 8 percent (CD model, table 4.9). The CES results are similar but more moderate, showing a decline of about 12 percent from baseline in the skilled/unskilled wage ratio by 2013.

Skill-Biased Technological Change

The next scenario (FS3) considers the impact of imposing skill-biased technological change onto the forecast. The same decadal increments in the elasticity for skilled labor, and reductions in that for unskilled labor, are applied as in the corresponding backcast counterfactual (CF9). This scenario also assumes that the 1993 base has skill-biased technological change, so the 1993 factor elasticities are already those applied in CF9 (table 4.7).

The consequence of imposing skill-biased technological change is almost uniformly to continue the time path of rising skilled/unskilled wage ratio deviation from the original (1973-93) baseline. Thus, whereas the impact on the wage ratio was about 6 percent by the end of the first decade (1984) and 12 percent by the end of the second (1993—see table 4.7), it reaches about 18 percent by the end of the third decade (2003) and 25 percent by the end of the fourth (2013—see table 4.9).[42]

The rise in the skilled/unskilled wage ratio results from an absolute reduction in the unskilled wage and increase in the skilled wage. It is also of note that there are induced effects on the return to capital. Countries specializing in skill-intensive goods (industrial countries and the G4) tend not to experience an impact on capital return, but the mainly developing countries specializing in unskilled-intensive exports experience a drop in the return to capital. The implication is that if technological change is biased against the country's abundant factor, the country's overall productivity of capital suffers.

Increased Protection

The next forecast scenario (FS4) considers the impact of higher protection against goods from developing countries. In this scenario, by 2003 and

---

42. Note that, correspondingly, if the scenario FS3 had been specified to begin in 1993 with the same factor elasticities as used in the baseline, the impact against the baseline would amount to about 6 percent increase in skilled/unskilled wage ratios by 2003 and 12 percent by 2013.

2013 all industrial countries impose uniform tariffs of 30 percent against all goods from developing countries, and Mexico loses its free entry into US and Canadian markets.

In the CD model, by 2013 high protection reduces the US skilled/unskilled wage ratio by about 4 percent from baseline, moving the relative factor price in the expected adverse direction for the relatively abundant factor. The wage of skilled labor falls 5 percent, and even the wage of unskilled labor falls, by 1 percent. In the CES version, both factors experience a wage loss of almost 4 percent from baseline values, and the decline in the skilled/unskilled wage ratio is negligible.

These results indicate that high protection against goods from developing countries would be a highly inefficient way to reduce domestic US wage inequality because both factors would lose in absolute terms, and even the reduction in the relative wage of skilled labor could be limited (only about 2 percent, the average of the two models). Higher protection means less efficiency, less to go around, and, hence, a drop in both the skilled and unskilled wage, albeit by a lesser amount for the latter. The results of this scenario contradict the popular view that there could be a major improvement in unskilled wages from much higher protection against developing countries.

Constant Transportation and Protection Costs

The final scenario (FS5) freezes both transportation costs and protection at their 1993 levels. The deviations from baseline in this scenario are generally close to those of the scenario freezing only protection (FS2), suggesting that the expected future decline of transportation costs by another 15 percent over 20 years has an even smaller impact than the prospective further reduction in protection.

The principal significance of this scenario is that, as in the case of the backcasts, it serves to identify the "impact of trade" on the future skilled/unskilled wage ratio. It indicates that if transportation and protection costs were to remain unchanged over the next two decades, this wage ratio for the United States would be only about 5 percent lower than in the baseline forecast for the CD model. For the CES version, the reduction from baseline would be only 1.7 percent by 2013. Defining the influence of trade as the impact of falling transport and protection costs, this future influence is moderate, at an average of about 3 percent for the two models. This impact is only about one-third as large as the corresponding impact of trade over the past two decades (10 percent increase in the skilled/unskilled wage ratio for both models—see tables 4.7 and 4A.6, CF4).

Model Sensitivity

All of the simulations considered above use the same sets of factor elasticities to distinguish between skilled and unskilled sectors. Kim and Mieszkowski (1995) have shown that in a simple general equilibrium formulation of trade, the impact of trade on relative factor prices diminishes as the gap between the sectoral factor elasticities diminishes. The experiments with the Krugman model in chapter 3 show the same thing. Thus, it is useful to consider the sensitivity of the TIDE model results to the particular choice of sectoral elasticities.

In the main simulations, the skilled-intensive sectors (1 and 4) always have an elasticity of 0.6 for skilled labor and 0.15 for unskilled labor, whereas the unskilled-intensive sectors (2 and 5) always have an elasticity of 0.15 for skilled labor and 0.6 for unskilled labor. To test the sensitivity of the results to the gap between these elasticities, the following tests set the skilled-intensive sectoral elasticities to 0.5 for skilled labor and 0.25 for unskilled labor and use the reverse values for the unskilled sectors. The sum of skilled and unskilled elasticities remains 0.75 as before, so the capital elasticities do not change. None of the elasticities change in the capital-intensive sector (3).

To gauge the impact of trade and, thus, test the Kim-Mieszkowski proposition, both the baseline backcasts and CF4 freezing protection and transport costs at 1973 levels may be run using the revised sectoral elasticities. In the original CF4, the skilled/unskilled wage ratio for 1993 falls by 10 percent from baseline in both the CD and CES variants, as a consequence of the constant transport and protection cost shock. In the sensitivity test with the smaller gap between sectoral elasticities, the drop is only 7.1 percent from the (revised) baseline for the CD model and 6.8 percent for the CES version. This result confirms the proposition that the narrower gap between sectoral elasticities means a lesser impact of trade on relative factor prices. In this case, the impact is about one-third smaller than in the main TIDE results. The reduction in the divergence between sectoral factor shares, from $0.6 - 0.15 = 0.45$ to $0.5 - 0.25 = 0.25$ is a proportionate cut of about 40 percent, somewhat larger than the proportionate reduction in the estimated impact of trade on the skilled/unskilled wage ratio.

As a second major sensitivity test, it is useful to consider the joint impact of trade and immigration. Thus, Borjas, Freeman, and Katz (1992) emphasize that because trade and immigration are potentially substitutes as alternative means of increasing the effective relative supply of the scarce domestic factor, their impact on relative wages should be examined jointly. The second sensitivity test combines CF4 and CF7. That is, 1973 transport and protection costs and nonimmigration for the United States after 1973 are applied jointly to 1993 global factor endowments to solve for optimal factor allocation and trade. This time once again the more moderate intersectoral factor elasticity divergence is applied (0.50/0.25 rather than 0.60/0.15).

This second sensitivity test finds that the ratio of US skilled to unskilled wages would have been 9.3 percent lower in 1993 than in the baseline (with the baseline also estimated using the lower elasticity divergence). This result is close to what would be expected with a linear effect of combining the "trade" (transport and protection cost) counterfactual with the "immigration" counterfactual. Namely, the former amounts to about a 7 percent reduction from baseline in the relative skilled wage. As for the latter, in the initial counterfactual (CF7 in table 4.7), using the larger sectoral elasticity divergence of the main TIDE model, the immigration impact is about 3 percent by 1993. From the first sensitivity test (for transport and protection costs only), narrowing the sectoral difference cuts the impact of the counterfactual shock by about one-third. So the immigration estimate using the narrower sectoral elasticity divergence would be about 2 percent as the contribution of US immigration to the increase in the skilled/unskilled wage ratio over the past two decades. Thus, the simple sum of the "trade" and "immigration" shocks is approximately the same as the result for the sensitivity test combining them jointly. This outcome is reasonable, given that each of the effects is modest so that interaction terms should be small.

An additional finding using the sensitivity-test parameters for sectoral factor elasticities is that for the projections through 2013, the influence of trade on the US skilled/unskilled wage ratio is likely to be an additional increase by 3 percent, based on the CD version of the TIDE model. This compares with an estimate of 5 percent in the unadjusted model (table 4.9, scenario FS5).

Estimates by Borjas, Freeman, and Katz (1997) provide a basis for a quasi-empirical estimate of the sectoral factor elasticities. They work at the three-digit industry level for US manufactures, for which they derive trade data based on four-digit SIC trade estimates. Their sectoral data on worker characteristics are from US Census Bureau estimates. The authors array the industries by import or export shares in sales (either for total trade or trade with LDCs). Using a cutoff point of 10 percent cumulative share of US manufacturing labor, they find that in 1990, 30.7 percent of labor in top export industries had education of 16 years or more, while only 9.7 percent had education of less than 12 years. If we use these categories as "skilled" and "unskilled," divide the rest of workers evenly between skilled and unskilled, and apply 1990 wages for less than 12 years, 12 to 15 years, and 16 or more years of education (table 1.2), we obtain the result that the wage bill in export industries was composed of 68.5 percent for skilled and 31.5 percent for unskilled labor. This sector would correspond to the skill-intensive tradable sector in the TIDE model (sector 1).

For the unskilled-intensive tradable good (sector 2), the appropriate comparison from Borjas, Freeman, and Katz (1997) is their preferred "middle" variant in which import-oriented factor shares for 1990 are drawn from 1980 data. The idea is that, somewhat in the spirit of Wood (1994), sectors intensive in imports from developing countries have more labor-intensive, earlier-vintage techniques in the goods actually traded than is characteristic of the same sectors on average. The Borjas, Freeman, and Katz (1997) estimates for 1980 for sectors intensive in imports from developing countries indicate that 44.4 percent of the workforce has fewer than 12 years of education and 6.3 percent has 16 or more years. Applying 1980 wage rates (table 1.2) and, once again, dividing the other workers evenly between skilled and unskilled, the result is that for the unskilled-intensive tradable sector the share of unskilled labor in the wage bill is 65 percent and that of skilled labor 35 percent.

Thus, it turns out that these Census-based estimates indicate that the skilled-labor-intensive tradable sector has a skilled-labor share that is about twice the unskilled-labor share, and the converse is true in the unskilled-labor-intensive tradable sector. If we set the capital share at 25 percent in both sectors, then this "double-share" rule implies a skilled-labor elasticity of 0.5 and unskilled elasticity of 0.25 for TIDE sector 1 and the reverse for TIDE sector 2. This turns out to be the same as the elasticities applied in the sensitivity tests of this section.

There is still some room to argue that the intersectoral difference of factor elasticities could be greater (and, thus, closer to the 0.6/0.15 dichotomy in the main TIDE estimates). The plant-level data of Bernard and Jensen (1994) suggest that the relevant factor combinations could diverge more between the export and import sectors than even indicated by applying 1980 aggregate factor shares for import-intensive industries, basically because aggregation masks differences in production techniques. Nonetheless, the data provided by Borjas, Freeman, and Katz (1997) suggest that the "double-share" sectoral divergence of the sensitivity test is closer to the mark than the "quadruple-share" divergence in the main TIDE estimates. Therefore, the policy conclusions of this study in chapter 5 will emphasize the findings of the sensitivity tests of this section, rather than the raw TIDE results. In general, on the basis of the sensitivity test for CF4, the shocks with the more moderate (double-share) sectoral elasticity differences could be expected to generate deviations from baseline that are about two-thirds to three-fourths as large as in the unadjusted TIDE simulations.

Conclusion

This chapter has applied a general equilibrium model to estimated actual data on endowments of skilled and unskilled labor to simulate the effect of trade and immigration on the ratio of skilled to unskilled wages in the United States and 12 other "countries." The factor data show a strong and persistent rise in the relative availability of skilled labor, not just in the United States but internationally, as well as a surprisingly large absolute stock of skilled labor in the populous LDCs.

When actual data on manufactured trade for 1973, 1984, and 1993 are classified into product categories intensive in the use of skilled labor, unskilled labor, or capital, they show strong patterns of comparative advantage that are consistent with trade theory. The United States has a pronounced comparative advantage in skilled goods, especially at the beginning of the period. There is some shift in US comparative advantage toward capital-intensive goods by the end of the period. The four East Asian "tigers" show a strong shift toward skill-intensive comparative advantage over the period.

The baseline backcast of the model, which does not incorporate skill-biased technological change, shows a persistent decline in the ratio of skilled to unskilled wages in the optimal solutions that maximize welfare subject to factor availability, production conditions, and plausible limits on trade. This decline is present in almost all of the countries in the model. It is the direct consequence of the application of a standard production function to a rising relative availability of skilled labor. This baseline is a stark reminder that there is an underlying puzzle in the subject of this study: the rise in the skilled/unskilled wage ratio rather than a decline that would be expected from factor availability trends. There is a variant in which skill-biased technological change is introduced, and this version substantially arrests the declining wage ratio.

The heart of the analysis, however, is not its baseline backcast but its tests showing the parametric response of skilled/unskilled wage ratios to alternative analytical shocks. These tests reveal the relative size of various influences that have been proposed for the impact of global forces on wage distribution.

The counterfactual backcast freezing transport and protection costs at their 1973 level finds that by 1993 the skilled/unskilled wage ratio would have been about 10 percent lower in the United States than in the baseline. If we accept as closer to reality the main "sensitivity" test, using a somewhat smaller divergence between sectoral factor shares, then this key result moderates to about a 7 percent increase as the central estimate for the impact of trade on the US skilled/unskilled wage ratio over the past two decades. Even the adjusted estimate strongly suggests a major influence of growing openness of the US economy on the path of relative wages, considering that the total rise in the skilled/unskilled wage ratio was in the range of 15 to 20 percent over this period.[43]

A counterfactual case freezing the stock of immigrant labor at its 1973 level causes the skilled/unskilled wage ratio by 1993 to be about 3 percent

---

43. However, as chapter 5 emphasizes, the relative importance of trade and immigration is more appropriately gauged against gross unequalizing forces than against the net relative wage change.

lower than in the baseline, suggesting a significant contribution of immigration as well to rising wage inequality. Applying the sensitivity adjustment of two-thirds, the adjusted estimate would be an increase of about 2 percent as the impact of immigration on the US skilled/unskilled wage ratio over the past two decades. A separate sensitivity test for the joint impact of "trade" (falling transport and protection costs) and immigration using the more moderate elasticity difference suggests that the combined effect of these forces over the past two decades was to increase the US skilled/unskilled wage ratio by about 9 percent. This estimate is approximately equivalent to a simple addition of the two effects separately, as might be expected given the relatively marginal magnitude of each individually.

If the immigration experiment is rerun freezing only the stock of unskilled immigrant labor at the 1973 level while allowing actual immigration in 1973-93, the reduction in the skilled/unskilled wage ratio from baseline by 1993 is larger. The US unskilled immigrant work force rose from 2.8 million in 1973 to 6.9 million in 1993, compared with a total unskilled work force of 51 million and 53 million in the two respective years. When the unskilled immigrant workforce is held constant at its 1973 level, by 1993 the absolute level of the US unskilled wage rises by 5 to 7 percent from its baseline value, and the ratio of skilled to unskilled wages falls by 7 to 10 percent from the baseline estimate. The larger impacts are those from the CES model, as is expected given its more limited scope for substitution between skilled and unskilled labor. Again, adjusted estimates using the sensitivity-test sectoral factor shares would be smaller, presumably about 4 to 7 percent impact.

One of the most important simulations reformulates the economy to make all goods and services tradable and remove sectoral trade constraints, whereas in the main model 60 percent of the economy is in nontradables (mainly services) and trade is limited to 50 percent of output or consumption in each of the tradable sectors. This variant shows a dramatic increase of over 100 percent in the skilled/unskilled wage ratio for the United States (and major reductions in this ratio for developing countries). About half of the increase in the wage ratio is attributable to turning nontradables into tradables, and about half is attributable to removing the sectoral trade constraints. Importantly, the large rise in the skilled/unskilled wage ratio comes from a massive increase in the skilled wage accompanied by a sizable increase in the unskilled wage, rather than from a decline in the latter.[44]

---

44. A sensitivity run of this counterfactual for 1993 using skilled/unskilled factor shares of 0.5/0.25 rather than 0.6/0.15, as described above for the sensitivity test on CF4, finds a more moderate increase in the relative skilled wage by 52 percent. This comes from an increase in the skilled wage by 152 percent and rise in the unskilled wage by 66 percent. The corresponding wage changes in the unadjusted TIDE-CD results are 182 percent and 28 percent, respectively.

This simulation suggests that the pessimism of economists steeped in the SS and FPE theories has been greatly exaggerated by the failure of those theories to take account of the natural buffer against international FPE provided by the facts that the bulk of the economy is nontradable and that there is a considerable "home orientation" of both consumption and production, even for tradables.

An encouraging finding in this simulation, furthermore, is that the tendency toward FPE (which remains incomplete because countries fully specialize) is accomplished by a large rise in unskilled wages in developing countries rather than a reduction in industrial-country unskilled wages (which show some increase themselves). This finding suggests that if the entire economy could be made tradable, the global efficiency gains would leave the scarce domestic factor (unskilled labor for the United States) better off rather than worse. Furthermore, whereas the simulation shows relative FPE across most countries, absolute skilled and unskilled wages remain much higher in industrial countries than in developing countries, because of the higher technological coefficient in production in the former group of countries (τ_i in equation 4.1a).

A simulation in which trade is completely suppressed causes the US skilled/unskilled wage ratio to fall by about 15 percent from the baseline in 1993. This extreme experiment places an outer limit on the equalization that might be accomplished by restrictive trade policies. In contrast, an experiment in which all protection and transport costs are eliminated shows an increase of only about 6 to 7 percent for the US relative skilled wage by 1993. The implication is that, by now, much of the relative wage effect of growing integration of the US economy into the world economy through rising trade has already occurred, as transport and protection barriers are now relatively low.

The estimates of this chapter then turn to forecasts over the next two decades. Once again, the driving force is the trend in factor endowments, as recent trends in skilled labor, unskilled labor, and capital are projected. Once again, the baseline shows a persistent decline in the skilled/unskilled wage ratio into the future as a consequence of the rising relative availability of skilled labor in the United States and abroad. Once again, this trend is arrested in a variant imposing substantial skill-biased technological change.

The baseline forecast assumes the presence of APEC and the FTAA, which by 2013 provide the United States with reciprocal free trade with Asia Pacific and Latin American countries. In an alternative scenario in which protection instead remains frozen at its 1993 levels, the wage of US unskilled labor remains virtually unchanged from its 2013 baseline, while the skilled wage falls by 3 to 4 percent. Thus, a standstill in trade barriers would cause overall US losses without increasing the wage of unskilled labor.[45] This experiment suggests that the opponents of APEC and FTAA have little basis for grounding their arguments in the name of wage equity.

A more extreme scenario raises US protection to 30 percent against all developing countries, including Mexico (i.e., an end to NAFTA). This case does reduce the US skilled/unskilled wage ratio by 0 to 4 percent from the 2013 baseline, but only by reducing skilled wages by 4 to 5 percent rather than raising unskilled wages significantly. This case again suggests protection is an inefficient way to achieve greater wage equality.[46]

On balance, the results of the TIDE model simulations suggest that trade and immigration (especially unskilled) have had a significant impact over the past decade in the observed rise of skilled wages relative to unskilled wages. Falling transportation costs and protection have driven the trade influence. In contrast, for the future the model suggests a much more benign outlook. Based on the deviation from the baseline in the future scenario freezing transportation and protection costs at 1993 levels, the further impact of trade (defined as the change brought about by growing global integration through the reduction in these physical and protective barriers) on the skilled/unskilled wage ratio for the United States is estimated at an increase of about 1.7 to 5 percent over two decades (or even less under smaller sectoral factor share differences), averaging only about one-third the estimated impact over the past two decades for the two models.

The central dynamic in the trade-equity connection is the following trade-off of forces operating in different directions. The force of increasing openness, whether because of improved transportation and communications technology or because of lower protection, causes a rising disparity between US skilled and unskilled wages. The reason is the classic economic theory that trade makes the factor that is relatively scarce at home less scarce. For the United States, unskilled labor is the relatively scarce factor. Trade essentially opens indirect access to the much larger pools of unskilled labor in developing countries.

Against this force, there is a second force working in the opposite direction. There has been a major trend toward greater dissemination of education among the labor forces of the world. The fraction of the labor force that is skilled has risen sharply almost everywhere. For example, in the East Asian G4, skilled labor has risen from about 9 percent to about

---

45. Note, however, that the model's simplistic treatment of the protection wedge as an outright loss, rather than incorporation of tariff revenue into welfare estimates, means that the TIDE model is not ideally suited to evaluate welfare changes from trade liberalization. Instead, it is designed to focus on changes in relative factor prices.

46. Moreover, for the various forecast scenarios, all changes from baseline would presumably be more moderate if the "sensitivity" factor share divergences were applied (0.5/0.25) rather than the corresponding unadjusted TIDE parameters (0.6/0.15).

41 percent of the labor force over the past two decades; in China, the increase has been from about 6 percent to about 11 percent (table 4.2). This systematic rise in the relative availability of skilled labor reduces the extremity of the US comparative advantage in skill-intensive exports and, thus, the tendency of greater openness to raise the skilled/unskilled wage ratio.

For the future, the analysis here suggests that the first, unequalizing force—greater openness—is likely to moderate, simply because protection and transport costs have already fallen to low levels. In contrast, the second, equalizing force—rising skill endowments abroad—is likely to persist. Within the confines of the TIDE model, the implication is that there should be more limited pressure on wage inequality from trade in the future than in the past.

Ironically, this result is almost the reverse of the popular view (and the implication of the analysis in chapter 3) that the unequalizing impact of trade is likely to be greater in the future. In part, this finding may reflect the model's inability to capture other important influences (such as the "Hicksian convergence" of LDCs toward industrial-country production capabilities, discussed in chapter 2). In part, however, it reflects an absence of focus in most of the literature on the formulation of the problem in terms of the two opposing forces just discussed and on the diminishing potential for further openness in an already open world economy as compared to the persistent pace of rising skill endowments globally. Chapter 5 further considers the proper balance in interpreting the divergent results of chapter 3 and chapter 4 about how much of the unequalizing impact of trade is already in the past and how much remains to be experienced in the future.

Appendix 4A

Table 4A.1 Classification of 2-digit SITC codes by major factor input

SITC	Description	Factor	Basis
5	**Chemicals and related products**		
51	Organic chemicals	K	L,IO
52	Inorganic chemicals	K	L,IO
53	Dyeing, tanning, and coloring materials	K	IO
54	Medical and pharmaceutical products	K	IO
55	Essential oils, resinoids, perfume materials; toilet, polishing, and cleaning preparations	K	L,IO
56	Fertilizers (other than those of group 272)	K	IO
57	Plastics in primary forms	K	IO
58	Plastics in nonprimary form	K	IO
59	Chemical materials and products	K	IO
6	**Manufactured goods classified chiefly by material**		
61	Leather, leather manufactures, n.e.s. and dressed furskins	U	SS
62	Rubber manufactures n.e.s.	U	C
63	Cork and wood manufactures (excluding furniture)	U	C
64	Paper, paperboard, and articles of paper pulp	K	L
65	Textile yarn, fabrics, and made-up articles n.e.s.	K	C
66	Nonmetallic mineral manufactures, n.e.s.	U	C
67	Iron and steel	U	L,IO,SS
68	Nonferrous metals	U	C
69	Manufactures of metal n.e.s.	S	L
7	**Machinery and transport equipment**		
71	Power-generating machinery and equipment	S	L
72	Machinery specialized for particular industries	S	L
73	Metal-working machinery	S	L
74	General industrial machinery and equipment n.e.s.	S	C
75	Office machines and automatic data processing machines	S	SS
76	Telecommunications and sound recording and reproducing apparatus and equipment	S	C
77	Electrical machinery, apparatus, and appliances n.e.s.	S	L
78	Road vehicles (including air-cushion vehicles)	K	L
79	Other transport equipment	S	L,SS
8	**Miscellaneous manufactured articles**		
81	Prefabricated buildings; sanitary plumbing, heating, and lighting fixtures and fittings n.e.s.	S	SS
82	Furniture and parts thereof; bedding, mattresses, mattress supports, cushions, and similar stuffed furnishings	U	L,SS
83	Travel goods, handbags, and similar containers	U	C
84	Articles of apparel and clothing accessories	U	L,SS
85	Footwear	U	L,SS
87	Professional, scientific, and controlling instruments and apparatus	S	L
88	Photographic apparatus, equipment and supplies, and optical goods, n.e.s.; watches and clocks	K	IO
89	Miscellaneous manufactured articles n.e.s.	U	C

Notes:
K: capital   U: unskilled labor   S: skilled labor
L: Leamer   SS: Sachs and Shatz   C: author   IO: input-output tables

Source: SITC (various years).

Table 4A.2 Actual exports and imports by product group (millions of dollars)

	1973			1984			1993		
	Exports	Imports	Trade balance	Exports	Imports	Trade balance	Exports	Imports	Trade balance
Skilled									
US	20,057.5	12,469.3	7,588.2	72,177.8	74,613.8	−2,436.0	162,165.8	199,447.2	−37,281.4
CA	2,860.4	6,446.0	−3,585.6	10,817.6	18,784.5	−7,966.9	22,670.0	43,484.2	−20,814.2
EU	59,555.4	44,263.2	15,292.2	155,797.9	122,740.3	33,057.6	396,910.2	345,468.2	51,442.1
JA	11,663.8	2,855.2	8,808.6	70,326.4	9,113.8	61,212.6	183,586.2	35,378.2	148,208.0
RO	11,496.9	13,333.7	−1,836.9	31,026.7	36,718.9	−5,692.2	74,482.5	82,409.5	−7,927.0
MX	390.3	1,697.2	−1,306.9	3,417.8	6,154.9	−2,737.1	21,110.6	24,282.4	−3,171.8
RL	412.4	5,273.0	−4,860.6	2,957.1	11,239.3	−8,282.2	6,690.8	30,509.6	−23,818.7
CH	187.8	321.2	−133.4	1,615.4	6,080.1	−4,464.7	18,401.1	44,459.1	−26,058.1
IN	132.9	659.9	−527.0	602.4	3,002.7	−2,400.3	1,481.0	6,065.2	−4,584.2
G4	3,213.3	4,794.2	−1,580.9	32,953.1	28,150.9	4,802.2	159,336.3	126,625.5	32,710.7
RA	139.0	2,527.3	−2,388.2	4,144.6	13,557.9	−9,413.4	33,824.7	53,246.2	−19,421.5
EE	5,034.1	8,871.0	−3,836.8	17,265.5	21,504.9	−4,239.5	11,503.9	34,129.4	−22,625.5
OPEC	114.0	5,821.7	−5,707.6	651.5	31,939.6	−31,288.2	2,305.5	40,611.9	−38,306.5
RW	306.3	6,007.5	−5,701.2	2,025.0	19,862.8	−17,837.8	7,099.6	30,126.7	−23,027.1
Unskilled									
US	6,049.45	14,641.3	−8,591.9	14,487.8	65,886.7	−51,399.0	47,282.2	127,222.5	−79,940.3
CA	2,978.5	3,087.6	−109.1	9,236.6	8,399.9	836.7	17,171.9	20,371.3	−3,199.4
EU	48,545.5	41,832.6	6,712.9	118,811.0	97,962.8	20,848.1	257,290.2	257,438.0	−147.9
JA	9,202.7	4,241.0	4,961.8	35,233.2	10,781.7	24,451.5	45,590.8	43,384.9	2,205.9
RO	8,929.0	11,020.8	−2,091.8	27,276.1	27,912.5	−636.4	54,016.0	57,226.4	−3,210.3
MX	536.3	482.2	54.1	1,954.6	1,545.8	408.8	7,630.9	9,049.1	−1,418.2
RL	2,449.6	2,840.7	−391.1	8,299.4	5,570.7	2,728.7	18,789.9	16,764.6	2,025.3
CH	819.5	1,204.7	−385.2	4,902.3	5,961.7	−1,059.3	40,936.9	23,673.2	17,263.7

continued next page

Table 4A.2 Actual exports and imports by product group (millions of dollars) (continued)

	1973			1984			1993		
	Exports	Imports	Trade balance	Exports	Imports	Trade balance	Exports	Imports	Trade balance
IN	638.4	536.1	102.3	2,858.8	2,021.3	837.5	10,139.0	4,318.6	5,820.5
G4	6,571.9	2,833.7	3,738.2	38,873.0	13,966.0	24,907.1	110,319.3	61,557.3	48,762.0
RA	1,182.8	1,344.2	-161.3	5,519.9	5,037.6	482.3	30,853.8	19,447.2	11,406.6
EE	5,233.5	6,172.2	-938.7	12,890.2	14,684.9	-1,794.7	29,935.6	20,791.4	9,144.1
OPEC	287.4	2,998.7	-2,711.4	3,033.3	17,334.7	-14,301.4	15,339.1	21,126.9	-5,787.8
RW	3,426.9	3,467.4	-40.5	3,975.4	8,817.6	-4,842.2	16,943.4	18,089.4	-1,146.0
Capital									
US	18,630.7	17,297.8	1,332.8	57,029.0	80,292.5	-23,263.5	129,551.8	142,970.9	-13,419.1
CA	7,855.5	7,251.4	604.2	32,321.6	22,158.5	10,163.1	53,949.5	41,856.4	12,093.1
EU	64,051.0	48,526.2	15,524.8	180,058.9	141,583.6	38,475.4	415,079.8	349,185.3	65,894.5
JA	14,022.2	3,329.3	10,692.9	59,470.4	11,626.7	47,843.8	119,229.8	30,596.6	88,633.2
RO	12,597.2	14,504.2	-1,907.0	34,946.9	34,985.1	-38.1	70,120.7	75,818.0	-5,697.2
MX	438.6	1,216.7	-778.1	1,793.9	3,876.4	-2,082.5	10,817.9	14,331.4	-3,513.5
RL	1,163.6	5,792.7	-4,629.1	6,131.1	16,510.8	-10,379.7	10,784.3	40,357.1	-29,572.8
CH	967.3	771.1	196.2	5,488.4	6,834.6	-1,346.3	15,454.4	36,991.6	-21,537.2
IN	798.5	601.7	196.8	1,743.8	3,346.6	-1,602.7	4,887.8	4,943.6	-55.9
G4	2,595.8	4,498.7	-1,902.9	19,675.5	19,729.9	-54.5	74,169.9	69,863.4	4,306.5
RA	689.5	2,956.7	-2,267.2	3,000.1	10,367.9	-7,367.8	11,594.8	34,601.1	-23,006.3
EE	3,936.0	6,589.3	-2,653.3	13,200.0	18,955.4	-5,755.4	18,798.9	31,910.3	-13,111.4
OPEC	452.9	4,922.4	-4,469.5	2,707.9	25,770.3	-23,062.4	6,247.6	35,107.0	-28,859.4
RW	846.0	9,608.9	-8,762.9	3,326.8	20,625.7	-17,298.9	8,713.6	35,419.0	-26,705.4
Total									
US	44,737.5	44,408.4	329.1	143,694.6	220,793.1	-77,098.5	338,999.8	469,640.6	-130,640.8
CA	13,694.5	16,784.9	-3,090.5	52,375.8	49,342.8	3,033.0	93,791.4	105,711.9	-11,920.5

EU	172,151.9	134,622.0	37,529.9	454,667.8	362,286.7	92,381.0	1,069,280.2	952,091.5	117,188.7
JA	34,888.7	10,425.4	24,463.4	165,030.0	31,522.1	133,507.9	348,406.8	109,359.7	239,047.1
RO	33,023.1	38,858.7	−5,835.7	93,249.7	99,616.5	−6,366.8	198,619.3	215,453.8	−16,834.5
MX	1,365.3	3,396.1	−2,030.8	7,166.3	11,577.1	−4,410.8	39,559.5	47,663.0	−8,103.6
RL	4,025.6	13,906.4	−9,880.8	17,387.6	33,320.8	−15,933.2	36,265.1	87,631.3	−51,366.2
CH	1,974.6	2,297.0	−322.4	12,006.1	18,876.4	−6,870.3	74,792.4	105,124.0	−30,331.6
IN	1,569.8	1,797.7	−227.9	5,205.1	8,370.6	−3,165.5	16,507.8	15,327.4	1,180.4
G4	12,381.0	12,126.5	254.5	91,501.6	61,846.8	29,654.8	343,825.4	258,046.2	85,779.2
RA	2,011.4	6,828.2	−4,816.8	12,664.5	28,963.4	−16,298.9	76,273.4	107,294.6	−31,021.2
EE	14,203.6	21,632.5	−7,428.9	43,355.7	55,145.2	−11,789.6	60,238.4	86,831.2	−26,592.8
OPEC	854.3	13,742.8	−12,888.5	6,392.7	75,044.7	−68,652.0	23,892.1	96,845.8	−72,953.7
RW	4,579.2	19,083.8	−14,504.6	9,327.2	49,306.1	−39,978.9	32,756.6	83,635.1	−50,878.5

Notes:
S: skilled   U: unskilled   K: capital

CA: Canada   CH: China   EE: Eastern Europe, including Russia
JP: Japan   IN: India   OPEC: Organization of Petroleum Exporting Countries
RO: rest of OECD   G4: Hong Kong, South Korea, Singapore, and   (including Venezuela)
MX: Mexico   Taiwan   RW: rest of world
RL: rest of Latin America except   RA: rest of Asia
Venezuela

Table 4A.3 Estimated distances between countries (miles)

	US	CA	EU	JP	RO	MX	RL	CH	IN	G4	RA	EE	RW
US (Chicago)	0	745	4,143	6,314	5,654	1,690	5,272	6,604	8,068	7,797	8,570	4,679	8,020
CA (Toronto)		0	3,432	6,471	5,261	2,317	5,078	6,519	7,521	7,736	8,338	4,022	7,269
EU (Paris)			0	6,053	2,558	5,725	5,684	5,120	3,561	5,990	5,877	852	3,607
JP (Tokyo)				0	5,517	5,062	11,532	1,307	4,193	1,791	2,865	5,347	7,001
RO (Vienna, Sydney)[a]					0	6,688	6,606	4,841	4,268	5,252	5,134	2,311	4,461
MX (Mexico City)						0	4,764	7,753	9,743	8,788	9,793	6,337	9,219
RL (Rio de Janeiro)							0	10,768	8,345	11,009	9,994	6,455	5,561
CH (Beijing)								0	2,960	1,217	2,046	4,325	5,732
IN (New Delhi)									0	2,698	1,868	3,604	2,818
G4 (Hong Kong)										0	1,077	5,147	5,471
RA (Bangkok)											0	5,033	4,484
EE (Warsaw)												0	3,816
RW (Nairobi)													0

a. The rest of the OECD is a weighted average of distances for relevant countries in Europe (centered at Vienna) and Australia-New Zealand (Sydney).

Notes:
CA: Canada
JP: Japan
RO: rest of OECD
MX: Mexico

RL: rest of Latin America except Venezuela
CH: China
IN: India
G4: Hong Kong, South Korea, Singapore, and Taiwan

RA: rest of Asia
EE: Eastern Europe, including Russia
RW: rest of world

Table 4A.4 Assumed tariff equivalents of total protection (percentages)

Year Product	Importer	Protection	Exporter
1973			
1, 3	DC1	12	All
	JP	15	All
	LDC	20	All
2	DC1	12	DC1
	DC1	15	JP
	JP	15	DC1
	DC1	30	LDC
	JP	35	LDC
	LDC	20	All
1984			
1, 3	DC1	9	All
	JP	12	All
	LDC	20	All
2	DC1	9	DC1, JP
	JP	12	DC1
	DC1	25	LDC
	JP	30	LDC
	LDC	20	All
1993			
1, 2, 3	US, CA, MX	0	US, CA, MX
1, 3	US, CA, RO	5	All exc. US, CA, MX
1, 3	JP	8	All
1, 3	EU	5	US, CA, LDC
1, 3	EU	7	JP
1, 3	EU	2	RO
1, 2, 3	G4	10	All
1, 2, 3	RL, CH, IN, RA, EE	15	All
1, 2, 3	MX	10	All exc. US, CA
2	US, CA, EU, RO	5	DC1[a]
2	JP	8	DC1
2	DC1	8	LDC[a]
2	JP	10	LDC
2	MX, G4, EE	10	All[a]
2	RL, CH, IN, RA, RW	15	All

1 = skilled intensive 2 = unskilled intensive 3 = capital intensive.
a. Except NAFTA partners.

Notes:
DC1: US, CA, EU, RO
LDC: all except DC1 and JP
JP: Japan
CA: Canada
MX: Mexico
CH: China
RO: rest of OECD
G4: Hong Kong, South Korea, Singapore, and Taiwan

RL: rest of Latin America
   except Venezuela
IN: India
EE: Eastern Europe,
   including Russia
RA: rest of Asia
RW: rest of world

Table 4A.5 Technical efficiency coefficients

	Cobb-Douglas[a]		Constant elasticity of substitution[b]	
	Constant	Coefficient on time	Constant	Coefficient on time
US	0.5208	0.0065	0.1137	0.0070
CA	0.4873	0.0017	0.0677	0.0018
EU	0.2815	0.0078	−0.1277	0.0070
JP	0.1285	0.0142	−0.2638	0.0132
RO	0.2889	−0.0017	−0.1208	0
MX	0.5083	−0.0144	0.0156	0
RL	0.2436	−0.0087	−0.1734	0
CH	−1.0913	0.0135	−1.0480	0.0029
G4	−0.0672	0.0125	−0.3247	0.0047
IN	−1.0032	0.0106	−1.0237	0.0049
RA	−0.6180	0.0066	−0.7017	0
EE	−0.3042	0.0004	−0.6118	0
RW	−0.3931	−0.0126	−0.6678	0

a. Scale parameter: 9.506.
b. Scale parameter: 2.952 × 18.149.

Notes:
CA: Canada
JP: Japan
RO: rest of OECD
MX: Mexico
RL: rest of Latin America except Venezuela
CH: China
G4: Hong Kong, South Korea, Singapore, and Taiwan
IN: India
RA: rest of Asia
EE: Eastern Europe, including Russia
RW: rest of world

Table 4A.6 Percent deviation of factor prices from baseline: backcast counterfactuals, TIDE-CES model

	1973 S	1973 U	1973 K	1973 S/U	1984 S	1984 U	1984 K	1984 S/U	1993 S	1993 U	1993 K	1993 S/U
CF1: Autarky												
US	0.18	0.32	−0.65	−0.13	−4.39	3.82	−0.42	−7.91	−9.56	4.47	−3.3	−13.44
CA	0	0	0	0	0.57	−0.72	0.07	1.29	−2.73	4.88	−7.15	−7.26
EU	0	0	0	0	0.23	0.24	−0.77	0.02	−0.6	2.12	−2.8	−2.66
JP	−1.35	1.15	−0.01	−2.48	−4.22	6.87	−4.36	−10.37	−4.36	4.41	−6.65	−8.41
RO	0.63	0.69	−0.19	1.33	6.57	−8.57	−1.69	16.56	6.93	−7.22	−2.44	15.25
MX	0.79	−1.06	−0.37	1.87	5.52	−8.23	−2.16	14.98	3.46	−15.86	−0.54	22.95
RL	0	0	0	0	2.17	−3.19	−0.62	5.54	5.92	−8.45	−2.08	15.69
CH	−1.64	−4.62	1.58	3.12	−1.84	−6.96	1.34	5.5	−1.74	−7.18	1.31	5.86
G4	0.78	−0.86	−0.26	1.66	0.36	−0.67	−0.03	1.03	−9.4	7.51	−1.46	−15.73
IN	0	0	0	0	−1.27	−6.31	2.36	5.38	0.63	−10.53	0.21	12.47
RA	0	0	0	0	5.06	−6.45	−1.39	12.31	4.02	−12.42	1.29	18.77
EE	0	0	0	0	0.35	−0.73	−0.05	1.09	3.47	−10.41	−3.08	15.5
RW	0.87	−0.9	−0.42	1.79	5.28	−7.82	−2.23	14.21	3.32	−14.78	−0.86	21.24
CF2: Constant transport cost												
US					−2.36	1.95	−0.29	−4.23	−2.67	−1.55	−1.27	−1.14
CA					0.57	−0.72	0.07	1.29	−3.07	5.97	−7	−8.53
EU					0.06	0.03	−0.38	0.02	−0.56	2.16	−1.75	−2.67
JP					−3.09	2.28	−0.37	−5.25	−1.76	−1.25	−0.55	−0.52
RO					0.45	−1.9	−0.76	2.4	3.38	−2.71	−1.69	6.25
MX					−0.14	−0.14	−0.14	0	1.96	1.78	2.27	0.18
RL					2.17	−3.19	−0.62	5.54	3.37	−4.44	−1.02	8.18
CH					−0.1	−0.87	−0.1	0.78	0.08	0	0.25	0.08
G4					0.36	−0.67	−0.03	1.03	−2.48	0.97	−0.8	−3.42
In					−0.69	−3.6	0.85	3.02	2.09	−4.61	−1.85	7.02
RA					4.42	−5.53	−1.25	10.53	0.25	−7.01	2.63	7.8

continued next page

Table 4A.6 Percent deviation of factor prices from baseline: backcast counterfactuals, TIDE-CES model (continued)

	1973				1984				1993			
	S	U	K	S/U	S	U	K	S/U	S	U	K	S/U
EE					0.35	-0.73	-0.05	1.09	-0.19	-1.08	0.45	0.91
RW					5.28	-7.82	-2.23	14.21	-1.47	-8.26	0.91	7.4
CF3: Constant protection												
US					-1.14	1	-0.13	-2.12	-4.03	-0.82	-1.15	-3.24
CA					0.57	-1.12	0.52	1.7	-2.82	4.81	-6.28	-7.27
EU					-0.04	-0.07	0	0.03	-0.64	2.07	-1.84	-2.66
JP					-3.41	3.32	-0.91	-6.52	-4.33	4.44	-5.65	-8.4
RO					-0.54	-0.44	-0.42	-0.1	0.48	2.02	-0.55	-1.51
MX					-0.36	-0.28	-0.28	-0.09	-2.19	-9.31	0.84	7.86
RL					1.81	-2.55	-0.6	4.48	5.03	-6.88	-1.72	12.79
CH					-0.1	-0.87	-0.64	0.78	-0.87	-1.44	-1.25	0.58
G4					0	-1.05	0.72	1.06	-4.92	-0.24	2.33	-4.69
IN					0.58	-1.8	-0.38	2.42	1.9	-4.61	-2.11	6.82
RA					4.72	-5.99	-1.35	11.39	2.47	-10.19	1.84	14.1
EE					0.35	-0.73	-0.05	1.09	-1.41	-1.95	-0.54	0.55
RW					0.42	-1.12	-0.51	1.56	2.34	-13.04	-0.39	17.69
CF4: Constant transport and protection cost												
US					-3.77	3.28	-0.42	-6.83	-7.33	2.61	-3	-9.69
CA					0.57	-0.72	0.77	1.29	-2.11	4.38	-7.19	-6.22
EU					-0.08	-0.1	-0.07	0.03	-0.87	1.82	-20.06	-2.65
JP					-3.81	4.71	-2.01	-8.14	-4.52	4.27	-5.82	-8.43
RO					6.05	-7.89	-1.67	15.14	6.52	-6.57	-2.41	14.02
MX					0.3	-1.31	-0.32	1.63	-2.28	-9.58	0.63	8.07
RL					2.17	-3.19	-0.62	5.54	5.92	-8.45	-2.08	15.69

CH					0.19	-2.61	-1.12	2.88	-1.1	-6.7	0.67	6
G4					0	-1.05	0.73	1.06	-5.09	1.85	-0.23	-6.81
IN					-0.58	-6.31	1.61	6.12	1.96	-6.58	-2.12	9.14
RA					5.06	-6.45	1.39	12.31	1.88	-9.87	1.76	13.04
EE					0.35	-0.73	-0.05	1.09	-1.79	-3.47	-1.5	1.74
RW					5.28	-7.82	-2.23	14.21	3.32	-14.78	-0.86	21.24

CF5: Zero transport and protection cost

US	11.29	-5.67	0.76	17.98	9.9	-1.68	0.13	11.78	7.33	0.08	-3.85	7.25
CA	11.6	-8.47	-1.41	-21.94	1.61	-4.76	8.54	6.68	4.98	0.83	-3.15	4.12
EU	-3.33	-5.4	10.14	2.19	-2.9	-3.36	12.34	0.48	-3.53	-0.49	10.34	-3.05
JP	18.6	-3.36	0.96	22.72	13.25	0.82	-5.64	12.33	0.96	1.03	0.47	-0.07
RO	-4.51	13.8	-1.97	-16.09	3.81	-11.54	10.32	17.36	4	-10.36	9.52	16.01
MX	-1.73	16.58	0.52	-15.7	2.34	6.57	-2.67	-3.97	-0.76	-2.41	-1.67	1.69
RL	-1.89	18.38	1.58	-17.12	-0.83	14.04	-0.21	-13.04	2.87	6.79	-2.01	-3.68
CH	-2.51	15.38	6.42	-15.51	-2.91	9.57	5.24	-11.39	-3.55	9.09	4.15	-11.59
G4	-1.84	17.24	1.69	-16.28	-3.88	15.22	-0.92	-16.58	5.74	0.79	-3.47	4.91
IN	0.62	20.97	5.53	-16.82	-1.5	11.71	7.17	-11.83	-0.25	7.24	4.55	-6.98
RA	-0.18	19.63	4.87	-16.56	4.23	11.52	2.33	-6.54	2.22	4.46	4.4	-2.14
EE	-2.91	17.92	1.3	-17.67	-3.16	15.37	-0.45	-16.07	2.23	6.72	-0.73	-4.21
RW	2.6	18.92	5.18	-13.72	6.39	10.61	2.52	-3.82	2.94	2.17	3.46	0.75

CF6: No nontradables or sectoral trade limits

US	98.44	-3.55	112.39	105.74	135.83	-2.11	97.45	140.91	145.38	4.33	97.76	135.19
CA	82.24	-10.23	83.83	103	98.62	-8.06	93.19	116.03	109.38	4.72	92	99.95
EU	49.73	-4.45	101.76	56.7	35.13	-1.73	132.9	37.52	44.8	4.79	134.43	38.18
JP	205.67	-17.73	60.34	271.53	161.54	-8.01	66.67	184.31	107.61	6.76	105.43	94.46

continued next page

Table 4A.6 Percent deviation of factor prices from baseline: backcast counterfactuals, TIDE-CES model (continued)

	1973				1984				1993			
	S	U	K	S/U	S	U	K	S/U	S	U	K	S/U
RO	3	44.96	117.92	−28.94	12.65	24.89	130.53	−9.8	13.65	21.44	133.91	−6.42
MX	2.06	149.42	72.8	−59.08	6.45	99.1	90.84	−46.53	−0.87	68.66	93.92	−41.23
RL	−10.8	201.07	64.46	−70.37	−7.21	156.06	75.76	−63.76	−7.43	133.36	69.52	−60.33
CH	−1.16	172.31	68.5	−63.7	3.59	148.7	63.34	−58.35	4.34	137.8	58.07	−56.12
G4	4.37	153.88	52.65	−58.89	14.34	111.8	45.23	−46.02	124.99	−13.55	60.46	160.26
IN	−3.39	232.26	82.85	−70.92	−9.05	203.6	81.31	−70.04	−10.77	184.21	72.71	−68.6
RA	−7.74	217.76	74.42	−70.97	−4.53	197.24	70.56	−67.88	−10.88	169.11	67.52	−66.88
EE	0.85	155.9	52.45	−60.59	0.82	130.31	57.11	−56.22	−4.38	188.29	68.76	−66.83
RW	10.23	246.85	95.33	−68.22	9.83	222.91	88.55	−65.99	−3.92	179.13	76.3	−65.58
CF7: No US immigration												
US					1.19	1.81	−3.56	−0.61	0.72	4.57	−6.44	−3.68
CA					0.02	0	0.02	0.02	0.03	0.08	0.07	−0.05
EU					0	0.03	0.02	−0.03	0.04	−0.17	0.12	0.21
JP					0	0	0	0	0	0	0	0
RO					0.02	0	0	0.02	0.27	−0.43	−0.25	0.7
MX					0	0.07	0.02	−0.07	−0.19	−0.16	−0.19	−0.03
RL					0.11	−0.21	−0.04	0.33	−0.14	−0.09	−0.11	−0.05
CH					0	0	0.01	0	0	0	0	0
G4					0	0	0	0	0	0	0	0
IN					0	0	−0.01	0	0	0	0	0
RA					0.04	0	0	0.04	0	0	0	0
EE					0	0	0	0	−0.13	−0.43	0.07	0.31
RW					0	0	0	0	−0.15	0	−0.11	−0.15

CF8: No US unskilled immigration

US	-1.9	3.27	-2.06	-5.01	-3.91	6.87	-4.32	-10.09
CA	0.02	0.02	0.04	0	0.08	0.17	0.15	-0.08
EU	0.02	0.03	0.02	-0.02	0.02	-0.12	0.07	0.14
JP	-0.04	-0.08	-0.04	0.04	0	0	0	0
RO	0.08	0.05	0.05	0.03	-0.07	-0.21	0.02	0.14
MX	0.03	0.07	0.04	-0.04	-0.19	-0.16	-0.24	-0.03
RL	0.04	0	0.02	0.04	-0.08	-0.08	-0.08	0
CH	0	0	0.03	0	0	0	0	0
G4	0	0	0.02	0	0	0	0	0
IN	-0.06	0	-0.08	-0.06	0	0	0	0
RA	0.15	0	0	0.15	0	0	0	0
EE	0.02	0	0.03	0.02	-0.11	-0.43	0.09	0.33
RW	0.02	0	0.01	0.02	-0.11	0	-0.08	-0.11

CF9: Skill-biased technological change

US	4.34	-2.19	0.95	6.67	8.23	-3.89	2.22	12.61
CA	3.73	-2.88	0.31	6.81	7.35	-5.08	0.93	13.09
EU	2.82	-3.68	-0.54	6.75	5.56	-6.54	-0.72	12.95
JP	4.34	-2.49	0.76	7	6.81	-4.62	1.82	11.98
RO	2.27	-4.24	-1.08	6.8	3.95	-7	-2.78	11.77
MX	1.44	-4.98	-1.86	6.76	2.87	-8.95	-3.11	12.98
RL	1.16	-5.21	-2.08	6.72	2.56	-9.49	-3.6	13.32
CH	1.94	-5.22	-1.48	7.55	3.23	-9.09	-3.03	13.56
G4	1.92	-4.66	-1.45	6.9	6.55	-5.68	0.23	12.97

continued next page

Table 4A.6 Percent deviation of factor prices from baseline: backcast counterfactuals, TIDE-CES model (continued)

	1973				1984				1993			
	S	U	K	S/U	S	U	K	S/U	S	U	K	S/U
IN					1.38	−5.41	−2.03	7.18	4.12	−11.84	−4.2	18.1
RA					1.32	−5.07	−1.98	6.73	2.47	−9.55	−3.56	13.29
EE					1.67	−4.98	−1.7	7	1.54	−8.89	−5.73	11.45
RW					0.69	−5.59	−2.68	6.65	1.88	−10	−4.19	13.2

Notes:
S: skilled   U: unskilled   K: capital
CA: Canada   RL: rest of Latin America except Venezuela   RA: rest of Asia
JP: Japan   CH: China   EE: Eastern Europe, including Russia
RO: rest of OECD   G4: Hong Kong, South Korea, Singapore, and Taiwan   RW: rest of world
MX: Mexico   IN: India

5

Conclusion

The first part of this study reviews trends in US wage inequality (chapter 1) and attempts to provide a thorough analytical survey of the now large economics literature on rising wage inequality and its link to global influences (chapter 2). The second part applies general equilibrium models of trade to evaluate the likely role of trade and immigration in rising inequality, first by extending the simple aggregative model proposed by Krugman (1995a) in chapter 3 and second by developing the more disaggregated and more empirically based (but still highly stylized) TIDE model (chapter 4). Several important themes emerge from this combination of review and research. However, several uncertainties remain about the causes of rising inequality, the influence of future trends in trade, and, especially, what can or should be done to moderate or reverse the trend toward wage inequality. This chapter first synthesizes the findings of the previous chapters and then briefly considers possible policy implications.

Overview of the Study

For the first quarter century after World War II, the US economy provided a favorable combination of rapid growth in per capita income and a reduction of income inequality. However, by a variety of measures, during the second quarter century there has been an unfavorable combination of slower growth and rising inequality. During this second period, the average income of the top 5 percent of American families rose from 7 times to about 10 times that of the bottom 40 percent. Inequality rose even faster for wealth than for income. The slowdown in productivity growth after 1973 meant that stagnation replaced rapid growth in real median family income, which reached its peak in 1989 and fell in the early 1990s (figure 1.1).

Social trends, no doubt, contributed to the deterioration. Whereas poverty incidence rose from 11.7 percent of the population in 1979 to 15.1 percent by 1993, about two-fifths of this increase can be attributed to shifting social patterns, especially toward female heads of households and households of unrelated individuals (figure 1.4). The influence of relative political power is reflected by poverty that was high and rising among children, but low and falling among those over 65.

Rising inequality does not seem to have come from redistribution away from labor to capital. Shares of labor compensation (including benefits) and profits in national income have been remarkably stable. Instead, much of the concentration of income has stemmed from rising wage inequality. Over the past two decades, the ratio of earnings at the 90th percentile to those at the 10th percentile has risen from about 360 percent to 520 percent for males and from about 340 percent to 420 percent for females (figure 1.6).

Human capital in the form of education and training seems to have played a critical role in widening wage inequality. The ratio of wages for those with at least some college education to those with high school or less education rose by 18 percent from 1973 to 1993 (figure 1.7), although this ratio had shown some decline from the late 1960s to the early 1970s.

The rise in inequality would have been less concerning had it been primarily the consequence of rising real wages at the top. Instead, it has resulted largely from falling real wages at the bottom: real wages appear to have fallen persistently and sharply over the past two decades for those with high school or less education (figure 1.10) and even for those with some college (figure 1.10). Correction for rising compensation in the form of health insurance and other fringe benefits does not substantially alter this diagnosis. It is only the persistent upgrading of the educational level of the American workforce that largely compensated the declining education-specific real wages to permit median real wages to hold about constant or decline only slightly.

The trend toward rising wage inequality has also been present, though less pronounced, in several other industrial countries. In Europe, wages have tended to increase or at least avoid decrease, but unemployment has risen. In the United States, stagnant or eroding real wages have helped keep unemployment low despite a rapid growth in the labor force (appendix A).

In the early 1990s, as the trend toward wage inequality in the 1980s became more widely documented, there was an outpouring of research from economists seeking to explain the phenomenon. Economists joined this search from two subdisciplines: labor and trade. That the debate that sharpened was not between the two subdisciplines but, rather, between two opposing schools of thought that had adherents within both groups, reveals the complexity of the issue. One approach heavily emphasized skill-biased technological change and minimized any role for trade and immigration; the other approach tended to allow considerably more impact of trade, immigration, and other international forces, while acknowledging a role for technological change as well.

The classic reason why trade might have increased wage inequality is the Stolper-Samuelson (SS) theory, whereby trade increases the price of the abundant factor of production and reduces that of the scarce factor. For the United States and other industrial countries, skilled labor is relatively abundant and unskilled labor relatively scarce. Opening the economy to trade provides more opportunity for skilled-intensive exports and increases competition from unskilled-intensive imports.

Labor economists in the camp skeptical of trade effects typically applied sophisticated econometric decompositions that did not find much impact from shifting sectoral composition, inferred therefore that trade must not have had much effect, and attributed the largely unexplained rise in inequality to technological change (e.g., Berman, Bound, and Griliches 1994). Only a few studies more directly measured the role of technology. However, a later study in the same tradition challenged the dismissal of trade on the grounds of limited intersectoral effects by identifying greater effects when using plant-level data (Bernard and Jensen 1994).

The second approach within labor economics focused on the effective supply of skilled and unskilled labor directly from domestic labor and indirectly through imports (an addition to supply) and exports (a subtraction). One prominent study concluded that trade and immigration had contributed up to 20 percent of the increase in the skilled/unskilled wage ratio and even more of the erosion of relative wages for high school dropouts (Borjas, Freeman, and Katz 1992). This finding was vulnerable to intermixing the effects of long-term trends in trade with the more transitory effects of the exaggerated US trade deficit associated with budget deficits and an overvalued dollar in the mid-1980s. Another study linked rising relative wage inequality to the undermining of monopoly power of unskilled workers in such sectors as automobiles and steel, as imports weakened these sectors (Borjas and Ramey 1994a, b), but the impressive correlations of this study began to break down by the late 1980s.

Next came the trade economists. Adherents to the first discipline-spanning approach, who emphasized technological change and minimized trade's role, attacked the labor economists of the second school for failing to conduct analysis consistent with trade theory. In a key study, Lawrence and Slaughter (1993) argued that the labor economists who had measured trade effects failed to realize that by the SS theory, two conditions would have to have held for trade to have been responsible for rising wage inequality. First, relative prices would have to have fallen for unskilled-intensive imports. Second, somewhat counterintuitively, the skilled/unskilled employment ratio would have to have fallen in all industries, to free up enough skilled labor from unskilled industries to permit the rapid expansion of exports in skilled industries. In contrast, they argued, relative prices for unskilled goods had not fallen, and skilled/unskilled employment ratios had risen in all industries. Bhagwati and Dehejia (1994) stressed that the theoretical conditions for Samuelson's classic factor price equalization (FPE) extension of SS were too unrealistic to justify concern that trade was likely to be having a major unequalizing effect.

At the same time, the second of the two approaches—emphasizing trade effects—had its own champions among the trade economists. In a series of articles, Leamer (1992, 1994, 1995) argued that not only could the trade "margin" drive falling unskilled wages in the economy, but also there was evidence of falling relative prices for unskilled goods and that it was theoretically incorrect that the ratio of skilled to unskilled employment must fall generally if trade were the source of erosion.[1]

Wood's exhaustive study (1994) even more dramatically supported the influence of trade. He argued that the usual "factor content of trade" studies failed to take account of goods no longer produced in the North because they had been transferred to the South. When he did so, and multiplied the effects by further considering induced technological change and trade in services, his stunning result was that almost the entire erosion of unskilled relative to skilled wages could be attributed to North-South trade. However, his methods, and especially his rough multiplication effects, would seem to exaggerate the effects substantially (chapter 2). Even so, his prominent study added weight to the second school.

By now the debate was heated, with some trade economists impugning labor economists' understanding of trade theory and other trade economists impugning that of the first group of trade economists. Paul Krugman, who had been an articulate participant in the critique of the labor economists favoring trade effects, then produced a new general equilibrium analysis concluding that they were probably right after all but that his own critic, Leamer, was wrong (Krugman 1995a, b). Krugman's general equilibrium approach essentially said that North-South trade was small enough relative to the OECD economies that the labor supply-demand calculations had been a good approximation. The main point, he empha-

---

1. Leamer's argument on the latter point is unnecessarily narrow. He invokes a special type of production (fixed coefficient) to argue that factor ratios would not necessarily change in the direction Lawrence and Slaughter postulate. A more general refutation is available simply by introducing shifting relative supply of skilled and unskilled labor, as is done in figure 2.9.

sized, was that even so, a general equilibrium analysis suggested that the skilled/unskilled wage ratio would have risen by only about 3 percent over the past two decades as a result of North-South trade—far from the bulk of the increase. He added that because trade theory says the wage change is larger than the product price change, the corresponding fall in the relative price of unskilled goods could easily have been small enough to be obscured by the noise in price movements. He added that Leamer's mistake had been to stick to the small-country trade model, where international prices set factor prices, whereas the US and OECD economies were large relative to world trade—as revealed by a general equilibrium approach.

The present study enters the fray at this point. Its critical survey of literature (chapter 2) rejects the extreme estimates on both sides of the issue. It concludes that the first school among both the labor and trade economists has understated the role of trade and immigration; the second school among the labor economists has probably estimated their impact at about the right level; and the second school among the trade economists has tended to exaggerate the impact of trade. The survey rejects the Wood estimates as overstated and sides with Krugman rather than Leamer in recognizing that a general equilibrium rather than small-country approach suggests moderate rather than severe trade effects. It critiques the original Lawrence-Slaughter analysis as failing to take account of the outward shift in skilled/unskilled endowments (the explanation for generally rising skilled/unskilled employment ratios). The survey critiques the first school of labor economists for assuming that what cannot be explained (which is most of the rise in wage inequality) was, by default, skill-biased technological change. Chapter 2 concludes that, on a balanced reading of the existing literature, about one-fourth to one-fifth of the nearly 20 percent rise in the skilled/unskilled wage ratio over the past two decades has been from the influences of trade and immigration.

The new research in the second part of this study explores areas that have so far been relatively less examined: general equilibrium modeling (as opposed to econometric estimation); forward-looking analysis (going beyond decomposition of past trends); and the estimation of actual factor-endowment trends by major world areas.

This analysis begins with chapter 3, which extends Krugman's (1995a) general equilibrium model. Krugman's ingenious device relies on a particular Cobb-Douglas (CD) production function, which has a high skilled-labor parameter (elasticity) in one sector and high unskilled labor parameter in the other. In an initial "general equilibrium," the countries of the Organization for Economic Cooperation and Development (OECD) produce an optimal amount of each of the two goods, given a CD consumption function. All units are defined so that the unskilled wage starts out equal to the skilled wage (by designating half a skilled worker as the unit equivalent to an unskilled worker), and the prices of the unskilled and skilled goods both start out at unity.

Krugman then shocks his model by postulating an increase in the relative wage of skilled labor by 3 percent. Since there has been no change in OECD labor or consumption preferences, this wage shock implicitly comes from less-developed-country (LDC) market penetration in unskilled goods, which drives down the unskilled wage in real terms and, by stimulating OECD skilled exports, drives up the skilled wage. He finds that when the amount of production and employment in each sector settles to new equilibrium levels, the value of production in the skill-intensive sector is higher than before. Since under the CD consumption function the fraction of consumption value in each sector remains unchanged, there must now be net exports of the skilled good to the South. It turns out that the amount of the net trade is 2 percent of GDP. Because this is just about the increase in OECD imports of manufactures from developing countries in the past two decades, Krugman concludes that trade has been responsible for an increase of only 3 percent in the relative wage ratio.

The model's extension in chapter 3 first considers a reformulation in another production function structure (constant elasticity of substitution [CES]) that can allow for less ease of factor substitution than assumed in the CD function. This revision concludes that the impact of North-South trade may have been a 4 percent rather than 3 percent increase in the skilled/unskilled wage ratio, using a somewhat lower degree of substitutability (elasticity of substitution of 0.7 instead of 1.0).

Chapter 3 also asks what might happen in the future. Its calculations consider the impact of a continuation of past trends in the share of manufactures in industrial-country GDP (falling), the ratio of manufactured imports to domestic production of manufactures (rising), and the share of developing countries in the supply of manufactured imports (rising). On this basis, chapter 3 projects that imports of manufactures from developing countries into industrial countries could approximately double, to slightly under 5 percent of GDP, by 2013.

In view of prospective real growth of industrial economies, this import penetration would be consistent with 6.5 percent annual real growth of these imports over two decades. Although this rate is lower than the average of 10 percent over the past two decades, it is relatively close to the real rate of 7.4 percent for 1988-93. Slower growth of manufactured imports from the group of four East Asian "tigers" (G4), Hong Kong, Taiwan, South Korea, and Singapore, is largely responsible for the lower recent rate. Such a slowdown is consistent with the relatively high incomes these economies now have, while their past impetus for export expansion based on low-priced unskilled labor has declined.

The model of chapter 3 predicts that with industrial-country imports of manufactures rising to 4.5 percent of OECD GDP by 2013, the impact of North-South trade on the ratio of skilled to unskilled wages would reach a total increase of about 9 percentage points, of which 4 already occurred from 1973 to 1993. In broad terms, then, the extended Krugman model of chapter 3 finds, first, that the effect of trade with developing countries on wage distribution in industrial countries has been a significant but not the principal source of widening inequality in the past two decades. Second, it finds that the prospective impact over the next two decades is likely to be slightly larger than that of the past two decades.

Chapter 4 develops a more comprehensive, but still highly stylized, general equilibrium model that finds a somewhat greater role for trade in the past than in the model of chapter 3, but a lesser role in the future in affecting US wage inequality. The model divides the world into 13 "countries," or regional groupings. It has three tradable goods (skilled-, unskilled-, and capital-intensive manufactures) and two nontradable goods (skilled and unskilled). The chapter develops databases on factor endowments and trade (by each broad product category) corresponding to the 13 countries.

The Trade and Income Distribution Equilibrium (TIDE) model alternatively uses CD or CES production functions. It postulates levels of transportation costs and trade barriers between each country pair for each of the three tradable goods. All analysis is for three benchmark years: 1973, 1984, and 1993. The model maximizes the (unweighted) world sum of consumption welfare in each country, for each year. This optimization is interpreted as replicating the market process. The optimal results generate "shadow prices" of the three factors that tell how much impact an additional unit of each factor would have on the welfare being maximized. The analysis shows that the ratio of the shadow prices for skilled and unskilled labor will equal the ratio of their wages.

Thus, the TIDE model is an instrument for predicting the expected behavior of the skilled/unskilled wage ratio over the past two decades in each of 13 global areas or countries. The driving forces in the model are the changing endowments of skilled labor, unskilled labor, and capital in each area and the changing levels of transportation costs and protection.

The conclusion of chapter 4 provides an extensive summary of the findings obtained with the TIDE model. Principal among them are the following:

■ The decline in transportation costs and protection over the past two decades raised the skilled/unskilled wage ratio by some 7 percent above the level it otherwise would have reached.[2]

---

2. Using the model adjusted to narrower intersectoral factor share differences. See the sensitivity analysis of chapter 4.

- Post-1973 immigration raised the relative wage by about 2 percent above what it otherwise would have reached. If unskilled immigration had been prohibited but skilled immigration had been at its actual levels, the skilled/unskilled wage ratio would have been 4 to 7 percent lower than in the actual-conditions reference path by 1993.

- There has been a rapid and pervasive rise in skilled relative to unskilled labor endowments over the past two decades, not only in the United States, but in most other areas as well. Because of this trend, the baseline estimate of the model shows a pronounced expected decline in the skilled/unskilled wage ratio over this period, amounting to over 40 percent for the United States. The contradiction between the baseline decline and the observed increase means much has been left out of the model (and the decline is substantially arrested in a variant that adds skill-biased technological change), but should not invalidate the individual experiments (such as "constant transport and protection costs") that are used to parametrically evaluate the impact of the various economic forces specifically considered.

- An experiment that makes the entire economy tradable and removes sectoral trade constraints limiting exports to half of output and imports to half of consumption yields an enormous jump (more than doubling) of the skilled/unskilled wage ratio for the United States. About half of the increase comes from making nontradables tradable, and about half stems from removal of the sectoral constraints. This experiment is close in spirit to the FPE theorem. By contrast with the main results, it reveals that economists preoccupied by FPE have failed to recognize the large cushion provided to US unskilled labor by the fact that nearly two-thirds of the economy is nontradable (mainly services), as well as by the "home orientation" of both production and consumption (proxied by the sectoral trade constraints). The experiment also suggests that if, somehow, the whole economy could become tradable, unskilled labor would gain in absolute terms because of large efficiency gains.

- In the same test, international relative wage equalization occurs, as the ratio of skilled to unskilled wages generally converges to an international norm. However, absolute wages of both skilled and unskilled workers remain much higher in industrial countries than in developing countries because of the higher technological efficiency of overall production in industrial countries.

- For the future, projected factor endowments, transport costs, and protection suggest a continuation of the expected trend of falling relative skilled wage. Freezing protection at 1993 (post-Uruguay Round) levels and, thereby, ruling out the Asia Pacific Economic Cooperation group (APEC) and the Free Trade Area of the Americas (FTAA) would have only minimal impact in boosting US unskilled wages. The model simulations also show unskilled labor would not gain from a protectionist scenario boosting tariffs of OECD countries against all LDCs to 30 percent, whereas skilled labor would experience a loss.

The analyses of chapters 3 and 4 show a substantial impact of trade on wage inequality. However, they show a different pattern of timing. In chapter 3, slightly more of the wage-concentrating impact lies in the future than in the past. In chapter 4, the reverse is true. In the model of chapter 4, the driving forces of growing world integration are falling transport and communication costs and declining protection. Because these costs and barriers are already at low levels by 1993, the model suggests little further impact from integration. Indeed, complete free trade would not have a major impact, because trade barriers are already low.

The analysis of chapter 4 identifies two opposing trends in the influence of trade on US wage inequality. An unfavorable trend in the past has been the growing internationalization of the economy through falling transport costs and falling protection. A favorable trend has been the briskly rising availability of skilled labor in developing countries, especially the G4. The former trend dominated in the last two decades, but the latter trend is likely to dominate in the next two.

The potential future impact of trade on wages in the projections of chapter 3 may be overstated in comparison with the estimates of chapter 4. The chapter 3 results find a smaller impact in the past and, by implication, may overstate future effects from what in some sense is a historical once-and-for-all shift from isolation to integration. Also, the estimates in chapter 4 are drawn from specific forecasts of factor endowments and may be a more robust basis for projection than the extrapolation of past trends for production and imports of manufactures. The factor-endowment projections incorporate the information that the relative abundance of skilled workers is rising rapidly in developing countries, taking pressure off competition from foreign unskilled workers through trade entering industrial-country markets.

Still another consideration is that the Krugman-based model of chapter 3 may understate the past influence of trade for US wage inequality by treating the OECD as homogeneous. The factor-endowment estimates of chapter 4 show that the European Union has a substantially smaller relative endowment of skilled labor than does the United States, and, in 1973, this divergence applied to Japan as well. Thus, the SS effects of falling transport and protection costs in 1973-93 should have had a greater relative wage impact on the United States than on the rest of the OECD. At the same time, convergence of factor-endowment profiles within the OECD (and especially convergence by Japan) means that this possible downward bias for US effects as measured by a model treating the OECD as a single country would be less in the future than in the past.

More specifically, the simulations of chapter 4 indicate that falling transport and protection costs raised the skilled/unskilled wage ratio over the period 1973-93 by about 2.5 times as large a proportion for the United States and Japan as for the European Union and Canada (tables 4.7 and 4A.6). Subject to the caveat of possible underestimation of skill density in the European Union (as discussed in chapter 4), the implication is that the US impact is about 40 percent higher than the OECD average.[3] This means that disaggregating the United States from the rest of the OECD in the Krugman-based model of chapter 3 could boost the US skilled/unskilled wage impact of trade from an estimated 4 percent increment to about 5.5 percent for the past two decades—relatively close to the adjusted TIDE model estimate of 7 percent in chapter 4.

At the same time, it is possible that the TIDE model results of chapter 4 overstate the impact of trade over the past two decades. The principal reason for a possible upward bias is that the TIDE model (adjusted to lower sectoral factor-share differences) predicts that in 1993 US manufactured imports from developing countries would have been 5.4 percent of GDP. Instead, these imports were an estimated 2.8 percent of GDP for the United States and Canada together (calculated from WTO 1997, 17; IMF 1996). However, the problem of excessive dampening of export and import factor-intensity differences that arises using aggregate sectoral averages rather than more detailed data may mean that the larger, unadjusted TIDE results (the initial results reported in table 4.7) may be more relevant than the adjusted results applying lower sectoral differences in factor shares. The unadjusted estimate of trade's impact on the US skilled/unskilled wage ratio is a 10 percent increase over the past two decades rather than 7 percent increase as in the adjusted estimates.

Thus, a balanced view of both the past and the future would probably be somewhere between the results of chapters 3 and 4. With respect to the future, although the projections in chapter 4 more explicitly estimate the outcome of evolving factor endowments and costs of transportation and protection, there are other forces that could also drive trade. Thus, the LDC mastery of sectors previously the domain of industrial countries (Hicksian convergence—see chapter 2) could mean that the implicit trade projections of chapter 4 are understated.

In terms of the debate in the literature summarized in chapter 2, the results of chapters 3 and 4 are closest in spirit to the (later) views of Krugman (1995a, b). They confirm the insight that moderate trade relative to the economy means moderate wage effects (as best highlighted by the converse experiment in which the entire economy is made tradable). Even so, the results here place considerably greater emphasis on the role of

---

3. Weighting effects by 1993 GDP.

trade and (not examined by Krugman) immigration in explaining the increase in US wage inequality in the past two decades.

An Illustrative Synthesis

It is by now conventional in this literature to attribute a given percentage of the observed increase in the skilled/unskilled wage ratio to international influences, primarily trade and immigration. This study has used the same shorthand. However, the dramatic decline in the expected relative skilled wage identified in the TIDE-model baseline (chapter 4) forces explicit recognition that not all forces work in the direction of increasing the wage differential. When there are forces working in opposite directions, it is misleading to compare one force with the net effect. Instead, it is more meaningful to compare the influence in question with the sum total of all of the forces working in the same direction as that influence. In short, the impact of trade should be compared not against the net increase in wage inequality, but against the gross increase in inequality that would have occurred if there had been nothing but unequalizing forces. Otherwise, the relative role of trade in the whole set of unequalizing influences will be exaggerated.

By far the single most important force implicit in the general equilibrium analysis of chapter 4 is the equalizing impact of rapid increases in the availability of skilled relative to unskilled labor. For the United States, the estimates of chapter 4 (table 4.2 and adjustments as discussed in the text) are that the ratio of skilled to unskilled labor stood at 0.59 in 1973 and rose to 1.28 by 1993. If the ratio of skilled to unskilled labor endowments approximately doubled, then in the absence of any other influence the ratio of the skilled wage to the unskilled wage should have approximately fallen by half under CD technology and by even more under CES technology.[4] Similarly, in the baseline backcast of the TIDE model, the ratio of the skilled wage to the unskilled wage for the United States falls by 47 percent for 1973-1993 in the main set of model results (table 4.5). Even with a higher degree of substitutability between skilled and unskilled labor, such as the elasticity of substitution of 1.41 at the economywide level estimated by Katz and Murphy (1992), the ratio of US skilled to

---

4. The wage is the marginal product. In the CD function with α as the elasticity of skilled labor and $(1 - \alpha)$ as the elasticity of unskilled labor, the marginal products are $\alpha Q/S$ for skilled labor (where S is the amount of skilled labor and Q is output) and $(1 - \alpha)Q/U$ where U is the amount of unskilled labor. The marginal product ratio (and, thus, wage ratio) is $[\alpha/(1 - \alpha)][U/S]$. The percentage change in the skilled/unskilled wage ratio thus equals the percentage change in the ratio of unskilled to skilled labor. In the US case, the decline in the unskilled/skilled labor ratio by about half would have meant reduction in the skilled/unskilled wage ratio by about half.

Table 5.1   Illustrative sources of increase in the ratio of skilled to unskilled wages in the United States (percentages)[a]

I. 1973-93	
A. Equalizing forces	
Increase in stock of skilled relative to unskilled labor	−40
B. Unequalizing forces	97
Trade: Stolper-Samuelson effects	6 [3–10]
Lower transport and communication costs	(3)
Trade liberalization	(3)
Trade: outsourcing, Hicksian convergence	1 ?
Immigration	2
Falling minimum wage	5
Deunionization	3
Skill-biased technological change	29
Other unexplained	29
C. Net effect	18
II. 1993-2013	
Trade: Stolper-Samuelson effects	4

a. Percentages for unequalizing forces must be chained, not simply added, to equal total unequalizing impact. Similarly, "A" and "B" must be chained to calculate "C."

unskilled wages would have been expected to fall by about 35 percent as the supply of unskilled relative to skilled labor fell by half.

If there was an equalizing force from factor endowments that should have reduced the skilled/unskilled wage ratio by, say, 40 percent (i.e., to only 0.6 of the level otherwise), then the observed actual increase of almost 20 percent means that the combined impact of all unequalizing forces must have been on the order of 100 percent, a doubling of the skilled/unskilled wage ratio from its level otherwise.[5] So, a particular force that contributes, say, 10 percentage points to a rise in the skilled/unskilled wage ratio is really only about one-tenth of the unequalizing force, rather than over one-half as gauged against the net effect.

Table 5.1 suggests an illustrative list of unequalizing forces to see how they might have overwhelmed the equalizing force of a rising relative skilled labor endowment. Several of the numbers are informed guesses from the literature, but key entries are from this study. The first entry suggests that in the absence of other forces, the skilled/unskilled wage ratio should have fallen by about 40 percent over the past two decades, as just discussed.

The first of the unequalizing forces is for the SS effects of trade as the economy becomes more integrated with the world economy and specializes more in skill-intensive goods. This impact has a range of 3 to 10

---

5. The specific increase from all unequalizing forces in the summary of table 5.1 is 97 percent. That is, $0.6 \times 1.97 = 1.18$.

percent (in brackets). The 3 percent figure is from the Krugman model, reproduced in chapter 3. The 10 percent figure is for the unadjusted TIDE model results in chapter 4 for the simulation of the impact of falling transport and protection costs.

The table also reports a preferred central estimate of 6 percent for the impact of SS effects. This is derived as a weighted average of the main chapter 3 and chapter 4 estimates. A weight of 1/3 is applied to the chapter 3 result of 4 percent, which refers to the Krugman model adjusted to lesser substitutability (elasticity of substitution of 0.7 between skilled and unskilled labor). As noted above, because that estimate is for the OECD, it probably understates the effect for the United States.

A weight of 2/3 is applied to the main chapter 4 result. This result is a central estimate of 7 percent as the impact of falling transport and protection costs on the US skilled/unskilled wage ratio.[6] The greater weight reflects the more complete and empirically based nature of the model in chapter 4. The overall result is a central estimate of an increase of 6 percent as the impact of trade on the US ratio of skilled to unskilled wages over the past two decades.

Table 5.1 also provides an illustrative division of the impact of trade between falling transport and communication costs on the one hand and falling protection on the other. The estimates in chapter 4 indicate that as of 1984, these two separate effects had a combined effect that was about linearly additive and that in that year the transport cost component accounted for about two-thirds of the total trade impact in both versions of the TIDE model (CD in table 4.7 and CES in table 4A.6). For 1993, the decomposition is more ambiguous, because the combined effect becomes strongly nonlinear, far greater than the simple sum of the two effects individually. For that year, the lower transport cost is more important in one version of the model, and lower protection is more important in the other version. In view of this ambiguity, the simplest estimate is that by 1993 about half the trade impact was attributable to lower protection and about half to lower transport and communication costs. This is the allocation imputed in table 5.1.

The next entry concerns other trade forces not examined directly in this study: Hicksian convergence and outsourcing (Johnson and Stafford 1992; Feenstra and Hanson 1995; see chapter 2). As the G4 and other developing countries master such sectors as semiconductors, there is a terms-of-trade and general real wage loss for industrial countries. When combined with a shift of domestic production from the North to the newly capable LDCs, upward pressure on the relative wage of skilled labor results, as unskilled

---

6. As discussed in chapter 4, this is from the sensitivity test adjusting the TIDE model to bring its intersectoral factor share differences into line with recent estimates provided by Borjas, Freeman, and Katz (1997).

tasks are now outsourced. In the absence of any clear estimate for this effect, the table includes a modest impact from this source of 1 percent.

The third unequalizing influence is immigration. The estimate of 2 percent is from the relevant experiment in chapter 4 (CF7).[7]

It is worth pausing at this point to compare the estimates in table 5.1 for trade and immigration with recent estimates provided by Borjas, Freeman, and Katz (1997). They now estimate that post-1979 immigration contributed 5 percent of the rise in the US ratio of college-and-higher to high school wages from 1980 to 1995, and developing-country trade contributed another 5 percent. Considering that their estimated total rise in the wage ratio was 21 percent (log wage difference of 0.191), their central estimate of the combined impact of trade and immigration is an increase of 2 percent in this wage ratio.[8] Their corresponding central estimate for the ratio of high school-and-higher to dropout wages (which rose by 11.5 percent) is much higher: 44 percent from immigration and 8 percent from developing-country trade, for a total increment of 6 percent in this wage ratio.[9]

The central estimate for the impact of trade and immigration in the present study, a total of 8 percent increase in the skilled/unskilled wage ratio, is thus about four times as large as the recent Borjas-Freeman-Katz estimate for the middle-upper end of the wage spectrum. Although the estimates are closer at the lower end, for that part of the wage distribution the results in Borjas, Freeman, and Katz give a much greater relative weight to immigration effects, whereas the results of this study give greater weight to trade.

The larger trade and immigration effects here occur even though the central adjusted TIDE model results adopt the sectoral factor share differences identified by Borjas, Freeman, and Katz (as discussed in chapter 4). Three differences seem to dominate the divergent results. First, the three authors use a higher elasticity of substitution between skilled and unskilled labor (1.41 instead of 1.0). Second, their trade estimate is based on an increment of 2 percent of US GDP for trade with developing countries from 1980 to 1996. In contrast, the adjusted TIDE model predicts imports from developing countries at 5.4 percent of GDP in the 1993 baseline and at zero in the counterfactual freezing transport and protection costs at their 1973 levels. So the relevant comparable shift in import penetration in the TIDE model is 5.4 percent of GDP, more than twice the Borjas-Freeman-Katz increment. Third, the TIDE model directly cap-

---

7. As adjusted in the sensitivity analysis to account for lesser divergence between sectoral factor shares.

8. This estimate is somewhat lower than in the earlier Borjas, Freeman, and Katz (1992) study, in part because of the smaller US trade deficit.

9. That is, 52 percent × 11.5 percent.

tures the influence of world factor price pressures, allowing for the influence of the "external margin" emphasized by Leamer (see chapter 2). The Borjas-Freeman-Katz approach does not do so, but relies instead on a domestic wage response to changes in total effective labor supplies incorporating supply removed by exports and added by imports.

Overall comparison to the recent Borjas, Freeman, and Katz (1997) estimates suggests that the central results of the present study may be on the high side for trade, but perhaps on the right order of magnitude for immigration (considering the measure of unskilled here includes both the high school educated and dropouts). The comparison also suggests, however, that the current state of the art in the literature may be understating rather than overstating the impact of developing-country trade on US wage inequality.

Returning to table 5.1, the next entry considers the impact of the minimum wage in the United States, which fell by 20 percent in real terms from its average in 1971-75 to its average in 1989-93 and by 31 percent from its 1979 peak to its 1989 trough (Mishel and Bernstein 1994-95, 172). Fortin and Lemieux (1997) work with samples of hourly wage data from the Current Population Survey to examine the impact of the falling real minimum wage on the US wage distribution. The 1979 minimum wage of $3.00 would have to have risen to $4.75 by 1988 to retain its real value. The authors compare the part of the 1988 wage distribution below $4.75 per hour with the corresponding part of the 1979 distribution below $3.00 per hour. This left tail of the distribution shows much less density for the 1979 distribution and a much greater spike at the level of the $3.00 cutoff, especially for women. To simulate the impact of holding the real minimum wage constant, Fortin and Lemieux replace the left tail (below the constant 1979 minimum wage) of the 1988 distribution with that from the 1979 distribution. Noting that the log variance of wages for men and women rose by 0.065 from 1979 to 1988, they calculate that 39 percent of the increase is explained by the decline in the real minimum wage (89).

Other studies also find substantial effects of the falling real minimum wage. The Fortin-Lemieux (1997) survey notes that Card and Krueger (1995) attribute 20 to 30 percent of the rise in wage dispersion during the 1980s to this influence and that Mishel, Bernstein, and Schmitt (1996) place the contribution even higher. In contrast, Freeman (1996) attributes 10 percent or less of rising US wage inequality to the falling real minimum wage. Overall, the central range of estimates in the studies of minimum wage impact seems to be on the order of 25 to 30 percent of the net rise in wage inequality. Compared to the estimated total rise of 18 percent in the skilled/unskilled wage ratio used in this study, this range would imply an impact of about 5 percentage points increase as the consequence of the falling real minimum wage (table 5.1).

Deunionization is the next entry in table 5.1. As discussed in chapter 2, the fraction of US nonagricultural workers in unions fell from 29 percent in 1969 to 16 percent in 1989. Fortin and Lemieux (1997) estimate that 21.3 percent of the rise in the log variance of US male wages from 1979 to 1988 is attributable to deunionization. They note that Card (1992) also arrives at an estimate of about 20 percent for US males.

However, the Fortin-Lemieux estimate for US females is zero. The variance of wages is lower in union sectors, and a falling incidence of unionization raises inequality from this standpoint. At the same time, union sectors have higher average wage rates, so there is an opposing effect on inequality: lower unionization reduces the divergence between sectoral wage averages. For US males, the first effect dominates, and deunionization is unequalizing. For US females, the two effects just cancel out each other. For both males and females, then, the Fortin-Lemieux estimate is that deunionization has been responsible for about 10 percent of the rise in wage inequality.

Freeman (1991, 1996) places the role of deunionization higher, in a range of 15 to 40 percent (1991), with a main estimate of 20 percent (1996). The entry in table 5.1 adopts a central estimate of 15 percent of the rise in inequality. Applied to the 18 percent rise in the skilled/unskilled wage ratio, this gives a contribution of about 3 percentage points from deunionization.

The cumulative effect of the first five unequalizing forces is an 18 percent increase in the skilled/unskilled wage ratio. The final two entries are for skill-biased technological change and "other" forces. The latter can include a widening wage differential for experience regardless of educational level. The spirit of the final two entries is simply to avoid allocating all of the unexplained residual to technological change, which is a common but questionable practice. The required total contribution from the final two influences is 67 percent, so the table allocates half to skill-biased technological change and half to other influences, for a contribution of 29 percent each.[10]

Viewed from this perspective *the overall influence of trade and immigration (9 percent increase including the guesstimate for outsourcing in table 5.1) amounts to about one-half of the observed net rise in the skilled/unskilled wage ratio (18 percent), but still accounts for only about one-tenth of the gross unequalizing forces (97 percent).* The basic implication is that it must have required numerous, strong unequalizing forces to overcome the powerful equalizing force from the side of relative supply of skilled labor.

In terms of the usual, but questionable, formulation solely against the net increase in the ratio of skilled to unskilled wages, this study finds an impact of trade and immigration that is considerably higher than most estimates in the existing literature. An equally important finding, however, is that on the basis of a careful examination of changing factor

---

10. That is, $1.18/(0.6 \times 1.18) = 1.67$; $1.67^{0.5} = 1.29$.

endowments in the United States and abroad, in the absence of these or other influences there should have been a reduction of about 40 percent in the US skilled/unskilled wage ratio because of the pervasive rise in the relative availability of skilled labor. Thus, the qualitative interpretation remains closer to that of the mainstream of the literature: trade and immigration contributed only a moderate part of the gross unequalizing forces in this period.

For the future, the estimates of chapter 3 suggest that there could be an additional increase of about 5 percent in the skilled/unskilled wage ratio from 1993-2013 as the result of North-South trade. The TIDE model of chapter 4 estimates a further trade impact of only 3 percent for the United States over the next two decades, measured by the difference between the baseline and a scenario in which protection and transport costs are held unchanged at 1993 levels.[11] Broadly, the TIDE model finds that the future equalizing forces of a more rapid increase in skilled labor endowments in the South substantially offset the unequalizing forces to be expected from further global integration, considering that transport and protection costs are already low.

This estimate range of 3 to 5 percent for the future unequalizing effect of trade on the skilled/unskilled wage ratio is not negligible, but it is a far cry from the specter of immiserization depicted by Perot-type politicians (and some economists).[12] Once again, giving 1/3 weight to the chapter 3 results and 2/3 weight to the chapter 4 results, the summary forecast estimate would be slightly under 4 percent as the impact of SS trade effects on the skilled/unskilled wage ratio over the next two decades, or about two-thirds as much as over the past two (table 5.1).

Absolute Versus Relative Wage

Suppose one accepts as a stylized fact that in the last two decades the skilled wage rose by about 18 percent relative to the unskilled wage and that trade accounted for about one-third of this increase, or 6 to 7 percent (table 5.1). Does this mean that trade made unskilled workers worse off in absolute terms? Whereas the literature is of many voices on the impact of trade on relative wages, it is surprisingly silent on the impact on absolute real wages of the unskilled. None of the empirical studies reviewed in chapter 2 attempts to calculate any offsetting changes in real wages provided through lower prices of imported goods. Nonetheless, it is useful to consider a rough approximation of this effect.

---

11. This is the estimate for the adjusted TIDE model using the more moderate intersectoral difference in factor shares. Using the unadjusted TIDE results, the estimate ranges from 2 percent in the CES version to 5 percent in the CD version.

12. In particular, see the discussion in chapter 2 of work by Leamer and Wood.

Whether unskilled workers suffered from trade in absolute terms depends on the counterfactual. From 1973 to 1993, imports of manufactures from developing countries into the United States and Canada have risen from 0.56 percent of GDP to 2.77 percent (WTO 1997; IMF 1996). Some of this increase was attributable to reductions in import barriers, but the bulk was probably the consequence of outward-shifting LDC supply as developing countries acquired industrial capacity, as well as falling transport costs. So the counterfactual question becomes: How much would US protection have to have increased to suppress this increase in imports? And, correspondingly, how much would this increase in protection have caused prices to rise for goods consumed by unskilled workers? This price increase can then be compared to the wage increase from protection to judge the net effect on real absolute wage.

If the increase in the relative skilled wage was about 6 percent, a first approximation would be that this wedge was divided evenly between a rise in the skilled wage and reduction in the unskilled wage from levels that otherwise would have been attained. On this basis, the gross reduction in the real unskilled wage before considering import price effects would be 3 percent.

What level of protection would have been necessary to suppress the rise in manufactured imports from LDCs? Import price elasticities in trade models tend to be in the range of one to two (Cline 1989; Hooper and Marquez 1995). Thus, suppression of these imports could have required increasing the tariff equivalent to perhaps 80 percent.[13] With an import price elasticity of two and a horizontal world supply curve, the traditional static welfare cost of a tariff of level t is $[t^2/(1 + t)]M$, where M is the import base value (Cline 1995). With M approximately 2 percent of GDP (the amount of the increase in LDC import penetration) and a required tariff of 80 percent in the counterfactual, the traditional static welfare cost of suppressing these imports would have amounted to 0.71 percent of GDP ($.8^2/1.8 \times 2$ percent). Allowing a doubling of welfare effects to take account of nontraditional effects (e.g., scale economies, stimulus to efficiency, reduction in monopoly power), the welfare cost would have been about 1.5 percent of GDP.

Considering that lower-income families have a much higher share in aggregate consumption than in aggregate income,[14] a welfare loss of 1.5 percent of GDP could have translated to a welfare loss for unskilled workers proportionately twice as large, or about 3 percent of their income.

---

13. Note that in trade retaliation cases, US authorities typically impose a 100 percent tariff on a group of goods with import value equal to the supposed loss of US exports, implying that they consider the trade-suppressing tariff to be 100 percent.

14. In 1984, the poorest 40 percent of US households accounted for 22.8 percent of consumption but only 11.7 percent of income (Cline 1987, 202).

On this basis, in the higher-protection counterfactual, *unskilled workers would have lost approximately as much from higher import prices as they would have gained from avoiding the downward pressure on their wages from import competition* if there had been a sufficient increase in protection against LDC imports to suppress their rise over the past two decades. Thus, suppression of manufactured imports from developing countries would have raised real unskilled wages directly by 3 percent, but reduced them indirectly by 3 percent because of higher import costs.[15]

This illustrative calculation stands somewhat in tension with the SS theorem, which requires that protection raise the real wage of the scarce factor (and holds that the magnification effect causes the percentage increase in the scarce factor's wage to exceed the price increase of the imported good caused by protection). That is, the SS theorem would generally be seen to allow much less real erosion of the scarce-factor gains from protection as a result of general costs of protection than suggested in this calculation.[16] The proximate explanation is that the inclusion of nontraditional welfare effects and of a higher share in consumption than in income for the low-income workers balloons the adverse impact of the import price effect relative to the favorable wage effect, as compared with the SS model.[17]

More detailed sectoral analysis of protection supports the diagnosis that it is a highly inefficient and potentially counterproductive instrument for income redistribution. Cline (1990, 201-06) estimates that the consumer costs of US textile and apparel protection in 1985 were proportionately the highest for the lowest-income groups. After taking account of government allocation of tariff revenue and increased profits of shareholders in textile and apparel firms, the study estimated that protection in this major sector caused a loss of real income of 3.6 percent for the poorest 20 percent (quintile) of households and about 1 percent for the next two quintiles, but a gain of 0.3 percent for the top quintile where equity ownership is concentrated. The implication was a substantially regressive incidence of protection in the sector.

---

15. A more complete analysis would distinguish between losses in consumer surplus and gains in producer surplus from higher protection. Because unskilled workers hold minimal equity, their participation in the latter would be small, suggesting another reason why losses from higher import prices and efficiency losses (including dynamic) would tend to offset direct gains to unskilled workers from higher protection.

16. Rodrik (1997) summarizes this phenomenon by the notion that protection has first-order redistribution effects but only second-order efficiency effects. Note, however, that Rodrik ignores dynamic welfare effects and considers only the static "welfare triangles."

17. The first of these two points is consistent with the Bhagwati-Dehejia (1994) observations noted above: economies of scale, rather than constant returns to scale as in SS, and X-efficiency gains from the stimulus of trade competition, mean that gains from trade could permit even the scarce factor to benefit rather than suffer from liberalization.

The TIDE model estimates the absolute impact of trade on low-skill wages. In the key experiment of chapter 4 holding transport and protection costs constant at their 1973 levels, the impact on the skilled/unskilled wage ratio by 1993 is divided between two-thirds in change of the absolute level of the skilled wage and one-third in change of the absolute level for the unskilled wage (table 4.7). Applying the overall (chapter 3 and chapter 4) central estimate of 6 percent as the impact of trade on the skilled/unskilled wage ratio, the implication is that trade caused the skilled wage to rise by 4 percent and the unskilled wage to fall by 2 percent. As discussed below, moreover, this trade impact is by no means synonymous with the effect of trade policy, because transport and communication costs would have fallen with technological advance regardless of the trade policies adopted.

In sum, there are substantial grounds for concluding that there was little reduction in the absolute level of US unskilled wages as a consequence of increased North-South trade over the past two decades. Moreover, it seems likely that any absolute reduction imposed by the liberalization of international trade (as opposed to the effect of falling transport and communication costs) was no more than about 1 percent or so and more probably close to zero once gains from trade (including dynamic gains) are taken into account.

Policy Implications

This study does not attempt to provide a rigorous evaluation of alternative policies to help strengthen the growth of low-end wages and to moderate or reverse the rising wage inequality of the past two decades. The observations here will be limited to the implications that flow most directly from the analysis in the preceding chapters, as well as some more informal intuitive judgments.

At the broadest level, both experience and economic theory suggest that the market process, and capitalism more specifically, provides the most certain basis for economic growth and efficiency. International trade and specialization are vital components of this market process. There is no assurance that market forces will lead to greater rather than less income and wage equality over time, however. The principal implication of this line of thinking is that a society adhering to free trade and other market-oriented policies will be well advised to make efforts in a whole array of other policies to assure that the resulting gains in efficiency and growth are shared in a fair way.

This broad approach also implies that any unequalizing effects of trade and immigration should not be viewed in a partial, restricted sense focusing only on directly affected parties. US Trade Adjustment Assistance (TAA) in the past has sought in various ways and degrees to provide for adjustment of workers displaced by imports. But this direct impact is only a part of the picture. If there is downward pressure on unskilled wages from trade, the impact spills over far beyond any workers that directly lose their jobs from the closing of a plant competing with imports. Broader effects imply the need for broader remedies.

One class of remedies involves an even more rapid increase in the supply of skilled labor relative to unskilled, through education and training. Tax credits and loans for college study are examples. It is beyond the scope of this study to identify which approaches to education and training are the most cost-effective, but this area surely must be at the forefront of policies designed to assure a more equitable evolution of US wages. Figure 2.9 illustrates how the rapid outward shift in the college-educated labor force in the 1960s and early 1970s contributed to a declining skilled/unskilled wage ratio even though skill-biased technological change could have been steadily shifting outward the demand for skilled relative to unskilled labor.

The seeming new vitality of labor unions in the United States could represent another source of wage equalizing influence in the future. So could the substantial increase in the US minimum wage adopted in 1996, raising it from $4.25 to $5.15 per hour and returning the real minimum wage from 75 to 85 percent of its 1979 peak.

However, both of these approaches, which push the supply curve of labor to the left (higher price for the same amount of labor), run the risk of increasing unemployment and nudging the United States away from its current set of problems to a more European dilemma of high unemployment albeit with higher wage growth for the employed (appendix A).

A painful policy implication of the analysis here is that the United States may need to reconsider its historic shift from skills to family ties as the basis for awarding immigration quotas. The experiments in chapter 4 indicate that if there had been no immigration of unskilled labor after 1973, the skilled/unskilled wage ratio would have been 4 to 7 percent lower by 1993 than otherwise, and the absolute level of the unskilled wage would have been 3 to 5 percent higher.[18] If the same amount of total immigration had been permitted, but allocated completely to skilled immigrants, these impacts would have been even greater.

This line of thinking is painful, because family ties seem to be a humanitarian way to allocate immigration quotas. It might be well, nonetheless, to reexamine the appropriateness of considering eligibility of relations beyond the immediate family (spouse, parent, or child).[19] There was

18. Impacts in CF8, tables 4.7 and 4A.6, as reduced by one-third to allow for lower intersectoral differences in factor shares.

19. A shift toward skill requirements in US immigration policy would seem unlikely to have much impact on the "brain drain" from developing countries. The estimates in chapter 4 place LDC skilled labor at a total of 188 million workers in 1993. The increase of unskilled

already a modest shift back toward skills and away from family ties in the immigration reform of 1990, and further revision in this direction could be appropriate.

The other major area of direct policy implications from the analysis of this study concerns what not to do. The forward-looking simulations of chapter 4 are uniform in showing that recourse to higher protection or even a protection standstill that jettisons APEC and FTAA would provide very little if any increase in the real unskilled wage, while causing net income losses from reduction in skilled wages. The illustrative calculation above on absolute as opposed to relative wages suggests that any attempt to suppress the increase in imports of manufactures from developing countries over the past two decades would have accomplished little if any net gain in real wages of the unskilled—considering the adverse side effects of higher import prices—while imposing substantial real wage losses on skilled workers.

In particular, if global protection were to be frozen at the 1993 level, by the year 2013 the absolute level of US unskilled wages would be virtually unchanged from the baseline that incorporates APEC and FTAA.[20] The ratio of skilled to unskilled wages might be about 2 to 5 percent lower than in the baseline, but only because of a sizable reduction in skilled wages from levels they would otherwise reach.

Similarly, if by 2013 a stiff tariff of 30 percent were imposed by industrial countries on imports from developing countries, the result would be a substantial cut in the absolute level of skilled wages without a significant rise (and possibly a decline) in unskilled wages.[21]

To recapitulate, the principal findings of this study and their policy implications are as follows:

■ The contribution of trade and immigration to rising US wage inequality has been somewhat larger than previously estimated in most of the literature.

■ Nonetheless, the bulk of increased inequality probably arose from skill-biased technological change, with additional significant contributions from the falling real minimum wage and the decline in unionization.

US immigrant workers from 1984 to 1993 was 1.8 million. So, if total immigration were kept constant and all unskilled shifted to skilled entrants, the resulting drain of skilled labor from the developing countries over an entire decade would amount to only 1 percent of the initial LDC stock of skilled labor.

20. The CD version of the TIDE model shows a minimal 0.8 percent increase in the unskilled wage from a trade standstill (chapter 4, table 4.9, scenario 2) while the CES version shows a 1.3 percent decrease (as discussed in chapter 4).

21. Table 4.9, scenario 4. Note, however, that tariff revenue would need to be incorporated into the TIDE model to obtain a more precise measure of the income effects of imposing additional protection.

- A doubling in the ratio of US skilled (some college or more) to unskilled (high school or less) labor supply over the past two decades should have caused the skilled wage to fall sharply relative to the unskilled wage, in the absence of other factors.

- As a result, whereas the impact of trade and immigration may have been as much as about half of the net increase in US wage inequality, these external-sector influences only contributed about one-tenth of the gross unequalizing forces on US wages.

- Trade liberalization in the past has probably caused little if any reduction in the absolute level of US unskilled wages, although by raising skilled wages it has contributed part of the rise in wage inequality associated with trade.

- At least an equal part of the impact of trade was attributable to falling transportation and communications costs rather than changes in trade policy.

- For the future, free trade under APEC and the FTAA should not cause much change in wage inequality and is unlikely to cause absolute reductions in unskilled wages.

- A policy of new, high protection against developing countries would cause serious losses to US skilled labor and either some loss or minimal gain to unskilled labor.

These broad policy conclusions will come as no great surprise to those familiar with mainstream trade economics. Yet at least one prominent trade economist, Edward Leamer (1992), has warned that by signing the North American Free Trade Agreement the United States threw away its option to successively raise protection in the future as a bulwark against the specter of FPE that otherwise would progressively depress US unskilled wages. As suggested in the preceding overview and detailed in chapter 4, the future threat of US unskilled wage reductions from world FPE through free trade is seriously exaggerated.

At the same time, the policy thrust of this study is that Americans cannot simply ignore unequalizing forces from integration into the global economy. There is considerably more to the trade-wage and immigration-wage connections than the early dismissal by school 1 of the trade economists allowed, as even some of this school's leading exponents now acknowledge. Thus, the basic policy conclusion is that a commitment to open trade needs to go hand in hand with a commitment to a whole array of domestic policies that help ensure that society evolves in an equitable rather than inequitable direction.

Appendix A
Employment and Wage Growth in Europe and the United States[1]

The unemployment rate in Europe rose from about 3 percent in 1970 to about 11 percent in the mid-1990s, while the rate in the United States was variable but trendless with a mean of about 6.5 percent. Not surprisingly, a debate emerged about whether excessive wage and labor rigidities or deficient macroeconomic policies were the primary cause of rising unemployment in Europe. At the same time, many Europeans were doubtful that the solution was to shift to US practices, which included lower social benefits and lower wage growth.

It became a stylized fact that, over the two decades before the mid-1990s, the United States had created far more jobs than Europe—some 40 million compared with only some 10 million—while real wages had risen briskly in Europe while stagnating in the United States. Many inferred that a flexible labor market made the US economy a powerful job machine, whereas labor rigidity in Europe meant ever higher unemployment.

Macroeconomic Influences

Solow (1994) has argued that the increase in Europe's unemployment was largely due to macroeconomic mismanagement rather than labor rigidities. He cites timing as evidence: Europe's unemployment rate remained relatively low until 1978-79 and then surged after the second

1. This appendix is drawn from Cline (1994b).

oil shock. After considering the slow upward drift of unemployment in earlier years, when most of the labor rigidities were already in place, Solow concludes that these supply-side factors accounted for only about a 6 percent unemployment rate by the early 1990s.

There should be little doubt that both macroeconomic and microlabor policies have contributed to high European unemployment, whether or not Solow's decomposition between the two is accurate. In the early 1990s Europe experienced a recession that stemmed primarily from the distorted nature of Germany's reunification, with a Reaganomic policy combination of loose fiscal and tight monetary policy. After a transitory stimulus to the exports of other European countries, the spillover effect for the EU was negative, because it was dominated by Germany's high real interest rates, which are characteristic of such a policy mix. Monetary institutions aggravated the spillover effect, because other European countries had become so attached to the disinflationary virtues of a rigidly fixed exchange rate against the deutsche mark, within the confines of the Exchange Rate Mechanism, that they were loath to permit Germany to revalue and, as a result, were forced to import Germany's high interest rates and their contractionary consequences.

Slow growth also plagued the United States and Japan in the early 1990s. In the United States, recession was fundamentally the price paid for fiscal excesses in the 1980s, but it was also marked by distinctive features that included downsizing in defense industries, adjustment to overindebtedness of households and firms, and the drag of asset market deflation for the first time since the 1930s.

For its part, Japan faced recession in the early 1990s as the aftermath of the bubble economy in the late 1980s. The bubble had seen not only an extreme run-up in stock market and land prices but also a massive boom in industrial investment that left a large lump of capacity to be digested and a corresponding hiatus for new investment. Fragility of the banking system once stock and land prices collapsed aggravated the situation. As for the origins of the bubble, an attractive candidate is the expansionary monetary policy associated with the attempt to sustain the dollar after the Louvre Agreement in early 1987.[2]

Microeconomic Influences

Despite recession in all three areas in the early 1990s, unemployment persisted at double-digit levels only in Europe. This suggests that structural as well as cyclical factors were at work. A major influence is that, in Europe, social charges cause a large wedge between what workers

2. However, the manifestation of loose money in asset rather than goods prices suggests that other factors, perhaps including liberalization of financial markets, were at work as well.

receive and what they cost employers. Employer contributions for social security and other payroll taxes are about 47 percent of total labor costs in Germany and France and 52 percent in Italy, compared with 28 percent in the United States; in Europe only the United Kingdom has moderate rates (30 percent) (*International Herald Tribune*, 10 March 1994).

Moreover, unemployment benefits are relatively high and have no time limit in Europe, whereas they are strictly limited in the United States. This means that the reservation price of labor is relatively higher in Europe, because the opportunity cost of not working is lower. Not surprisingly, one consequence is that the share of long-term unemployment is much higher. In Europe, typically half of the unemployed have been out of work more than one year, compared with only one-tenth or less in the United States (OECD 1992a).

Demographics, Wages, and Jobs

One factor often left unmentioned in the paeans to the US job machine is that the actual and potential labor force has grown more rapidly in the United States than in Europe. More jobs were created in part because more people were available to work. From 1970 to 1990, the population of age 15 to 64 rose by 29 percent in the United States and 20 percent in Japan, but only by 13 percent in Europe (OECD 1992b). From this standpoint alone, one should have expected the US economy to generate more than twice as large a percentage increase in employment than the European economy. Considering that Europe's labor force in 1970 was 50 percent larger than that in the United States, age composition (essentially the baby-boom phenomenon in the United States) should have meant that the absolute number of new jobs created in the United States over the period should have been about 50 percent larger than that in Europe ([29/13]/1.5).

Quasi-demographic influences widened the gap further, as the adult labor force participation rate rose in the United States from 67 percent in 1970 to 77 percent in 1990, whereas the rate held constant at 66 percent in Europe (Cline 1994a). The rise came primarily from women. The ratio of employed to population for white women rose from 40 percent in 1972 to 55 percent in 1993 and from 46 percent to 54 percent for black women (CEA 1994, 107). The favorable interpretation is that women's liberation and reduced job discrimination opened up new opportunities; the unfavorable interpretation is that stagnant or even falling real wages forced households to send wives into the job market. The rise in single-parent households also probably played a role.

If the quantity of labor available was rising more rapidly in the US economy, its price was rising much more rapidly in Europe. Figure A.1 shows the path of real wages in manufacturing, deflating by consumer

Figure A.1 Real wages for the G6 countries, 1970-93 (1970 = 100)

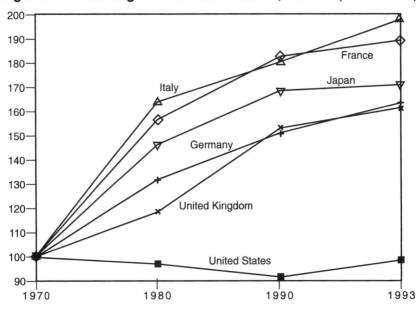

prices (IMF 1992, 1994a). From 1970 to 1990, real wages in Italy and France rose by 80 percent, in Germany and the United Kingdom by 50 percent, and in Japan by two-thirds. In contrast, real wages actually declined in the United States over the same period.[3] By 1993, the US-EU wage gap had widened further.

Real wages are the equilibrium-price outcome of demand and supply in the labor market. Figure A.2 shows what happened in the past two decades to wages and jobs in the United States (panel A) and Europe (panel B). The horizontal axis shows the size of the labor force, in index form with 1970 equal to 100; the vertical axis shows a similar index for the real wage. In the United States, demographic and cultural factors have shifted out the labor supply curve (SS) by about 50 percent. The labor demand curve (DD) has also shifted outward by a large amount but by somewhat less. The result has been a slight decline in the real wage (with the caveat noted above). The amount of unemployment is the horizontal gap between the labor supply curve and the labor demand curve at the going wage. The fraction of the labor force unemployed has stayed about constant, although the larger base of the labor force means the absolute number of unemployed has risen from u_0 to u_1.

---

3. In this data set. Broader data pertaining to total compensation (including health and other benefits), all sectors of the economy, and all workers rather than just production workers show moderately increasing rather than falling trends.

Figure A.2 Wages and job creation, 1970-90

A. United States

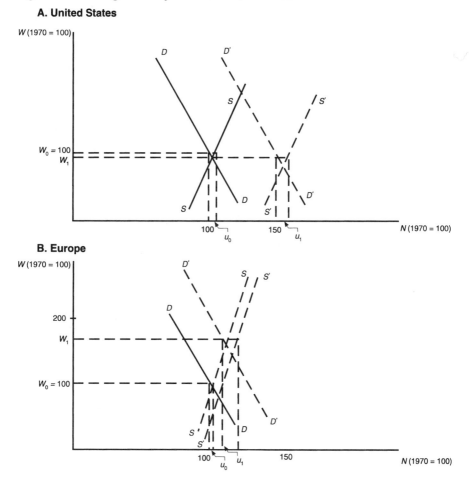

B. Europe

In Europe (panel B), there has been a much smaller outward shift of the labor force, so the horizontal distance between SS and $S'S'$ is narrower. However, wages have risen by much more (with w_1 about two-thirds higher than w_0, rather than slightly below as in the US case). The labor demand curve has shifted out substantially, though not as much as in the United States. The resulting equilibrium shows a small expansion of total jobs and a significant widening of the horizontal gap between the labor supply and demand curves at the going wage: from u_0 to u_1.

Figure A.2 reveals several important points. First, the potential job creation capacity of the US economy has been somewhat greater than that of the European economy, but the difference is considerably smaller than indicated by the proportionate rise in actual employment. Job creation capacity is reflected by the horizontal outward shift in the labor demand curve. As depicted, this was less unfavorable for Europe in comparison with the United States than might be suspected from the proportionate increase in actual employment.

Second, the figure suggests that it would take far less draconian a wage reduction than cutback to the base year level to reduce Europe's unemployment rate to the base period level. Thus, the horizontal gap between $D'D'$ and $S'S'$ disappears at a wage rate that is somewhat closer to w_1 than to w_0. This simply means that with a smaller increase in labor supply than in the United States, Europe could have held the unemployment rate unchanged and still have experienced substantial wage increases.

Third, from the standpoint of a labor representative, it is not obvious that the US outcome was superior to that in Europe. The total wage bill rose by the amount indicated by the area of the rectangle, with height shown by the wage and width shown by the number employed. In the United States, this expansion was accomplished solely by increasing the size of the employed labor force; in Europe, it was accomplished primarily by raising wages. The total proportionate increase in the real wage bill was actually greater in Europe: an 80 percent rise from 1970 to 1990, compared with a rise of only one-third in the United States. Dividing the wage bill by the labor force (including the unemployed), wage income per potential worker rose by 55 percent in Europe from 1970 to 1990 but fell by 10 percent in the United States.[4]

Thus, a labor representative might well say that labor as a group did better in Europe than in the United States. Of course, the implication would be that in Europe there were institutional arrangements to carry out transfers from those fortunate enough to be employed at high wages to those out of a job. Although in principle the counterpart of the high cost of social charges is precisely that such mechanisms do exist, in fact there is concern in Europe that the benefits are not being shared adequately with the unemployed and that their employment is essential to social solidarity (Commission 1993).

The advantages of job expansion versus wage increase depend, of course, on the elasticities of demand and supply for labor. If labor demand is more elastic than depicted here, then the calculus of the labor representative must shift in the direction of favoring more job expansion and less wage increase; otherwise, the total wage bill rectangle can actually fall because of elastic (price-responsive) labor demand.[5] Moreover, there is growing concern in Europe that the high-wage strategy is pricing its firms

4. Again using the IMF wage data. US labor compensation data would show a greater rise.

5. Similarly, if the labor supply curve is more elastic, a high-wage strategy will widen the horizontal unemployment gap between the labor supply and demand curves.

out of the international market, with the implication that the labor income expansion record shown in figure A.2 might not be sustainable into the future. Despite these caveats, the analysis here suggests that neither the US nor the European outcome has been unambiguously more favorable from the standpoint of labor. There has been less unemployment in the United States, but more wage gain in Europe.

EC White Paper

The Commission of the European Communities (the Commission) has issued a White Paper on employment (Commission 1993). Along with much broader diagnoses and analyses, the study singles out the relatively high cost of social charges in payroll taxes as a deterrent to employment of low-skilled workers. It notes that statutory labor charges (including income taxes) rose from 34 percent of GDP to 40 percent between 1970 and 1991 in Europe but remained at only 30 percent in the United States. It cites studies showing that a reduction of 30 to 40 percent in social security contributions for low-paid workers would increase employment by 2 percent. The white paper proposes that the nonwage costs of unskilled and semiskilled labor be reduced by an amount equivalent to 1 to 2 percent of GDP by the year 2000. It suggests that almost one-third of the associated need for replacement revenue would be made up by increased activity and that the remaining revenue costs might appropriately be raised by levying the carbon-energy tax already proposed by the Commission on environmental grounds (Commission 1993, 15). Divorcing social funding from the price incentive facing firms in the hiring decision could be an important way to address the problem of structural unemployment in Europe, and the Commission's suggestions make eminent sense. The politics of raising a carbon-energy or other tax are, however, difficult.

For microeconomic employment problems, the United States needs to emphasize training, in view of falling real wages for unskilled workers. In Europe, such reforms as the Commission's proposed cut in social charges for unskilled workers, financed by general revenue (and ideally such taxes as environmental levies that remove existing price distortions) seem important to reduce the rigidity that has contributed to minimal job creation. However, Europeans would do well to think twice before dismantling the social safety network and wage policies that played a role in what appears to have been larger growth in the total wage receipts than in the United States, despite larger growth in the US labor force.

References

Abowd, John M. 1991. Appendix: The NBER Immigration, Trade, and Labor Markets Data Files. In *Immigration, Trade, and the Labor Market*, ed. by John M. Abowd and Richard B. Freeman. Chicago: University of Chicago Press.

Abowd, John M., and Richard B. Freeman, eds. 1991. *Immigration, Trade, and the Labor Market*. Chicago: University of Chicago Press.

Atkinson, Anthony B. 1970. On the Measurement of Inequality. *Journal of Economic Theory* 2, no. 3 (September): 244–63.

Balassa, Bela. 1986. The Employment Effects of Trade in Manufactured Products between Developed and Developing Countries. *Journal of Policy Modeling* 8, no. 3 (Fall): 371–90.

Baldwin, Robert E., and Glen G. Cain. 1994. Trade and US Relative Wages: Preliminary Results. Madison: University of Wisconsin. Photocopy.

Batra, Ravi, and Daniel J. Slottje. 1993. Trade Policy and Poverty in the United States: Theory and Evidence, 1947–1990. *Review of International Economics* 1, no. 3 (October): 189–208.

Bergstrand, Jeffrey H., Thomas F. Cosimano, John W. Houck, and Richard G. Sheehan, eds. 1994. *The Changing Distribution of Income in an Open US Economy*. Amsterdam: North-Holland.

Berman, Eli, John Bound, and Zvi Griliches. 1994. Changes in the Demand for Skilled Labor within US Manufacturing: Evidence from Annual Survey of Manufacturers. *Quarterly Journal of Economics* 109, no. 2 (May): 367–97.

Bernard, Andrew B., and J. Bradford Jensen. 1994. *Exporters, Skill Upgrading, and the Wage Gap*. Discussion Paper No. 94–13. Washington: Bureau of the Census, Center for Economic Studies (November).

Bhagwati, Jagdish. 1991. *Free Traders and Free Immigrationists: Strangers or Friends?* Working Paper No. 20. New York: Russell Sage Foundation (April).

Bhagwati, Jagdish. 1995. Trade and Wages: Alternative Theoretical Approaches. Paper prepared for Brookings Conference on Imports, Exports, and the American Worker, Washington (2–3 February).

Bhagwati, Jagdish, and Vivek H. Dehejia. 1994. Freer Trade and Wages of the Unskilled: Is Marx Striking Again? In *Trade and Wages: Leveling Wages Down?*, ed. by Jagdish Bhagwati and Marvin H. Kosters. Washington: American Enterprise Institute.

Bhagwati, Jagdish, and Marvin H. Kosters, eds. 1994. *Trade and Wages: Leveling Wages Down?* Washington: American Enterprise Institute.

Bhagwati, Jagdish, and T. N. Srinivasan. 1983. *Lectures on International Trade.* Cambridge, MA: MIT Press.

Blau, Francine D., and Lawrence M. Kahn. 1996. *Wage Inequality: International Comparisons of Its Sources.* Washington: American Enterprise Institute.

Bluestone, Barry. 1994. Old Theories in New Bottles: Toward an Explanation of Growing World-Wide Income Inequality. In *The Changing Distribution of Income in an Open US Economy,* ed. by Jeffrey H. Bergstrand et al. Amsterdam: North-Holland.

Borjas, George J. 1994. The Economics of Immigration. *Journal of Economic Literature* 32 (December): 1667–717.

Borjas, George J. 1995. The Internationalization of the U.S. Labor Market and the Wage Structure. *Economic Policy Review* (Federal Reserve Board of New York) 1, no. 1 (January): 3–8.

Borjas, George J., and Valerie A. Ramey. 1993. *Foreign Competition, Market Power, and Wage Inequality: Theory and Evidence.* Working Paper No. 4556. Cambridge, MA: National Bureau of Economic Research (December).

Borjas, George J., and Valerie A. Ramey. 1994a. The Relationship between Wage Inequality and International Trade. In *The Changing Distribution of Income in an Open US Economy,* ed. by Jeffrey H. Bergstrand et al. Amsterdam: North-Holland.

Borjas, George J., and Valerie A. Ramey. 1994b. Time-Series Evidence on the Sources of Trends in Wage Inequality. *American Economic Review* 84, no. 2 (May): 10–15.

Borjas, George J., Richard B. Freeman, and Lawrence F. Katz, eds. 1992. *Immigration and the Work Force: Economic Consequences for the United States and Source Areas.* Chicago: University of Chicago Press.

Borjas, George J., Richard B. Freeman, and Lawrence F. Katz. 1997. How Much Do Immigration and Trade Affect Labor Market Outcomes? *Brookings Papers on Economic Activity,* no. 1: 1–67.

Bosworth, Barry, and George L. Perry. 1994. Productivity and Real Wages: Is There a Puzzle? *Brookings Papers on Economic Activity,* no. 1: 317–44.

Bound, John, and Richard B. Freeman. 1992. What Went Wrong? The Erosion of Relative Earnings and Employment among Young Black Men in the 1980s. *Quarterly Journal of Economics* 107, no. 428 (February): 201–32.

Bound, John, and George Johnson. 1992. Changes in the Structure of Wages in the 1980s: An Evaluation of Alternative Explanations. *American Economic Review* 82, no. 3 (June): 371–92.

Bourguignon, François, and Christian Morrison. 1989. *External Trade and Income Distribution.* Paris: Organization of Economic Cooperation and Development, Development Centre.

Bourguinon, François, William H. Branson, and Jaime de Melo. 1989. *Adjustment and Income Distribution: A Counterfactual Analysis.* Working Paper No. 2943. Cambridge, MA: National Bureau of Economic Research (April).

Bowman, Charles T. 1993. Trends in Industry Employment, 1990–2005. *The Service Economy* 7, no. 3 (July): 1–8.

Branson, William H., and James P. Love. 1987. *The Real Exchange Rate and Employment in US Manufacturing: State and Regional Results.* NBER Working Paper No. 2435. Cambridge, MA: National Bureau of Economic Research.

Brauer, David A., and Susan Hickok. 1995. Explaining the Growing Inequality in Wages across Skill Levels. *Economic Policy Review* (Federal Reserve Bank of New York) 1, no. 1 (January): 61–72.

Brooke, Anthony, David Kendrick, and Alexander Meeraus. 1988. *GAMS: A User's Guide.* Redwood City, CA: Scientific Press.

Brown, Drusilla K., and David M. Garman. 1989. *A Review of the Role of Labor in Recent International Trade Models.* Seminar Discussion Paper No. 252. Ann Arbor: University of Michigan, Research Seminar in International Economics (August).

Brown, Drusilla K., Alan V. Deardorff, and Robert M. Stern. 1993a. *Protection and Real Wages: Old and New Trade Theories and Their Empirical Counterparts.* Discussion Paper No. 331. Ann Arbor: University of Michigan, Research Forum on International Economics (May).

Brown, Drusilla K., Alan V. Deardorff, and Robert M. Stern. 1993b. *International Labor Standards and Trade: A Theoretical Analysis.* Discussion Paper No. 333. Ann Arbor: University of Michigan, Research Forum on International Economics (July).

Buron, Lawrence, Robert Haveman, and Owen O'Donnell. 1994. *Recent Trends in US Male Work and Wage Patterns: An Overview.* Jerome Levy Economics Institute Working Paper No. 122. Madison: University of Wisconsin.

Burtless, Gary. 1995a. International Trade and the Rise in Earnings Inequality. *Journal of Economic Literature* 333 (June): 800–16.

Burtless, Gary. 1995b. Widening U.S. Income Inequality and the Growth in World Trade. Washington: Brookings Institution. Photocopy (September).

Card, David. 1992. *The Effect of Unions on the Distribution of Wages: Redistribution or Relabeling?* NBER Working Paper No. 4195. Cambridge, MA: National Bureau of Economic Research (October).

Card, David, and Alan B. Krueger. 1992. School Quality and Black-White Earnings: A Direct Assessment. *Quarterly Journal of Economics* 107, no. 428 (February): 151–200.

Card, David, and Alan B. Krueger. 1995. *Myth and Measurement: The New Economics of the Minimum Wage.* Princeton, NJ: Princeton University Press.

Carliner, Geoffrey. 1980. Wages, Earnings, and Hours of First, Second, and Third Generation American Males. *Economic Inquiry* 18, no. 1 (January): 87–102.

Chiang, A. 1984. *Fundamental Methods of Mathematical Economics.* New York: McGraw-Hill.

Chiswick, Barry R. 1978. The Effect of Americanization on the Earnings of Foreign-Born Men. *Journal of Political Economy* 86, no. 5: 897–921

Clarete, Ramon L., Irene Trela, and John Whalley. 1994. *Evaluating Labour Adjustment Costs from Trade Shocks: Illustrations for the US Economy Using and Applied General Equilibrium Model with Transactions Costs.* Working Paper No. 4628. Cambridge, MA: National Bureau of Economic Research (January).

Cline, William R. 1972. *Potential Effects of Income Redistribution on Economic Growth: Latin American Cases.* New York: Praeger.

Cline, William R. 1975. Distribution and Development: A Survey of Literature. *Journal of Development Economics* 1, no. 4 (February): 359–400.

Cline, William R. 1979. Imports and Consumer Prices: A Survey Analysis. *Journal of Retailing* 55, no. 1 (Spring): 3–24.

Cline, William R. 1982. Can the East Asian Model of Development Be Generalized? *World Development* 10, no. 2 (February): 81–90.

Cline, William R. 1984. *Exports of Manufactures from Developing Countries.* Washington: Brookings Institution.

Cline, William R. 1989. *United States External Adjustment and the World Economy.* Washington: Institute for International Economics.

Cline, William R. 1990. *The Future of World Trade in Textiles and Apparel,* rev. ed. Washington: Institute for International Economics.

Cline, William R. 1992. Optimal Carbon Emissions Over Time: Experiments with the Nordhaus DICE Model. Washington: Institute for International Economics. Photocopy (August).

Cline, William R. 1994a. A Note on Job Creation in Europe and the United States. Washington: Institute for International Economics. Photocopy (March).

Cline, William R. 1994b. Policies for Global Employment Growth. Washington: Institute for International Economics. Paper prepared for the International Labor Office. Photocopy (April).

Cline, William R. 1994c. *International Economic Policy in the 1990s.* Cambridge, MA: MIT Press.

Cline, William R. 1995. Evaluating the Uruguay Round. *The World Economy* 18, no. 1 (January): 1–23.

Commerce, US Department of (DOC). 1975. *Historical Statistics of the United States: Colonial Times to 1970*. Washington: Bureau of the Census.

Commerce, US Department of (DOC). 1982. *Statistical Abstract of the United States*. Washington: Bureau of the Census.

Commerce, US Department of (DOC). 1983. *Statistical Abstract of the United States*. Washington: Bureau of the Census.

Commerce, US Department of (DOC). 1992. *Statistical Abstract of the United States*. Washington: Bureau of the Census.

Commerce, US Department of (DOC). 1994. *Statistical Abstract of the United States*. Washington: Bureau of the Census.

Commerce, US Department of (DOC). 1995. *Income, Poverty, and Valuation of Noncash Benefits: 1995*. Current Population Reports, Consumer Income, Series P60–188. Washington: Bureau of the Census.

Commission of the European Communities. 1993. *Growth, Competitiveness, Employment: The Challenges and Ways Forward into the 21st Century*. Brussels: EC Commission (December).

Cooper, Richard N. 1994. Foreign Trade, Wages, and Unemployment. Cambridge, MA: Harvard University. Photocopy (October).

Council of Economic Advisers (CEA). 1990. *Economic Report of the President*. Washington: CEA (February).

Council of Economic Advisers (CEA). 1991. *Economic Report of the President*. Washington: CEA (February).

Council of Economic Advisers (CEA). 1993. *Economic Report of the President*. Washington: CEA (February).

Council of Economic Advisers (CEA). 1994. *Economic Report of the President*. Washington: CEA (February).

Council of Economic Advisers (CEA). 1995. *Economic Report of the President*. Washington: CEA (February).

Cutler, David M., and Lawrence F. Katz. 1991. Macroeconomic Performance and the Disadvantaged. *Brookings Papers on Economic Activity*, no. 2: 1–74.

Davidson, Carl, Lawrence Martin, and Steven Matusz. 1988. The Structure of Simple General Equilibrium Models with Frictional Unemployment. *Journal of Political Economy* 96, no. 6 (December): 1267–93.

Davis, Steven J. 1992. Cross-Country Patterns of Change in Relative Wages. In *NBER Macroeconomics Annual*. Cambridge, MA: National Bureau of Economic Research.

de Melo, Jaime, and Sherman Robinson. 1986. The Treatment of Foreign Trade in Computable General Equilibrium Models of Small Economies. Report No. DRD189. Washington: World Bank (June).

Deardorff, Alan V. 1993a. *Exploring the Limits of Comparative Advantage*. Discussion Paper No. 335. Ann Arbor: University of Michigan, Institute of Public Policy Studies, Research Forum on International Economics (August).

Deardorff, Alan V. 1993b. *Overview of the Stolper-Samuelson Theorem*. Discussion Paper No. 345b. Ann Arbor: University of Michigan, Institute of Public Policy Studies, Research Forum on International Economics.

Deardorff, Alan V., and Dalia Hakura. 1994. Trade and Wages: What Are the Questions? In *Trade and Wages: Leveling Wages Down?*, ed. by Jagdish Bhagwati and Marvin H. Kosters. Washington: American Enterprise Institute.

Deardorff, Alan V., and Jon D. Haveman. 1991. *The Effects of US Trade Laws on Poverty in America*. Discussion Paper No. 285. Ann Arbor: University of Michigan, Institute of Public Policy Studies, Research Forum on International Economics (June).

Deardorff, Alan V., and Robert W. Staiger. 1988. An Interpretation of the Factor Content of Trade. *Journal of International Economics* 24, no. 1/2 (February): 93–107.

Deardorff, Alan V., and Robert M. Stern. 1993. *The Stolper-Samuelson Theorem: A Golden Jubilee*. Discussion Paper No. 344. Ann Arbor: University of Michigan, Institute of Public Policy Studies, Research Forum on International Economics (December).

Ehrbar, Al. 1994. Working Under Different Rules: Why the Lowest-Paid US Workers Are So Poor, and What Can Be Done about It. *Ford Foundation Report* 25, no. 1 (Spring): 22–25.

Ethier, Wilfred J. 1984. Higher Dimensional Issues in Trade Theory. In *Handbook of International Economics*, vol. 1, ed. by Ronald W. Jones and Peter B. Kenen. Amsterdam: Elsevier.

Fallon, Peter, and Richard Layard. 1975. Capital-Skill Complementarity, Income Distribution, and Output Accounting. *Journal of Political Economy* 83, no. 2 (April): 279–302.

Feenstra, Robert C., and Gordon H. Hanson. 1995. *Foreign Investment, Outsourcing and Relative Wages*. NBER Working Paper No. 5121. Cambridge, MA: National Bureau of Economic Research (May).

Fortin, Nicole M., and Thomas Lemieux. 1997. Institutional Changes and Rising Wage Inequality: Is There a Linkage? *Journal of Economic Perspectives* 11, no. 2 (Spring): 75–90.

Frank, Charles R. Jr. 1977. *Foreign Trade and Domestic Aid*. Washington: Brookings Institution.

Frankel, Jeffrey A. 1997. *Regional Trading Blocs in the World Economic System*. Washington: Institute for International Economics.

Franklin, Howard N. Jr. 1993. Industry Output and Employment. *Monthly Labor Review* 116, no. 11 (November): 41–57.

Freeman, Richard B. 1975. Overinvestment in College Education? *Journal of Human Resources* 10, no. 3 (Summer): 287–311.

Freeman, Richard B. 1991. *How Much Has De-Unionization Contributed to the Rise in Male Earnings Inequality?* NBER Working Paper No. 3826. Cambridge, MA: National Bureau of Economic Research.

Freeman, Richard B. 1995. Will Globalization Dominate US Labor Market Outcomes? Paper prepared for Brookings Conference on Imports, Exports, and the American Worker, Washington (2–3 February).

Freeman, Richard B. 1996. When Earnings Diverge: Causes, Consequences, and Cures for the New Inequality in the U.S. Paper prepared for Council on Foreign Relations Study Group on Global Trade and Wages, New York (4 November).

Fullerton, Howard N. 1993. Another Look at the Labor Force. *Monthly Labor Review* 116, no. 11 (November): 31–40.

General Agreement on Tariffs and Trade (GATT). 1993. *International Trade 91–92*. Geneva: General Agreement on Tariffs and Trade.

Gottschalk, Peter. 1997. Inequality, Income Growth, and Mobility: The Basic Facts. *Journal of Economic Perspectives* 11, no. 2 (Spring): 21–40.

Grinols, Earl L., and Erik Thorbecke. 1978. The Effects of Trade between the U.S. and Developing Countries on U.S. Employment. Paper presented to the International Economic Association Conference on Unemployment in Western Countries Today, Strasbourg (28 August–2 September).

Grossman, Gene M. 1987. The Employment and Wage Effects of Import Competition in the United States. *Journal of International Economic Integration* 2, no. 1 (Spring): 1–23.

Hall, Robert E. 1993. Comment. *Brookings Papers on Economic Activity*, no. 2: 211–13.

Hamermesh, Daniel S. 1986. The Demand for Labour in the Long Run. In *Handbook of Labor Economics*, vol. 1, ed. by Orley Ashenfelter and Richard Layard. Amsterdam: North-Holland.

Hamermesh, Daniel S. 1993. *Labor Demand*. Princeton, NJ: Princeton University Press.

Haveman, Jon D. 1993. The Effect of Trade Induced Displacement on Unemployment and Wages. Lafayette, IN: Purdue University, Krannert School of Management. Photocopy (October).

Heckman, James J., Rebecca L. Roselius, and Jeffrey Smith. 1994. US Education and Training Policy: A Reevaluatiion of the Underlying Consensus behind the New Consensus. Washington: American Enterprise Institute. Conference on Job Change and Federal Labor Policies (March).

Heckscher, Eli. 1919. The Effect of Foreign Trade on the Distribution of Income. *Ekonomisk Tidskrift* 21: 497–512. Reprinted in American Economics Association, *Readings in the Theory of International Trade*, vol. 4. Philadelphia: Blakiston Co., 1949.

Henderson, James M., and Richard E. Quandt. 1980. *Microeconomic Theory: A Mathematical Approach*. New York: McGraw-Hill.

Hicks, John R. 1953. An Inaugural Lecture: 2. The Dollar Problem. *Oxford Economic Papers* 5 (June): 117–35.

Hooper, Peter, and Jaime Marquez. 1995. Exchange Rates, Prices, and External Adjustment. In *Understanding Interdependence: The Macroeconomics of the Open Economy*, ed. by Peter B. Kenen. Princeton, NJ: Princeton University Press.

Hufbauer, Gary C. 1994. The Coming Boom in Services Trade: What Will It Do to Wages? *Law and Policy in International Business* 25, no. 2 (Winter): 433–38.

International Monetary Fund (IMF). 1991. *International Financial Statistics, Yearbook*. Washington: International Monetary Fund.

International Monetary Fund (IMF). 1992. *International Financial Statistics, Yearbook*. Washington: International Monetary Fund.

International Monetary Fund (IMF). 1994a. *International Financial Statistics, Yearbook*. Washington: International Monetary Fund.

International Monetary Fund (IMF). 1994b. *Balance of Payments Yearbook*. Washington: International Monetary Fund.

International Monetary Fund (IMF). 1996. *International Financial Statistics, Yearbook*. Washington: International Monetary Fund.

International Monetary Fund (IMF). 1997. *World Economic Outlook*. Washington: International Monetary Fund (May).

Johnson, George E. 1970. The Demand for Labor by Educational Category. *Southern Economic Journal* 37, no. 2 (October): 190–204.

Johnson, George E., and Frank P. Stafford. 1992. *Models of Real Wages and International Competition*. Discussion Paper No. 314. Ann Arbor, MI: Research Forum on International Economics (July).

Johnson, George E., and Frank P. Stafford. 1993. International Competition and Real Wages. *American Economic Review* 83, no. 2 (May): 127–30.

Johnson, George E., and Frank P. Stafford. 1995. *The Hicks Hypothesis, Globalization, and the Distribution of Real Wages*. Discussion Paper No. 373. Ann Arbor: University of Michigan, Institute of Public Policy Studies.

Jones, Ronald W. 1965. The Structure of Simple General Equilibrium Models. *Journal of Political Economy* (December): 557–72.

Jones, Ronald W. 1971. A Three-Factor Model in Theory, Trade, and History. In *Trade, Balance of Payments, and Growth: Essays in Honor of C. P. Kindleberger*, ed. by Jagdish Bhagwati et al. Amsterdam: North-Holland.

Juhn, Chihui, and Kevin M. Murphy. 1995. Inequality in Labor Market Outcomes: Contrasting the 1980s and Earlier Decades. *Economic Policy Review* (Federal Reserve Board of New York) 1, no. 1 (January): 26–32.

Juhn, Chihui, Kevin M. Murphy, and Brooks Pierce. 1993. Wage Inequality and the Rise of Returns to Skill. *Journal of Political Economy* 101, no. 3 (2 June): 410–42.

Karoly, Lynn A. 1988. A Study of the Distribution of Individual Earnings in the United States from 1967 to 1986. Ph.D diss., Yale University, Department of Economics (December).

Karoly, Lynn A., and Jacob Alex Klerman. 1994. Using Regional Data to Reexamine the Contribution of Demographic and Sectoral Changes to Increasing U.S. Wage Inequality. In *The Changing Distribution of Income in an Open US Economy*, ed. by Jeffery H. Bergstrand et al. Amsterdam: North-Holland.

Katz, Lawrence F. 1992–93. Understanding Recent Changes in the Wage Structure. *NBER Reporter* (Winter): 10–15.

Katz, Lawrence F., and Kevin M. Murphy. 1992. Changes in Relative Wages, 1963–1987: Supply and Demand Factors. *Quarterly Journal of Economics* 107, no. 428 (February): 35–78.

Katz, Lawrence F., and Lawrence H. Summers. 1984. Can Interindustry Wage Differentials Justify Strategic Trade Policy? In *Trade Policies for Industrial Competitiveness,* ed. by Robert Feenstra. Chicago: University of Chicago Press.

Katz, Lawrence F., and Lawrence H. Summers. 1989. Can Interindustry Wage Differentials Justify Strategic Trade Policy? In *Trade Policies for International Competitiveness,* ed. by Robert Feenstra. Chicago: University of Chicago Press.

Kennickell, Arthur B., Martha Starr-McCluer, and Annika E. Sunden. 1997. Family Finances in the U.S.: Recent Evidence from the Survey of Consumer Finances. *Federal Reserve Bulletin* 83, no. 1 (January): 1–24.

Kim, Dae Il, and Peter Mieszkowski. 1995. The Effects of International Trade and Outsourcing on Relative and Real Factor Prices. Houston, TX: Rice University. Photocopy (May).

Kletzer, Lori. 1994. International Trade and Job Loss in US Manufacturing, 1979–91. Paper prepared for Brookings Conference on Imports, Exports, and the American Worker, Washington (2–3 February).

Kohler, Wilhelm K. 1991. Income Distribution and Labor Market Effects of Austrian Pre- and Post-Tokyo Round Tariff Protection. *European Economic Review* 35, no. 1 (January): 139–54.

Komiya, Ryutaro. 1967. Non-Traded Goods and the Pure Theory of International Trade. *International Economic Review* 8, no. 2 (June): 132–52.

Kosters, Marvin H. 1994. An Overview of Changing Wage Patterns in the Labor Market. In *Trade and Wages: Leveling Wages Down?* ed. by Jagdish Bhagwati and Marvin H. Kosters. Washington: American Enterprise Institute.

Krueger, Alan B. 1992. How Computers Have Changed the Wage Structure: Evidence and Implications. In *Brookings Papers on Economic Activity, Microeconomics*: 209–10

Krueger, Anne O. 1978. Impact of LDC Exports on Employment in American Industry. Paper presented to the Annual Conference of the International Economics Study Group, Sussex (24–26 September).

Krugman, Paul R. 1979. A Model of Innovation, Technology Transfer, and the World Distribution of Income. *Journal of Political Economy* 87, no. 2 (April): 253–66.

Krugman, Paul R. 1980. Scale Economies, Product Differentiation, and the Pattern of Trade. *American Economic Review* 70, no. 5 (December): 950–59.

Krugman, Paul R. 1992. Does the New Trade Theory Require a New Trade Policy? *World Economy* 15, no. 4 (July): 423–41.

Krugman, Paul R. 1993. *Inequality and the Political Economy of Eurosclerosis.* Discussion Paper No. 867. London: Centre for Economic Policy Research (November).

Krugman, Paul R. 1994. Competitiveness: A Dangerous Obsession. *Foreign Policy* 73, no. 2 (March/April): 28–44.

Krugman, Paul R. 1995a. Growing World Trade: Causes and Consequences. *Brookings Papers on Economic Activity,* no. 1: 327–77.

Krugman, Paul R. 1995b. Technology, Trade, and Factor Prices. Stanford, CA: Stanford University, Department of Economics (October).

Krugman, Paul R., and Robert Z. Lawrence. 1993. *Trade, Jobs, and Wages.* Working Paper No. 4478. Cambridge, MA: National Bureau of Economics (September).

Krugman, Paul R., and Robert Z. Lawrence. 1994. Trade, Jobs and Wages. *Scientific American* 270, no. 4 (April): 44–49.

Kutscher, Ronald E. 1993. Historical Trends, 1950–92, and Current Uncertainties. *Monthly Labor Review* 116, no. 11 (November): 3–10.

Kuznets, Simon. 1955. Economic Growth and Income Inequality. *American Economic Review* 45, no. 1 (March): 1–28.

Lawrence, Robert Z. 1994. *The Impact of Trade on OECD Labor Markets*. Washington: Group of Thirty.

Lawrence, Robert Z. 1995. US Wage Trends in the 1980s: The Role of International Factors. *Economic Policy Review* (Federal Reserve Bank of New York) 1, no. 1 (January): 18–25.

Lawrence, Robert Z., and Matthew J. Slaughter. 1993. Trade and US Wages: Great Sucking Sound or Small Hiccup? *Brookings Papers on Economic Activity*, no. 2: 161–226.

Layard, P. Richard G., and Alan A. Walters. 1978. *Micro-economic Theory*. New York: McGraw-Hill.

Leamer, Edward E. 1993. Wage Effects of a US-Mexican Free Trade Agreement. In *The Mexico-U.S. Free Trade Agreement*, ed. by Peter M. Garber. Cambridge, MA: MIT Press.

Leamer, Edward E. 1994. *Trade, Wages, and Revolving Door Ideas*. Working Paper No. 4716. Cambridge, MA: National Bureau of Economic Research (April).

Leamer, Edward E. 1995. A Trade Economist's View of US Wages and 'Globalization.' Paper prepared for Brookings Conference on Imports, Exports, and the American Worker, Washington (2–3 February).

Lenz, Allen J. 1992. *Narrowing the US Current Account Deficit: A Sectoral Assessment*. Washington: Institute for International Economics.

Leontief, Wassily W. 1953. Domestic Production and Foreign Trade: The American Capital Position Re-examined. *Proceedings of the American Philosophical Society* 97: 332–49. Also published in *Input-Output Economics*, 2d ed. 1986. New York: Oxford University Press.

Levy, Frank. 1987. *Dollars and Dreams: The Changing American Income Distribution*. New York: Russell Sage Foundation.

Levy, Frank, and Richard J. Murnane. 1992. US Earning Levels and Earnings Inequality: A Review of Recent Trends and Explanations. *Journal of Economic Literature* 30: 1333–81.

Lewis, H. Gregg. 1986. Union Relative Wage Effects. In *Handbook of Labor Economics*, vol. 2, ed. by Orley Ashenfelter and Richard Layard. Amsterdam: North-Holland.

Linder, Steffan B. 1961. *An Essay on Trade and Transformation*. London: John Wiley & Sons.

Love, Roger, and Michael C. Wolfson. 1976. *Income Inequality: Statistical Methodology and Canadian Illustrations*. Ottawa: Statistics Canada (March).

Maddison, Angus. 1970. *Economic Progress and Policy in Developing Countries*. New York: Norton.

Martin, John P., and John M. Evans. 1981. Notes on Measuring the Employment Displacement Effects of Trade by the Accounting Procedure. *Oxford Economic Papers* 33, no. 1 (March): 154–64.

Martins, Joaquim Oliveira. 1994. Market Structure, Trade and Industry Wages. *OECD Economic Studies*, no. 22 (Spring): 131–54.

Matusz, Steven J. 1985. The Heckscher-Ohlin-Samuelson Model with Implicit Contracts. *Quarterly Journal of Economics* 100, no. 4 (November): 1313–29.

Matusz, Steven J. 1986. Implicit Contracts, Unemployment and International Trade. *Economic Journal* 96, no. 382 (June): 307–22.

McKibbin, Warwick J. 1993. *Integrating Macroeconometric and Multisector Computable General Equilibrium Models*. Discussion Papers in International Economics No. 100. Washington: Brookings Institution (February).

Mincer, Jacob. 1958. Investment in Human Capital and Personal Income Distribution. *Journal of Political Economy* 66, no. 4: 281–302.

Mincer, Jacob. 1991. *Human Capital, Technology, and the Wage Structure: What Do Time Series Show?* NBER Working Paper No. 3581. Cambridge, MA: National Bureau of Economic Research.

Mishel, Lawrence. 1992. The End of the White-Collar Job Boom. *International Economic Insights* 3, no. 5 (September/October): 9.

Mishel, Lawrence, and Jared Bernstein. 1994–95. *The State of Working America: 1994–95*. Washington: Economic Policy Institute.

Mishel, Lawrence, Jared Bernstein, and John Schmitt. 1996. *The State of Working America, 1996–97.* Armonk, NY: M. E. Sharpe, Economic Policy Institute.

Murphy, Kevin M., and Finis Welch. 1991. The Role of International Trade in Wage Differentials. In *Workers and Their Wages: Changing Patterns in the United States,* ed. by Marvin Kosters. Washington: American Enterprise Institute.

Murphy, Kevin M., and Finis Welch. 1992. The Structure of Wages. *Quarterly Journal of Economics* 107, no. 428 (February): 285–326.

Nehru, Vikram, and Ashok Dhareshwar. 1993. A New Database on Physical Capital Stock: Sources, Methodology, and Results. *Revista de Análisis Económico (Journal of Economic Analysis)* 8, no. 1 (June): 37–59.

Nehru, Vikram, Eric Swanson, and Ashutosh Dubey. 1995. A New Database on Human Capital Stock in Developing and Industrial Countries: Sources, Methodology, and Results. *Journal of Development Economics* 46, no. 2 (April): 379–401.

Ohlin, Bertil. 1933. *Interregional and International Trade.* Cambridge, MA: Harvard University Press.

Orcutt, Guy H. 1950. Measurement of Price Elasticities in International Trade. *Review of Economics and Statistics* 32 (May): 117–32.

Organization for Economic Cooperation and Development (OECD). 1979. Measuring the Employment Effects of Changes in Trade Flows: A Survey of Recent Research. *The Impact of the Newly Industrialising Countries on Production and Trade in Manufactures.* Paris: Organization for Economic Cooperation and Development.

Organization for Economic Cooperation and Development (OECD). 1980. *Trade by Commodities: Jan–Dec 1980,* 2 vols. Paris: Organization for Economic Cooperation and Development .

Organization for Economic Cooperation and Development (OECD). 1984 (for 1982). *Foreign Trade by Commodities* (formerly *Trade by Commodities*). Paris: Organization for Economic Cooperation and Development.

Organization for Economic Cooperation and Development (OECD). 1989. *Mechanisms for Job Creation: Lessons from the United States.* Paris: Organization for Economic Cooperation and Development.

Organization for Economic Cooperation and Development (OECD). 1991. *Foreign Trade by Commodities: 1988,* vol. II. Paris: Organization for Economic Cooperation and Development.

Organization for Economic Cooperation and Development (OECD). 1992a. *Employment Outlook.* Paris: Organization for Economic Cooperation and Development.

Organization for Economic Cooperation and Development (OECD). 1992b. *Historical Statistics 1960–90.* Paris: Organization for Economic Cooperation and Development.

Organization for Economic Cooperation and Development (OECD). 1995. *Income Distribution in OECD Countries.* Social Policy Studies No. 18. Paris: Organization for Economic Cooperation and Development.

Penn. 1994. *Penn World Tables.* Mark 5.6. New York: United Nations and the University of Pennsylvania.

Pierce, Brooks, and Finis Welch. 1994. Dimensions of Inequality in Labor Income. In *The Changing Distribution of Income in an Open US Economy,* ed. by Jeffrey H. Bergstrand et al. Amsterdam: North-Holland.

Pryor, Fredric L., and David Schaffer. 1997. Occupation and Wage Changes among the College Educated: A New Explanation to the Paradox. *Monthly Labor Review.* Forthcoming.

Revenga, Ana L. 1992. Exporting Jobs: The Impact of Import Competition on Employment and Wages in US Manufacturing. *Quarterly Journal of Economics* 107, no. 428 (February): 255–84.

Revenga, Ana L., and Claudio Montenegro. 1995. North American Integration and Factor Price Equalization: Is There Evidence of Wage Convergence between Mexico and the

United States? Paper prepared for Brookings Institution conference on Imports, Exports, and the American Worker, Washington (2–3 February).

Richardson, J. David. 1995. Income Inequality and Trade: How to Think? What to Conclude? *Journal of Economic Perspectives* 9, no. 3 (Summer): 33–55.

Rodrik, Dani. 1997. *Has Globalization Gone Too Far?* Washington: Institute for International Economics.

Rybczynski, T. M. 1955. Factor Endowment and Relative Commodity Prices. *Economica* 22, no. 84 (November): 336–41.

Sachs, Jeffrey D., and Howard J. Shatz. 1994. Trade and Jobs in US Manufactures. *Brookings Papers on Economic Activity*, no. 1: 1–84.

Sachs, Jeffrey D., and Howard J. Shatz. 1995. Trade and Manufacturing Jobs. Oral presentation at Brookings Institution Conference on Imports, Exports, and the American Worker, Washington (2–3 February).

Samuelson, Paul A. 1948. International Trade and the Equalization of Factor Prices. *Economic Journal* 58, no. 230 (June): 163–84.

Samuelson, Paul A. 1949. International Factor-Price Equalization Once Again. *Economic Journal* 59, no. 234 (June): 181–97.

Samuelson, Paul A. 1971. An Exact Hume-Ricardo-Marshall Model of International Trade. *Journal of International Economics* 1, no. 1 (February): 1–18.

Saunders, Norman C. 1993. The US Economy to 2005: Framework for BLS Projections. *Monthly Labor Review* 116, no. 11 (November): 11–30.

Silvestri, George T. 1993. Occupational Employment: Wide Variations in Growth. *Monthly Labor Review* 116, no. 11 (November): 58–86.

Slaughter, Matthew J. 1993. International Trade, Multinational Corporations, and American Wage Divergence in the 1980s. Cambridge: Massachusetts Institute of Technology. Photocopy (November).

Solow, Robert M. 1994. *Is All That European Unemployment Necessary?* Robbins Lecture. Claremont, CA: Claremont Graduate School.

Stolper, Wolfgang, and Paul A. Samuelson. 1941. Protection and Real Wages. *Review of Economic Studies* 9, no. 1 (November): 58–73.

Taiwan, Central Bank, Taiwan District, Republic of China. 1995. *Financial Statistics*. Taiwan: Economic Research Department, The Central Bank of China (August).

Topel, Robert. 1994. Why the Natural Rate of Unemployment Has Risen. *Jobs and Capital* 111 (Fall): 18–21.

Varian, Hal. 1978. *Microeconomic Analysis*. New York: W. W. Norton.

Weicher, John C. 1996. *The Distribution of Wealth: Increasing Inequality?* Washington: American Enterprise Institute.

Williamson, Jeffrey G., and Peter H. Lindert. 1980. *American Inequality: A Macroeconomic History*. New York: Academic Press.

Wolff, Edward N. 1994. Trends in Household Wealth in the United States: 1962–83 and 1983–89. *Review of Income and Wealth* 40, no. 2 (June): 143–74.

Wood, Adrian. 1991. The Factor Content of North-South Trade in Manufactures Reconsidered. *Weltwirtschaftliches Archiv* 127, Heft 4:719–43.

Wood, Adrian. 1994. *North-South Trade, Employment and Inequality: Changing Fortunes in a Skill-Driven World*. New York: Oxford University Press.

Wood, Adrian. 1995. How Trade Hurt Unskilled Workers. *Journal of Economic Perspectives* 9, no. 3 (Summer): 57–80.

World Bank, 1995a. *World Tables: 1995*. Washington: International Bank for Reconstruction and Development (May).

World Bank, 1995b. *World Development Report 1995*. Washington: International Bank for Reconstruction and Development (June).

World Trade Organization (WTO). 1997. *Annual Report 1996*, vol. 2. Geneva: World Trade Organization.

Index

Abowd, John M., 75n
Accounting decomposition method, 47
Active labor market hypothesis, 70
AFL-CIO, 46
African Americans
  family income, 5-6
  poverty rates, 8-9, 10-11
Aggregate employee compensation, 81, 81n
Annual Survey of Manufacturers (ASM), 60-61, 100-101
Asia
  factor endowments and output, 183t
  immigrants, 86
  optimal trade matrix, 204t
  US deficit, 192
  See also Gang of Four
Asia Pacific Economic Cooperation (APEC) forum, 224, 227, 237
Atkinson, Anthony B., 20
Autarky, 206-14
Auto workers, 46

Baby boom, college education, 26
Backcasts, 202
Balassa, Bela, 48-49, 106n
Baldwin, Robert E., 61n, 89n, 106-10, 107n, 142
Berman, Eli, 60-63, 62-63, 63n, 88-89, 106, 119-20, 122, 139, 140, 255

Bernard, Andrew B., 87-89, 139, 141, 255
Bernstein, Jared, 6, 7, 8n, 21, 22, 23, 26, 148, 267
Bhagwati, Jagdish, 43, 45, 90, 95-97, 97-98, 97n, 98, 99n, 100, 110, 141, 256, 271n
Blau, Francine D., 32
Bluestone, Barry, 16n, 43
Borjas, George J., 35, 56, 74-79, 75n, 78-82, 79n, 81, 81n, 84, 84n, 85-87, 86, 86n, 90n, 95, 98, 99n, 100, 136, 137, 141, 144, 220, 232, 255, 266-67
Bosworth, Barry, 6n, 28, 30, 31, 50
Bound, John, 50-54, 53, 56, 57, 60-63, 62-63, 63n, 65, 67-68, 67n, 88-89, 106, 119-20, 122, 139, 140, 255
Branson, William H., 82-83
Brooke, Anthony, 178
Burtless, Gary, 16-17, 18, 20n, 21, 26, 28, 28n, 61, 81, 92, 131, 136-39, 140, 145

Cain, Glen G., 61n, 89n, 106-10, 107n, 142
Canada
  capital, 184t
  factor endowments and output, 183t
  optimal trade matrix, 204t
  purchasing power parity, 185t
  skilled labor, 184t
  trade by factor intensity and partner, 188t

unskilled labor, 184t
Capital
    accumulation, 54
    income distribution and, 14-15
    services, 198
    stocks, 180, 182
    TIDE model, 198
Card, David, 267, 268
Carliner, Geoffrey, 85
Changing factor endowment, 107-08
Chiang, A., 159
Children, poverty rates, 10-11
China, 103
    capital, 185t
    factor endowments and output, 183t
    optimal trade matrix, 204t
    purchasing power parity, 185t
    skilled labor, 184t
    trade by factor intensity and partner,
        189, 190t
    unskilled labor, 184t
Chiswick, Barry R., 85
Civil War, 2
Cline, William R., 2, 46, 47, 47n, 48, 96,
    117, 117n, 131, 182, 205, 270, 271,
    277n, 279
Cobb-Douglas (CD) functions
    production function, 120, 125, 152, 158,
        257
    production and expenditure functions,
        108-09
    TIDE model, 208-13t
    utility function, 175
Coefficients, 108
Comparative advantage, 37, 108, 187,
    192-93
    manufacturers, 192t
    model conclusions, 235
Compensation
    aggregate employee, 81, 81n
    historical trends, 254
    real, 30
Computers
    investments in, 62
    US price data, 101
Cone of diversification, 170
Constant elasticity of substitution (CES),
    96, 158-61
Consumer deflator, 30
Consumer goods, 30
Consumer price index (CPI)
    deflator, 50
    family income data, 6, 6n

weekly earnings, 50
Cooper, Richard N., 103-06, 104n, 112,
    117n, 141, 144
Counterfactual, 83
Cutler, David M., 14, 14n

Davis, Steven J., 32
Deardorff, Alan V., 37, 38, 42, 43, 44, 73,
    76n, 96, 100, 107, 108-09, 122
Debt, consumer, 13
Decomposition analysis
    changing relative wages, 50
    rising wage inequality, 59
Defense industry buildup, 62
Dehejia, Vivek H., 43, 95-97, 98, 99n, 110,
    141, 256, 271n
Deunionization, 64-65
Development economists, 46-49
Dhareshwar, Ashok, 180
Diminishing marginal productivity, 41
Direct labor coefficients, 47, 48-49
Dollar, overvaluation of, 82-83
Domestic consumption, 62, 63
Dubey, Ashutosh, 179

Eastern Europe
    capital, 185t
    factor endowments and output, 183t
    optimal trade matrix, 204t
    purchasing power parity, 185t
    skilled labor, 184t
    trade by factor intensity and partner,
        190, 191t
    unskilled labor, 184t
Economic growth, historical trends, 29-30
Education
    college differential, 54
    college education and gender, 26
    college enrollment in US, 26, 27
    college-equivalent worker demand, 70
    college premium, 24n, 90n, 101
    demand and average wages, 51
    historical trends, 72t
    human capital, 3
    immigrants, 76, 86
    income differentials, 18, 19, 20
    income differentials (female), 25
    income differentials (male), 24-25
    real wages, 4
    skills and, 106
    student loan availability, 99
    trade and immigration impact, 76-77
    union premium, 65
    upgrading, 26-27

widened inequality, 57-59
years of schooling, 179
Elderly, poverty rates, 11
Employment
    construction trade, 69, 78
    dollar overvaluation, 82-83
    domestic demand, 47
    exports and, 47
    historical trends, 72t
    imports from LDCs and job loss, 46, 82
    manufacturing decline, 104
    sectoral change, 61-62, 73-74
    unskilled categories, 102
    and wage shares, 88
Employment cost index (ECI), 31
Ethier, Wilfred J., 44, 111
Ethnicity, poverty rates, 10-11
Europe, 182
    GNP growth, 2
    unemployment, 33
    unskilled labor, 33
    wage distribution, 254
    wage inequality, 31-32
European Economic Community (EEC),
    liberalization of 1960s, 46
European Union (EU), 181
    capital, 184t
    factor endowments and output, 183t
    purchasing power parity, 185t
    skilled labor, 184t
    trade by factor intensity and partner,
        189t
    unskilled labor, 184t
Evans, John M., 47
Experience, 50
    differential, 28-39
    factor, 70
    widened inequality, 57-59
Exports
    growth, 93

Factor content of trade, 95n, 108, 135-36,
    137, 144, 256
    approaches compared, 90, 109-10
    job loss, 109
Factor endowments, 178-82
    TIDE model, 195
    trends
    Krugman model, 157
Factor-price equalization (FPE), 36, 36n,
    40-41, 43
    Samuelson's diagram for, 41-42
    TIDE models, 218-20, 237
    theorem criticized, 95-96

Factor reversal, 43, 96
Factors
    factorial elasticities, 157-58
    prices/price ratios, 107, 112, 198
    in reality, 43
    specific-factors model, 44
    substitution elasticity, 158
Fallon, Peter, 161
Families
    poverty rates, 7-11
    income, 4-7
    ethnicity, 5-6
    growth rate, 6
    historical trends, 254
Feenstra, Robert C., 110, 119-24, 142, 144,
    265
Fiscal redistribution, 7
Fortin, Nicole M., 267, 268
France, GNP growth, 2
Frank, Charles R. Jr., 46-47
Freeman, Richard B., 35, 63-65, 64n, 73,
    74-79, 75n, 81, 86n, 90n, 95, 98, 100,
    136, 137, 141, 144, 220, 232, 255, 266-
    67, 267, 268
Free trade, 36
    core concept, 36-37
    future predictions, 113
    TIDE model, 227
Free Trade Area of the Americas
    (FTAA), 224, 227, 237

General Algebraic Modeling System
    (GAMS) optimization methodology,
    178
Gang of four (G4), 48
    capital, 185t
    comparative advantage, 193, 235
    factor endowments and output, 183t
    imports from, 168
    optimal trade matrix, 204t
    purchasing power parity, 185t
    skilled labor, 184t
    trade by factor intensity and partner,
        189, 191t
    unskilled labor, 184t
    US comparative disadvantage, 192
    US deficit, 187
    See also Hong Kong; Singapore; South
        Korea; Taiwan
Gender
    age composition, 83-84
    college premium, 101
    partial gender offset, 17-18
    skills and trade, 138

trade deficits and unemployment, 69-70

trade impacts, 137-38

wage gap, 17

wage trends, 82

General equilibrium analysis, 38

Krugman, 256-57

Krugman model, 151-72

quantity formulation, 176

General equilibrium model, 133, 134, 135, 257

TIDE model, 234

wage levels, 45

Germany

domestic manufacturing prices, 122

GNP growth, 2

wage inequality, 31-32

Gini coefficient

household income, 15

(in)equality shown by, $4n$

wage inequality, 15, 20

wages and salaries, 16

wealth, 12

Global competitiveness, $144n$

Global integration, 45

Globalization, 57

wage erosion, 124

Goldsmith, James, 33

Gottschalk, Peter, $24n$, $28n$, 29, 32

Gravity trade model, 103

Griliches, Zvi, 60-63, 62-63, $63n$, 88-89, 106, 120, 122, 139, 140, 255

Grinols, Earl L., 47

Gross domestic product (GDP)

deflator, 30

economic welfare and, 31

GDP deflator, 30, 31

historical trends, 29-30

lower-income families, 6

period of 1947-93, 3

Gross national product (GNP)

trend from 1870 to 1965, 1-2

Hakura, Dalia, 73, $76n$, 100, 122

Hall, Robert E., 92

Hamermesh, Daniel S., 161, $161n$

Hanson, Gordon H., 110, 119-24, 142, 144, 265

Haveman, Jon D., 96

Heckscher-Ohlin (HO) model, 46, $56n$

technology, $91n$

(HO) proposition, 45

(HO) theorem for North-South trade, 91

(HO) trade, 37-46

Heckscher, Eli, 37

Henderson, James M., 160, 171, 196

Hicks, John R., 124-27

Hicksian regressive wage convergence, 94, 125-27, $127n$, 135, 262, 265

Higher dimensionality literature, 111

Hispanic Americans, 10-11

family income, 6

Historical trends in US income, 1-4

Hong Kong, 258

imports from, 168

protectionism, 48

See also Gang of Four

Hooper, Peter, 270

Households

income, 4

net worth falling, 13

unrelated individuals, $4n$

wealth, 11, 13

Housing

real estate market, 13

residence as wealth, 13

Human capital, 3, 254

income and, 15

Immigration

effects on wage ratio, 255

effects questioned, 112

historical trends, 85

illegal, 85

labor-supply effect, 76

policy shifts, 85, 87

skilled/unskilled wage ratio, 145

TIDE model conclusions, 235-36, 238

TIDE models, 220-22

unskilled-intensive production, 99

wage distribution, $82n$, 145, 255

wage inequality, 78, 85

welfare burden thesis, 86

Immigration Reform and Control Act (IRCA) (1986), 85, 87

Imports

competition and wage equality, 81

competitive and quality upgrading, 104-05

competitive pressure, 96

domestic manufacturing versus, 122

employment and, 47, 82

growth, 93, 167, 258

Krugman projections, 165-70, 258

manufacturing, 33

slowing rates, 168, 258

SS theorem, 38

tariff revenue, 175
value 1980-92, 104
wage changes vis-à-vis, 122-23
wage decline, 111
Income
male/female differentials, 17-18
part-time (female), 16
Income distribution
family, 4-7
historical trends, 2, 253-54
period of 1947-70, 3, 3n
postwar trends, 2-3
trends, 1-34
Index number problems, 47
India
capital, 185t
factor endowments and output, 183t
optimal trade matrix, 204t
purchasing power parity, 185t
skilled labor, 184t
trade by factor intensity and partner,
189, 191t
unskilled labor, 184t
Indirect labor coefficients, 47
Industrial countries
imports and job loss, 47
intraindustry trade, 102
specialization cone, 117-18
US position as ordinary, 117
wage inequality, 31-32, 254
Inequality
four measures of wage, 20
general patterns, 32-34
increase since 1980, 4
part-time income, 16
wage and gender, 21
wage distribution, 2, 14, 50
wealth, 2, 12
Inflation, 12, 30
Integrated development, 117
Interest rates, 77-78
Intermediate goods, 120
Intermediate inputs, 93
Intermediate sectors (ITA), 136-39
International Standard Industrial
Classification (ISIC), 48
Investment and government goods and
services, 30
Inward-oriented development, 117
Isovalue curve, 38-39, 38n

Japan, 182
capital, 184t
domestic manufacturing prices, 122

factor endowments and output, 183t
GNP growth, 2
optimal trade matrix, 204t
purchasing power parity, 185t
skilled labor, 184t
trade by factor intensity and partner,
189t
unskilled labor, 184t
US comparative disadvantage, 192
US deficit, 187
Jensen, J. Bradford, 87-89, 139, 141, 255
Johnson, George, 50-54, 53, 56, 57, 60, 62,
65, 67-68, 67n, 87, 110, 124-27, 139-
142, 161, 265,
Jones, Ronald W., 40, 91
Juhn, Chihui, 2, 17n, 18, 21, 24, 28, 56-60,
65, 140

Kahn, Lawrence, M., 32
Karoly, Lynn A., 15-16, 20, 21, 83-85, 84n,
139, 141
Katz, Lawrence F., 14, 14n, 17n, 24, 35,
65-71, 73, 74-79, 75n, 81, 86n, 90n, 95,
97, 99n, 100, 105, 136, 137, 140, 141,
144, 147n, 149-50, 162, 220, 232, 255,
266-67
Kendrick, David, 178
Kennedy Round, 46, 57
Kennickell, Arthur B., 13
Kim, Dae Il, 155n, 230-31
Klerman, Jacob Alex, 83-85, 84n, 139, 141
Korea, 83n
Kosters, Marvin H., 24, 29, 61, 65n, 145
Krueger, Alan B., 267
Krueger, Anne O., 47, 53
Krugman, Paul R., 33, 91, 92, 93, 93n,
95n, 100, 106, 110, 114, 115, 124, 133-
36, 135n, 139, 141, 142, 144, 151-72,
256-57, 256n
Krugman model, 133-34, 151-72, 253, 257-
59, 261
experimental results, 156t
Kuznets, Simon, 2
Kuznets-Lampman, 2

Labor coefficients, 48
Southern versus Northern, 128-29
Labor economists, 136-39, 255
literature review, 49-88
Labor efficiency units, 75
Labor force
age composition, 83-84
demand structure, 132
hours worked, 30

immobility, 81
job loss, 109
labor shedding, 118-19, 138
labor supply, 107n
nonproduction, 61, 75
price of unobservable skills, 60
production, 60-61
production and nonproduction
    workers, 19-20, 92, 100-101, 114-115
skill dimensions, 60
skilled/unskilled, 18-20
white collar, 60
Labor market flexibility, 33
Labor migration, 144
Labor unions
    auto workers, 46
    influence declining, 63-65
    union premiums, 63
    wage inequality and, 63-65
    wage levels and, 32
Latin America
    capital, 184t
    factor endowments and output, 183t
    optimal trade matrix, 204t
    purchasing power parity, 185t
    skilled labor, 184t
    trade by factor intensity and partner,
        189t
    unskilled labor, 184t
Latin American immigrants, 86, 87
Lawrence, Robert Z., 35, 77, 89-93, 93,
    93n, 95n, 100, 103n, 106, 110, 111,
    112, 113n, 114n, 117, 118, 120, 122,
    136, 139, 141, 165, 255-56, 256n, 257
Layard, Richard, 161
Leamer, Edward E., 54n, 90, 91n, 92, 98,
    106-07, 110-18, 111n, 113n, 115n, 134-
    35, 139, 142, 144, 158, 165, 170, 186,
    256, 257, 269n, 275
Least trade affected (LTA), 136-39
Lemieux, Thomas, 267, 268
Lenz, Allen J., 63n
Leontief, Wassily W., 121, 159
Leontief paradox, 96
Less-developed-countries (LDCs)
    Asian output, 181
    development orientation, 117
    exports and US employment, 103
    manufacturing exports, 94
    merchandise exports, 131
    skilled labor, 181
    trade size and wage inequality, 134
Levy, Frank, 3n, 15-16, 17, 20, 21, 21n, 24,
    29, 30

Linder, Steffan B., 91
Lindert, Peter H., 2, 3
Lorenz curve, 4n
Love, James P., 82-83
Love, Roger, 20
Low income, wage concentration, 23
Low-income groups, family income, 5

Magnification effect, 40
Manufacturing
    actual trade by factor intensity and
        partner, 188-91t
    average wages, 104
    durable goods vis-à-vis imports, 79-81
    factor shares, 116
    GDP share, 93
    historical, 88, 93
    labor shedding, 118-19
    North-South labor forces, 179
    North-South trade, 48-49
    OECD, 1972-85, 112
    output and imports, 1971-93, 166f
    TIDE model, 185-86
    trade balance, 93
    trade effect on wages, 119
    trade impacts on skills, 101-02
    unskilled wages, 104
    wage distribution, 84, 85
    wage loss, 94
    weighted average wages, 95
Maquiladora assembly plants, 123
Marquez, Jaime, 270
Martin, John P., 47
Measure of trade impact, 149
Meeraus, Alexander, 178
Mexico
    capital, 184t
    comparative advantage, 217
    factor endowments and output, 183t
    free trade and wages, 96
    optimal trade matrix, 204t
    purchasing power parity, 185t
    skilled labor, 184t
    TIDE model, 227, 230
    trade by factor intensity and partner,
        189, 190t
    unskilled labor, 184t
    US deficit, 187
    US-Mexico trade and investment, 123-
        24
Middle class
    income gains slow, 7
    income share and growth, 4-5
    wage concentration, 21, 23

white collar, 64
Mieszkowski, Peter, 155n, 230-31
Mincer, Jacob, 3, 54-56, 54n, 55n, 56n, 57, 79n, 140
Minimum wage, 267
Mexico, 123
Mishel, Lawrence, 6, 7, 8n, 21, 22, 23, 26, 148, 267
Monopoly rents, 79
Montenegro, Claudio, 187n, 215
Most trade affected (MTA), 136-39
Multi-Fiber Arrangement (MFA), 46
Multinational competition, 87
Multinational corporations, 75, 103
Murnane, Richard J., 15-16, 17, 20, 21, 21n, 24, 29, 30
Murphy, Kevin M., 2, 6, 17n, 18, 21, 24, 28, 55, 56-60, 65-71, 71-74, 105, 137, 140, 147n, 149-50, 157, 162

National accounts, GDP deflator calculation, 30n
National Bureau of Economic Research, 60
Nehru, Vikram, 179, 180
Neoclassical economics
  income equalization hypothesis, 2
  synthesis, 3
Newly industrialized countries (NICs), 57
Nonproduction workers, 122, 123
Nontradable goods
  TIDE models, 217-20
Nontradables, 69, 157, 170
  induced employment, 77
  interest rates, 78
  wage inequality, 71
Nontradable sectors, TIDE model, 193
Nordic countries, wage inequality, 31-32
North American Free Trade Agreement (NAFTA), 96
  bitter debate, 1
  future predictions, 113
  wage erosion, 110-11
North-South trade
  capital flow, 122
  effects per Krugman model, 163-64, 258
  sectoral nature, 91
  wage inequality, 127

Ohlin, Bertil, 37
Oil price shock, 93
Oligopoly rents, 79

Omnibus Budget Reconciliation Act of 1993, 7
Optimal tariff, 36, 36n
Optimal trade matrix, 203-06, 204t
Orcutt, Guy H., 162n
Organization for Economic Cooperation and Development (OECD)
  Asian exports to, 169
  cone of diversification, 170
  factor endowments and output, 183t
  import rate slowing, 169
  income levels, 117
  Krugman model, 152-58, 257
  manufacturing, 1972-85, 112
  optimal trade matrix, 204t
Organization of Petroleum Exporting Countries (OPEC)
  capital, 185t
  factor endowments and output, 183t
  purchasing power parity, 185t
  trade by factor intensity and partner, 190, 191t
  unskilled labor, 184t
Outsourcing, 87, 144

Partial equilibrium analysis, 134-35
Perot, H. Ross, 33, 89
Perry, George L., 6n, 28, 30, 31, 50
Pierce, Brooks, 17n, 21, 24, 28, 56-60, 65, 140
Populism, 89
Poverty, 7-11
  growing rates, 7
  historical trends, 8, 254
  incidence 1959-93, 3
  US poverty line, 8n
Principles of Political Economy and Taxation (David Ricardo), 37
Production, neoclassical model of, 2
Productivity, 47
  diminishing marginal, 41
  goods *versus* services, 93
  historical trends, 254
  hours worked, 30
  import pressure, 47
  real wages, tradables and nontradables, 125
  wage inequality, 89
  wage levels, 29-31
Product specialization, 96
Protection functions, 48
Protectionism, 97n
  costs per TIDE model, 215-17, 231, 235
  estimates, 102

factor intensity, 102
free trade *versus*, 36
income redistribution, 110
nontariff barriers, 48
TIDE model, 230-31
Pryor, Frederic L., 145*n*
Purchasing power parity (PPP), 180, 182

Quandt, Richard E., 160, 171, 196

Ramey, Valerie A., 56, 78-82, 79*n*, 81*n*,
    84, 84*n*, 99*n*, 141, 255
Reaganomics, 77-78
Real wages
    decline, 23-24, 31, 50, 58, 254
    education, 26
    free trade and, 37-38
    historical trends, 30, 254
    labor economists on, 50
    period 1964-88, 58
    terms of trade, 94
    young workers, 58
Recession, 3, 6
    of 1974-75, 46
Research and development (R&D), 62
    skill-based technical change, 54
    wage differentials calculated, 79*n*
Revenga, Ana L., 82-83, 83*n*, 141, 187*n*,
    215
Ricardo, David, 37, 44, 118
Richardson, J. David, 106, 145
Rodrik, Dani, 144*n*, 271*n*
Russia
    factor endowments and output, 183*t*
    optimal trade matrix, 204*t*
Rybczynski, T.M., 44-45, 99, 112-113,
    113*n*

Sachs, Jeffrey D., 56*n*, 61, 91, 93*n*, 100-
    103, 104, 109, 110, 115, 118-19, 137,
    141, 142, 162, 186
Samuelson, Paul A., 36, 36*n*, 40-41, 41-42,
    95
Samuelson's factor price equalization
    (FPE), 256
Saving, personal saving rate, 13
Scale economies, 96
Schaffer, David, 145*n*
Schmitt, John, 267
Sector-specific model, 91
Services
    nontradable, 43
Service sector
    demand structure, 60

OECD (*See also* Nontradables)
Services sector
    wage distribution, 84, 85
Shadow prices, 198-202, 200-201, 226*t*
Shatz, Howard J., 56*n*, 61, 91, 93*n*, 100-
    103, 104, 109, 110, 115, 118-19, 137,
    141, 142, 162, 186
Singapore, 258
    imports from, 168
    protectionism, 48
    See also Gang of Four
Skilled labor availability, 234-35
Skill educational differential, 29
Skilled/unskilled labor
    constant-elasticity-of-substitution (CES)
        function, 158-61
    developing countries, 45
    elasticity of substitution, 161-63
    factor endowment trends, 184-85*t*
    labor economists view, 49
    labor supply, 107*n*
    product price calculations, 90
    skill augmentation differentiation, 99*n*
Skilled/unskilled workers
    availability of skilled, 145
    changing ratios, 138-39
    demand structure, 65
    effective supply, 97
    European Union, 181
    falling trade prices, 92
    less developed countries (LDCs), 181
    manufacturing and nonmanufacturing,
        118-19
    North/South, 179
    sectoral changes, 66
    sectoral ratios, 91
    trade effects, 91-92
    trade size and, 69
    US, 181
    US exports, 106
    wage distribution, 78
    wage gap calculated, 109
Skills demand structure, 60
Slaughter, Matthew J., 35, 77, 89-93, 95*n*,
    100, 103*n*, 106, 110, 111, 112, 113*n*,
    114*n*, 117, 118, 120, 122, 136, 139,
    141, 165, 255-56, 256*n*, 257
Smith, Adam, 35
Social structure, 137
Social trends, 254
Solow, Robert M., 277
South Korea, 180, 258
    imports from, 168

protectionism, 48
See also Gang of Four
Specialization cone, 117
Specific-factors model, 44, 118-19
Srinivasan, T.N., 45, 134*n*
Stafford, Frank P., 87, 110, 124-27, 142,
 265
Staiger, Robert W., 76*n*, 107, 108-09
Standard Industrial Classification (SIC)
 level, 47
Standard International Trade
 Classification (SITC), 186
 classification by factor input, 240
Starr-McCluer, Martha, 13
Stern, Robert M., 43
Stock prices, 12
 surge 1995-97, 13
Stolper, Wolfgang, 36, 36*n*
Stolper-Samuelson (SS) effects, 56
Stolper-Samuelson (SS) framework, 45
 domestic prices, 105
 labor economists using, 90
Stolper-Samuelson (SS) theorem (theory),
 36, 37-46, 255
 strawman version, 90
 Lerner-Pierce diagram, 38-40
Strategic trade, 36, 36*n*
Summers, Lawrence H., 99*n*
Sunden, Annika E., 13
Swanson, Eric, 179

Taiwan, 258
 imports from, 168
 protectionism, 48
 See also Gang of Four
Tariff equivalents, 194-95
Tariff revenue, 175
Tariffs, 38
Taxes, family income and, 7
Technological change
 between-industry demand shift, 67-68
 computer-related, 62
 computers, 53
 demand shifts *versus*, 88-89
 factor price trends, 107
 globalization effects *versus*, 115-16
 globalization price impact, 116-117
 import-substitute-biased, 124
 methodological dilemmas, 51
 sector-specific approach, 51*n*
 skill-biased, 54, 60, 255
 trade economists' view, 255-56
 unexplained residuals, 62, 51, 53-54,
 144

wage levels, 114
Technological change, skill-biased
 importance, 135
 scenarios given, 108
 TIDE model, 222-23, 230
Technology
 factor-price ratios, 41
Terms of trade, 94
 falling relative prices, 92-93
 fixed-weight, 92-93
 labor production and consumption, 89
 oil prices, 93*n*
Textiles, apparel, and leather (TAL), 104,
 105
Textiles and apparel
 falling prices, 117, 117*n*
Thorbecke, Erik, 47
Total factor productivity (TFP), 55
Tourism, 131
Tradables
 wage inequality, 71
Tradable sector
 TIDE model, 193
Trade
 balance or deficit effects calculated, 73
 deficit, 74, 77, 94, 255
 deficits and labor demand, 69, 71
 direct labor calculations, 74-76
 durables, 81
 effects on wage ratio, 255
 employment and, 46, 62
 employment in import-competing
 industries, 46
 factor demand impact calculated, 68-69
 factor prices and, 97*f*
 globalization and, 120
 inequality and, 35
 intraindustry, 63, 102
 job creation or loss, 48-49
 labor demand and, 102-03
 labor intensities, 48
 manufacturers, 48
 manufacturers by factor intensity and
 partner, 188-91*t*
 North-South, 157, 256
 role in US economy, 32
 sectoral change, 62
 sectoral divergences, 78
 skilled/unskilled wage ratio, 145
 surplus and negative impact, 69, 149-
 50
 surplus scenarios, 48
 technological change vis-à-vis, 55-56

TIDE model conclusions, 238
unskilled labor, 100, 103, 238
US peak, 68n
wage erosion, 110-18
wage inequality, 57, 71
Trade Adjustment Assistance (TAA), 272
Trade and Income Distribution
    Equilibrium (TIDE) model, 173-252,
    253, 259-60, 262
    forecast assumptions, 224-25
    forecast baseline, 225
    model sensitivity, 231-34
Trade data for TIDE model, 182-93
Trade economists, 255-57
Trade-equity connection, 238
Trade gap factor, 49n
Trade matrix in TIDE model, 203-06, 204t
Trade specialization, 178-82
Transnational corporations. See
    Multinational corporations
Transport costs, 194
    TIDE model, 214-15, 217, 231, 235

Unemployment, 3
    Europe, 32
    Third World imports and, 33
Unionization. See Labor unions
Union premiums, 63
United Kingdom
    GNP growth, 2
    postwar slowdowns, 124
    productivity and import growth, 47
    wage inequality, 31
United States
    capital, 184t
    comparative advantage, 187
    optimal trade matrix, 204t
    trade by factor intensity and partner,
        188t
    domestic manufacturing prices, 122
    factor endowments and output, 183t
    historical trends, 1-4
    purchasing power parity, 185t
    skilled labor, 184t
    textile sector, 47n, 48n
    unskilled labor, 184t
Unskilled labor
    marginal demand, 118
    wage decline, 103-06

Varian, Hal, 153n, 154n, 159, 171n
Viner, Jacob, 44, 118

Wage differentials

trade and immigration impact, 76
Wage distribution
    college differential, 54, 55
    compensation and, 80-81
    dollar overvaluation, 82
    experience differential, 28-29
    free trade and, 36
    fringe benefits, 23
    globalization, 94
    historical trends, 57-60, 72t
    immigration, 82, 86-87
    immigration and trade impacts, 76, 78-
        79
    inequality issue, 14
    international comparisons, 32
    labor immobility, 81
    market concentration, 79
    overall income and income
        distribution, 145
    production/nonproduction, 19-20
    real wage decline, 23-24
    skilled/unskilled, 18-20
    social structure, 136-37
    union premium, 63, 65
Wage inequality
    age composition, 83-84
    calculations for 1963-88 period, 79-81
    decomposition analysis, 59
    demand structure and, 56-60
    durable goods imports, 84, 85
    exporting industries, 89
    globalization, 115, 124
    historical trends, 57-60
    import competition, 255
    international patterns, 31-32
    price issue, 101
    sectoral changes, 84, 255
    shift-shares and regression analysis of
        trends, 83-85
    social structure, 136-37
    supply-demand interaction
        summarized, 146-48f
    supply of skilled and unskilled labor,
        255
    TIDE model conclusions, 235
    timing of imports, 103
    trade, 95-97, 115, 124, 136, 256
    traded versus nontraded goods, 137
    trade impact, 89-93
    trade (overview), 139-40
Wage levels
    labor demand, 103
    productivity, 29-31

technological change, 56
Third World trade, 43
Wage rents, 99n
Wages
    at external margin, 158
    trends, 1-34
Wealth
    concentration increasing, 11-12
    distribution, 11-13
    historical trends in distribution, 11
Wealth of Nations (Adam Smith), 35-36

Weicher, John C., 12
Welch, Finis, 6, 55, 71-74, 137, 140, 157
White collar workers, 64
Williamson, Jeffrey G., 2, 3
Wolff, Edward N., 4, 11-12, 13, 15
Wolfson, Michael C., 20
Wood, Adrian, 33, 49, 121, 127-33, 127n, 129n, 130n, 132n, 136, 137, 139, 143, 144, 158, 179, 179n, 233-34, 256, 257, 269n

Other Publications from the Institute for International Economics

POLICY ANALYSES IN INTERNATIONAL ECONOMICS Series

1 **The Lending Policies of the International Monetary Fund**
John Williamson/*August 1982*
ISBN paper 0-88132-000-5   72 pp.

2 **"Reciprocity": A New Approach to World Trade Policy?**
William R. Cline/*September 1982*
ISBN paper 0-88132-001-3   41 pp.

3 **Trade Policy in the 1980s**
C. Fred Bergsten and William R. Cline/*November 1982*
(out of print)   ISBN paper 0-88132-002-1   84 pp.
Partially reproduced in the book *Trade Policy in the 1980s.*

4 **International Debt and the Stability of the World Economy**
William R. Cline/*September 1983*
ISBN paper 0-88132-010-2   134 pp.

5 **The Exchange Rate System,** Second Edition
John Williamson/*September 1983, rev. June 1985*
(out of print)   ISBN paper 0-88132-034-X   61 pp.

6 **Economic Sanctions in Support of Foreign Policy Goals**
Gary Clyde Hufbauer and Jeffrey J. Schott/*October 1983*
ISBN paper 0-88132-014-5   109 pp.

7 **A New SDR Allocation?**
John Williamson/*March 1984*
ISBN paper 0-88132-028-5   61 pp.

8 **An International Standard for Monetary Stabilization**
Ronald I. McKinnon/*March 1984*
(out of print)   ISBN paper 0-88132-018-8   108 pp.

9 **The Yen/Dollar Agreement: Liberalizing Japanese Capital Markets**
Jeffrey A. Frankel/*December 1984*
ISBN paper 0-88132-035-8   86 pp.

10 **Bank Lending to Developing Countries: The Policy Alternatives**
C. Fred Bergsten, William R. Cline, and John Williamson/*April 1985*
ISBN paper 0-88132-032-3   221 pp.

11 **Trading for Growth: The Next Round of Trade Negotiations**
Gary Clyde Hufbauer and Jeffrey J. Schott/*September 1985*
(out of print)   ISBN paper 0-88132-033-1   109 pp.

12 **Financial Intermediation Beyond the Debt Crisis**
Donald R. Lessard and John Williamson/*September 1985*
(out of print)   ISBN paper 0-88132-021-8   130 pp.

13 **The United States-Japan Economic Problem**
C. Fred Bergsten and William R. Cline/*October 1985, 2d ed. January 1987*
(out of print)   ISBN paper 0-88132-060-9   180 pp.

14 **Deficits and the Dollar: The World Economy at Risk**
Stephen Marris/*December 1985, 2d ed. November 1987*
(out of print)   ISBN paper 0-88132-067-6   415 pp.

15 **Trade Policy for Troubled Industries**
Gary Clyde Hufbauer and Howard F. Rosen/*March 1986*
ISBN paper 0-88132-020-X   111 pp.

16 **The United States and Canada: The Quest for Free Trade**
Paul Wonnacott, with an Appendix by John Williamson/*March 1987*
ISBN paper 0-88132-056-0   188 pp.

17 Adjusting to Success: Balance of Payments Policy
in the East Asian NICs
Bela Balassa and John Williamson/*June 1987, rev. April 1990*
ISBN paper 0-88132-101-X   160 pp.

18 Mobilizing Bank Lending to Debtor Countries
William R. Cline/*June 1987*
ISBN paper 0-88132-062-5   100 pp.

19 Auction Quotas and United States Trade Policy
C. Fred Bergsten, Kimberly Ann Elliott, Jeffrey J. Schott, and
Wendy E. Takacs/*September 1987*
ISBN paper 0-88132-050-1   254 pp.

20 Agriculture and the GATT: Rewriting the Rules
Dale E. Hathaway/*September 1987*
ISBN paper 0-88132-052-8   169 pp.

21 Anti-Protection: Changing Forces in United States Trade Politics
I. M. Destler and John S. Odell/*September 1987*
ISBN paper 0-88132-043-9   220 pp.

22 Targets and Indicators: A Blueprint for the International
Coordination of Economic Policy
John Williamson and Marcus H. Miller/*September 1987*
ISBN paper 0-88132-051-X   118 pp.

23 Capital Flight: The Problem and Policy Responses
Donald R. Lessard and John Williamson/*December 1987*
(out of print)   ISBN paper 0-88132-059-5   80 pp.

24 United States-Canada Free Trade: An Evaluation of the Agreement
Jeffrey J. Schott/*April 1988*
ISBN paper 0-88132-072-2   48 pp.

25 Voluntary Approaches to Debt Relief
John Williamson/*September 1988, rev. May 1989*
ISBN paper 0-88132-098-6   80 pp.

26 American Trade Adjustment: The Global Impact
William R. Cline/*March 1989*
ISBN paper 0-88132-095-1   98 pp.

27 More Free Trade Areas?
Jeffrey J. Schott/*May 1989*   ISBN paper 0-88132-085-4   88 pp.

28 The Progress of Policy Reform in Latin America
John Williamson/*January 1990*
ISBN paper 0-88132-100-1   106 pp.

29 The Global Trade Negotiations: What Can Be Achieved?
Jeffrey J. Schott/*September 1990*
ISBN paper 0-88132-137-0   72 pp.

30 Economic Policy Coordination: Requiem or Prologue?
Wendy Dobson/*April 1991*
ISBN paper 0-88132-102-8   162 pp.

31 The Economic Opening of Eastern Europe
John Williamson/*May 1991*
ISBN paper 0-88132-186-9   92 pp.

32 Eastern Europe and the Soviet Union in the World Economy
Susan M. Collins and Dani Rodrik/*May 1991*
ISBN paper 0-88132-157-5   152 pp.

33 African Economic Reform: The External Dimension
Carol Lancaster/*June 1991*
ISBN paper 0-88132-096-X   82 pp.

34 Has the Adjustment Process Worked?
Paul R. Krugman/*October 1991*
ISBN paper 0-88132-116-8   80 pp.

35 **From Soviet disUnion to Eastern Economic Community?**
Oleh Havrylyshyn and John Williamson/*October 1991*
ISBN paper 0-88132-192-3   84 pp.

36 **Global Warming: The Economic Stakes**
William R. Cline/*May 1992*
ISBN paper 0-88132-172-9   128 pp.

37 **Trade and Payments After Soviet Disintegration**
John Williamson/*June 1992*
ISBN paper 0-88132-173-7   96 pp.

38 **Trade and Migration: NAFTA and Agriculture**
Philip L. Martin/*October 1993*
ISBN paper 0-88132-201-6   160 pp.

39 **The Exchange Rate System and the IMF: A Modest Agenda**
Morris Goldstein/*June 1995*
ISBN paper 0-88132-219-9   104 pp.

40 **What Role for Currency Boards?**
John Williamson/*September 1995*
ISBN paper 0-88132-222-9   64 pp.

41 **Predicting External Imbalances for the United States and Japan**
William R. Cline/*September 1995*
ISBN paper 0-88132-220-2   104 pp.

42 **Standards and APEC: An Action Agenda**
John S. Wilson/*October 1995*
ISBN paper 0-88132-223-7   176 pp.

43 **Fundamental Tax Reform and Border Tax Adjustments**
Gary Clyde Hufbauer assisted by Carol Gabyzon/*January 1996*
ISBN paper 0-88132-225-3   108 pp.

44 **Global Telecom Talks: A Trillion Dollar Deal**
Ben A. Petrazzini/*June 1996*
ISBN paper 0-88132-230-X   128 pp.

45 **WTO 2000: Setting the Course for World Trade**
Jeffrey J. Schott/*September 1996*
ISBN paper 0-88132-234-2   72 pp.

46 **The National Economic Council: A Work in Progress**
I. M. Destler/*November 1996*
ISBN paper 0-88132-239-3   90 pp.

47 **The Case for an International Banking Standard**
Morris Goldstein/*April 1997*
ISBN paper 0-88132-244-X   128 pp.

48 **Transatlantic Trade: A Strategic Agenda**
Ellen L. Frost/*May 1997*
ISBN paper 0-88132-228-8   136 pp.

49 **Cooperating with Europe's Monetary Union**
C. Randall Henning/*May 1997*
ISBN paper 0-88132-245-8   104 pp.

50 **Renewing Fast-Track Legislation**
I.M.Destler/*September 1997*
ISBN paper 0-88132-252-0   72 pp.

BOOKS

IMF Conditionality
John Williamson, editor/*1983*   ISBN cloth 0-88132-006-4   695 pp.

Trade Policy in the 1980s
William R. Cline, editor/*1983*
(out of print)   ISBN paper 0-88132-031-5   810 pp.

Subsidies in International Trade
Gary Clyde Hufbauer and Joanna Shelton Erb/*1984*
ISBN cloth 0-88132-004-8   299 pp.

International Debt: Systemic Risk and Policy Response
William R. Cline/*1984*   ISBN cloth 0-88132-015-3   336 pp.

Trade Protection in the United States: 31 Case Studies
Gary Clyde Hufbauer, Diane E. Berliner, and Kimberly Ann Elliott/*1986*
(out of print)   ISBN paper 0-88132-040-4   371 pp.

Toward Renewed Economic Growth in Latin America
Bela Balassa, Gerardo M. Bueno, Pedro-Pablo Kuczynski,
and Mario Henrique Simonsen/*1986*
(out of stock)   ISBN paper 0-88132-045-5   205 pp.

Capital Flight and Third World Debt
Donald R. Lessard and John Williamson, editors/*1987*
(out of print)   ISBN paper 0-88132-053-6   270 pp.

The Canada-United States Free Trade Agreement: The Global Impact
Jeffrey J. Schott and Murray G. Smith, editors/*1988*
      ISBN paper 0-88132-073-0   211 pp.

World Agricultural Trade: Building a Consensus
William M. Miner and Dale E. Hathaway, editors/*1988*
      ISBN paper 0-88132-071-3   226 pp.

Japan in the World Economy
Bela Balassa and Marcus Noland/*1988*
      ISBN paper 0-88132-041-2   306 pp.

America in the World Economy: A Strategy for the 1990s
C. Fred Bergsten/*1988*   ISBN cloth 0-88132-089-7   235 pp.
      ISBN paper 0-88132-082-X   235 pp.

Managing the Dollar: From the Plaza to the Louvre
Yoichi Funabashi/*1988, 2d ed. 1989*
      ISBN paper 0-88132-097-8   307 pp.

United States External Adjustment and the World Economy
William R. Cline/*May 1989*   ISBN paper 0-88132-048-X   392 pp.

Free Trade Areas and U.S. Trade Policy
Jeffrey J. Schott, editor/*May 1989*
      ISBN paper 0-88132-094-3   400 pp.

Dollar Politics: Exchange Rate Policymaking in the United States
I. M. Destler and C. Randall Henning/*September 1989*
(out of print)   ISBN paper 0-88132-079-X   192 pp.

Latin American Adjustment: How Much Has Happened?
John Williamson, editor/*April 1990*
      ISBN paper 0-88132-125-7   480 pp.

The Future of World Trade in Textiles and Apparel
William R. Cline/*1987, 2d ed. June 1990*
      ISBN paper 0-88132-110-9   344 pp.

**Completing the Uruguay Round: A Results-Oriented Approach
to the GATT Trade Negotiations**
Jeffrey J. Schott, editor/*September 1990*
      ISBN paper 0-88132-130-3   256 pp.

Economic Sanctions Reconsidered (in two volumes)
Economic Sanctions Reconsidered: Supplemental Case Histories
Gary Clyde Hufbauer, Jeffrey J. Schott, and Kimberly Ann Elliott/*1985, 2d ed. December 1990*
      ISBN cloth 0-88132-115-X   928 pp.
      ISBN paper 0-88132-105-2   928 pp.

Economic Sanctions Reconsidered: History and Current Policy
Gary Clyde Hufbauer, Jeffrey J. Schott, and Kimberly Ann Elliott/*December 1990*
      ISBN cloth 0-88132-136-2   288 pp.
      ISBN paper 0-88132-140-0   288 pp.

Pacific Basin Developing Countries: Prospects for the Future
Marcus Noland/*January 1991*   ISBN   cloth 0-88132-141-9   250 pp.
(out of print)   ISBN paper 0-88132-081-1   250 pp.

Currency Convertibility in Eastern Europe
John Williamson, editor/*October 1991*
ISBN paper 0-88132-128-1 396 pp.

International Adjustment and Financing: The Lessons of 1985-1991
C. Fred Bergsten, editor/*January 1992*
ISBN paper 0-88132-112-5 336 pp.

North American Free Trade: Issues and Recommendations
Gary Clyde Hufbauer and Jeffrey J. Schott/*April 1992*
ISBN paper 0-88132-120-6 392 pp.

Narrowing the U.S. Current Account Deficit
Allen J. Lenz/*June 1992*
(out of print) ISBN paper 0-88132-103-6 640 pp.

The Economics of Global Warming
William R. Cline/*June 1992* ISBN paper 0-88132-132-X 416 pp.

U.S. Taxation of International Income: Blueprint for Reform
Gary Clyde Hufbauer, assisted by Joanna M. van Rooij/*October 1992*
ISBN cloth 0-88132-178-8 304 pp.
ISBN paper 0-88132-134-6 304 pp.

Who's Bashing Whom? Trade Conflict in High-Technology Industries
Laura D'Andrea Tyson/*November 1992*
ISBN paper 0-88132-106-0 352 pp.

Korea in the World Economy
Il SaKong/*January 1993* ISBN paper 0-88132-106-0 328 pp.

Pacific Dynamism and the International Economic System
C. Fred Bergsten and Marcus Noland, editors/*May 1993*
ISBN paper 0-88132-196-6 424 pp.

Economic Consequences of Soviet Disintegration
John Williamson, editor/*May 1993*
ISBN paper 0-88132-190-7 664 pp.

Reconcilable Differences? United States-Japan Economic Conflict
C. Fred Bergsten and Marcus Noland/*June 1993*
ISBN paper 0-88132-129-X 296 pp.

Does Foreign Exchange Intervention Work?
Kathryn M. Dominguez and Jeffrey A. Frankel/*September 1993*
ISBN paper 0-88132-104-4 192 pp.

Sizing Up U.S. Export Disincentives
J. David Richardson/*September 1993*
ISBN paper 0-88132-107-9 192 pp.

NAFTA: An Assessment
Gary Clyde Hufbauer and Jeffrey J. Schott/*rev. ed. October 1993*
ISBN paper 0-88132-199-0 216 pp.

Adjusting to Volatile Energy Prices
Philip K. Verleger, Jr./*November 1993*
ISBN paper 0-88132-069-2 288 pp.

The Political Economy of Policy Reform
John Williamson, editor/*January 1994*
ISBN paper 0-88132-195-8 624 pp.

Measuring the Costs of Protection in the United States
Gary Clyde Hufbauer and Kimberly Ann Elliott/*January 1994*
ISBN paper 0-88132-108-7 144 pp.

The Dynamics of Korean Economic Development
Cho Soon/*March 1994* ISBN paper 0-88132-162-1 272 pp.

Reviving the European Union
C. Randall Henning, Eduard Hochreiter and Gary Clyde Hufbauer, editors/*April 1994*
ISBN paper 0-88132-208-3 192 pp.

China in the World Economy
Nicholas R. Lardy/*April 1994*
ISBN paper 0-88132-200-8 176 pp.

Greening the GATT: Trade, Environment, and the Future
Daniel C. Esty/*July 1994*   ISBN paper 0-88132-205-9   344 pp.

Western Hemisphere Economic Integration
Gary Clyde Hufbauer and Jeffrey J. Schott/*July 1994*
                    ISBN paper 0-88132-159-1   304 pp.

Currencies and Politics in the United States, Germany, and Japan
C. Randall Henning/*September 1994*
                    ISBN paper 0-88132-127-3   432 pp.

Estimating Equilibrium Exchange Rates
John Williamson, editor/*September 1994*
                    ISBN paper 0-88132-076-5   320 pp.

Managing the World Economy: Fifty Years After Bretton Woods
Peter B. Kenen, editor/*September 1994*
                    ISBN paper 0-88132-212-1   448 pp.

Reciprocity and Retaliation in U.S. Trade Policy
Thomas O. Bayard and Kimberly Ann Elliott/*September 1994*
                    ISBN paper 0-88132-084-6   528 pp.

The Uruguay Round: An Assessment
Jeffrey J. Schott, assisted by Johanna W. Buurman/*November 1994*
                    ISBN paper 0-88132-206-7   240 pp.

Measuring the Costs of Protection in Japan
Yoko Sazanami, Shujiro Urata, and Hiroki Kawai/*January 1995*
                    ISBN paper 0-88132-211-3   96 pp.

Foreign Direct Investment in the United States, Third Edition
Edward M. Graham and Paul R. Krugman/*January 1995*
                    ISBN paper 0-88132-204-0   232 pp.

The Political Economy of Korea-United States Cooperation
C. Fred Bergsten and Il SaKong, editors/*February 1995*
                    ISBN paper 0-88132-213-X   128 pp.

International Debt Reexamined
William R. Cline/*February 1995*
                    ISBN paper 0-88132-083-8   560 pp.

American Trade Politics, Third Edition
I. M. Destler/*April 1995*   ISBN paper 0-88132-215-6   360 pp.

Managing Official Export Credits: The Quest for a Global Regime
John E. Ray/*July 1995*   ISBN paper 0-88132-207-5   344 pp.

Asia Pacific Fusion: Japan's Role in APEC
Yoichi Funabashi/*October 1995*
                    ISBN paper 0-88132-224-5   312 pp.

Korea-United States Cooperation in the New World Order
C. Fred Bergsten and Il SaKong, editors/*February 1996*
                    ISBN paper 0-88132-226-1   144 pp.

Why Exports Really Matter!   ISBN paper 0-88132-221-0   34 pp.
Why Exports Matter More!   ISBN paper 0-88132-229-6   36 pp.
J. David Richardson and Karin Rindal/*July 1995; February 1996*

Global Corporations and National Governments
Edward M. Graham/*May 1996*
                    ISBN paper 0-88132-111-7   168 pp.

Global Economic Leadership and the Group of Seven
C. Fred Bergsten and C. Randall Henning/*May 1996*
                    ISBN paper 0-88132-218-0   192 pp.

The Trading System After the Uruguay Round
John Whalley and Colleen Hamilton/*July 1996*
                    ISBN paper 0-88132-131-1   224 pp.

Private Capital Flows to Emerging Markets After the Mexican Crisis
Guillermo A. Calvo, Morris Goldstein, and Eduard Hochreiter/*September 1996*
                    ISBN paper 0-88132-232-6   352 pp.

The Crawling Band as an Exchange Rate Regime:
Lessons from Chile, Colombia, and Israel
John Williamson/*September 1996*
  ISBN paper 0-88132-231-8   192 pp.

Flying High: Civil Aviation in the Asia Pacific
Gary Clyde Hufbauer and Christopher Findlay/*November 1996*
  ISBN paper 0-88132-231-8   232 pp.

Measuring the Costs of Visible Protection in Korea
Namdoo Kim/*November 1996*
  ISBN paper 0-88132-236-9   112 pp.

The World Trading System: Challenges Ahead
Jeffrey J. Schott/*December 1996*
  ISBN paper 0-88132-235-0   350 pp.

Has Globalization Gone Too Far?
Dani Rodrik/*March 1997*   ISBN cloth 0-88132-243-1   128 pp.

Korea-United States Economic Relationship
C. Fred Bergsten and Il SaKong, editors/*March 1997*
  ISBN paper 0-88132-240-7   152 pp.

Summitry in the Americas: A Progress Report
Richard E. Feinberg/*April 1997*
  ISBN paper 0-88132-242-3   272 pp.

Corruption and the Global Economy
Kimberly Ann Elliott/*June 1997*
  ISBN paper 0-88132-233-4   256 pp.

Regional Trading Blocs in the World Economic System
Jeffrey A. Frankel/*October 1997*
  ISBN paper 0-88132-202-4   346 pp.

Sustaining the Asia Pacific Miracle: Environmental Protection and
Economic Integration
André Dua and Daniel C. Esty/*October 1997*
  ISBN paper 0-88132-250-4   232 pp.

Trade and Income Distribution
William R. Cline/*November1997*

  ISBN paper 0-88132-216-4   296 pp.

SPECIAL REPORTS

1   **Promoting World Recovery: A Statement on Global Economic Strategy**
    by Twenty-six Economists from Fourteen Countries/*December 1982*
    (out of print)   ISBN paper 0-88132-013-7   45 pp.
2   **Prospects for Adjustment in Argentina, Brazil, and Mexico:**
    Responding to the Debt Crisis   (out of print)
    John Williamson, editor/*June 1983*
                            ISBN paper 0-88132-016-1   71 pp.
3   **Inflation and Indexation: Argentina, Brazil, and Israel**
    John Williamson, editor/*March 1985*
                            ISBN paper 0-88132-037-4   191 pp.
4   **Global Economic Imbalances**
    C. Fred Bergsten, editor/*March 1986*
                            ISBN cloth 0-88132-038-2   126 pp.
                            ISBN paper 0-88132-042-0   126 pp.
5   **African Debt and Financing**
    Carol Lancaster and John Williamson, editors/*May 1986*
    (out of print)   ISBN paper 0-88132-044-7   229 pp.
6   **Resolving the Global Economic Crisis: After Wall Street**
    Thirty-three Economists from Thirteen Countries/*December 1987*
                            ISBN paper 0-88132-070-6   30 pp.
7   **World Economic Problems**
    Kimberly Ann Elliott and John Williamson, editors/*April 1988*
                            ISBN paper 0-88132-055-2   298 pp.
    Reforming World Agricultural Trade
    Twenty-nine Professionals from Seventeen Countries/*1988*
                            ISBN paper 0-88132-088-9   42 pp.

8   Economic Relations Between the United States and Korea:
     Conflict or Cooperation?
     Thomas O. Bayard and Soo-Gil Young, editors/*January 1989*
                    ISBN paper 0-88132-068-4   192 pp.

9   Whither APEC? The Progress to Date and Agenda for the Future
     C. Fred Bergsten, editor/*October 1997*
                    ISBN paper 0-88132-248-2   272 pp.

WORKS IN PROGRESS

The US - Japan Economic Relationship
C. Fred Bergsten, Marcus Noland, and Takatoshi Ito

China's Entry to the World Economy
Richard N. Cooper

Liberalizing Financial Services
Wendy Dobson and Pierre Jacquet

Economic Sanctions After the Cold War
Kimberly Ann Elliott, Gary C. Hufbauer and Jeffrey J. Schott

Trade and Labor Standards
Kimberly Ann Elliott and Richard Freeman

Forecasting Financial Crises: Early Warning Signs for Emerging Markets
Morris Goldstein and Carmen Reinhart

Global Competition Policy
Edward M. Graham and J. David Richardson

Prospects for Western Hemisphere Free Trade
Gary Clyde Hufbauer and Jeffrey J. Schott

Trade Practices Laid Bare
Donald Keesing

The Future of U.S. Foreign Aid
Carol Lancaster

The Economics of Korean Unification
Marcus Noland

Foreign Direct Investment in Developing Countries
Theodore Moran

Globalization, the NAIRU, and Monetary Policy
Adam Posen

The Case for Trade: A Modern Reconsideration
J. David Richardson

Measuring the Cost of Protection in China
Zhang Shuguang, Zhang Yansheng, and Wan Zhongxin

Real Exchange Rates for the Year 2000
Simon Wren-Lewis and Rebecca Driver

Canadian customers	RENOUF BOOKSTORE
can order from	5369 Canotek Road, Unit 1, Ottawa, Ontario K1J 9J3, Canada
the Institute or from:	Telephone: (613) 745-2665 Fax: (613) 745-7660

Visit our website at: http://www.iie.com   E-mail address: orders@iie.com